KICKING OFF

KICKING OFF

OFF

How women in sport are

changing the game

SARAH SHEPHARD

BLOOMSBURY

LONDON · NEW DELHI · NEW YORK · SYDNEY

Bloomsbury Sport
An imprint of Bloomsbury Publishing Plc

50 Bedford Square
London
WC1B 3DP
UK

1385 Broadway
New York
NY 10018
USA

www.bloomsbury.com

BLOOMSBURY and the Diana logo are trademarks of
Bloomsbury Publishing Plc

First published 2016

British Library Cataloguing-in-Publication Data
A catalogue record for this book is available from the British Library.

Library of Congress Cataloguing-in-Publication data has been applied for.

ISBN: Print: 978-1-4729-1383-8
ePDF: 978-1-4729-1385-2
ePub: 978-1-4729-1384-5

2 4 6 8 10 9 7 5 3 1

Typeset in Archer by Deanta Global Publishing Services, Chennai, India
Printed and bound in Great Britain by CPI Group (UK) Ltd. Croydon, CR0 4YY

To find out more about our authors and books visit www.bloomsbury.com.
Here you will find extracts, author interviews, details of forthcoming
events and the option to sign up for our newsletters.

CONTENTS

Chrissie Wellington

FOUR-TIME IRONMAN WORLD CHAMPION

Sport and physical activity change lives.

That fact is irrefutable.

Yet, statistics tell of falling participation in physical activity and sport among women, and growing disengagement of young girls. Not that we need data to tell us of the deep-rooted, endemic problem. We only have to look around us to see sedentary lifestyles, obesity and a vast array of other health problems. The benefits of regularly participating in sports and physical activity are well known and unequivocal. Increasing participation in physical activity and sport by all – men and women – is an investment in the overall economic, cultural and social health of our nations, and world.

I have gone from being a relatively sporty school girl, to a disengaged 16–23 year old, a relatively unsporty university student, a 'running mad' civil servant, an amateur triathlete, a professional and finally a retired athlete. For me, school was a key channel for developing, cultivating and nurturing my passion for sport and the skills, physiology and characteristics necessary to succeed in sport at a higher level.

It also installed activity in my own daily lifestyle up until the age of 16 or 17. I was fortunate to be taught by passionate, enthusiastic and well-trained PE teachers, who stimulated my sporting passion and ability. My parents tirelessly ferried me to and from activities, and humoured me as I ran around the garden barefoot trying to emulate my idol, Zola Budd. I gave up structured sport aged around 16, and only took it up again during my Master's degree when I discovered running. From there a passion for endurance sport was born and resulted in a foray into triathlon, which was to become my career. I achieved more than I could have ever imagined as a professional triathlete and have now retired, convinced more than ever before of the power of sport to change lives.

Overall I feel that I am one of the lucky ones. While, yes, there have been hurdles to overcome, I feel that my gender has never held me back from achieving my dreams. As an athlete I was fortunate to take part in a sport

7

that, despite its faults, is relatively egalitarian from a gender perspective. Women race on the same day and over the same course as men. At the professional level, the prize purse is the same for men and women, opportunities for sponsorship and media coverage are, in my view, equal between the sexes, and the ratio of men to women (at the shorter races and within triathlon clubs) is becoming increasingly even.

The reasons are many, but include the fact that triathlon is a relatively new sport, and that from its genesis women have participated with men at the professional and amateur level. The amateurs race simultaneously with the professionals (hence the male and female amateurs see professional women competing and can be inspired by our performance). Women hold high-level positions on the various national and international federations, while editors and journalists for a number of triathlon publications and websites are women. At the grassroots level in the UK, the 600 or so triathlon clubs that currently exist welcome women and families, and offer a cocoon of support and encouragement which is backed up by extensive online information resources.

As this thought-provoking book shows, we have a wealth of athletes at the elite level who have helped to create this platform of opportunity for athletes like me. We see pioneers like Billie-Jean King and Roberta Gibb who paved the way for women to have an opportunity to take part, both at an amateur level and professionally. We have women who are carving out a path in male-dominated arenas such as cycling, football and cricket. We see those who are challenging stereotypes and cultural barriers simply by taking part. These women are leaving a legacy that goes far beyond times or medals. It's a legacy that will endure and help change the face of the global sporting landscape.

However, despite the rays of light, we know that the overall picture is far from rosy and we see many sports that are languishing far behind in terms of equality in governance, participation, event and race opportunities, and commercial sponsorship.

Ask yourselves … How can it be right for the champion of the most prestigious multi-stage female cycling race, the 10-day Giro Rosa, to be awarded €525 when the winner of the Tour de France pockets €450,000? How can it be right to have to search with a fine-tooth comb to see a story on a sportswoman on the back pages of a mainstream newspaper? How can it be right that only 27 per cent of the boards of National Governing Bodies for sport in the UK are female?

The impact of these rules and traditions are grave, and go far beyond the professional sporting sphere. This book casts a thorough, much-needed eye on many of these questions. It is only by having such a spotlight shone on this subject that we can begin to find lasting solutions.

Let us not look back in 10 or 20 years' time and rue the day that we did not strive to change the status quo. When it was normal for women to be told, as the former managing director of Birmingham City FC, Karren Brady, was, that: 'You are going to have to be twice as good as the men to be considered even half as good.' Or a time when we rested on our laurels and looked around us saying that 'this isn't a problem', or 'this isn't *my* problem'.

We all have a role to play – elite athletes, the general public, government, national governing bodies, the media, sports managers and agents, facility providers, event organisers and other delivery bodies.

As Sarah so eloquently shows in *Kicking Off*, we can turn the tide. We can all make a difference. And we must all strive towards a situation when we no longer need a book about 'women in sport' to raise awareness about this hugely important issue and are able to look around and see a playing field that truly is level and open to all.

Introduction

It was February 2014 when I was granted the opportunity for an interview with the legendary Brazilian female footballer Marta Vieira da Silva (or Marta, as she is widely known). For five years in succession, from 2006 to 2010, she was named as the best female footballer in the world by the sport's international governing body, FIFA. To many she is quite simply the best woman ever to have played the game. It has been quite the journey for a woman who left her small town of Alagoas at the age of 14, to 'really try to make something of [her] life in football'.

But to many, Marta remains a relative unknown. Not because of any fault on her part but because she happens to excel at football – a sport that in her lifetime has existed largely for the benefit of men. Consider this: The best female footballer in the world has played for 10 different teams since her career began in 2000. Her time at five of those clubs ended because the clubs could no longer afford to exist. She has been involved in two different professional women's soccer leagues in the USA that both failed to make it into a third season before they too fell foul of dire finances. She has moved from Brazil to Sweden, to the USA, to Brazil, to the USA again and, finally, back to Sweden where at time of writing she plays for the nine-time Swedish champions, FC Rosengard.

None of the above has dimmed the passion Marta has for the sport she first played as a child on the grassless fields of Alagoas. It has marked her in some ways though, as becomes clear as I ask her to ponder the future of her sport. What would she change about it if she had the power, and ten years from now, how would she like to see women's football looking? The word 'structure' features heavily in her answer to both questions. 'I would like for the main countries to have really strong, professional and well-structured leagues', she says. 'And for women to be able to make a good life – an honourable career – from the game. Just like men.'

This book was already underway at the time Marta answered my questions. But hearing her reflect on the failure of her sport to provide a stable, sustainable career for even the most exceptional of its exponents reinforced why I was writing it. I could not shake the thought that if Marta's name had been Lionel Messi or Cristiano Ronaldo – two players who combined have won

FIFA's top award as many times as Marta has on her own – her career (not to mention her bank balance) would look so very different.

It is not only in the football world that such inconsistencies exist of course. But it is the sport that presents the widest discrepancies between the men and women who play it, to the extent that the men who do it best are rewarded with long term contracts worth millions of pounds a year, while the women who excel are forever aware that their career is built upon shifting sands.

'It's harder for women,' Marta told FIFA in 2011. 'The men earn a lot of money, and they have a lot of clubs they can choose to play for. We work very hard, but we're always thinking about what might happen next year — if there's going to be a team or a place for me.'

For the past nine years, I have worked on a weekly sport magazine. Its target readership is males aged between 18 and 40. We have often been asked why it should be that a sport magazine is only aimed at half the general population. Can't women like and want to read about sport, too?

Of course, the answer to this is a resounding yes. The reason why *Sport* magazine is targeted at men comes down to one rather predictable factor: money. As a free publication, *Sport* relies on advertising spend to make a profit, and the fact remains that there is far more money in men's sport than in women's.

This was proven to us in 2008 when *Sport* launched a female-specific supplement called *Sport Woman*, with the intention of running one of these every quarter. The first issue went down well. Readers provided positive feedback and industry types expressed their pleasure at seeing a rare focus on sportswomen. But while the big brands like Nike and Adidas were happy to put athletes forward for interview and for their kit to be featured, they were less willing to back up their support with cold, hard cash.

This reluctance to invest in women's sport is only one part of the story. Over the following eight chapters, I will endeavour to fill you in on the rest. It's not all bad news though, I promise. In recent years there have been many positive moments and significant steps forward for women involved in sport. Even in the course of writing this book, changes have occurred: Another male-only golf club has emerged from the dark ages and opened its doors to women, while FIFA has introduced quotas for female coaches at its most junior women's competition – the under 17 Women's World Cup – in 2016.

Over the following pages you'll read stories about women in sport that will make you chuckle at their absurdity, quotes that will make you twitch with rage, and tales that will make you wonder just how much things have changed since the days when women were told sport was 'not for girls'. As a girl who grew up loving all the things my mother believed I shouldn't – 'Wrestling? It's just a phase', she reassured my worried grandmother as I sat in front of the TV, transfixed by Hulk Hogan body slamming and clothes lining his opponents – I have never really paid any attention to what was or wasn't meant for me. But I have always wondered whether the day might come when sport – ALL sport – would be considered as much for women as it is for men.

We're not there just yet, but the sound of female voices can finally be heard punctuating the booming male din that has dominated the sports world for so long. This book is one of those female voices, so put it in the middle of the room and turn the volume up, because I've got plenty to say …

1: Who's that girl?

How do editors decide which sports people are worthy of splashing all over a front cover and which are not? Before entering the publishing industry I – a fresh-faced graduate with very little knowledge of the world I would soon be entering – believed that popularity and success were the key factors in determining who became a 'cover star' and who was left in the shadows. But after spending almost a decade writing for a weekly sport magazine, I now know there is a third word that is even more significant: recognisability. Whether that comes as a result of fame or infamy, having it can make all the difference to an athlete who is trying to make a living from their sport.

The key question then is this: How many sportswomen are truly recognisable to the average sports fan? Wherever you are in the world, the Williams sisters, Venus and Serena, are probably among the best-known female faces from the world of sport, with fellow tennis star Maria Sharapova tracking them every step of the way. In Britain, Olympic champions Jessica Ennis-Hill and Nicola Adams have also reached that sweet spot where sport and celebrity become intertwined, while in America it's the likes of WNBA star Candace Parker, UFC's Ronda Rousey and NASCAR driver Danica Patrick who have managed to achieve levels of fame to match their sporting achievements.

Ask the same question about sportsmen though, and the list becomes long; too long to include in all its glory here. Success rapidly brings worldwide fame to male football/soccer stars, boxers, tennis players and golfers, whose names and faces appear regularly in newspapers and magazines, as well as in adverts and on TV shows across the globe.

The imbalance in numbers is easily explained. Read any newspaper in the UK on any given day of the week and the back pages will be divided largely like this: 70 per cent Premier League football; 10 per cent cricket; 10 per cent rugby; with the remainder comprising a mishmash of motorsport, golf, tennis, athletics, cycling and any other 'minority' sports occurring at that time. Of course, this does alter on occasion. Tennis grabs a larger share of the column inches during each of the season's four Grand Slams, as does golf for the Majors and cycling for the duration of the Tour de France. There's also that fortnightly blip that occurs once every four years, when the Olympics gives sports like swimming, equestrian, rowing and hockey their moment in the sun – a moment that can even be prolonged beyond the closing ceremony if Team GB has tasted success.

Although even that does not last for long, according to a study by the University of Birmingham. Researchers there wanted to use the UK's hosting of the Olympic Games in 2012 to find out whether there was a boom in coverage of women's sports in the build-up to the Games and, crucially, whether it was sustained afterwards. They looked at six key national publications on weekend days in a three-week period in February 2012 and again in February 2013, counting the numbers of articles devoted to women's sport and measuring the article areas.

Their findings revealed a decline in coverage across all newspapers. In 2012, articles about women's sport accounted for 4.5 per cent of specialist sports sections and supplements, but a year later that figure dropped to 2.9 per cent. In terms of space, that meant a drop from 3 per cent of the area in these sections that was allocated to women, to 1.9 per cent. For Senior Clinical Lecturer in Public Health Dr Claire Packer, who led the study, these findings have potentially worrying implications for the numbers of women and girls taking part in sport: 'Despite the success of our female athletes both at the 2012 Games and since, women's sport, at least in the eyes of the print media we studied, remains a minority sport. Until we change this perception, the levels of participation of girls and women in sport will continue to suffer – as will public health as a result.'

Although the researchers do recognise the 'wider societal issues at play', they claim that such results are evidence of a deep-rooted gender bias in sports reporting – a bias which they believe is not fully understood by sports editors and their colleagues.

To find out how much of this is true, I put the question to the sports editors at the *Mail on Sunday* and the *Guardian*, who both said that the disparity in coverage is something they recognise and certainly do understand. They are willing to amend it too, when the time is right. Alison Kervin became Fleet Street's first female sports editor when the *Mail on Sunday* appointed her to the role in 2013. When I spoke to her about the calls for newspapers to increase coverage of women's sport, she said that those asking the question are missing a wider point: 'Before I started this role, I had this idea that if you just put more women into the papers that would solve things. They would be seen, people would have role models and more women and girls would do sport. But I don't think that's true now.'

Kervin is voicing a belief that is shared by many: Put more women's sports stories in front of more people and the profile of sportswomen will automatically be raised. But her time on Fleet Street has convinced Kervin that coverage isn't the magical cure-all many believe it to be: 'It's more complicated than just putting something in the paper that most people aren't really interested in. If I put a story in about women's hockey on a Sunday, I don't think it makes any difference. It doesn't have the impact you think it's going to have. It's just a patronising effort to give them publicity.

'It's the same with women's rugby. But something like the England women's rugby team winning the World Cup [as they did in 2014] does make a difference because that's a proper story. That's what women's sport needs: For them to create their own stories. It needs to be a story worth telling before you can tell it.'

The *Guardian*'s sports editor, Ian Prior, agrees, telling me: 'Stars make sport, and that's a fairly organic process from sport itself. There's no particular mystery to why athletes from the Williams sisters to Jessica Ennis-Hill to Paula Radcliffe have had huge amounts of coverage. They became superstars because they are extraordinary at what they do. They are at the top of their field and are dominant figures in their sport and attract attention accordingly. Nothing drives coverage like stars.

'For example, look at the coverage in the Irish media of the women's rugby team during the 2014 Rugby World Cup. Between Ireland beating the Black Ferns [New Zealand] and playing the semi-final against England, there was blanket, wall-to-wall coverage across all outlets for a solid week, purely as a result of their success. That team had been ignored for the past five years, but you beat New Zealand – a team that hadn't suffered defeat in a World Cup for 23 years – and suddenly everyone wants to know about you.'

But then you lose to England (as Ireland did), and, as quickly as the coverage arrived for them, it disappeared twice as fast. That is something that rings true for most sports outside of the 'big three' of men's rugby, cricket and football, because the media is a fickle beast. The hope is, though, that in those seven short days of blanket coverage earned by Ireland's stunning victory over the four-time world champions, something will have stuck. Whether it's the name of the captain (Fiona Coghlan, in case you're wondering), or simply the memory of a great game of rugby that ended with a historical win, what surely matters most is that women's rugby will have worked its way into the consciousness of more people in that week than ever before.

Such an audience is invaluable no matter what length of time they hang around for, says Kervin, who edited *Rugby World* magazine for three years from 1994 to 1997. During her time in charge, Kervin says the publication 'campaigned like mad' for women to be allowed to play rugby at Twickenham, either before or after a men's game. And in 2003, it happened. England played France at HQ as part of the Women's Six Nations tournament, with the game being played immediately prior to England's men launching their own Six Nations campaign against the same country on 15 February.

Both England teams won, and Kervin says she's 'convinced it made a huge difference' to have the women's game on the same bill as the men's: 'Normally, half the problem is that people don't see it. Even when women's rugby is televised, it's tucked away because there isn't the audience for it. But putting it on before or after the men, so people see it and say, actually, this isn't bad, can really help. People start to recognise players and know what's going on. It's the same patriotism, whether women or men are on the field. If England women are playing Wales at Twickenham, the predominantly English crowd will still cheer for England, won't they? It still has that sporting edge to it. So it's just being a bit clever about how you present it, really.'

While more people might have seen the game live than they would if it had been held away from Twickenham, there is no evidence of any increase in press coverage, despite the match representing such an historic moment. And the one report that can be found, on espn.co.uk, covers it in just three brief sentences:

'England's women's team marked their Twickenham debut in style with a 57–0 victory over France. England, playing the game as a curtain-raiser to the men's RBS 6 Nations showdown with France, ran in 10 tries. Sue Day and Chris Diver both scored hat-tricks as France found themselves totally outplayed.'

Still, the Rugby Football Union (RFU) clearly decided this combination approach was the way forward and have continued with it since then, with England's women playing many of their Six Nations home games on the same day as the men. It doesn't work for everyone, though. The *Guardian's* Sports Editor Ian Prior says he was at HQ in the autumn of 2013 to see England's men take on the All Blacks. A crowd of 80,000 gathered to watch the world champions pushed hard by England, but when the final whistle blew and it was time for the women's match to start, not everyone was prepared to hang around. 'It was a freezing cold day with temperatures hovering around zero', recalls Prior. 'By the time the men's game was finished no one could feel their fingers and toes. You just wanted to get out of there, not hang around for another game.

'In any sensible system the women's game would have been a curtain raiser, not on after the main event. If you put it on beforehand, even if you're not getting half the crowd you're getting at least a third which in a stadium like Twickenham is 20–25,000 people. You also introduce the possibility that TV will show a decent chunk of it as a preliminary. It really isn't rocket science. I don't know what the argument would be for not doing that, it's certainly not to do with the pitch cutting up, because pitches are much better than that these days.'

Prior's argument is hard to refute, especially for anyone who has been at Twickenham and observed the mass exodus that takes place at the end of the men's game, despite the impending kick-off of an England women's match. It's something the England and Wales Cricket Board (ECB) seem to understand a little better than the RFU. Women's Twenty-20 internationals are now played immediately prior to men's matches, with Sky Sports broadcasting both. Not only has this ensured that cricket fans are given the opportunity to watch the women's game, but it has also led to the England Women's team earning a first-ever standalone sponsorship deal. Signed in July 2014, the two-year deal means Kia cars are the sole title sponsor of England women's home Test matches.

For ECB chief executive, David Collier, it's a deal that proves how crucial media exposure is when it comes to making the sponsorship case for women's sport. He made his gratitude clear when announcing the partnership, thanking both Sky Sports and BBC Radio, whose coverage, he said, 'plays such a vital role in making the sport attractive to potential business partners'.

Another positive step came in November 2014, when the ECB announced that Sky Sports would be showing live coverage of every ball of the 2015 Women's Ashes for the very first time. The summer of 2015 also marked the first time a women's Test match was televised. This seems little to shout about given that the first men's Test match to be televised was in 1938, but for the Head of England Women's Cricket, Clare Connor, the progress – however slow it has been in coming – is hugely significant. She said: 'The level of broadcast coverage that the England women's team now gets is exceptional, and I am thrilled that the ECB, in partnership with Sky Sports, continues to lead the way in this respect within international women's team sport. It is this level of exposure and support that will ensure that the women's game continues to grow, and that will inspire the next generation of England women's cricketers.'

If there is a regret, it is one that is shared with the men's game: that cricket is no longer the preserve of terrestrial television. Imagine the reach and impact that women's cricket could have if it was available for all to view instead of being reserved for those with the will and finances to pay an annual subscription to Sky Sports.

Media exposure is something women's football has traditionally faced a titanic struggle with, particularly at club level where it is constantly overshadowed by the behemoth of the Premier League. It was this overshadowing that led the FA to make a revolutionary decision when they launched the new Women's Super League (FA WSL), in 2011. Instead of matches being played throughout the winter months, in direct competition with the men's leagues, they would be played from April until October. It was hoped that this cunning plan would fill the sad emptiness that appears in the lives of football fans between the end of May and the start of August (unless there's a World Cup or European Championship to get excited about of course).

The FA hoped that this plan would help women's football to build the audience it had lacked since its halcyon days during the First World War (when thousands would flock to watch the women play). Is it working? Well, the league is now well established and about to enter its sixth season, but it took until its fourth for the first real signs of change to emerge.

The 2014 FAWSL season was the most closely contested one yet. It was also the best attended, with crowd numbers 30 per cent higher than in 2013. 'The clubs are working hard to build local fanbases, engage sports fans and their communities, and it's paying off,' said Kate Brazier, the FA's head of women's leagues and competitions. 'The quality of the league has improved since we established the FA WSL, and fans are responding to that.'

That much is true, but the numbers themselves are still not where they should be considering the quality on show. The average WSL attendance in 2014 increased to 728, from 562 in 2013. Compare that to the second tier of men's football – the Championship – where the average attendance at games in the 2014/15 season was 17,847, and it's clear there is still a very long road ahead.

Brazier was right to laud the rise in quality though. It meant that unlike previous years when Arsenal Ladies were so far ahead of every other team they could almost be named champions on the first day of the season, the competition for the League title was still going strong with just one game left of the 2014 season. Going into the final day, three teams still had a chance of lifting the trophy: Chelsea, Birmingham City Ladies and Liverpool Ladies.

Despite starting the day in third place, behind Chelsea and Birmingham, it was Liverpool who ended the day as league champions, beating Chelsea into second only by virtue of a slightly better goal difference (both teams finished the season with 26 points). It was the most thrilling climax to a season that women's football had ever experienced. It was also the perfect way to begin the league's four-year television deal with BT Sport that was signed in 2013, and which sees the subscription channel commit to showing exclusively live games throughout the season as well as a weekly review show.

In the same year that BT Sport announced their deal with the FAWSL, the BBC also stepped up their game when it came to broadcasting women's football, promising to devote more air time and coverage to the sport than ever before across its TV, radio and online platforms. And to their credit, they delivered, broadcasting 16 matches on BBC Radio during the 2014 season and screening eight episodes of *The Women's Football Show* (a highlights programme in the *Match of the Day* vein) on BBC Three.

The BBC also showed England's 2015 World Cup qualifiers and the FA Cup Final. This is all great and to be applauded, but we should also put it into some sort of context. Try to find the semi-finals of the women's FA Cup on TV, for example, and, well, you won't. While matches in the men's version of the competition are considered worthy of televising from the third round onwards, female footballers must be an FA Cup finalist before they are deemed deserving of a slot on the television schedules. So well done and everything on reaching the semi-finals, girls, but it's still not quite good enough, sorry.

Despite such shortcomings, former England captain and Arsenal defender Casey Stoney focuses on the forward steps that have been taken. I caught up with her ahead of the 2015 Women's World Cup and she agreed that the media are picking up on women's football more than they ever have done: 'I think there's a lot of contributing factors to that, including moving the league to the summer months and the fact it is being marketed more. I also put it down to the 2012 Olympics, which gave us a platform to showcase our sport that we had never had before. When we played against Brazil at Wembley I think over 3.8 million people tuned into that on BBC Three. That's a vast number for us.'

England's women also attracted a record crowd for their match against Germany at Wembley Stadium in November 2014. Some 55,000 tickets were sold for a friendly against the European champions. Although London's rickety public transport system prevented around 10,000 from actually making it to the game, the final attendance of 45,619 still dwarfed the previous best for an England women's game of 29,092, recorded when England played Finland at Manchester City's Etihad Stadium in 2005, as part of the European Championships.

For Stoney, those numbers only serve to highlight the scarcity of women's sport coverage in the written press: 'When you think that even now, such a small percentage of articles in the media are focused on women's sport, there's still a lot of work to do. I think the media have a responsibility but it's also up to us as players, when it is on TV, to make sure it's a good advert.'

When the Women's Sport and Fitness Foundation (WSFF), now Women in Sport, conducted their most recent research in 2014 they found that women's sport received just seven per cent of total sports coverage in the media (in the US that number drops to an even more shocking four per cent). And when you consider that much of that seven per cent is likely to be dedicated to sports like tennis and athletics, where the women's programmes are given relatively equal billing to the men's, it doesn't leave a whole lot of air time for the rest.

The *Guardian*'s sports editor Ian Prior is in no doubt as to the consequences of this, telling me: 'You have to look at what distinguishes those women's sports that we do cover a lot of in the paper from the women's sports that we don't. To me there's one very constant factor. Championship athletics and tennis are the runaway successes of women's sport in terms of audience and athlete profile because the programming of women's sport is on a par with the men's. That's really no coincidence.'

It's the reason why the likes of the Williams sisters, Venus and Serena, and Jessica Ennis-Hill (or for example Allyson Felix in the US) are household names, while Casey Stoney and her replacement as England captain, Steph Houghton, are not. Every Grand Slam event brings the world's best female tennis players into our living rooms for two weeks at a time, while the athletics season provides multiple opportunities for female athletes to showcase their talents on national television.

As a result, female tennis players and athletes are far more visible and accessible to the average sports fan than women competing in other sports. For the *Mail on Sunday*'s sports editor Alison Kervin, that visibility provides tennis players and athletes with a golden opportunity to reveal their characters and personalities, so we know who they are, as well as what they can do. And it's that knowledge that is so crucial to building a rapport with viewers, Kervin tells me: 'In most women's sport there's no narrative because the characters aren't as established.

'Every weekend, we're all wondering things such as how will Wayne Rooney do? Or, what will Petr Čech be like when he's playing against his former team, Chelsea? The characters in women's sport haven't come to life in the same way – certainly in team sports – and that's because of lack of publicity. These things feed themselves. Until people start really wondering whether the England women's star striker is going to score in her next league game, it's very hard for the sport to become as engaging.

'When we run interviews with people, we're asking the questions we think readers would want to ask. It's genuinely quite hard to think what readers would want to ask of the women's volleyball team, for example. Readers haven't got the questions, and don't have a particular interest in them because they don't know the characters.

'In terms of working out who's famous and who's not, I do what a lot of journalists do – you think about what you'd tell your mum. If the captain of the England men's football team died and I rang my mum to tell her, she'd be shocked because you almost feel like you know these people. If I rang her and said it was a woman who plays hockey for England, she wouldn't respond in quite the same way. The public haven't formed a relationship with these characters like they have in the men's game.'

The launch of BT Sport in August 2013 appeared to spark some movement towards correcting this, with the channel committing itself to covering 21 tournaments live from the women's tennis tour and 12 live FA WSL games per season. They also hired Clare Balding, whose stellar work during the London 2012 Olympics ensured that she ended the Games as much of a household name as those who won gold medals for their efforts. Her weekly programme, cunningly titled 'The Clare Balding Show', was launched with the stated aim of featuring a female guest every week and, for the most part, has succeeded in fulfilling that aim (and, on the odd occasion it doesn't, you can be sure she hears about it from her legions of followers on Twitter).

Balding's skill during London 2012 was to make whichever sport she happened to be presenting – which could be anything from swimming to equestrianism – instantly appealing to a broad TV audience. It's a skill that has much to do with her own obvious and genuine passion for sport. Since that Olympic summer Balding has used her strengthened position to try and drive real change in the media's attitude towards women's sport, with her sights set firmly on those in the most powerful positions.

'You need your editor to be demanding women's sport coverage', she told the *Evening Standard*. 'Whether on (BBC Radio) 5 Live sports bulletins or in newspapers. The editor needs to be looking for it and saying: "Make sure I have a full page of women's sport every day. Make sure women's sport is in the sports bulletin every hour." Things become important because we make them important.'

Kervin, though, says this type of quota-filling approach could actually be counter-productive: 'It's a delicate balance. Women's sport has to earn its place otherwise it's just lip service.' I appreciate Kervin's point but it is difficult to align with a world in which sportswomen often receive a fraction of the coverage for achieving the same things (if not more) than their male counterparts. If they cannot "earn their place" by excelling at their sport, then how can they?

The *Guardian*'s sports editor, Ian Prior, is in the same camp as Balding. He tells me that a focused determination to close the gap in coverage between women's and men's sport is the only way to make changes happen. He says he is certain that his paper is covering more women's sport now than it was before London 2012, and puts that certainty down to the 'conscious effort' that has been made to do so. 'But that effort is guided far more by what we think is right than by anything that's happening in terms of our audience. And let's make no bones about it, that's positive discrimination.

'Why do we do it? Because I genuinely think that the balance in sports pages is wrong, and that it does need an artificial correction that's driven by something other than the brute market forces. It's wrong to say there's no audience for women's sport because there is, and you could even call it significant. But the audience for women reading men's sport is a lot greater than the audience for anyone reading women's sport.'

Prior's last point is one on which he and Kervin do agree. As the first female sports editor on Fleet Street, Kervin admits she feels more responsibility to cover women's sport than perhaps her male predecessors might have, but says it's a responsibility that's tempered by the one she also feels with regards to her position as editor: 'You feel responsibility to do your job well and to not mess it up by filling the paper with things that you fancy filling it with, rather than what people want. I did a lot of research when I started the job which showed that predominantly, everyone is interested in men's football, men's rugby and men's cricket. To ignore that completely would be really unprofessional. But I do feel a responsibility, and I'm sure there is more women's sport in since I've been sport editor. I think that comes down to me being more aware of it rather than me trying to create stories that fit my agenda, though. I think that would be a huge mistake.'

Giving readers and viewers what they want is one of the most frequently proffered explanations for men's sport receiving more coverage than women's. Indeed, Ian Prior describes the small number of people wanting to read about women's sport as the 'principle overwhelming obstacle' to it getting more coverage. 'There is a fiction abroad', he says, 'that sports editors don't do enough women's sport for reasons that are entirely to do with being the victim of their own prejudices. I wouldn't claim that every sports editor is of an entirely open mind, but at the same time editors aren't particularly stupid with regards to knowing what their audiences want to read and how much of it. And without doubt, a willingness to read more is the single biggest barrier.'

How can he be so sure that the interest isn't there? Prior says that knowing what readers want is a lot more straightforward now than it used to be: 'Back in the days when we did nothing but produce print papers, if there were biases in the coverage, the problems were far more to do with personal preferences and convictions of editors. These days we monitor traffic [on the internet] remorselessly. We know an awful lot about our audiences. We know exactly what they're reading at any given moment, in what numbers they're reading it, and the factors that are influencing them to read it. I think the days where you could possibly validly argue that there was a silent majority out there that you weren't listening to are gone. We know exactly what they're reading.'

Prior's own newspaper published a blog on the topic in 2013, primarily to explain why a weekly women's football report had been scrapped. 'When there are signs of increasing popularity in a women's sport we try to react to that. But it's difficult to keep putting things up that aren't being read', wrote Prior at the time. He argued that the 50 per cent of the *Guardian*'s sports coverage that is devoted to men's football would actually be even higher if editors were entirely governed by market forces (the piece went on to claim that in such a scenario, 'probably 75 per cent of resources and coverage would go to football and 25 per cent to everything else').

With the written press being forced to cut costs – and sometimes corners – to preserve struggling profits these days, Prior explains that commercial factors cannot be ignored: 'The *Guardian* is not a charity. We live in the same commercial environment as everyone else. Ok, we're not answerable to shareholders but at the same time we're not publically subsidised either. We have to make money. I need readers, and I need readers in great volume, particularly in the digital world.'

The numbers game is rarely one that has female winners, especially when there are targets to be hit. The BBC has no such worries when it comes to viewing figures – in theory, at least. But that can also leave the broadcaster vulnerable to fierce scrutiny. In recent years though, there has been a significant increase in women's sport appearing across the BBC's services.

BBC Sport reporter Karthi Gnanasegaram started her broadcasting career at the BBC, before leaving to gain more experience elsewhere. She tells me that when she returned to the national broadcaster in time for the build-up to the 2012 Olympics there was a noticeable shift in how much more women's sport they were showing compared to her earlier time there: 'Whereas most other networks only really mentioned women when it came to tennis (and then only the top few names that people would recognise) and athletics, there seemed to be a concerted effort at the BBC to boost the profile of women's sport and put sportswomen on level terms with sportsmen in a variety of sports.'

Gnanasegaram says she doesn't consider this increased focus on women's sport as positive discrimination because, in her view, it was 'a mistake to not report on women's sport as a matter of course for such a long time'. She adds that the BBC keeps across a much greater number of sports now than it used to, and that in turn means that women's sport gets more of a mention.

Not everyone has been satisfied with the BBC's coverage, however. In 2014, the 2008 Olympic cycling champion Nicole Cooke called on the broadcaster to give the same amount of coverage to women's sport as it does to men's, citing the example of the USA where a law passed in 1972 called Title IX (more on this in Chapter 6) requires equal funding for men's and women's university sport scholarships. 'We could do the same with TV time', said Cooke. 'If the BBC is paid for by the public, then maybe equality there could be brought in.'

The BBC responded with a statement declaring: 'We broadcast around 1,000 hours of women's sport every year on BBC television, meaning almost

20 per cent of our coverage is dedicated to women's sport.' It's not exactly the 50 per cent Cooke is calling for just yet, then, but as the likes of Sky Sports and BT Sport continue to wrap up the rights to more and more live sport, the BBC is left with an ever dwindling selection – something which could end up pushing that 20 per cent a little higher.

The situation is something Cooke touches on in her 2014 autobiography, *The Breakaway*, when she writes of the increasing coverage given to track cycling following the success of the GB cycling team at the 2008 Olympics: 'The BBC was undergoing change as satellite channels outbid them for so many of the sporting jewels they took for granted. The Corporation started trawling for sports that were easy to cover and did not come with a high price tag, and in which … British success was frequent. Track cycling was about to fit the bill perfectly.'

While Cooke is right to label the USA as a fine example in terms of the way university sports are funded, she would be disappointed to learn that when it comes to media coverage of her fellow sportswomen, there is little for the USA to boast about.

In 1989, a group of American sociologists began a study of gender in US sports coverage, releasing reports into their findings every five years. In the latest report, released in 2009 (the 2014 results were not available at time of writing), they discovered that women's sports accounted for less than two per cent of network news and highlight programmes (they focused on ESPN Sportscentre, which is a nationally televised programme similar to Sky Sports News in the UK). That figure is a significant drop from the 6.3 per cent they found in 2004.

Cheryl Cooky, Associate Professor of Women's Gender and Sexuality Studies at Purdue University in Indiana, was one of the sociologists responsible for putting together the 2009 study. When I caught up with her for a chat between her classes, she told me that that the decline was particularly surprising considering the participation figures: In 1971, 294,000 high-school girls played interscholastic sports. Today that number is up to 3.1 million. 'More women than ever are participating in sport at all levels', says Cooky, 'with collegiate women's sports growing in popularity. So it was a bit surprising not to see an increase in coverage.'

While on the whole it was a huge disappointment to see such a drop, Cooky and her colleagues found one positive from the decline when they dug deeper into the numbers: 'What we saw was that while the total amount of coverage had declined over that timeframe, there was also a drop in the amount of humorous sexualisation of women's sports and athletes. We saw fewer trivialised stories. It almost felt to me that the mainstream sports news media don't really know how to talk about women's sports unless they're sexualising female athletes, trivialising them or making fun of them. They don't have a narrative framework to talk about female athletes in a respectful way, which is why we saw that decline. From that standpoint the results are not that surprising because sports journalism in the US, as it is elsewhere, is very much male dominated and still has that very hyper masculine culture about it.'

The picture becomes bleaker still when I talk to Joe Fleming, who is the Deputy Sports Editor at daily newspaper *USA Today*: 'I know that 10 years ago I think we felt an obligation to balance our coverage', he says. 'It wasn't 50-50, but it was probably around 75 per cent men's sport and 25 per cent women's. For example, women's college basketball used to have a weekly presence via a column in the daily section, but we just don't do that anymore.

'Part of the reason for that is we're a bottom-line business in a lot of ways nowadays, and the traffic online doesn't support some of the coverage we used to give. Women's tennis does well because of Serena Williams and Maria Sharapova, but the traffic numbers online just aren't there for most women's sports in our publication. How we end up handling that is by putting our resources more and more into the NFL, college football and NBA. We put more of our people on those sports and ... that's where the traffic is coming from.'

From the UK, across the Atlantic to the USA, the argument put out by those within mainstream media is the same: we are giving readers and viewers what they want. Not only does this attitude ensure women's sport doesn't get the chance to prove otherwise but also, says Cooky, 'it helps to maintain the myth that sports are exclusively by, about and for men.'

If this is the scale of the problem then, what is the solution? Fleming points to the unassailable rise of digital media, and says that while women's sports might struggle to find a home in the mainstream press, new media offers a viable alternative: 'There are all kinds of niche websites out there for people to get the information they want and read the stories they want. So it is more accessible than before.'

He's talking about websites like Womentalksports.com in the US, which offers an online space connecting the best blogs relating to women's sports. In the UK, Sportsister.com has been giving women's sport a voice in a similar way since its launch in 2008. While these sites do an excellent job of covering women's sport for those who know about them, Cooky does not see them as the solution: 'These are niche outlets that are almost alternative spaces. You have to really be in the know to know about them, or really seek them out, whereas coverage of men's sport is just a part of the media landscape that exists out there.

'I don't have to seek it out, it's in front of me. I can't avoid it in some ways. If these sites are the future, then it's unfortunate because I don't think it bodes well for women's sports in terms of generating and sustaining interest, meeting the needs of fans and expanding to new markets and new fan bases.'

She's got a point. It seems like a backward step to take women's sport out of the mainstream and put it into these 'niche' places where only those who are actively seeking it (and are therefore already fans) will be able to find it. Sure, it's better than nothing, but not by much.

In the UK, Sky Sports have offered a broadcasting-based solution in the form of their weekly *Sportswomen* programme. The 30-minute long show, launched in November 2013 and broadcast on a Tuesday morning (with repeats at 6.30pm on the same day), delivers interviews with sportswomen or those involved with promoting women's sport, as well as updating viewers with the latest women's sports news. It is the one time and place on the Sky Sports News channel where women's sport has guaranteed coverage.

While it can be considered a 'win' for women's sport to have this ring-fenced time, Cooky tells me she has mixed feelings about media outlets that are solely dedicated to women's sport: 'I feel very ambivalent about them. On the one hand they are a way and a space for women to get coverage. And more importantly, they are a way for fans of women's sports to follow teams and for people to see women playing sport, which I think is a powerful message for society that has important implications in terms of gender equality.

'At the same time, having a separate format to cover women's sport really leaves the male dominance of the mainstream media intact. Ideally we would want to see more coverage of women in those spaces – on *Sports Centre* and on the nightly news, and in the newspapers and in *Sports Illustrated* and other media outlets. But until that happens, I guess this is a necessary evil.'

Cooky is right. When the battle is proving to be so incredibly difficult for women to win, it would seem foolish not to take any route possible to gaining some precious ground – even if that route does appear to be a scenic one at best.

While the governing bodies of some sports have taken criticism for failing to help their female competitors to raise their public profile, others have taken steps that can be seen as strategically pretty smart. In the US, Joe Fleming points out the US Golf Association (USGA)'s leverage of its prize asset – the US Open – to encourage the national NBC network to show the equivalent women's tournament. He tells me that 'NBC paid to cover the men's US Open and as part of that package the USGA said they also have to televise the Senior Open and the Women's Open. That's why the US Women's Open was on NBC all these years, because it was part of the package. If the US Women's Open was on its own trying to sell itself, it would be a much harder sell. So I think it would help if more governing bodies did what the USGA have done.'

In the UK, the RFU utilised a similar strategy to try and build a profile for the England women's rugby team during the Six Nations. When planning media appearances, they ensured the men's and women's press conferences were conducted back to back. By doing it this way, they found the women received more press coverage than they would by holding a standalone women's team press conference. If you get the journalists there in the first place, it seems that is half the battle won (not that we're a lazy breed, but giving sports reporters the opportunity to get a lot of interviews done without the need for moving too far is always an attractive option. Actually it's true, we are a lazy breed).

This is one of the many reasons why it was so crucial for the annual Women's Boat Race to be moved, as it was in 2015. Originally held in Henley a week before the world-famous men's Boat Race, 11 April 2015 saw it held on the same stretch of the River Thames and on the same day as the men's, for the first time in the event's history. Despite the predictable Oxford victory (the Dark Blues had won seven of the previous 10 races), it was a momentous day for women's sport in Britain.

Symbolically it showed that the women were finally level pegging with the men, after years of being treated like second-class citizens. But just as – if not more – importantly than its symbolic importance, the move to the Tideway was crucial to securing television coverage for the women's race. While the BBC has televised the men's race since 1938, the 2015 event was the first time the women's race was broadcast live, with the BBC committing to cover it from 2015 until 2021. Paul Davies, Executive Producer for the BBC's coverage, spoke proudly of the BBC's intentions when the planned coverage was announced in February 2012, promising to 'cover [the women's event] as a proper race, that's for sure.' How very good of them.

On the surface it looked like the BBC was finally moving into the 21st century, but the reality was that it had been left with little choice in the matter thanks to some smart negotiating by a woman called Helena Morrissey. As chief executive of investment firm Newton Asset Management, Morrissey had been behind the firm's initial decision to sponsor the Women's Boat Race in 2011. Shocked at the vast inequalities in funding and facilities that the women received compared to the men, she made it her mission to achieve parity for the female rowers who exerted the same effort and suffered the same blistered hands as their male counterparts.

When Newton's parent company, BNY Mellon, took over sponsorship of the men's race a year later in 2012, Morrissey spied her opportunity. She made sure that her call for the women's race to receive equal billing to the men's was made a key condition of the deal. There were some raised eyebrows among the traditionalists, but Morrissey's hunch that the money would talk loudly enough to drown out any doubts proved to be correct. And once the confirmation came that the women's race would take place on the same day and in the same place as the men's, any refusal by the BBC to cover both would have been a major PR fail.

If it had not been for Morrissey's foresight and determination, the Women's Boat Race would most likely have remained an out-of-the-way and out-of-sight event. Because while some in the media might feel a sense of obligation to cover women's sport – that it is something they really *should* be doing – that feeling is all too easily overcome when the so-called 'bottom line' comes into play.

'I feel some obligation myself as a member of the media', says *USA Today*'s Joe Fleming, 'but I don't know if that feeling is as broad as it used to be because the people who are making decisions can see the bottom line nowadays. They can see the numbers. Outside of some occasional stories – just throwing a bone to some women's sports – they make the case that there's just not enough interest to spend too many resources on it. So yes, I do feel an obligation but I also understand that people making the decisions have numbers backing them up.'

Ah yes, the all-important numbers. Cooky sites some of her own in response to these, asking: 'What responsibility does the media have in terms of reporting on what's happening in the world? I don't know how you can report on what's happening in the world of sport while ignoring 40 per cent of its participants.'

The bottom line? I think that's probably it.

Billie Jean King

'I always told people that one day, we're going to be playing for millions of dollars and be truly global. I can see us playing all over the world.' Billie Jean King is talking in the overly air-conditioned press room of the Singapore Sports Hub stadium, where the 2014 Women's Tennis Association (WTA) Championships are being held for the first time. The 44th edition of the prestigious tournament, which acts as the climax to the women's tennis season, saw more than 129,000 fans flock to see the world's top eight female players play for the honour of lifting the Billie Jean King trophy. It was Serena Williams who emerged on top and got her hands on a trophy bearing the name of perhaps the only female tennis player who can rival her in the fame stakes.

The victory took Williams's prize money earnings to $9,317,298 for 2014, and saw her career winnings hit an astronomical $63,500,779. For King, whose early days in the sport saw her make $14 per day as an amateur, such figures must be almost beyond comprehension.

'When I see these players making big money, I feel proud,' King tells me when we chat a few days into the tournament. 'That's what we always wanted for the future generations so when I speak to them I say: "You're living our dream." It's great to see a dream come true through the future generations.'

King's presence at the WTA Championships in Singapore is reflective of the unbreakable tie between her and the association she formed in 1973, when she and 63 other women gathered in a London hotel to make decisions that would change the course of women's sport forever. The origins of the WTA can be traced back even further though, to another historical event in 1970, this one taking place at the New York residence of *World Tennis Magazine*'s founder and editor, Gladys Heldman.

'At that time', King recalls, 'we were having tournaments taken away from us. When tennis went professional in 1968 the women started losing opportunities to even play — forget the money, we didn't have places to compete. So the writing was on the wall. We were going to have nothing, eventually. It was going to be all guys competing.'

The start of the Open era had shown in no uncertain terms where women's tennis stood, and it wasn't even in the same postcode as the men's game. By the time King won the women's singles title at Wimbledon in 1968, she was already a four-time Grand Slam champion, having won the two previous Wimbledon singles titles, the 1967 US Championships and the 1968 Australian Championships. In short, she was one of the game's biggest stars. And yet, lifting the Venus Rosewater Dish for a third time saw King collect winnings of just £750, while the men's champion Rod Laver (also winning a third Wimbledon singles title in 1968) received £2,000.

Matters came to a head two years later when King and co. discovered that an upcoming tournament in Los Angeles was paying the men eight times as much as the women. When they approached the event chairman, former tennis player Jack Kramer, and asked him to reduce the disparity in prize money, he refused.

King and her eight allies – Rosie Casals, Nancy Richey, Kerry Melville, Peaches Bartkowicz, Kristy Pigeon, Judy Dalton, Valerie Ziegenfuss and Julie Heldman (daughter of Gladys) – gathered at the Heldman home to discuss what they could do about the situation. Now known as the 'Original Nine', the women knew that if women's tennis was to have any sort of a future, they would have to break away from the tennis establishment and do it on their own.

'I remember saying to the others: "Here's the deal: If we do this, do not do it for applause and do not do it for money. Do it because it's the right thing to do." We talked about what we wanted and I said: "I'm going to tell you what I want and then you guys can tell me if you agree or not and we can have a discussion. I want for any girl in the world if she's good enough, to have a place to play, to be recognised – really recognised – and to make a living. I want her to be a professional athlete." They said: "Yeah, we like that too, Billie." Everyone agreed so we said: "Let's go for it."'

The task of setting up a women's event then fell to Gladys Heldman, a woman who her daughter Julie says 'knew everyone in tennis'. In a speech she made at a reunion of the Original Nine in 2012, Julie recalled that a matter of days after the meeting Gladys had gained verbal permission from the men in power at the United States Lawn Tennis Association (USLTA), contacted people in Houston to run the tournament, and rounded up the players. 'Yet when the Houston tournament was about to start, the USLTA made an about face, threatening to suspend any player who competed in Houston. Those suspensions could cause havoc for the players and the club.'

Gladys was quick to react, coming up with a solution that made clever use of the complex rules distinguishing amateurs and professionals in 1970. 'To make the tournament work, my mother creatively made all the players contract professionals for one week by signing them up for $1. That solution protected the players and the club.'

Heldman also brokered a deal with Joseph Cullman III, who was then President of a company called Philip Morris USA and, as luck would have it, also a big tennis fan. She persuaded Cullman that his new women's cigarette brand, Virginia Slims, should sponsor a new women's tennis tournament and thus win over a host of new female fans. He was convinced and the Virginia Slims Invitation was born. 'It was the tournament that would forever change tennis and open the doors for generations of women professional tennis players to make a living playing the sport they love', wrote King in her 2008 book, *Pressure is a Privilege*.

After the final, which saw Rosie Casals beat Judy Dalton in three sets, the women gathered at the Heldman house and talked about their next steps. For King, it was simple: 'I remember asking Gladys, could you go get us money for a tour next year? She went back to Slims and said: "Hey, I've got an even better idea for you, instead of one tournament why don't we do a series of tournaments?"'

The Virginia Slims Series started small, but by the end of 1970 it had grown from nine to 40 members who travelled the US (plus one event in Puerto Rico), playing anywhere a big enough crowd could be gathered to enable prize money to be paid. 'Some of the places we played were really not equipped for tennis', recalled Rosie Casals in the PBS documentary, *American Masters: Billie Jean King*. On occasion the players would arrive at arenas that didn't have any tennis balls, having to dispatch someone to a sports shop to buy them, other times they would arrive at the venue to find the court hadn't been laid yet.

The players even got involved in finding spectators: 'We'd stand out in the street and stop cars and give out tickets', says King. 'We didn't care, it was fun.' The media were unsure what to make of it all, often sending their 'society' reporters to cover events instead of the sports writers. The bemused journalists would ask King and co.: 'Just how long do you think you can keep this up?'

Despite the uncertainty from some quarters, Virginia Slims had the marketing and advertising know-how – both from within, and from its advertising agency, Leo Burnett – to ensure the series grew. The brand had been using women's liberation slogans since 1968 to build a modern female image, and now it was throwing its full weight and influence behind King and her colleagues, who were the epitome of the Slims slogan: 'You've come a long way, baby.'

By 1973 there were 22 US-based tournaments on the schedule offering $775,000 in prize money, while the USLTA's threat to ban those playing on the Virginia Slims Tour from Grand Slam events had failed to materialise. Progress had been made, but King knew there was still a long way to go for women's tennis.

'We were empowered by the Virginia Slims Tour but I wanted all the women to be together', says King, pointing to the fact that by 1973 the USTA (United States Tennis Association, formerly USLTA) had set up their own, official, women's tour to rival Virginia Slims. 'When the USTA heard about the Virginia Slims circuit, they saw the handwriting on the wall … they got Evonne Goolagong, Chris Evert, Margaret Court and Virginia Wade – all the players who wouldn't go with us. The only reason the USTA organised the circuit was because they didn't want to lose control.'

King and her Original Nine colleagues tried to influence key players on the USTA's Tour, even visiting Evert and her father Jimmy (who was also her coach) in Florida to try and convince them to join their circuit. In Lynn Gilbert's biography of King, called *Particular Passions* (2012), King recalls saying to Evert: 'We're hurting tennis by being divided. Please come with us because we're really the future.' Chris said: 'It's unfair to the USTA. I don't want to rock the boat.' Her father agreed. I said to her: 'Chris, I'll talk to you ten years from now and you'll think differently … the only reason any of us are getting any money is because Gladys [Heldman] and Joe [Cullman, the CEO of the company that owned the Virginia Slims brand] were willing to take a risk. Do you think USTA would have started a circuit unless they were forced to?'

'I don't know', she said.

King did, and she remained determined to unite all the women. A week before Wimbledon in the summer of 1973, King hosted a meeting for 64 top female players in a room at London's Gloucester Hotel. 'If we can't make this happen today,' began an exhausted King, 'then I'm finished, because I cannot spend one more ounce of my life on this.' With the doors locked and the tall, imposing figure of Dutch player Betty Stove guarding the exit, the women discussed and debated their future. They voted too, electing leaders, a treasurer and a secretary.

King had come prepared with legal documents for everyone to sign, ensuring that the meeting would end with concrete foundations in place: 'I knew not to let them out until they'd signed up and we had our officers, because I knew if they didn't have something legal to sign, that maybe it could fall apart after they left. The media thought we were going to boycott Wimbledon. I said no: 'We've got our association. It's the Women's Tennis Association.'

The minutes of that meeting on 20 June 1973 fill three pages of A4 paper and begin with the emphatic words: 'Well, we've finally done it!' It lists the officers and committee members and names King as President with Virginia Wade as her Vice President. The minutes conclude with the emphatic words: 'We are 64 members strong, our members come from 18 countries and five continents!'

'We were in business', says King who went on to win the 'triple crown' of the women's singles, women's doubles and mixed doubles at Wimbledon that year (a feat that won her a total of £3,550, while the men's singles champion, Jan Kodes took home £5,000). With 81 of the top men's players boycotting the 1973 tournament in a stand against the ban placed on Yugoslavia's Nikola Pilic by the International Lawn Tennis Federation (ILTF) for his refusal to play in a Davis Cup tie, King remembers it as 'a great Wimbledon for women that year. We got a lot of attention'.

More attention had not equalled more money though – something King remained determined to change. At her home Grand Slam, the US Open, King had won $10,000 for securing the women's singles title in 1972, while the men's winner, Ilie Nastase had earned $25,000. In 1973, bolstered by the successful creation of the WTA, King returned to New York for a meeting with the US Open tournament director, Billy Talbert. A legendary doubles player during his own career, Talbert served as the Open's tournament director from 1971–75 and then again from 1978–87, and was never one to shy away from making big calls. In 1971 he took the rare decision to put a 16 year old making her Grand Slam debut on Stadium Court for her first-round match. Chris Evert didn't let him down, thrashing 34-year-old Edda Buding in 42 minutes to kick-start a remarkable run that took America's newest tennis sweetheart all the way to the semi-finals (where she was beaten by the more experienced King).

Some three years after Talbert took a risk that helped to propel the career of a teenage sensation, he took another one that helped to propel women's tennis as a whole. Receiving a visit from an almost 30-year-old King whose will to win on the tennis court was nothing compared to her determination to ensure women were no longer the poorer sex, Talbert listened intently to her arguments for equal pay at the US Open. King backed up her words by producing a survey conducted by the WTA that showed tennis fans had a strong interest in the women's game. Finally, King concluded with the announcement that she had already put sponsors in place who had agreed to pay the difference between the men's and women's purses.

Talbert was won over, and with extra funds donated by a deodorant brand called 'Ban', the US Open became the first Grand Slam to offer equal prize money to men and women. When asked if there would be any complaints from the male players, Talbert answered simply: 'If there are, I'll just tell the men to go out and sell their product better.'

In July 1973, beneath the headline *Tennis Decides All Women are Created Equal, Too*, the New York Times reported: 'Stepping in to rectify a situation that Mrs Billie Jean King once said "stinks", Ban deodorant announced yesterday it would donate $55,000 in prize money to make the women's purse at the 1973 US Open tennis championships equal to the men's.'

King recalls how that period in time was the height of the women's movement, and that there was considerable social pressure to start doing things differently. But even so, she praises the USTA for acting so quickly: 'They broke new ground by paying the women the same as the men, well before that was the popular thing to do. I was proud that the US championship was the first to take this important step towards equality.'

Margaret Court won the 1973 US Open women's singles title and the $25,000 that went with it, but King had won something far more valuable. She had set women's tennis on the path to equal prize money at all four of the Grand Slams. It was to prove a long one, though. The US Open stood alone in offering equal prize money until 1984 when the Australian Open followed suit. But the Aussies had a change of heart in 1995 when the tournament organisers said that men's matches earned higher ratings. Years of lobbying from the WTA followed until 2001, when the Australian Open returned to its equal pay policy offering US$450,000 to the winners of the men's and women's singles crowns.

It was another six years before Wimbledon and the French Open ensured equality across the board, with Wimbledon announcing their intention to do so in February 2007, and the French Open joining them a month later. After years of resisting calls to make rewards for men and women equal, Chairman of the All England Club Tim Phillips seemed to have finally grasped the full implications when he said: 'We hope it will also encourage girls who want a career in sport to choose tennis as their best option. In short, good for tennis, good for women players and good for Wimbledon.'

With many other women's sports still lagging behind in the prize-money stakes (an issue that I'll delve deeper into in Chapter 5), the current stars of women's tennis are well aware that their situation could be so very different had it not been for King and her colleagues. 'I have so much respect for Billie Jean King and her generation', says former world number one, Caroline Wozniacki. 'Because of the way they fought, my generation is now living the dream.' Wozniacki's gratitude is echoed by Serena Williams who calls King her 'inspiration', and Maria Sharapova who credits the 12-time Grand Slam singles champion with encouraging her to think more about the future generations: 'I think that's one of the best gifts that Billie has taught so many players; that what you do today will eventually affect the players that you don't even know today, in the years to come. When you look back at what she did, her motivation and work helped us today. It gives us a pretty good reason to look at it unselfishly for the future and I hope all of us are able to do that for the girls that are young right now.'

By the time King secured the historic win of equal pay in New York, she had already committed to play in a match that would go down in history. In a press conference that July, a $100,000 winner-takes-all match between King and a 55-year-old former Wimbledon champion called Bobby Riggs had been announced to take place in September 1973. 'I'll tell you why I'll win,' sneered the self-described male chauvinist pig. 'She's a woman and they don't have the emotional stability.'

Riggs had been one of the greatest tennis players in the world. In 1939 he won the men's singles, doubles and mixed doubles titles at Wimbledon, and spent part of his career as the number one ranked player in the world. By 1973, Riggs had been retired from professional tennis for 22 years and, depending on who you believe, was either craving a return to the spotlight or chasing a sizeable pay out to get himself out of some serious debt with the Mob.

Early in the year, Riggs identified a wishlist of female opponents who he felt could help propel him back into the big time. King was right at the top of that list, with Chris Evert and Margaret Court not far behind.

King felt it was a no-win situation. Win, and it would be dismissed as an easy victory over a 55-year-old retiree. Lose, and her efforts at winning women's tennis the respect it deserved would be severely damaged. She was also rather busy, playing regularly, working to get the women's professional tour started and helping to get Title IX – the ground breaking legislation that would require all high schools, colleges and universities receiving federal funds for education to spend those funds equally on boys and girls – passed in Congress. King knew there was no way she could devote the time she would want to training and preparing for a match against Riggs – a match that could have a significant impact on the progress of women's sports.

'I did not want anything to set back the struggle that I and so many other women were enduring, and I wondered what would happen if I – or any other woman – lost to Bobby.'

When Riggs realised he was chasing a lost cause he turned his attentions to a young Chris Evert, or to her dad, at least. With Evert not yet 20, her father declined on her behalf, sending Riggs to Margaret Court, who in 1970 had become the first woman to win the Grand Slam during the open era. She had taken a year off to give birth to her first child in 1972, but returned in 1973 to win three of the four Grand Slam women's singles and women's doubles tournaments, ending the year as the top-ranked female player.

Court signed up, apparently oblivious to the potentially damaging consequences. While King was acutely aware this was a match that was about more than just tennis – 'it was about social change, about women's sports and women's rights' – Court saw it as an exhibition, and an opportunity to silence a man with a rather big mouth.

Finally, Riggs had his 'Battle of the Sexes', which would be played against Court on Mother's Day (13 May) 1973 in California. Throughout the build-up to the match Court was confident she would not be troubled by him, boasting: 'I've beaten better men in practice matches.' Not this time. In front of 3,200 fans in makeshift bleachers and with a national television audience watching on, it took Riggs just 57 minutes to secure a 6-2, 6-1 victory. In the press conference that followed he had one thing on his mind: 'Now I want King bad. I'll play her on clay, grass, wood, cement, marble or roller skates', he declared.

King had been playing at a tournament in Japan at the time of Court's defeat and was boarding a plane back to the US when a flight attendant filled her in on the score. 'I could not believe what I had heard', she recalls, of a match that became known as the 'Mother's Day Massacre'. King knew what she had to do if the women's movement was to maintain its forward momentum: 'I had no choice – I had to play Bobby, and I had to beat him.'

On 10 September 1973 – 10 days before he was due to meet King in a $100,000 winner-takes-all match at the Houston Astrodome – a caricature of Riggs adorned the cover of *Time* magazine. Inside, he was quoted as saying: 'Billie Jean King is one of the all-time tennis greats, she's one of the superstars, she's ready for the big one, but she doesn't stand a chance against me. Women's tennis is so far beneath men's tennis, that's what makes the contest with a 55-year-old man the greatest contest of all time. I went to Wimbledon this year to watch her play, I wasn't scared before, but after watching the girls at Wimbledon I may even be overconfident.'

It was nothing King hadn't been hearing for months already. Ever since the match-up with King was first announced at a press conference in July, Riggs had used every opportunity he could to talk as loudly and obnoxiously as possible. The build-up was unlike anything King had ever experienced, with the event being hyped on every television channel as well as in newspapers and magazines for weeks. As she travelled to tournaments on the Virginia Slims Tour, she was followed by reporters who had little interest in her 'day job' but an insatiable fascination with Riggs and the upcoming 'Battle of the Sexes: Part II'.

'The stakes were high', says King, 'and the media pressure made them even higher. If I lost, it was going to be an even bigger blow for women's rights than Margaret's loss had been – Bobby would now have proved his point by beating not one but two of the top-ranked women in the sport.'

The night of 20 September 1973 was to be the one that changed King's life forever. It was also a night that impacted on millions of people around the world as a television audience of more than 30 million was estimated to have tuned in to watch King take on Riggs. The Houston Astrodome itself was filled with almost 31,000 spectators, with those in courtside seats paying $100 to get close to the action.

ABC's television coverage opened with Irving Berlin's 'Anything You Can Do', setting the tone for the announcer's introductions and the entrances that followed: 'So this is what it has come down to', began ABC's Howard Cosell, 'a long-awaited match. Hustled and promoted ceaselessly and shrewdly by Bobby Riggs. Excitement engendered all over the country … And here comes Billie Jean King – a very attractive young lady; if she ever let her hair grow down to her shoulders and took her glasses off, you'd have someone vying for a Hollywood screen test.' What a charmer.

The match got off to a nervy start with both players making uncharacteristic errors beneath the glare of the stadium's bright lights. Riggs struck the first blow, however, breaking King's serve in the fifth game to take a 3-2 lead. 'That was my moment of truth', reflects King. 'I had to regain control.' Changing her game from her usual attacking style to one that mixed up the speed and power and relied on her accuracy to manoeuvre the ball from one side of the court to another, King had Riggs covered in sweat and breathing heavily within minutes, striking back and wrapping up the first set 6-4. Although she lost her serve in the first game of the second, King went on to win that one, too.

With Riggs visibly tiring in the third set, King ignored her cramping calves to take a 5-3 lead and found herself at match point. 'I completely choked', she says. 'On my second match point I recall hitting a forehand so low it hit the bar at the bottom on the net – how tight was I! I thought to myself, when I get the next match point I'm going to put the ball so high over the net that he has to hit it.' King did exactly that, and when Riggs hit his high backhand volley straight into the net, she flung her racket into the air in celebration.

Riggs leaped over the net to shake King's hand and offered her words that she says still resonate loudest with her today: 'I really underestimated you.' In one of the last interviews he gave before his death in 1995, Riggs went further, telling the Tennis Channel: 'I was so confident, I made the classic mistake that anyone can make when they think they're so good and they underestimate their opponent … I figured, she's got two chances – slim and none, and slim just left town. That was my attitude going into it.'

For King, the relief was enormous. 'I thought it would set us back 50 years if I didn't win that match. It would ruin the women's tour and affect all women's self-esteem.' While her supporters flooded the streets in celebration, she gave a press conference revealing what the victory meant to her: 'I love tennis very much, I wanted it to change ever since I started in the sport. I thought it was just for the rich and just for the white and ever since that day when I was 11 years old and wasn't allowed in a photo because I wasn't wearing a tennis skirt, I knew that I wanted to change the sport.'

Riggs, meanwhile, was surprisingly gracious in defeat: 'I'd say Billie was too good. I played my game, she didn't let me play any better.' His words represented a vast change in tune from the bluster he had spread beforehand, including one quote that would return to haunt him: 'Women play about 25 per cent as good as men, so they should get about 25 per cent of the money men get.'

'Billie Jean King didn't just raise consciousness, which was the feminist mantra then', Frank Deford wrote in a *Sports Illustrated* piece reflecting on the match in 1998. 'No, she absolutely changed consciousness.' In the UK meanwhile, the *Sunday Times* referred to King's victory as: 'The drop shot and volley heard around the world.' Indeed, King tells me: 'People can remember exactly where they were that day, it's really amazing. I get men and women coming up to me saying, "It changed my life". President Obama said it changed the way he raised his daughters – he was 12 years old when he saw that match. Guys come up to me with tears in their eyes and say, "I have a daughter now". Women come up to me and say, "You gave me more self confidence to ask for a raise", or to do something they didn't think they could do before. So both genders got a lot out of it.'

While the Battle of the Sexes is an eye-catching, headline moment in King's career, her influence doesn't begin or end with that unforgettable September evening in 1973. The following year she founded the Women's Sports Foundation (WSF), an organisation dedicated to advancing the lives of girls and women through sports and physical activity.

She also launched the first magazine ever to be dedicated to women's sports. The inaugural issue of *WomenSports* featured King herself on the cover (well you would, wouldn't you?) and gave King the opportunity to explain her motivations in her debut publisher's letter: 'I am proud to be a woman athlete. My hope is that through *WomenSports* many more women will take pride in their performance in sports and take pride in the enjoyment a well-toned body can bring them.'

Despite early teething issues based around the fact that the magazine appeared a little too much like a promotional vehicle for King (aside from gracing the cover, King was also mentioned 40 times in a 96-page magazine and appeared in six of the 20 adverts), the publication initially proved popular with editors, distributing 300,000 copies to newsstands in October 1974. But it wasn't long before problems began to surface.

By the summer of 1975 the magazine was in trouble, with falling sales and a narrow demographic meaning it was struggling to attract advertisers. King attempted to change its direction, firing her first editor, Rosalie Wright and telling staff they needed to include more fashion, health, travel and beauty articles. Her suggestions led to a mass resignation, with six members of the editorial team following Wright through the exit door. Further change was still to come, with Charter Publishing (the same company behind *Redbook* magazine) reaching an agreement with King to take over the publishing side of the business.

A new editor, Cheryl McCall, was installed with King retaining overall editorial control, but by 1978 the magazine was still running a $1.5million deficit. In January of that year, King put the writing on the wall for her readers, saying she was tired of the slow but steady progress. She wanted big growth and she wanted it now: 'If I had that kind of patience, I'd be a golfer – or at least be able to outlast Chris Evert in a baseline rally on clay. But let's face it, I'm not that kind of person.'

King knew from the participation figures that there were huge numbers of women and girls in the US who were interested in sports, so she suggested a grassroots subscription drive enlisting current readers to put forward five friends to receive a free copy of the magazine. The idea was that it would broaden the reach of *WomenSports*. It was too little too late though, and when Charter Publishing merged with Downe Communications later in 1978, the deficit was considered too much of a liability.

The February edition was to be the final one but King ensured the magazine did survive, albeit in a slightly different incarnation. It got a new name – *Women's Sports* – and a new publisher in the Women's Sports Foundation who put out an issue every month, until 1984 when it was altered again. This time it became a bimonthly called *Women's Sports and Fitness,* which lasted four years before being acquired by publishing giant, Condé Nast.

But even they could not support the title. Following publication of the September 2000 issue, *Women's Sports and Fitness* was closed, with Condé Nast's editorial director James Truman saying the magazine never really found an audience: 'We felt we were publishing a very good magazine, and we had been really holding on with it for a long time, 18 months. We kept hoping the audience would materialise, but it did not.'

Away from the bottom-line world of publishing, King's influence remained strong. In 1974 she co-founded World Team Tennis, a competition which sees mixed teams of two men and two women contest five sets that include singles, doubles and mixed doubles matches.

The team event epitomises the way that King believes sport can work: 'It's the way I want the world to look: men and women working together, championing each other, helping each other, promoting each other. We're all in this world together and any time you don't take advantage of both genders you probably weaken what you're going to do in the long run. Diversity equals strength. If you really want to win in business and in other areas, you need everyone to work together.'

It's the reason why, as she sits in the Singapore Sports Hub Stadium preparing to watch multimillionaire tennis player Serena Williams add yet another title to her growing legacy as another of tennis' game-changing women, King is determined to get one final point across.

'I understand people's intentions when they say to me, "Thank you for what you've done for women's tennis,"' says King, fixing me with a trademark look of steely determination. 'But at the same time, it drives me crazy. Every time we talk solely about helping women it cuts our market place in half. I think women influence both genders, but people present it as women only influencing women. Mothers influence both boys and girls, and I know that the Kings versus Riggs match influenced both genders. We need to have our marketplace as big as the guys have it. I don't think people think about that, yet. I've been thinking about it for years.'

King's role now is as important as it has ever been, according to the current chairman and CEO of the WTA (at time of writing), Stacey Allaster, who tells me: 'She's as engaged today in being our hero and champion for the growth and development of women's tennis as she was in 1970. She's my mentor. She knows it's not easy and she has this special gift with the young players. She educates them and shares the journey and history with them.'

It was a journey that King admits was often difficult. But for her, the end result was the only thing that ever mattered: 'I felt very alone, very isolated at times but you know what – I always felt like we were trying to do the right thing. And then I didn't care so much what people thought.'

2: Girls not allowed

While Billie Jean King was responsible for breaking down barriers in women's tennis that many believed would never be shifted, other obstacles to women's participation in sport have proved more stubborn. Some of the ridiculous medical beliefs might have evaporated (cycling, for example, was once believed to be an activity far beyond a girl's strength and one which made women incapable of bearing children), but they have left behind a sticky residue that is proving tough to shift where some sports are concerned. In place of the outrageous predictions of exhaustion and wombs dropping out, we now have rules, regulations and simple, old-fashioned attitudes preventing many sports women from reaching their full potential.

This chapter focuses on five sports – golf, football, American football, boxing and ski jumping – in which at least one of the above applies. In all five disciplines, women have had to fight long and hard for the right to compete, and despite the wars being won before the start of this century, the battles have raged on. Some of the women who compete in these sports are professionals, some are semi-professionals and some are amateurs – no matter which world they operate in, the struggles still apply.

The golf world is one that's particularly stuck in its old-boy ways. It wasn't until September 2014, for example, that Scotland's Royal and Ancient Golf Club (R&A) agreed to let women become members for the first time in its 260-year history. The vote in favour of ending the exclusion came two years after Augusta National – home of the Masters – did the same. With only three women confirmed as Augusta members at time of writing though (those being former US Secretary of State Condoleezza Rice, South Carolina financier Darla Moore, and IBM CEO Virginia Rometty), the decision is largely a symbolic one. That's not to say their memberships are meaningless, but just a reminder that the job is far from complete.

Further reminders can be found right here in Britain, where two of the most high-profile golf clubs are clinging on to a single-sex agenda. Male-only memberships are still in place at Open venues Muirfield and Royal Troon (the latter has separate men's and women's clubs). Outside of these prominent venues, around 30 clubs in the UK (one per cent of the nation's 3,000 golf clubs) have single-sex membership policies, with some of these being female-only.

The United States has more than 20 golf clubs that still exclude women from becoming members, including the prestigious Pine Valley in New Jersey and Burning Tree in Maryland where former Speaker of the House John Boehner is a member. What kind of message does it send, asked *USA Today* columnist Christine Brennan in April 2014, that the Speaker of the House feels comfortable being a member of somewhere that discriminates against 51 per cent of the population? 'It sends the message that men don't want women around them when they are playing golf, that's what it sends', wrote Brennan. 'Discriminatory, male-only clubs put out a big stop sign that has a chilling effect on girls' and women's participation in the game when golf needs them the most. Private clubs can do what they want, of course, but those decisions are not without consequences'. Boehner resigned in October 2015.

We got a glimpse of these consequences when Muirfield hosted The Open in 2013. One of Britain's best-loved sports presenters, Clare Balding, registered her dissatisfaction by declining her invitation to host the event's coverage, and politicians including Maria Miller (then Secretary for Culture, Media and Sport) and Alex Salmond (then Scotland's First Minister), refused to attend. 'The Open Championship is the biggest tournament in golf, and it sends out completely the wrong message for it to be held at clubs that don't allow women members', said Miller. 'Sports governing bodies should be doing all they can to promote equality and address the sexism that still exists in some quarters, not turning a blind eye to it.'

Muirfield began a consultation process with its members on the issue in 2014, saying they would have a report completed by spring of 2015. At time of writing, however – and even after I gave them the opportunity to provide an update – the only thing emerging from the club is a deafening silence.

In the wake of Augusta's historic about-turn, Royal Troon (hosts of the 2016 Open) also appeared determined to keep their outdated policy in place. They insisted that their situation was different to other single-sex clubs because the club shares its facilities with The Ladies Golf Club Troon, whose members (according to a club spokesman) 'have no desire to become full members of Royal Troon Golf Club.'

In January 2015, however, Royal Troon made two announcements that suggested their stance was softening. They revealed that they would be hosting the 2016 Open on a joint basis with Troon Ladies' Golf Club – the first time in history that such a set-up has been in place for the world's oldest major. Royal Troon also announced that the club would follow Muirfield in 'undertaking a comprehensive review to consider the most appropriate membership policy for the future'. Should their review – which was given no timescale – lead to a reversal of the club's traditional membership policy, the members of the Ladies Golf Club Troon will finally get to express their real desires.

While both Muirfield and Royal Troon both remain men-only clubs at time of writing, one bookmaker is offering odds of just 1/10 that Royal Troon will still be an all-male club by the end of 2015, and odds of 8/15 that Muirfield will finish the year the same way. By now, you should be in a position to decide whether the bookies were putting too much faith in the power of peer pressure.

Shona Malcolm, who serves as chief executive of the Ladies' Golf Union (LGU), believes the best approach female golfers can take is not to turn their backs on the men-only clubs, but to embrace them: 'I would be very happy to take our Open to a male-only club', she says of the LGU's flagship major championship. 'I think you are far better influencing from the inside. Look at the Women's Amateur at St George's. We take 144 young girls from a whole new generation, who can hit the ball a mile and will play the course beautifully. It doesn't matter how a club is constituted, we just want to go to the best courses and show what these girls can do. The message to the members would be that they are not a threat.'

Malcolm's experiences do at least suggest that such clubs have become more accustomed to females being in their midst. When Britain's most successful female golfer, Laura Davies, was a young player still finding her way into the game in the late 1970s, things were rather different. She recalls: 'I remember when I was about 15, you weren't even allowed to walk in front of the window [of the clubhouse]. You were allowed on the course but not in front of the men's bar.

'Myself and [fellow future pro-golfer], Julie Brown were brought in front of the secretary because we had walked in front of the men's members' lounge at one club. We weren't members there and were in a junior competition ... we weren't allowed in certain parts of the clubhouse and yet we were playing in one of the biggest amateur women's tournaments you could possibly play in. It's one of those things, but was a bit weird, I have to say.'

Less than 30 years after Davies and Brown were reprimanded, a 14-year-old American schoolgirl made headlines when she became the youngest female to play in a PGA tour event. Michelle Wie's performance at the 2004 Sony Open where she shot a second-round score of 68, missed the cut by a single shot and finished ahead of 47 male players, had the golf world dreaming of a female prodigy in the same mould as Tiger Woods.

'She's a true phenomenon', gushed South African golfer Ernie Els after sharing his practice round with Wie at the Sony Open. 'I was lucky enough to be around when Tiger Woods came out, I saw him when he was an amateur, and a lot of what I saw from Michelle reminds me of what Tiger used to do. I don't think I have ever seen a lady golfer who swings the club as well as she does.'

The opportunities for such a talented young player appeared to be limitless. But it was not long before Wie and her father, B.J. Wie, were shown exactly where Michelle's limits were. Shortly after Wie's astonishing display at the Sony Open, B.J. Wie contemplated entering his daughter in The Open, but he only made it as far as page three of the R&A's rulebook before discovering it was not going to happen. The meaty tome produced by the R&A states that entry for The Open 'will be accepted from any male professional golfer or from a male amateur golfer'.

B.J. Wie was stunned. 'I couldn't believe it when I discovered that the rules specifically state it is a men-only event', he said. At the time, R&A secretary Peter Dawson was non-committal when asked whether Michelle Wie might one day be allowed to take part in The Open. 'Never say never', he blathered.

A few months later the R&A relented, saying that the word 'male' would be removed in time for the 2006 Open and that, in the meantime, Wie could play in the 2005 Open providing she qualified for it. With the about-turn coming in late April, just a few months before The Open took place, Wie's only route to qualification was by winning or finishing high up the leaderboard at the PGA Tour's John Deere Classic – a tournament held in Illinois a week before The Open every year. In the event, Wie missed the cut by two strokes. She tried again in 2006 but was forced to withdraw from the event with heat exhaustion after finishing the opening day 13 strokes behind the leaders.

In the same year though, Wie did make history at the Asian tour's SK Telecom Open, becoming the first woman to make the halfway cut in a men's tour event since the Second World War. It remains the only time in 13 attempts that Wie has done so though and, despite the R&A opening up entry to women from 2006, no female golfer has attempted to qualify for The Open since Wie's failed attempts.

Golf journalist Matthew Cooper believes this is partly because of Wie's unsuccessful ventures between 2003 (when she first played in a PGA event at just 13 years old) and 2008 when she last entered a PGA Tour event. 'Wie's protracted involvement with men's tours is widely thought to have distracted her from competing on the LPGA' says Cooper. 'Because for all her abundant promise it took her until 2009 to win at that level.'

He also says that other players in the women's game have been put off because of Wie's experiences: 'This is not just because Wie's adventures have hung over her ever since, but a wider acknowledgement that if anyone had the game to make the cut on a main tour, she did – and she couldn't do it.'

Cooper doesn't rule out the idea of a female golfer trying again in future, though. He believes that if Wie finds a run of form sufficient to give her the confidence, she could give it another go and that younger players like America's Lexi Thompson and Britain's own Charley Hull might have the game to do the same. But, he adds that if any of these players do give it a go, they are more likely to follow the example of Britain's Laura Davies and retired Swedish golfer, Annika Sorenstam, and play in PGA Tour events as one-off occasions, as opposed to Wie's more persistent efforts.

Golf's re-admittance to the Olympics in 2016 adds a new dimension to the fight against the sport's archaic attitudes. The International Olympic Committee (IOC) says it is satisfied that 'both women and men have access to play all courses in the UK', and to a degree they are correct – women have always been able to play on the public courses at St Andrews, and can play at Muirfield too, but the club itself only permits male golfers. This can lead to embarrassing situations, as golf journalist Matt Cooper tells me: 'A friend who plays on the Ladies European Tour tells me she has experienced the anecdotal classic of playing there [Muirfield] and then having to sit on a bench outside while the member she played with fetched drinks afterwards. Indeed, in some anecdotes – possibly urban myths – the member will take a dog into the clubhouse while the lady awaits her drink.'

While clubs stand firmly by their right to do what they like in a private setting, the issue becomes more complicated when these private clubs fulfill a public function, as any golf club does when it hosts The Open. The former Minister for Sport, Hugh Robertson, made his point clear ahead of the 2013 Open at Muirfield, saying: 'I would really encourage the R&A, when they next come to allocate The Open, to look at this, simply because of the message that it sends out.'

His attitude is echoed by some of golf's biggest names. In 2013, British golf star Rory McIlroy said of men-only clubs that such blatant discrimination 'shouldn't happen these days. It's something that we shouldn't even be talking about, so that's why I guess a lot of people don't want to talk about it. Obviously it's an issue in some golf clubs. But in terms of life in general, I think men and women are treated equally for the most part these days. And that's the way it should be.'

And when 2013 US Open champion Justin Rose was asked in his press conference ahead of the 2014 Ryder Cup whether the policy of taking the Open to men-only golf courses should be changed, he replied: 'I think there's definitely a situation there where if you're going to host such high-profile events, you need to conform a little bit more with what's acceptable in mainstream society.'

Rose's bottom line, uttered in front of the world's press, won't have been missed by those at Muirfield and Royal Troon. But just in case it was, Laura Davies was on hand to ensure it hit home: 'We're in the 21st century, and it's about time clubs like Muirfield caught up. Women are not second-class citizens any more.'

Golf journalist Matt Cooper agrees that male-only clubs reinforce the impression that golf is 'covered in cobwebs and smells of pipe tobacco'. But he also tells me that they are an unhelpful distraction from a far more serious issue: 'If I were a girl, the Muirfield issue might frustrate and anger me, but at least I'd know exactly what prejudices I was up against. What would have a far more dispiriting effect would be the notion of joining a golf club where I was permitted to play but was treated like a second-class citizen in a far more subtle and damaging fashion. People (in this case women) know when they are unwelcome in a social situation, and it is achieved with petty bureaucracies, insider-jokes and nasty little put-downs. *This* is the glass ceiling: male-only clubs have ceilings you can see.'

Student Natalie Jones is all too familiar with this glass ceiling. Now studying at St Andrews University, where she plays on the women's golf team, she tells me that she first started playing in her home town of York at the age of 16 after injury and illness ended her burgeoning athletics career.

'I sort of fell into the sport', Jones says, explaining that her dad – a frequent golfer – invited her along to play with him. 'But to start with I found it very intimidating', she says of playing at her local club. 'I was petrified of stepping out onto the course when anyone else was there because there was just an abundance of older men who didn't seem to want me to be there. There were some who were very welcoming, but there were definitely a few negative comments from some of the men when I was learning. It was only because I was so determined to do it that I carried on.

'Although I wasn't aware of the wider picture at the time in terms of there being men-only golf clubs around, I knew that it was quite an old-fashioned club. When my dad first started going there they had a room that only men could go into. That played a role in making me feel like it wasn't a sport that I was naturally fitting into. It didn't help that I was the only junior girl there.'

Jones tells me that at St Andrews University she is one of 200 members of the women's golf club (around 160 of whom are beginners). She's keen to point out that they are very well supported by the R&A, even if, unlike the University's men's team they have not yet received an invite to play at the R&A Golf Club. 'Not much has changed since the vote [to allow female members to join the R&A]' says Jones, 'although they are apparently building ladies locker rooms. A lot of my friends still say they wouldn't play golf because of the way it is. They feel like they wouldn't be welcome. Overall though I do think the vote was good for the game's image. It's a positive signal from the top that can hopefully influence the other Open courses, too.'

While St Andrews is considered to be the 'home of golf', Jones says the game there is a more relaxed affair in some ways than it is south of the border. 'In England – especially the north where I'm from – they like their rules. There's one club in Yorkshire where you're not allowed to change your shoes in the car park, for example. It's the same club where they have a separate lunchroom for men and women. Often at a match I'll be the only girl so I'll have to eat in a separate room unless we all change into our formal wear so we can go into the dining room where we are allowed to eat together.'

Some clubs are starting to understand, however, that if they want to survive, they are going to have to start working harder to attract younger members. 'My local club has definitely realised that since the days I was a junior', says Jones. 'So there are more young players at the club now but still only two girls that are members.' Jones was given a clue as to why the game is struggling to attract junior girls when she went to the World Golf Business Conference in St Andrews during her first year: 'I was just there to hold the microphone and get some experience, but it was interesting listening to the delegates – almost all of whom were male and of a certain age bracket – discussing how to get more girls into golf. I stood there thinking "why don't you ask us?"

'What I would like to see are more relaxed rules regarding things like dress codes and mobile phones. But the people who are making the decisions believe if they relax the rules then it's like they are "lowering the sport". Really it's just that you don't want to have to think about all these things you must abide by when you go to play golf. Also, being able to go to any club in the country is hugely important. I understand the traditions behind some clubs being male-only but I don't think it's acceptable any more.'

Cooper has been given a slightly different insight into why the numbers of junior girls joining golf clubs are so small. He tells me about the many times he has found himself in conversation with club secretaries who are almost universally perplexed about dwindling membership numbers. His response is to query the number of girls in their junior section or young women in the main section. 'Oooh, we're not sure about that direction', they've replied. To which his answer is: 'Don't moan about low numbers if you limit who you let in.'

'They say – and I largely believe them, even if I disagree with them – that they're scared of women being slow', says Cooper. 'But it's self-perpetuating. Women golfers have traditionally been slow because they only started playing in their late 50s or 60s and it's a very difficult game to begin late in life. Men who start at that age are slow golfers, too. Age is the key, not sex.

'If you believe the industry, golf is not exactly a sport that's flourishing (indeed, the latest figures from the KPMG Golf Participation Survey report a drop of 2.7 per cent in junior golf in 2013). Golf bigwigs like to boast about being great businessmen, so where's the sense in limiting what demand they've got? The debate is a complex one but ultimately it should be simple: if you want to play golf, the sport needs you and you should be welcomed.'

For now though, the majority of golf clubs remain committed to preserving the status quo. But something will surely have to change if the sport is to avoid becoming marginalised in a world that is moving far quicker than golf ever has.

Football was once a sport that – like some golf clubs – decided it definitely did not need women. On 5 December 1921, the FA banned women's teams from playing on League and Association-affiliated grounds, claiming that the game was 'quite unsuitable for females and ought not to be encouraged'. Their claims were backed by respected physicians, including Dr Mary Scharlieb of Harley Street, who said football was the 'most unsuitable game, too much for a woman's physical frame'.

According to some, the FA's real motive had little to do with the health of women, and everything to do with the health of the women's game. It might seem incredible now to think that the behemoth that is the men's game could ever feel threatened by women's football, but in the early 1920s the women's game – led by the world-famous Dick, Kerr Ladies FC – was booming. Formed in 1917 from a group of munitions workers who were filling in at the Dick, Kerr & Company factory in Preston while the nation's men were away fulfilling their wartime duties, Dick, Kerr Ladies FC was the best-known team in Britain. On Boxing Day 1920, they attracted a crowd of 53,000 to Goodison Park for a match against St Helen's Ladies, while another 14,000 were locked outside of the ground trying to get in.

'The FA got frightened', says June Gregson, who played for the team from 1949 to 1957. 'Women's football was getting too popular. My own dad thought women should be as near the kitchen sink as possible. He even burnt my football boots on a bonfire when I was 16.'

This fear gripped the FA so tightly that it was 50 years before they lifted the ban on women playing football on their grounds. In 1971, affiliates of UEFA (football's European governing body) voted in favour of all member states bringing the control of women's football under their respective national governing bodies. The FA wasn't quite ready to open its doors to the women's game, but it did take one small step in the right direction by lifting the ban on women playing football on the grounds of affiliated clubs.

The FA was still reluctant to get too involved with the women's game, however, leaving the day-to-day running of it to the Women's Football Association (WFA), which had been formed in 1969. Meanwhile, other European countries were a step ahead. In Germany, Norway, Denmark and Sweden, the women's game was welcomed by their respective national governing bodies in the early 1970s, giving them access to resources and financing that the WFA could only dream of.

That was until 1993 when FIFA finally raised its voice to declare that a single body in each nation should run all football. Suddenly the FA was left with little choice but to take direct control of the women's game – an action that meant the WFA was swiftly dissolved.

Despite the obvious advantages in funding and facilities that came with being taken under the FA's wing, there were many who remained suspicious of the ruling body's motives. 'The FA has taken over to control us, to keep us in our place', said Sheila Edmunds, one of the founding members of the

Doncaster Belles women's team, in an interview with the *Independent* in 1994. Her view wasn't a lone one, either. Linda Whitehead, who was secretary of the WFA for 13 years before the FA disbanded it, said: 'A lot of people felt very bitter [about the FA takeover]. It wasn't what they wanted to do. It was the way they did it – they just rode roughshod all over us.'

Today, the FA's relationship with the women's game – and with women full stop – remains a complicated one. Coming under the jurisdiction of the FA had the potential to give women's football a sense of legitimacy, but in reality, during the 10 years that followed the FA takeover, very little changed.

This was despite the fact that more and more females were starting to play the game. In the two years between the 1998–99 and 2000–01 seasons, the number of girls under the age of 16 playing football rocketed by 87 per cent according to research by the FA. And by 2002, football had overtaken the schoolgirl's favourite, netball, as the most popular sport for women. So despite their lack of support for women at the top of the game, it seems the FA's work at grassroots level, where centres of excellence and academies were set up to help identify and develop young talent, was paying off.

The next step, said the FA, was to 'professionalise the game'. It was the right sentiment, made at the right time, but the FA failed to deliver the right results. In 2005, England played host to the UEFA European Women's Championship but the tournament did not go well for the home nation. After a winning start against Finland, England lost their next two games against Denmark and Sweden, leaving them bottom of their group and ensuring they were nothing more than interested observers for the rest of the competition.

The FA chose to ignore the disappointing performance, and instead got busy talking up the impressive crowds (a combined total of almost 70,000 attended England's three group games) and encouraging television audiences (the BBC showed England's games live, with three million tuning in to watch their final group game against Sweden on BBC Two). If distracting from England's failure was the FA's aim, they failed.

Perturbed by what they saw as a mismatch between the overwhelming enthusiasm for women's football from young girls and the opportunities that were available to women who actually wanted to make a career out of it, the House of Commons took action. In March 2006 they appointed the Culture, Media and Sport Committee to launch an inquiry into women's football in England. The report that emerged was published in July, one year after

England's dismal Euros display. It explained that despite the tremendous growth of the game, its expansion was 'being hindered by various barriers, many of which are rooted in cultural attitudes'.

The report expressed 'extreme concern' over the disparity in funding given to the Centres of Excellence for boys and girls, and criticised the inequalities that appeared in all sorts of other areas. These included the lack of women in governance roles and access to facilities with the Football Foundation finding that in 2003, 94 per cent of changing rooms had no facilities for females. Out of all the recommendations the report made, however, it was those relating to the elite level of the game that would have the biggest impact.

After labelling the Women's Premier League 'unstable', the report praised the FA's plans for a shake-up of the domestic scene in England. Their proposed Super League promised better quality of competition, improved revenues via sponsorship, gate receipts and media rights and more visibility of role models. But the report made clear that the FA's request for public funding – £3million every year for five years – to put this plan into effect was not something they would support. Instead, they called on the FA to make a financial commitment of its own to women's football. In other words, the FA was told: 'Put your money where your mouth is.'

The FA was left with little choice but to fall in line. And so plans were made for an FA-funded introduction of England's first semi-professional football league for women (by comparison the top level of men's football is largely funded by the sale of television rights, which for the 2016–17 season amounted to an astronomical cost of £10.2million per Premier League game). Plans were put in place for an eight-team Women's Super League (WSL) to launch in the summer of 2010.

But almost as soon the excitement started to build, the door of opportunity seemed to slam shut again. In March 2009 the FA announced that the league would be delayed until 2011, causing an audible sigh of frustration to echo loudly from everyone in and around the women's game.

The reason for the hold up? The usual: money. The FA blamed the global financial downturn for forcing it to 'review planned financial commitments'. Unsurprisingly, women's football was at the top of the FA's expendable list when it was looking for areas to save some cash.

'If anybody wanted a clear indication of the FA's regard for women's football, this is it', said Sue Tibballs, who was then Chief Executive of the Women's Sport and Fitness Foundation (WSFF). 'They were looking at their budgets to see what they could cut, and women's football was an easy option. You have to question their fitness to run the women's game.'

It took six months for the FA to announce that the WSL was back on their agenda and would finally launch in 2011, by which time the damage had been done. Some 38 years after the FA had lifted their ban on women's football, a whole new generation of female footballers had been shown that their game was disposable.

Even so, when the England team departed for the Women's World Cup in Germany in the summer of 2011, they did so amid optimism that attitudes towards women's football were starting to change. The launch of the WSL had been well received, with ESPN broadcasting Chelsea's game against Arsenal on the opening day (one of six matches they paid for the right to show during the season), and 2,510 paying spectators turning up to watch.

Once the World Cup got underway, it too was lauded by the media for the quality of football on display and the competitiveness of the games. Indeed, 'dogged and dazzling' was the *Guardian*'s description of England's performance in their final group game victory against Japan. It was a shame, then, that the BBC had elected not to show any of England's matches live. They were available to watch via the BBC's website and interactive service, but not on any of the main channels, meaning that only those actively looking to tune in were likely to watch (whereas putting games on BBC One/Two means more chance of enticing 'opportunist' viewers to tune in).

This lack of mainstream coverage was 'a huge step backwards for the profile of women's football', according to Jo Welford and Carrie Dunn, who co-authored *Football and the FA Women's Super League* in 2014. And many others, from inside and outside of the game, agreed with them. The FA, however, remained silent on the situation, apparently unperturbed that the efforts of England's women were going largely unnoticed on home soil.

Once England reached the quarter-final stage of the competition, the BBC's decision to continue limiting the Lionesses' matches to their interactive service attracted even more criticism. Instead of showing the World Cup quarter final between England and France on one of their main channels, the BBC scheduled golf on BBC One and repeats of Ronnie Barker's comedy *Porridge*, and antiques show, *Flog It!* on BBC Two during the time of the match.

It would be funny if it wasn't quite so sad. Just imagine the same situation occurring during a men's World Cup tournament in which England reached the quarter-final stage. You can't, right? Because it would never, ever happen.

It was, said the BBC, an unavoidable situation. They were contracted to show the golf (the Scottish Open) and were hamstrung by a longstanding policy not to show sport on both of its main channels at the same time. The FA remained a bystander in the whole argument, with their commercial director at the time, Stuart Turner, giving the verbal equivalent of a shrug. 'Without the BBC,' he said, 'these games would not be on free-to-air at all and at a time when they're also showing Wimbledon, the British Grand Prix and The Open, there were always going to be scheduling pressures.'

The BBC was urged by MPs and the WSFF to reconsider. Shadow education secretary, Andy Burnham, and the Tory MP Tracey Crouch wrote a letter to the corporation arguing that showing the match on the red-button service would not build momentum and wider public support for the women's game. It proved to be the final push that was needed. The BBC backed down, releasing a statement paying heed to the 'growing public interest in this national football match', and agreeing to move it to BBC Two. It was not a victory that England could repeat on the pitch though as the team were beaten by France on penalties – not something for which the BBC can be held accountable, sadly.

While the BBC was applauded for reversing its decision, the whole episode only served to reinforce the position of women as outsiders in the world of English football. Most concerning, say Welford and Dunn, was the refusal of the FA to get involved, 'even justifying the BBC's decision – despite their commitment to enhancing the profile of women's football.'

One possible explanation for this could be found behind the doors of the FA itself, where those in positions of power remained mostly male (the balanced tipped slightly in January 2013 when after more than 20 years working at the FA, Kelly Simmons was made Director of the National Game and Women's Football). But without a strong female influence over decision making at the FA, it is hardly surprising that a conflict of interests emerged between football's female participants and the men charged with running their game.

One year after the 2011 World Cup debacle, the FA learned the extent to which these 'outsiders' had made their way into the public consciousness. During the London 2012 Olympics a crowd of 70,584 filled Wembley for Team GB's momentous victory over Brazil in their final group match. It was, said the FA, 'the largest crowd to watch a women's game in this country since 1920'. It wasn't a record that would last for long though, with 80,203 fans packing out the stadium for the Olympic final between USA and Japan.

While the numbers can in part be explained by the huge demand for tickets overall at London 2012, that doesn't alter the fact that a large number of people – many of whom would never have seen a game of women's football before – were exposed to the game at its highest level. The chances are that at least some of those will have been converted into fans (my own mother was in the crowd for England vs. Brazil at Wembley – it was her first visit to the stadium and her first experience of women's football. She has raved about it ever since).

Players and administrators alike have labelled the Games a 'watershed moment' for women's football in the UK, and with an Olympic record of 740,000 people attending the 26 women's matches during the Games, it is hard to argue. Finally, the sport had the kind of exposure that could really make a difference. To their credit, the FA acted swiftly to take advantage of this momentum. In October 2012 they launched a five-year plan to grow the women's game, which involved creating an Elite Performance Unit, appointing a Head of Elite Development and expanding the WSL.

This expansion led to the launch of a second division in 2014, imaginatively titled: WSL2. Along with it came the introduction of promotion and relegation between the top division, WSL1, and this new second division. After spending its first three seasons concentrating on becoming more established and growing its fan base, this expansion was the logical next step for the league.

What happened next, however, rocked the foundations of the football world. In April 2013, with the third WSL season just one game old the FA told Doncaster Rovers Belles they would be demoted to WSL2 at the end of the season to open up space at the top level for Manchester City Ladies. The FA casually dropped this news into a brief statement, simply listing which clubs had been selected for WSL1 and WSL2 beneath the bland headline 'FA Selects Clubs for WSL Licenses.' There was no immediate explanation, no apology and no indication that they even recognised the significance of their decision.

As one of the founder members of the WSL and with a long, successful history in the women's game (they have twice won the league and FA Cup double), the Belles were outraged. And one can understand why – they were being demoted to make space for a team that had never before played in the top tier of the women's game.

At the time their entry into WSL1 was announced, Manchester City were competing in the Women's Premier League National Division which was one tier below the WSL (when the WSL was first launched it became the top division, followed by the WPL National and then the WPL North and South divisions). City had only recently been promoted into that division, too. In April 2012, City won the Premier League Northern Division to secure their elevation to the second highest tier in women's football for the first time in their history. Just one year later they were going up again. Only this time, they hadn't earned it. Not in the traditional football sense, anyway.

City finished the 2013 season in fourth spot in the WPL, 20 points behind the league winners Sunderland, and 13 points shy of Watford and Leeds, who finished in second and third place respectively. Why then were they being elevated into the top flight ahead of those teams? And why were the Belles being demoted, with the current season only one game old?

After the WSL expansion into two tiers was announced in 2012, the FA invited applications from all clubs who wanted to be part of either tier, including those who were already part of the WSL. A selection panel assessed each bid, looking at their financial sustainability and factors like management, marketing and the quality of their coaching staff and facilities.

The panel concluded that while Manchester City's bid met all the required standards for a WSL1 team, the Belles' did not. The FA based their objections to the Belles' bid on three key factors: lack of assurance that the Belles would have sufficient access to enable them to play their games at Keepmoat Stadium (the home of Doncaster Rovers men's team); the Belles' failure to submit a satisfactory commercial and marketing plan; and finally, their intent to spend 11 per cent of their turnover on players' salaries – a figure the FA said it did not consider sufficient to 'support the development of professional football as strongly as other applicant clubs'.

Belles' boss, John Buckley, called the FA's decision 'the most farcical thing I've ever heard'. Others were even more dismissive, with Vic Akers, the manager of rival team Arsenal Ladies, labelling it as 'morally scandalous'. The club itself did the only thing it could and launched an appeal. Some 9,000 people signed a petition against the Belles' demotion, while a more visual protest was planned for the FA Cup final game between Arsenal Ladies and Bristol Academy, which was – somewhat ironically – to be held at the Keepmoat Stadium in May.

Belles fans turned up for the game with flyers, bells (which they traditionally rang to support their team), and a banner that read: 'Doncaster Belles. 22 years in the top division ended by the FA's gr££d.' Stewards muted the protest pretty swiftly and confiscated the offending banner. But the fuss was all for nought as the Belles' appeal was quashed by the FA (yes, the very same organisation that made the decision in the first instance).

The Belles fans at the FA Cup final blamed the FA's 'greed' for their demotion, but it seems less a case of the FA chasing cash than the FA trying so hard to advance women's football (and make up for their own previous failings) that they were willing to do it at any cost.

At the time, the *Telegraph* wrote: 'Much of the appeal of women's football comes from its lack of self-regard, its closeness to fans, the approachability of the players, its affordability, its spirit, its roots. Does success have to mean surrendering to rampant capitalism and all it entails?' While everyone at Doncaster Rovers would probably have answered that question with a resounding 'no' at the time of their demotion, the progress of the club and women's football as a whole in the ensuing years suggests that while the FA might have been heavy handed in their approach, their actions have left the game on a more stable footing than ever before.

Two years after their relegation to WSL2 the Belles' president and founding member, Sheila Edmunds, believes that the demotion actually saved the club. They had been struggling financially in WSL1 and while the FA's decision initially compounded their financial strife, leading to the loss of a long-term sponsor, it also encouraged the local community to step up their support of the club. 'The fact that it became very public knowledge that Doncaster Belles were not going to be in WSL1 really opened up the media', Edmunds told the BBC. 'We had to restructure and look at what we were doing and where we were going. We've got a very rich history in the club, but you can't live on your history. Changing our ideas really made us work much harder. Sometimes you coast along when you think you're safe, when in fact you're not; you have to change with the times and move forward.'

The Belles came close to securing immediate promotion back into the top tier in 2014, but were pipped to the top spot by Sunderland, who moved up into WSL1 for the 2015 season (thereby avoiding many red faces at the FA). But in 2015 they secured back to WSL1, finishing behind Reading on goal difference alone.

Manchester City Women meanwhile have proven their ability to compete with the best in the women's game (aided to no small extent by the financial support of their mega wealthy men's team). With England captain Steph Houghton also wearing the armband for her club side, they finished fifth in their first season in the top flight, and won their first piece of silverware by beating Arsenal to the League Cup trophy.

Many still believe the FA were wrong to demote the Belles in the way they did, however (at the beginning of the season and with such little regard for their history or stature within women's football). And while Manchester City clearly had everything in place to be a success at the top level, one has to question why the FA didn't just let nature take its course and wait for them to work their way up through the system. That surely would have been the fairest way of advancing the women's game.

The current relationship between women's football and the governing body at the top level might be stronger than it has ever been, but the association remains an uneasy one. Clubs and players are constantly told that the FA is committed to growing the game and capitalising on its popularity at grassroots level, but their treatment of a club that helped to build the foundations for where the game is today is difficult to justify. 'You cannot just rip the heart out of a game to justify the ugliest of phrases in sport: "a new franchise", wrote Laura Williamson in the *Daily Mail*. 'That is not progress – it's going backward.'

There's more to come on the tricky relationships surrounding women's football in the UK later on in the book, when I'll delve deeper into the FA's approach to marketing the women's game and discuss the sexism that still plagues the sport at every level. But for now I'll move on to another type of football – one that will let women play, but only if they agree to do so wearing what amounts to little more than a bikini.

In 2004, a young advertising executive named Mitchell Mortaza came up with an idea for filling the halftime break of the annual Super Bowl (an American football match that's often the most watched sporting event of the year in the US). Noting that the halftime shows were leaving television audiences cold, Mortaza created an alternative – the Lingerie Bowl. First held in 2004, it was an American football match played between two teams of scantily clad swimwear models and broadcast on pay-per-view TV. 'It will play well with men and women', Mortaza told the *New York Times*. 'With men, for the obvious reasons, and for women it's an incredible lingerie fashion show, with red carpet arrivals and more.'

He was proved right, with millions reportedly paying out $19.95 to tune in. For the next two years, the Lingerie Bowl filled the Super Bowl halftime break with women playing football wearing less material than it takes to make an NFL player's underwear. For most of the models, it led to nothing more than a pay cheque, but for the organisers, the success was enough to convince them there was more to be gained.

In 2009 Mortaza launched the Lingerie Football League (LFL), a competitive, 10-team league featuring teams like Los Angeles Temptation and San Diego Seduction. Players were paid a percentage of the ticket sales (minus the cost of stadium rental) and the games were broadcast on the US network MyNetworkTV. But in 2011 the league stopped paying players and started charging them a $45 fee to compete, with Mortaza claiming it was a necessary step for a league that was trying to stay alive in a tough economic environment. In a letter sent to league players in March 2011, Mortaza said the plan was to eventually revert back to paying players but that, in the meantime, 'we will create an environment and culture that will cater to only those who love the game, while weeding out those doing it for a pay cheque'.

At time of writing, players are still playing for nothing. So, why do they do it? In short, it's their only option if they want to play football in big arenas and in a competitive league that gets TV coverage. In 2015, ESPN's sports blog site, Grantland, published an article in which numerous players talked about their reasons for taking part in the LFL (the acronym now stands for Legends Football League after being rebranded in 2013 when organisers said they were ditching the lingerie for 'performance wear'. In reality, the uniforms remain little more than bikinis topped off with a pair of shoulder pads).

In the piece, Chicago Bliss player Heather Furr explains that playing in the league gave her the same competitive thrill that she had experienced at college, where she'd played on the basketball team and competed in athletics. She had always been the type of person who defined herself by the sports she played, but since leaving college she had failed to find the same level of intensity among the amateur athletes playing in weekend leagues. It was only when she joined the Bliss in 2010 – ahead of the league's second season – that Furr felt like that college athlete again. And that, finally, she was surrounded by like-minded women. She recalls making 'a few hundred bucks per game' in her first season and doing interviews and photo shoots just like the pros. Now though, the money has gone. 'That's the hardest thing', says Furr. 'If we were being paid, there's so much more we could put into it.'

Some believe that in continuing to play for nothing, players are adhering to what society has led them to believe – that they aren't really worthy of the money.

'Women athletes are accustomed to playing for less than men, or for nothing at all', says Charlene Weaving, a university professor who has written widely about sports and gender, in Grantland's article. She argues, that even in childhood, boys receive more external rewards — attention, popularity, praise — for athletic achievement than girls do, so women become accustomed to the lack of it. 'It seems to be, "Is this all we're going to get? Well, OK then"', says Weaving.

Over the last few years the league has been sued by a handful of former players. Mortaza and his organisation are accused of wrongly classifying players as independent contractors when they are actually employees. This makes a significant difference to players' rights. Employment law dictates that independent contractors can control the terms of the services they provide, but don't have to earn the minimum wage and have no right to earn overtime. Employees, meanwhile, are subject to terms set out by their employer and are covered by the Fair Labor Standards Act.

At time of writing Mortaza has evaded sanction, and the league seemingly goes from strength to strength, with a new Texas franchise planned for the 2016 season.

American football is perhaps the only sport that rivals professional boxing in its reluctance to allow women a seat at the top table. 'Boxing is not a sport for women' is the long-held view of one of boxing's best-known promoters, and former manager of heavyweight champ Lennox Lewis, Frank Warren. Two years after women's boxing made its Olympic debut at London 2012, Warren explained his view on his website, frankwarren.com: 'It is not a chauvinistic stance because I'm all for equality in sport and in life, but I am just not comfortable seeing girls attempting to belt bits off each other in the ring, no more than I am knowing they are now fighting on the frontline in wars.

'Apart from anything else I worry about the effect being repeatedly hit in the stomach might have on their reproductive system. There have been cases of women boxers turning up at a weigh-in and found to be pregnant. Obviously they were not allowed to fight, but what was happening to their bodies in all the sparring sessions beforehand?'

Alongside his concerns for their wellbeing, Warren also expresses fears for the bank balances of female fighters, saying he believes that women's boxing 'is not something the average fan would pay to watch. As a promoter I don't think it is commercially viable in this country. The interest is not there and never has been going back to the days when Jane Couch was a pioneer female professional.'

Couch is a former five-time World Boxing Champion who made history in 1997 by becoming the first woman to be granted a licence to box legally in England. Already a world welterweight champion having fought as a professional in America and Europe (Couch won her title in Copenhagen in 1996), she then entered into one of the toughest battles of her career – against the British Boxing Board of Control (BBBC).

The board refused to grant Couch a professional licence in June 1997, basing their decision on flimsy medical grounds (the highlight of which was their claim that pre-menstrual tension made women too unstable to box). It was a position that Couch knew would never stand up in court, so that's where she took the fight, suing the BBBC for gender discrimination. The six-month court case gave Couch one of her most famous victories when, in March 1998, she won her claim and was finally able to fight professionally in her own country. She wasn't done fighting just yet though, going on to sue the BBBC for loss of income.

'While I was going through the case I wasn't thinking about breaking down barriers and making things easier for up and coming women boxers', says Couch. 'I just had a passion for what I was doing and wanted to be accepted in England.' A step towards that acceptance came in November 1998 when Couch faced Germany's Simona Lukic in the first women's professional boxing bout in Britain. Couch won, stopping her younger opponent in the second round, but she knew there were still many battles ahead for women's boxing, saying after the fight: 'It is now accepted and things are a little easier, but it's still very new to England and we don't have the base of boxers here like in the USA. It still has a long way to go.'

Just how far was something boxer Cathy 'The Bitch' Brown soon discovered. As the second British female to get her professional licence (she followed Couch in August 1998), the 5'1" flyweight had to battle for everything, including finding willing opponents, as she told me when I met her at the London gym where she now works as a trainer and coach: 'I had to pay men to spar with me out of my own pocket as nobody wanted to hit a woman, and if I did find someone, they wouldn't hit me properly so I wasn't learning what I should have been. Paying them helped, as they knew they would only get paid if they sparred with me fully.'

The lack of female fighters in Britain can be explained by the fact that for 116 years the Amateur Boxing Association of England (ABAE) had banned women from boxing. It was only in 1996 that they voted in favour of ending the ban and finally allowed women to glove up. With so few opponents in the UK, Brown says she often had to look abroad for people to fight, with promoters insisting that she then sell enough tickets to the show to cover the costs: 'That would include the cost of flights for the fighter and her trainer, accommodation, food and purse [the amount of money a boxer is paid for taking a fight], but also money in the promoter's pockets. So I had to sell over £5,000 worth of tickets, which along with training twice a day and working full time was very tiring.'

There was a ban on women's amateur boxing in the USA too until 1993, when a 16-year-old called Dallas Malloy became the first female to challenge the ban in a federal court. Two months after the lawsuit was filed a US judge ruled in Malloy's favour. Later that same year, she found herself in the centre of the ring and the centre of attention as she fought in the first sanctioned amateur women's boxing match in the US, beating her opponent Heather Poyner in a college gymnasium in front of 1,200 people.

Different states across the USA had been granting professional licences as and when they felt like it over the years, with Yorkshire-born Barbara Buttrick becoming one of the best-known female fighters of the 1950s. She took up the sport in her teens after spotting a story in the *Sunday Dispatch* (which would later become the *Sunday Express*) about Polly Burns – a female prize-fighter of the early 1900s. Then 15, Buttrick's curiosity was piqued.

After buying herself a pair of boxing gloves and a book called *The Noble Art of Self-Defence*, Buttrick started spending her evenings in the gym. She'd be there for hours hitting punch bags, skipping and sparring with her coach, Len Smith (who she eventually married). 'I was small, but I was mean', says Buttrick. Her husband would undoubtedly agree, having suffered a broken nose from one of his wife's blows during a sparring session.

Buttrick was labelled as 'monstrous' and 'an insult to womanhood' by her critics at home. Such slurs, combined with the difficulty of finding opponents in a country that refused to recognise female boxers, persuaded Buttrick and Smith to pack up and move to America in 1952. There, the 4'11" fighter, nicknamed 'The Mighty Atom of the Ring', won eight fights in a row and knocked out the US female bantamweight champion. Buttrick also made US television history when in 1954 she took on Joann Hagen in the first women's bout to be nationally broadcast.

The eight rounder went the way of the taller – and reportedly 33lb heavier – American, but Buttrick refused to be undone by her first defeat. In 1957 she beat Phyllis Kugler for the World Bantamweight title in a six rounder that

Buttrick calls 'the most memorable fight of my career'. She retired three years later with a record of just one defeat in more than 30 fights. Her love affair with boxing wasn't over though, as Buttrick founded the Women's International Boxing Federation (WIBF) – one of the more recognised fight-sanctioning bodies in women's boxing – in 1990. Now 85, Buttrick lives in Miami, Florida where she still takes an active role in the boxing community. Most recently, she put in an appearance at a gym where Britain's Olympic champion boxer, Luke Campbell, was training for his next fight. 'It was great to have her along to one of our sessions and hear about her experiences and success', said the Yorkshireman, some 57 years Buttrick's junior.

The 1990s was the decade in which women's professional boxing in the USA hit new heights. The momentum was kick-started by a gruelling fight between America's Christy Martin and Ireland's Deirdre Gogarty that took place at the MGM Grand in Las Vegas in March 1996. The fight was on the undercard of a world championship bout between star heavyweights Mike Tyson and Frank Bruno, with few expecting it to match the headline act for entertainment value.

As it turned out, Tyson and Bruno had nothing on Martin and Gogarty. The two women traded vicious blows for six fierce rounds before Martin, who was bleeding heavily from a nose that had been broken in the fourth round, was awarded the unanimous decision. It was, in boxing parlance, 'a proper scrap'. And quite the contrast to what happened later that evening between two of boxing's star heavyweights.

Over 30 million people had coughed up to watch a night of boxing that was supposed to climax with Tyson vs. Bruno, but after the notorious American eased Bruno aside in just three rounds, the women's bout was the one that left a lasting impression. Indeed, many of the female boxers who emerged in the following years credited Martin vs. Gogarty with igniting their passion for the sport.

Since then, however, boxing in the USA has been through a down period, when it was shunted to the margins of the nation's sporting interests. Viewers had become disillusioned with a sport where the best fighters very rarely faced each other and when they did, it was made into a pay-per-view production. With the emergence of mixed martial arts (the UFC franchise in particular), in which competitors are matched by the organisation (in whose best interest it is to have the best fighting the best), the future of boxing looked bleak in the mid-2000s.

Things have improved for men's boxing since then, with one of the main television networks, NBC, teaming up with legendary promoter Al Haymon to launch a series called Premier Boxing Champions in January 2015. It has brought boxing out from behind the paywall and is delivering it to the masses once more, with 20 shows scheduled to take place in its first year on air.

But women's boxing is nowhere to be seen in this resurgence, in professional terms at least. Bouts are rarely televised and female fighters earn far less than their male counterparts. In an interview with a British newspaper in 2012, American boxer Lisa Garland who turned professional in 2007 said: 'Once I got just $500 – less than I spent on air travel – for a belt. I am a world champion but you wouldn't know it from my bank account.'

And according to President of the Women's International Boxing Council, Don 'Moose' Lewis, the money isn't the worst of the sport's issues: 'Women's professional boxing is even more unscrupulous than men's', he said in the same newspaper. 'Sexism is rife – men want to see pretty girls fighting.' He also claims the fights are often run in a less than professional manner, explaining: 'Women's weight often varies by several pounds, so they are switched from lightweight [132lb] to welter weight (145lb). You get some poor little girl being pummeled by someone 10lb heavier and they don't stand a chance.'

So while women's amateur boxing has undoubtedly made progress since Couch's landmark victory against the BBBC, becoming an Olympic sport for the first time in 2012 and providing more opportunities for female boxers to compete, the professional sport has moved in the opposite direction. For Olympic champions Nicola Adams, Katie Taylor and Claressa Shields (who hail from Britain, Ireland and the USA respectively), it means that their options for progressing in the sport are limited.

All three women made history at the London 2012 Olympics by winning gold in their relevant weight categories, while Taylor and Shields are also world champions (Taylor a five-time one at that). Most male boxers with such an impressive amateur CV would be fighting off the contract offers from professional promoters. Indeed, both of Great Britain's male Olympic boxing champions, Anthony Joshua and Luke Campbell, have become professional boxers since London 2012, signing up with one of the UK's biggest promoters, Eddie Hearn. Conversely, all three women are likely to be back on the Olympic stage in 2016 to defend their titles in Rio.

'I could turn pro if I wanted to', insisted Nicola Adams when I interviewed her in 2014. Her Olympic performance turned her into a household name in Britain, and Adams says she actually has been approached by promoters wanting to represent her: 'I've had a couple of offers but I've still got a lot to offer as an amateur. I want to go on to Brazil [for the 2016 Olympics] and hopefully be the first boxer from GB to be double Olympic champion.'

I don't know exactly what those offers consisted of that Adams received, but it's fair to assume they would not have made her rich. Nor even a little bit wealthy. So despite what she says, it's hard to imagine that if Adams had the same opportunities available to her as those that have been available to her male counterparts, who are now frequently seen in huge boxing events at places like Wembley Stadium and the O2 Arena, she would choose to remain an amateur. An Olympic double is a great prize, but it only comes at the end of a tough four-year cycle during which Adams is mostly grafting at the GB Boxing training centre in Sheffield, or competing in low-profile amateur events that merit a few lines of coverage in the press.

Ireland's Katie Taylor has also flirted with, and then dismissed, the idea of joining the professional ranks. She arguably has even more reason than Adams to make the leap after adding a fifth World Championship gold medal to her collection in 2014. But despite Taylor's continued dominance of the amateur scene, *Boxing News'* amateur expert, John Dennen believes Taylor is right to steer clear of the professional ranks, telling me: 'Katie Taylor is a huge star in Ireland ... There's fame and acclaim in women's amateur boxing. On the other hand, you don't really see a lot of women's professional boxing, so it's hard to know who's who or who's any good. For these Olympic-standard boxers, the level of competition is much higher – and Katie Taylor is the best we've seen.'

There is one female fighter who has bucked the trend, achieving fame, fortune and acclaim for her undisputed talent. The only difference is that Ronda Rousey complements her boxing skills with moves taken from wrestling, jiu-jitsu, judo and various other fighting arts. She's a mixed martial artist (MMA), and since becoming the first female fighter to sign with the Ultimate Fighting Championship (UFC) in 2012, many believe that Rousey has become the sport's biggest star (yes, even bigger than its male champions).

After initially being wary of getting involved in women's MMA, the UFC has come to see the value in using Rousey's fame to add to its stable of female fighters (how could they not when a fight she was expected to win easily attracted more than 90,000 pay-per-view buys in August 2015?). At present, the others fall way behind Rousey when it comes to making headlines and drawing crowds but her success has created more career opportunities for women who want to fight for a living than boxing has ever done. If those female fighters can attain the same level of success in the octagon (where

MMA fights take place as opposed to a ring) as Rousey, then the UFC has already proven they are willing and able to give women the platform and support they need to turn it into a viable career.

Female boxers have been forced to accept the idea that they deal in medals while their male counterparts deal in championship belts, worldwide fame and relative fortune. The hope is, however, that with participation figures continually rising (the number of registered female boxers in Britain rose from 70 in 2005 to more than 900 in 2009, while women's boxing was one of the few sports to see participation increases after London 2012, according to a 2013 Sport England survey), the quality and quantity of women's boxing will demand that the professional code raises its game. It won't happen quickly or easily if Frank Warren's views are anything to go by, but even he realises that his opinions carry an expiry date: 'Call me an old git, but that's how I see it. It is probably a generation thing because my two sons Francis and George who work with me on Queensberry Promotions say they would happily put female boxers on the bill.'

Warren might not know it, but he has a kindred spirit in the Russian men's ski jumping team. 'I admit, I'm not a fan of women's ski jumping', said the Russian men's ski jumping coach Alexander Arefyev in a newspaper interview a week before the women's event made its Winter Olympics debut at the Sochi 2014 Games. 'It's a pretty difficult sport with a high risk of injury. If a man gets a serious injury, it's still not fatal, but for women it could end much more seriously.' Arefyev simply cannot comprehend how the fragile and weak female form would be able to cope with the inevitable bumps and bruises involved in ski jumping. "If I had a daughter (it's perhaps fortunate for him that he did not), I'd never let her jump — it's too much hard labour. Women have another purpose — to have children, to do housework, to create hearth and home.'

Arefyev wouldn't have been around in 1862, but if he had, he would almost certainly have been outraged by the actions of a Norwegian woman called Ingrid Olavsdottir Vestby. At the first recorded event dedicated to ski jumping, Vestby soared almost 20 feet, 'past the point where many a brave lad had lost his balance earlier in the competition', according to eyewitness reports. And she did it all while wearing a skirt of 19th-century proportions.

Vestby's feat was followed in 1911 by Austrian baroness Paula Lamberg, who set a world record of 22 metres, earning her grudging admiration in her home country: 'Jumps of this length are very good, *even for men*', read a report in *Illustrierte Zeitung* magazine. 'It is understandable that ski jumping is performed very rarely by women, and taking a close look, not really a recommendable sport. One prefers to see women with nicely mellifluous movements, which show elegance and grace … and it is not enjoyable or aesthetic to see how a representative of the fair sex falls when jumping from a hill.'

Aesthetic preferences aside, the typical medical reasoning for excluding women emerged in the 1920s when concerns were raised over how the 'female organism' would cope with the impact from a hard landing or fall (one wonders why they never thought to invent a little crash helmet for these delicate organisms us women need to protect so dearly). Given these fears it's hardly surprising that when the first Winter Olympics took place in 1924 with ski jumping included on the programme, it was deemed a men-only event.

Women continued jumping though, either on their own or in informal sporting groups, and in 1994 an Austrian called Eva Ganster, who had been hurling herself from slopes in her home country since she was 10, made a breakthrough. She had been competing in men's events for some time, either as a pre-jumper (someone who 'tests' the hill before the actual competition begins), or jumping against the men when permitted. Finally in 1994, the same year in which the International Ski Federation (FIS) set up a women's ski jumping working group to look at the feasibility of holding women's competitions, Ganster was invited to start as a pre-jumper at the Winter Olympics in Lillehammer – the first woman ever to fulfil such a role.

Female ski jumpers took heart from Ganster's Olympic inclusion and launched a petition for their sport to be given a place in the Winter Olympics in time for Nagano in 1998 – the same year in which the FIS first sanctioned a women's Grand Prix series. The IOC was not to be moved, though. Nor were they convinced when another petition was submitted four years later or indeed for a third time in 2006, by which time the female ski jumping community was, frankly, expecting the rejection.

After all, what else could come after the President of the FIS at the time (and member of the IOC) Gian-Franco Kasper had said this about ski jumping in 2005: 'It's like jumping down from, let's say, about two metres on the ground about a thousand times a year, which seems not to be appropriate for ladies from a medical point of view.'

His fears were based on the antiquated belief that partaking in such rigorous endeavours could have a disastrous impact on a woman's uterus (ah yes, the delicate organism). It was a notion popularised by English magistrate and author Donald Walker in his book, *Exercises for English Ladies,* written in 1836. His argument was that women should engage in 'restrained and non-violent' exercise to protect their 'peculiar function of multiplying the species'. Clearly, the man had never been present at an actual birth or he'd know that while it may be peculiar, giving birth (or multiplying the species) is rarely a restrained event. Heck, sometimes it isn't even a non-violent one.

US ski jumper Lindsey Van found Kasper's comments infuriating, saying: 'It just makes me nauseous. I'm sorry, but my baby-making organs are on the inside. Men have an organ on the outside. So if it's not safe for me jumping down, and my uterus is going to fall out, what about the organ on the outside of the body?'

In 2009, with the Vancouver Winter Olympics on the horizon, female ski jumpers were finally given a world championship-level competition. With such an international event now established, the American winner Van felt it was the perfect time to ramp the Olympic fight up a notch. She joined forces with nine other female jumpers from five different nations to sue the Vancouver Organizing Committee (VANOC) for violating the ban on gender discrimination in Canada's Charter of Rights and Freedoms.

While the British Columbia Supreme Court ruled that the IOC was indeed discriminating against the women because of their gender, it also claimed that, as an international organisation, the IOC was not bound by Canada's laws, meaning the court had no right to tell them which sports they should include. The world champion, Van turned her back on the sport for a season – furious, frustrated and drained from the legal battle.

Ironically it was Van who held the record jump (105.5m) on the Olympic course in Vancouver at the time the Games started. 'It was a little strange,' she said. 'It was as if the IOC were saying: "You're not good enough to be here, but you're good enough to test out the hill to see if it's good enough for men."'

Little more than a year after the Vancouver Games, the IOC finally saw sense. With almost 100 women competing in FIS-sanctioned ski-jumping competitions by 2011, and with at least 30 top-tier jumpers from 11 different nations consistently proving the sport was of undeniable Olympic quality, the IOC could shut it out no longer. On 6 April 2011 the committee's members voted to include one women's ski-jumping event in the Winter Olympics, beginning in Sochi 2014.

Van finished out of the medals in Russia, but that was of secondary importance to her: 'It's overwhelming, I can't put it into words', she said after her emotional final jump in Sochi. 'It's been a really long journey. I've been ski jumping for 22 years and I've always wanted to go to the Olympics.'

The sport's Olympic debut is only the beginning of its journey to catch up with the men, though. At present, women are allowed to compete in just one event on the 'normal' hill, while the men compete in two more events: the large hill and the team event. While a lack of numbers could explain the omission of women from the team event (four women from each country would be required), there is little reason to exclude them from the large hill. Women competed on a large hill at two World Cup events in 2014, while the United States national championship has been held on one for many years.

People within the sport feel it could take another eight years (two Olympic cycles) before women get the opportunity to compete in a large hill Olympic event though. In fact Peter Jerome – the father of top US jumper Jessica Jerome, and himself an instrumental figure in the effort to get women's ski jumping into the Games – is resigned to the fact: 'It's just an old boys' club making decisions', he told the *New York Times* in Sochi. 'That's why it takes so long for everything.'

His words are equally applicable to a number of other sports that are by no means limited to those featured in this chapter. But the experiences of female golfers, footballers, boxers and ski jumpers described here are indicative of the struggles sportswomen have faced and continue to face in the fight to compete – or in some cases, just to play – on an equal footing with men. Where change has come, it has come gradually and required a mammoth effort from those driving it.

Some have taken their battle into the courtroom, seeing it as their only route to changing years of exclusion and inequality. Others have waged tireless campaigns lasting for many years against those holding them back. And some have gathered more and more support for their cause, not stopping until ignoring them became more difficult than heeding their calls for fairness.

However progress might have come, the contributions of those women (and men) that made it happen is all the motivation current competitors need to push for more, for what sportswomen deserve – which is to have the same opportunities as their male equivalents.

Roberta Gibb

THE RUNNING RULE BREAKER

Her name might not be as well known as some of the other women who feature in this book, but Roberta Gibb's story is one that can give inspiration to every woman who has ever laced up a pair of running shoes (or even thought about doing so).

Now in her 70s, Gibb can look back on a life in which she has worked as a horse-riding instructor, a sculptor, a lawyer and an associate in a neuroscience laboratory. She has written books about inflation and economics. She is currently putting together a collection of essays and a children's book. She is collaborating on a film project. She is a mother, which she says is 'the best thing' she ever did. And in 1966, Gibb became the first woman ever to run the Boston Marathon – the world's oldest annual 26.2-mile race.

Not that many people know it. In fact, there are many who believe that a woman by the name of Kathrine Switzer was actually the first female to run the Boston Marathon (when she in fact ran it a year after Gibb, in 1967). Why the confusion? Well, it has much to do with the main difference between these two very determined women. While Gibb has always lacked any real appetite for the media spotlight, Switzer has revelled in it.

On her own website, Switzer is described thus: 'An iconic athlete, sports and social advocate, author, and Emmy award-winning television commentator, Kathrine Switzer was the first woman to officially enter and run the Boston Marathon.' While the early parts of this sentence ring true, the latter rings alarm bells.

At the time that both Gibb and Switzer ran the Boston Marathon, women were forbidden from entering the race for fear of what it would do to their fragile physiology. But both were determined to take part nevertheless. Gibb had been focused on taking part ever since she had caught sight of the race on a drab April morning in 1964. Standing alongside her dad at around the halfway point of the famous Boston course, Gibb watched in awe as the runners involved in the 68th Boston Marathon streamed past her.

'I've never seen people run like this before', Gibb wrote in her autobiography, remembering her excitement at seeing the race up close. 'How strong they are! They run with such grace, balancing the motions of their arms and legs – their heads scarcely bobbing. I'm surprised at how quiet their foot falls are … They are like wild animals running. I know how they feel; it is the way I feel when I run, turned inward, listening to the inside of their bodies. Here at last are people who feel the same way I do … Something shifts deep inside me. At this moment I know that I am meant to run this race.'

For Switzer, the desire to run in Boston came from her coach, Arnie Briggs (himself a veteran of 15 Boston Marathons). Switzer had taken up running in high school as a means to make the field hockey team and quickly discovered that the further she went, the stronger, more powerful and more liberated she felt. The marathon distance intrigued her more and more, but it was the Boston Marathon in particular – this race that allowed 'normal' people to run alongside the greatest runners in the world – that really captured her imagination.

In an article printed in *Runner's World* magazine in 2007 and headlined 'The Girl Who Started it All' (in itself a problematic title – did Switzer really 'start' it?), Switzer describes an argument she had with her coach during a six-mile run in December 1966 (eight months after Gibb had become the first woman to run the Boston Marathon). At the time, Switzer was a 19-year-old journalism student at Syracuse University where – like everywhere else – there was no women's running team. It was while training unofficially with the men's cross country team that Switzer met 50-year-old Briggs, who took her under his wing and regaled her with his Boston Marathon adventures. When Switzer suggested to him that they should stop talking about it and 'run the damn thing', Briggs scoffed, telling her, 'no woman can run the Boston Marathon'.

Switzer told her coach that she had heard a woman called Roberta Gibb had 'jumped into the race and finished it the previous April', but Briggs remained adamant it was simply not possible. 'If *any* woman could do it, you could', said Briggs, but you would have to prove it to me'. The pair struck a deal – if Switzer could cover the 26.2-mile marathon distance in a training session, then Briggs would take her to Boston. Her goal was set.

Gibb had also met a running companion while at university, a cross-country runner who would routinely race over five miles – a distance Gibb was initially awed by. But within six months of training with him she was right alongside as he ran five, six and even ten miles. 'I seemed to have a knack for it and a lot of stamina', she recalls.

To Gibb, the world's best known 26.2-miler (outside of the Olympic marathon), that so captivated her for the first time in 1964, was less about racing than about a group of like-minded individuals engaging in their favourite pastime: 'It hardly even occurred to me that it was an actual sporting event. To me, it was like a celebration of spring.'

When she made the decision to run, Gibb had no coach, no real idea of how to train for a marathon and no overpriced, weather-proof-sweat-wicking kit to wear while she was doing it. What she did have was a pair of nurse's shoes ('I had worked as a nurse's aide one summer … and they were sturdy shoes'), a tank top black bathing suit, and either shorts and a cotton shirt or 'layers of long underwear and leggings', depending on the season.

Her training was driven by curiosity: How far could she go? And how fast? At first her ventures stayed relatively close to home, with her boyfriend taking her out on his motorcycle so they could measure the mileage before he dropped her off and she would run home. Each time out they would go a little bit further than the last. With her confidence building by the summer of 1964, Gibb decided to take her training into new surrounds. She packed up her VW van with the bare essentials and her favourite running companion, her puppy Moot, and set off across the continent, from Massachusetts to California.

Every day she would run for hours in a new place, covering miles of ground. At night she would sleep out under the stars alone – totally out of tune with the prevailing beliefs that women needed protecting and guiding at all times. 'That's part of what I was trying to change and to find for myself', explained Gibb in a 2011 interview with the website of former American record holder for the marathon, Bill Rodgers. 'I was looking for a sense of authentic autonomy and freedom as a person, as a woman, as a human being.'

Gibb's guess is that she was covering between 15 and 20 miles at a stretch, every day for just over a month. Returning to Boston in time for the new school year and a new direction (in 1964 Gibb transferred to the Boston Museum of Fine Arts, where she studied sculpture), she was in fantastic shape. Her initial plan was to run the Boston Marathon the following year, in April 1965. But a few weeks before the race, Gibb slipped and fell, spraining both ankles. She harboured hopes of healing in time but come Marathon day, she was on crutches watching from the sidelines, with tears of disappointment stinging her eyes. Her marathon would have to wait another 12 months.

That autumn, Gibb's training reached levels that few would consider achievable, or even sensible. Allying herself with the Woodstock Vermont hundred-mile equestrian event, in which the horses ran 40 miles on the first day, 40 miles on the second and 20 miles on the third, she woke at dawn on the first day of the event and set off with the first horses. She ran all day, navigating rugged terrain, dirt roads and mountain trails. The following day she planned to do it all over again, but was forced to stop after 25 miles with pain in her knee (unsurprisingly). Still, running 65 miles in two days proved that she would have no problems running the Boston Marathon – physically speaking, at least.

Gibb remained blissfully ignorant of the one major obstacle that did stand in her way of running – the exclusion of women – until just two months before the race. In January 1966 she moved to California and became friendly with runners from the San Diego Track Club, including founding member Bill Gookin. It was the well-informed Gookin who first told Gibb that if she wanted to run the Boston Marathon, she would have to apply. 'I had no idea', she recalls, 'I had thought that people just went out to Hopkinton [where the race started] and kind of got together and ran to Boston.'

Heeding Gookin's advice, Gibb wrote to the Boston Athletic Association requesting an application in February 1966. The letter she got back from Will Cloney, the Race

Director, left her reeling. It explained that women were not physiologically able to run marathons and that furthermore, they were not *allowed* to do so. Coney added that under the rules of the Amateur Athletic Union, the longest sanctioned women's division race was a mile and a half and that they simply couldn't take the medical liability.

'I was thunderstruck', remembered Gibb in a 2011 interview. 'I had heard that the Marathon was open to every person in the world. It had never crossed my mind to consider myself different from the other runners … If you were a woman, it seemed you weren't allowed to do anything.'

Gibb's anger and hurt turned into a renewed sense of focus as she realised that there was now an even greater reason for her to run. She wanted to prove that women were capable of running a marathon in the belief that once she crossed that finish line, the race would open up. 'They just didn't know', she says. 'Women themselves didn't know they could do this.'

Switzer's discussions with her coach Arnie Briggs are proof that some people would take more persuasion. But as they stepped up their training with the aim of testing how much Switzer could handle, Briggs was forced to accept the reality. Three weeks before the 1967 Boston Marathon the duo completed their 26-mile trial. It wasn't enough for Switzer though, who insisted on adding another five-mile loop to the run.

This is the point at which Gibb's and Switzer's stories take divergent paths. Gibb's tactic was to run the race 'undercover'. She knew that if anyone spotted her before the start gun went off, she would be stopped before she could even get going. A plan was hatched, but Gibb would need the help of her (traditionally minded) parents to make it work. In the week leading up to the 1966 Marathon, Gibb departed her San Diego home and boarded a Greyhound bus bound for Boston. For the four days and three nights it took her to reach her childhood home, Gibb mused over what the reaction of her unknowing mother and father would be when she revealed her intention to run the famous Boston Marathon.

Arriving the day before the race, Gibb revealed her gatecrashing plan to her disbelieving parents: 'They thought I'd gone nuts. My dad actually thought I was delusional. They were very worried about me.' Gibb took her mother aside, explaining that she had been training for this for two years and was not just doing it for herself, but for all women, to set women free. On the morning of the race, Gibb's father reinforced his disapproval by storming out of the house to attend a sailing regatta, while her mother drove her to the start line. 'The look on my mother's face as she dropped me off reflected pride and concern, a combination of "I know you can do it", and "Will you be all right?"'

Dressed in a pair of her brother's Bermuda shorts and a blue hooded jumper, with the hood pulled up to try and conceal her gender, Gibb even wore a pair of boys' running shoes in place of the sturdy nurse's ones that had seen her through much of her training. Her one major fear was that she might be arrested or prevented from running, so she did whatever she could to hide herself away. Finding a clump of bushes near the start, Gibb hunkered down and waited.

'Bang! When the starting gun fired, Gibb watched the first surge of runners move away, and waited until half the pack remained before leaping out from the bushes and merging into the moving masses. As she did so, it crossed her mind that if she completed the race without anyone spotting her, how would anyone know she had done it at all? She would not be left wondering for long. A few minutes after starting her race, with her mind frantic with the implications of what she was attempting, Gibb became aware of an odd silence behind her, followed by murmurs: 'Is that a girl?'

'It is a girl!' She turned around and smiled at them, knowing her fate was now at least partly in their hands. To her great relief, they were friendly, asking: 'Are you going to run the whole way?' When she answered that yes, she certainly hoped to, they were impressed. 'Gee, I wish my girlfriend would run', said one of the men. Gibb could see that they wanted to share their love of running with the women in their lives.

Gibb had survived her first test, but soon there was another. She was warm in her heavy hooded jumper, but feared that removing it would not reveal not only her body shape but also her long, blonde hair. Her new male running buddies reassured her, saying they would not let her get thrown out.

So off came the sweater. When the crowds saw a woman running they cheered, says Gibb. 'The men clapped and said, "Atta go, girly!" And the women screamed and shouted.' Reporters for a local radio station quickly recognised they had a story on their hands, and before long, the progress of 'the girl' was being relayed to captivated listeners on the wireless. Some of them left their houses to join the crowds at the roadside, intent on cheering her along as she passed. Gibb felt the emotion urging her on but was determined to run conservatively, aware that, if she failed to finish the race, it could leave women's running in an even more hopeless place than it was before she started.

For many miles she ran 'stride for stride' with a man from Connecticut who had been among the group that had spotted her at the start of the race. The two chatted on and off, but for the most part, his mere presence alongside her was enough for Gibb, whose dream was that men and women could run together. The pair rattled off each mile in just under seven minutes – a pace Gibb says she was more than comfortable with. 'Most of the race was easy for me. I never got out of breath. It was fun. I was holding myself back, saving my energy. I talked with the runners around me. I was holding a sub three-hour pace without much effort.'

At 20 miles Gibb still felt strong. What was another six miles? She felt as though she could run 20 more. But as she hit the marathon's famous incline (known as Heartbreak

Hill) she felt her energy levels start to drop for the first time. As soon as that happened she became aware of a burning sensation on the soles of her feet. 'I wasn't used to running on pavement and my new shoes hurt. Each step sent a searing jolt of pain to my brain. My pace dropped off. I set each foot down as if on tacks.'

Gibb had learned the golden rule of marathon running: Always respect the distance. Later, she learned another one: stay hydrated. The last two miles seemed interminable to Gibb not only because of the blisters on her feet, but also because she was severely dehydrated. She had been led to believe that drinking while exercising would give her cramps, and so had avoided all the water stations throughout the race. For the first time, Gibb started to feel like a failure, wondering whether anyone would be left at the finish line by the time she got there.

'This is where I learned the real meaning of fortitude', says Gibb of those excruciatingly long, final miles. 'To keep on in the face of disappointment, to continue to do your best even when others are passing you. To see your hopes crushed and yet continue.'

As she entered the final approach to the finish line, Gibb was greeted by thousands of people cheering and yelling their encouragement. 'I ran across the finish line, with a sense of elation welling up inside me. I'd done it! I'd pursued my dream despite overwhelming obstacles. I'd run the Boston Marathon. I felt a great sense of triumph. The press closed in around me and whisked me off to a hotel room with cameras flashing and pens scribbling on note pads. I'd finished in three hours, 21 minutes and 40 seconds, ahead of two thirds of the pack. Not one of my better runs … but ok, given all the handicaps.'

The next day, Gibb was front-page news of the *Record American* (which would later become the *Boston Herald*), with the headline reading: Hub Bride First Gal to Run Marathon. 'It's silly that there aren't more distance races for women', she was quoted as saying. 'They may not be as fast as men, but I think it's been proved many times that they have just as much endurance and stamina.'

A week after the race she was the subject of an article in *Sports Illustrated*, titled: 'A game girl in a man's game.' The report referred to the 'shapely blonde housewife who came out of the bushes to crush male egos and steal the show', with the writer, Gwilym S. Brown, explaining that this 'tidy-looking and pretty 23-year-old blonde' had 'not only started but also covered the 26-mile, 385-yard course at a clip fast enough to finish ahead of no fewer than 290 of the event's 415 starters.

He concluded that even if Gibb had failed to 'convince a single housewife that she is as capable as her husband of spading up the garden, the performance should do much to phase out the old-fashioned notion that a female is too frail for distance running.'

The response from the general public was positive, and reports followed that the New England Amateur Athletic Union was planning to contact the organisation's national headquarters to see whether the rules could be amended so that a female who wished to compete in the race could do so. But for the man who had first told Gibb she could not enter the race back in February, nothing had changed: 'Mrs Bingay did not run in the Boston Marathon', insisted race director, Will Cloney, referring to Gibb by her married name. 'She merely covered the same route as the official race while it was in progress. No girl has ever run in the Boston Marathon', he insisted. Gibb, and all those men who had run alongside her in 1966, knew just how wrong Cloney was.

This brings us back to Switzer and her coach Briggs, who held the same view as Cloney ahead of the 1967 Boston Marathon. Although, once his athlete had proven to him that she was more than capable of running 26.2 miles, Briggs had agreed to take her to Boston. He wanted to do it the 'proper way' though, insisting that Switzer should sign up for the race. Otherwise, he said, she could find herself in hot water with the sport's governing body, the Amateur Athletic Union.

'We checked the rule book and entry form', wrote Switzer in her 2007 autobiography, 'there was nothing about gender in the marathon.' Attaching her $3 entry fee and signing, as she says she always did, with her initials: 'K.V. Switzer', she mailed off her entry. A few weeks later she arrived in in Boston accompanied by Briggs, her boyfriend (235lb, nationally ranked hammer thrower, Tom Miller) and a runner from the university cross-country team, John Leonard – all of whom were signed up to run.

While Gibb has always been clear that she was running to prove a point, Switzer says she wasn't running to prove anything: 'I was just a kid who wanted to run her first marathon.'

At the start area, Arnie Briggs collected race numbers for Switzer and the others in the group. With the number 261 pinned to the grey sweatshirt that she had accepted was the only way she would keep warm in the sleet and snow, Switzer followed the throng of people making their way into the starting 'pen', moving unchecked past race officials whose job it was to mark off runners' bib numbers. It was here where the presence of a female should have been noticed, but amid the moving mass of sodden, freezing cold bodies, Switzer somehow eluded detection by the authorities.

Those who did spot her were supportive and pleased to have a woman in their presence, as they had been with Gibb a year earlier. And until the fourth mile, Switzer was enjoying the race much as Gibb had. But then came the moment that changed everything, when a vehicle carrying the race photographers passed right by Switzer and her companions before slowing to a crawl right in front of them. The photographer's lenses fixated on Switzer, who smiled and waved: 'It was our "Hi-Mom-on-the-nightly-news" moment, and it was fun', recalls Switzer.

Moments later the fun was over as Switzer found herself being pursued by race officials, yelling at her to 'Get the hell out of my race!' They clung on to her sweater, trying to rip the number from her (the photographs of this have become legendary, and are often mistakenly labelled as showing the first woman to run the Boston Marathon).

Switzer wondered if she should step off the course, but only for a brief moment: 'I knew if I quit, nobody would ever believe that women had the capability to run 26-plus miles. If I quit, everybody would say it was a publicity stunt. If I quit, it would set women's sports back, way back, instead of forward. If I quit, I'd never run Boston. If I quit, co-race Director Jock Semple and all those like him would win.'

She later came to understand that Semple's anger was not only to do with her gender, but also with her having managed to secure an official race number (though the two factors are obviously inextricably linked): 'Jock probably would have left me alone if I was just running along like Bobbi', she told Deadspin in 2015. 'It was the number that got him. I had made him look like a fool.'

At the finish line, a group of reporters was waiting for Switzer, and peppered her with questions as soon as she stopped running: 'What made you do it?' (I like to run, the longer the better.) 'Oh come on, why Boston, why wear numbers?' (Women deserve to run, too. Equal rights and all that, you know.) 'Will you come back to run again?' (Yes.) 'They will ban your club.' (Then we'll change the name of our club.) 'Are you a suffragette?' (Huh? I thought we got the right to vote in 1920!)

Once again, a woman had made headlines at the Boston Marathon. The *New York Times* report ran under the headline: 'Lady with Desire to Run Crashed Marathon', following it with a subheading that left readers in no doubt as to who the victim in the story was: 'Officials at Boston Shaken when Entry 261 Started Race.'

The report asked what a girl, and a former beauty contestant at that, was doing in a marathon? Switzer's response was simply that she loved to run. When confronted with the question of the rules that forbid women from running, she said: 'They are archaic. Women can run, and they can still be women and look like women. I think the AAU will begin to realise this and put in longer races for women.'

Noting that Switzer spoke in a high-pitched voice filled with girlish enthusiasm, the reporter expressed his admiration that this woman with 'soft brown hair' and a 'winsome look' could be 'more than peaches and cream', detailing how she had been the sports editor of her university paper and had occasionally been drafted in to the men's track team when they were short on numbers.

Not everyone was won over though. The article concluded with a quote from Boston's Race Director Will Cloney, who said that while the rules stayed as they were he would continue to try and carry them out. 'We have no place in the marathon for any unauthorised person, even a man', said Cloney. 'If that girl were my daughter, I would spank her.'

Gibb had also run in Boston that year, though she had done so without a race number. Unlike the previous year there had been no need to hide herself away in the bushes this time, with Gibb allowed to run in what was technically (if not yet officially), the women's division Boston Marathon (the lack of drama over Gibb's participation proving Switzer correct in her belief that it was her race number more than her gender that had so angered Jock Semple). Gibb finished around an hour ahead of Switzer, unaware of the other woman's presence until after she returned home and read the newspaper reports (in which her own run garnered barely a passing mention).

While Gibb was pleased to see that another woman had followed her lead in wanting to prove women capable of running a marathon, she was not entirely happy with Switzer's methods. 'I didn't like to see the negativity that surrounded her approach' she told the Bill Rodgers Running Centre in 2011. 'I felt that it would end up setting women's running back. This was exactly what I was trying to avoid. I wanted to keep it upbeat and inspirational.'

The following year, Gibb returned to run for a third time. Switzer was nowhere to be seen, but a total of five women ran the race. 'The unpleasantness of the year before seemed to have disappeared', says Gibb. 'The women entered in various places near the start, wherever they could do so without drawing attention. In my case, I entered from the bushes, because after the negative reception the year before, I wasn't sure if they'd try to stop me.'

Gibb was once again the first woman across the line in three hours, 30 minutes and 17 seconds, but that was to be her final appearance in her beloved Boston Marathon until much later in her life. By 1969 she had graduated from the University of California with a Major in philosophy and went to law school. She continued to run, but returned to the 'quiet places' she had left, writing in her autobiography: 'The mountain trails, the vast blue sky, the nameless clouds, forests, deserts and beaches … Once again running became a way to express joy.'

Switzer stayed in the spotlight though. Driven by her experience in Boston, she has devoted her life to creating opportunities for other women in running. She started by helping to lead the campaign to get official status for women in distance races – a feat achieved at the Boston Marathon in 1972, some six years after Gibb emerged from the bushes to run. And when the women's marathon was finally included in the Olympic Games in 1984, that too was partly thanks to Switzer and her efforts in launching the international Avon Running Circuit in 1978.

A media favourite, Switzer has spent the last few decades working in radio and television, building her brand into one that is so well known, it has often threatened to totally eclipse the story of Roberta Gibb. It is perhaps easy to understand the overshadowing of Gibb when you read Switzer refer to herself (correctly) as the first woman to officially enter and run the Boston Marathon. There is nothing false about that statement, but it is easily misconstrued. In April 2015, for example, I heard a BBC Radio programme called *The Kathrine Switzer Story* refer to her as 'the first woman to run the Boston Marathon'. There might only be a few words missing from that sentence, but they are crucial ones.

It is equally crucial, though, to recognise the impact that both these women have had on women's lives. Today, women's participation in marathons and beyond (Ironman triathlons, ultramarathons and the like) has become so commonplace it is almost hard to comprehend that it was ever any different. And for all their differences, Gibb and Switzer can both feel satisfied that their efforts have proved more worthwhile than they ever could have expected, however widely their names are known (or not, as the case may be).

3: Money talks

Women's sport is trapped in a vicious cycle. No one knows exactly where it starts or where it ends, but everyone knows the exasperating details that keep it spinning. One such detail – the lack of media coverage women's sport receives – was discussed in the first chapter. But this dearth of exposure can't be viewed in isolation for it is a result of – and a factor in – another part of the vicious cycle: The sponsorship black hole.

In 2014 the UK's Women's Sport and Fitness Foundation (now known as Women in Sport), reported that women's sports accounted for a pitiful 0.4 per cent of the commercial investment going into all sport in Britain. It's a number that tallied depressingly well with their finding that women's sports received seven per cent of total sports coverage in the media. After all, what kind of sponsor wants to invest precious time and money in something or someone without any guarantee of a reasonable return?

Reluctant investors point the finger at the editors, broadcasters and directors who pack their schedules with men's sport. Meanwhile, those media types will point the finger right back and say that without the marketing and sponsorship support to ensure that people know about it and want to see it, women's sport will remain a side note among mainstream sports coverage.

Caught in between the two are the governing bodies, whose desire to promote their sportswomen is often stymied by a lack of resources and limited expertise. This was something I had an insight into after the England women's football squad returned from the World Cup in the summer of 2015, when having won an historic bronze medal – the first World Cup medal for any England football team since 1966 – there was a real surge in demand from the media for time with the players. Brilliant news, you might think; at last the media are starting to pay attention to these talented footballers who just happen to be women.

And it was brilliant news. Less brilliant was the response from the FA who were simply not prepared for the frenzy. One PR contact I spoke to, who was trying hard to line up media coverage for the Women's FA Cup final that came just weeks after the World Cup ended, told me that the number of requests going into the FA for player interviews was piling up and they were too slow to react. Not because they didn't want the coverage but because there simply weren't enough people working on women's football in the FA's communications team. Throughout the months leading up to the World Cup, everyone within the FA had been excited about the impact that a successful campaign could have on the women's game in this country, yet when it happened, they still weren't ready for it. Brilliant.

How can this frustrating cycle be stopped? One woman who has some ideas is Sally Hancock, the Chair of Women in Sport. She has an extensive background in sponsorship planning, strategy and delivery and has seen first-hand how brands approach their partnerships with sport, so I decided to pick her brains on how women's sport can start taking a larger share of the sponsorship pie. Hancock told me that in the lead up to the London Olympics in 2012, there was actually 'something of a spike in expenditure on women's sport, in keeping with the fact that the whole market grew in the years leading up to the Games.

'What we've seen since is that although the market has dropped off, it is still growing. Even so, the money going into women's sport remains a tiny proportion of the total for the sector as a whole which is really poor.'

Hancock's words are supported by a 2014 report by Women in Sport, which found that although the number and value of deals for women's sport increased five-fold in 2011 and 2012, men's sport also benefited from an upsurge in that period, so the proportion of funding going into women's sport remained similar. In the post-Olympic lull, 2013 sponsorship levels for women's sport declined considerably.

The gaping chasm that exists in sports sponsorships between the genders becomes painfully clear when looking at a list of the most valuable deals across men's and women's sports.

In 2013, the top five women's sponsorship deals totalled £1.4million. See Figure 1.

Team/Athlete	Sponsor	Length of deal	Amount
FA Women's Superleague	Continental	5 years	£450,000 ($697,252)
Netball Superleague	Zeo	1 year	£390,000 ($604,285)
Laura Robson	Virgin Active	2 years	£195,000 ($302,142)
Christine Ohuruogu	Virgin Media	1 year	£195,000 ($302,142)
Jessica Ennis-Hill	Santander	1 year	£195,000 ($302,142)

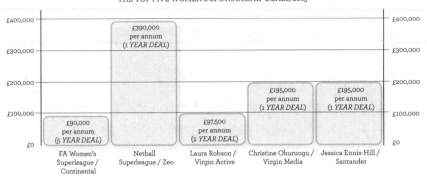

THE TOP FIVE WOMEN'S SPONSORSHIP DEALS, 2013

FA Women's Superleague / Continental: £90,000 per annum (5 YEAR DEAL)

Netball Superleague / Zeo: £390,000 per annum (1 YEAR DEAL)

Laura Robson / Virgin Active: £97,500 per annum (2 YEAR DEAL)

Christine Ohuruogu / Virgin Media: £195,000 per annum (1 YEAR DEAL)

Jessica Ennis-Hill / Santander: £195,000 per annum (1 YEAR DEAL)

FIGURE 1

The top five men's deals, meanwhile, totalled a staggering £590 million. See Figure 2.

Team/Athlete	Sponsor	Length of deal	Amount
Chelsea FC	Adidas	10 years	£280million ($434million)
Rory McIlroy	Nike	19 years	£150million ($232million)
Manchester United	AGON	8 years	£110million ($170million)
Football League	Sky Bet	5 years	£27.5million ($42.6million)
Premier League	Carlsberg	3 years	£23million ($36million)

In addition to the financial mismatch, there is also a noticeable difference in the length of commitment from sponsors, with deals lasting five years or more common among men's sports, compared to one- or two-year deals in women's. Not only do longer deals mean increased financial benefits for the athlete or sport involved (allowing them to focus on training without worrying about where the next deal is coming from), they also allow for better forward planning, which helps to build events and partnerships and gives sponsors a better return on their investment.

While the problem is evident, the solution is harder to fathom, says the Chief Executive of Women in Sport, Ruth Holdaway. When her organisation released their

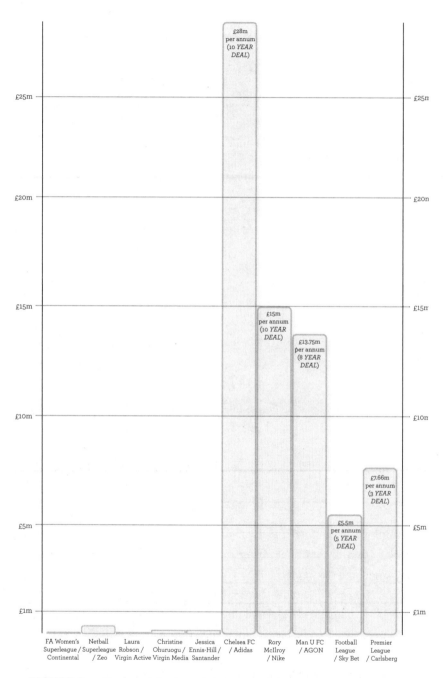

FIGURE 2

report on the commercial value of women's sport in March 2014, they promised to use their position to bring sponsors, sports and the media together and show them how they can benefit from a successful women's sport event.

'Broadcasters and investors have told us there simply aren't enough high-calibre women's sport events between Olympic cycles to justify greater investment and dedicated media coverage', said Holdaway, 'so we choose to tackle the problem at its root and bring more women's sport to the fore.'

Holdaway's mission is one that she says will take 'compromise, commitment and the occasional leap of faith'. But she realises the challenges are daunting: 'It will involve breaking the pervading culture which allows men's sport to dominate. We recognise it will need progressive thinkers and those with influence to take brave decisions.'

These decisions are likely to require those making them to alter a way of thinking that has become deeply ingrained. It's a way of thinking that prioritises viewing figures, crowd attendances and column inches way above almost anything else when it comes to deciding where the cash should go. But Hancock tells me she is starting to see signs that some 'insightful brands' are finally starting to see the bigger picture. 'Of course there are some sectors and brands for whom the "eyeball count" is still a major attraction, but I'd suggest that insightful brands are starting to see that there is a connection between doing the right thing in sponsorship and doing the right thing for business.

'That means there is a stronger connection between what might be thought of as corporate social responsibility and sponsorship. In some of the good businesses I get involved with, there's not much of a distinction. If you look at some of the activity that Lloyds [bank] are now undertaking, it's very much community driven. Is it sponsorship or is it community? Does it matter?'

Not everyone is so keen for sponsorship and social responsibility to merge completely, though. Take Bank of America's Global Strategy and Marketing Officer, Anne Finucane, for example. At a 2013 conference titled 'Game Changers' hosted by the *Sports Business Journal* in New York, she gave a blunt response when asked whether top corporate sponsors should do more to support women's sports: 'What is the responsibility of corporate America to sponsor women's sports?' asked Finucane (who politely declined my request to discuss her thoughts with me in further detail for this chapter). 'Corporate America sponsors sports because we're looking for branding, revenue, customer engagement, employee engagement, community engagement. We're not doing it because we're trying to advance the sport itself, honestly. So I don't think we see it as a moral imperative.'

Her view is echoed by the Executive Editor of *Sports Business Journal*, Abraham Madkour, who believes that women's sport shouldn't be positioned as a philanthropic commitment: 'Today's chief marketing officers don't have an obligation to support women's sports. They are representing businesses, and businesses fail across the US on a daily basis. They will succeed or fail based on the quality of the product and the customer experience.'

Madkour adds that the onus should be on the sports themselves to 'deliver on brand and business objectives for their sponsors and elevate themselves by delivering better ratings and promotional value.'

Delivering promotional value is something that the former Chairman and CEO of the Women's Tennis Association (WTA), Stacey Allaster, prioritised when she took on the role in 2009, and it has paid dividends. During her tenure the WTA secured a record number of new sponsors, ensuring the financial success of the sport and securing the position of tennis as the world's leading professional sport for women.

I meet her in Singapore at the end of 2014, when the WTA's end of season championships are beginning a five-year run at the 7,500-seater Singapore Sports Hub stadium. The event itself – a 10-day extravaganza combining music and entertainment with world-class tennis – is indicative of the WTA's forward-thinking approach when it comes to selling their sport. As is Allaster's response when I ask her to explain why women's tennis has succeeded where so many other women's sports have failed.

She answers without hesitation, telling me there are five reasons for the WTA's success, starting with Billie Jean King and the 'Original Nine'. 'In them we had courageous women who had the vision and the belief and who stood up to the establishment.' Secondly, Allaster says, are the tournament promoters who have 'made the investment, taken the risk and believed that women's professional tennis would be commercially successful'.

Allaster's third reason is the sponsors, going all the way back to Virginia Slims who sponsored the first independent women's professional tennis tour in 1970. 'All through our journey we've had the type of sponsors who certainly want a return on their investment from their partnership with the WTA, but they see a much larger picture too, as a contributor to the empowerment of women.

'Kraft [who sponsored the women's tour from 1990 until 1994] and Sony Ericsson [whose £56.3 million contract to be title sponsor of the WTA Tour was the largest in the history of women's professional sports when it was signed in 2005] wanted a strong WTA brand because that would positively reflect on their brand.'

The fourth point relates to the sheer number of events the WTA now boasts: 'We have five "Olympics" every year', says Allaster. 'Four Grand Slams and the WTA Finals. Then I have 53 other WTA tournaments. Consistent exposure breeds success. We all fall in love with women's sports during the Olympic Games, and then they go out of sight. Women's sport lacks consistent media exposure but women's tennis has it, so we can stay connected with our fans.'

Finally, Allaster points to what she calls the 'gender neutrality' of women's tennis. 'In many societies around the world it's accepted that women can play tennis. Whereas putting a hockey helmet or football pads on them [or boxing gloves, as discussed in Chapter 2] ... I don't think all countries around the world are as accepting of women playing those types of sports.'

In 2013 the WTA signed multi-year, global sponsorship deals with Xerox and SAP, adding to existing deals with BNP Paribas and Rolex. It also partnered with Singapore, where the WTA Finals are being held for five years from 2014 to 2018, a deal that Allaster says was 'the largest financial partnership ever completed in the history of the WTA' at the time it was agreed.

The end of 2014 brought even bigger news for the women's tour when it signed a £340 million ($535million) deal with British media company Perform. The deal gives Perform broadcasting rights to every tournament on the WTA calendar for 10 years from 2017, meaning the company is obligated to arrange coverage of all 2,000 or so singles matches a year on the tour as well as semi-finals and finals in the doubles. In turn it will sell the footage on to TV companies, websites and mobile operators. Billed as the biggest single commercial contract in the history of women's sport, Allaster calls it a 'game changer and an historic moment for the WTA and women's sport'.

It's a deal that moves women's tennis out of the vicious circle that has prevented most women's sports from thriving. By ensuring that the sport is beamed into peoples' homes more often than ever before, Allaster knows the sport's attraction to potential investors will only rise: 'Without question, women's sports needs consistent, year-round exposure in order to compete for the fans' attention, their engagement and disposable income', she says. 'More exposure, more fans, more sponsorship revenues.'

But Allaster admits that even with the increased profile of women's tennis compared to other women's sports, finding willing investors has always been a challenge. 'We've come a long way but we have a long way to go. It's time for leaders in corporations to stop talking about how great women's sport is and dedicate resources to promote women's sport because they are amazing athletes and role models for youth. It takes leadership, and for people to put their money where their mouth is. We're fortunate but even for us, with the most popular female athletes in the world, it's not easy.'

There are reasons to be positive about the future though, says Allaster, starting with the 'she-conomy'. It's a term that has emerged to describe the economy in a world where women have a greater control of incomes and spending, both in households and wider society. While it has long been known that women make most of the purchasing decisions in households (85 per cent is the figure most often quoted), the difference in recent years has been that women are now also the ones earning the money. In October 2009, the US workforce became nearly half female, while in the UK, figures released in 2014 showed that women made up 46 per cent of the workforce (the number of women in work was reported to have risen to 14 million – the highest figure since the Office for National Statistics began).

For Allaster, these facts have the potential to change the future of women's sport. 'Because of the she-conomy and government leaders and CEOs now understanding that the female is driving this economy, companies are going to have to start aligning their brand with things of interest to their customer, as opposed to the guys just picking their male sports because they like them.

'The evaluation process for women's sport has to go beyond eyeballs. It needs to be more strategic, looking at return on objectives with the brand alignment, with the intangibles, with those money can't buy experiences that women's sport will give a brand far superior access to than male sports.'

Women in Sport Chair, Sally Hancock, agrees, telling me: 'There is a greater recognition of the role of women in purchasing decisions, and because of that you are starting to see things like more of the car companies taking an interest in women's sport.' She highlights Kia Motors as one example – the car manufacturer became the first official partner of England women's cricket when they signed a two-year deal to be the official car of the team in 2014.

Previous sponsorship deals involving the England women's team had been part of contracts with the entire England set up, so the Kia partnership was considered to be an historic moment, showing that women's cricket was a strong enough proposition alone to attract investment. And from a major player in sports sponsorship, too. Kia are an official FIFA Partner, sponsor the Australian Open in tennis and have boasted multiple Grand Slam champion Rafael Nadal as an ambassador since 2006.

For the ECB's Head of England Women's Cricket, Clare Connor (who tells me all about her incredible journey from England captain to boardroom later on in the book), getting such a major brand on board was just as important as what they can offer in a practical sense: 'Kia are a big global brand. Whatever the amount, however many cars they give us, for me it's about the fact that as a brand, they have such a pedigree already in terms of being a sponsor of sport.'

Connor knows it's the kind of deal that gets other brands thinking about their own sponsorship strategies. Where Kia have led, others are likely to follow and that can only lead to bigger and better things for England's women. It's something that women's basketball – the world's longest established professional team sport for women, via the Women's National Basketball Association (WNBA) – saw some years ago.

From the time of the league's launch in 1997 teams in the WNBA had followed their NBA colleagues in having the team's name emblazoned across the front of their jerseys. Then in 2009, things changed. During an off-season when one franchise (the Houston Comets) folded and the remaining 13 cut their squads to 11 players from 13, the WNBA authorised its teams to do what European football clubs had been doing since the late 1970s and surrender their jersey space to companies in exchange for a generous sum of money.

The first team to take the leap was Phoenix Mercury in June 2009, when they signed a three-year deal with identity-theft protection company Life Lock, worth at least $1million per year. It wasn't just a big leap for women's sport but for US sport too, as Mercury became the first team in a major American sports league to add a sponsor name to their uniform.

'This is inventory that's not available any other place', said Rick Welts, president of (male) NBA team, Phoenix Suns, which owns the Mercury. 'Every photograph, every piece of game footage becomes part of the picture.'

Players effectively become moving billboards, providing sponsors with almost continuous exposure. Even taking into account the WNBA's lower profile compared to the major men's team sports in the USA, the co-founder and chief executive of Life Lock, Todd Davis, was convinced of the benefits on offer from investing in a team with 'fanatical' supporters who appreciate the role of sponsors in the league: 'Mercury fans have a real affinity for the sport', he said. 'They just go above and beyond to support it.'

Mercury's move divided fan opinion at first. Some felt the club was selling out, while others simply disliked the look of the new uniform. But those who understood the financial strain under which WNBA teams had been operating (during the league's 11th season in 2007, clubs were estimated to be losing $1.5 to $2million per year), were happy to celebrate new revenue streams rather than scrutinise them.

A matter of days after Mercury's deal was signed, a second WNBA team followed suit. One of the most successful teams in WNBA history, the Los Angeles Sparks, announced a multi-year marketing partnership with Farmers Insurance that would also include jersey branding. The deal made perfect sense for Farmers Insurance Executive Vice President Kevin Kelso, who said: 'The Sparks reach a primary demographic in our marketing strategy – the women's market – not only in LA, but throughout our operating territory. In recognition of a growing women's market and internal initiatives to target this market, this is a perfect arrangement for us to be associated with a quality franchise.'

At time of writing, six teams in the league have multi-year jersey sponsorship deals (San Antonio Stars, Phoenix Mercury, Minnesota Lynx, Indiana Fever, Tulsa Shock and Washington Mystics). While some fans might still pine for the days when team uniforms were free from the clutches of the money men, the significance of WNBA teams attracting this kind of investment is clear.

Even the NBA is starting to take notice. Thus far, NBA teams have steered clear of allowing sponsor names to appear on team jerseys (all the teams have sponsors, but they are limited to displaying adverts in stadiums as opposed to on players' uniforms). But in 2015, the league's commissioner Adam Silver admitted that it was an inevitability: 'As we look to generate other forms of revenue and also as we listen to the marketplace, the companies that are involved with the NBA want to get closer to the game, want to get closer to our players.'

For Alex Chambers, who writes for women's basketball website Full Court, the WNBA's jersey sponsorships reflect the value that the WNBA has built over the years. She says, 'The companies that have decided to sponsor these teams have one goal with this level of advertising – to generate revenue. If the visibility of the WNBA did not have this kind of value, these multi-million dollar companies would not be signing on as quickly as they are.'

Karen Bryant, who was the CEO of WNBA team Seattle Storm when they signed a four-year deal with the Microsoft-owned brand Bing in 2010 agrees. 'I can't think of one WNBA jersey partner that is doing this because they are taking pity or because it's the right thing to do. They're running businesses. They're making these investments because they believe it's good for their business. In that way *it is* the right thing to do because it is an opportunity to associate yourself with an avid and loyal fan base of women, who are the most powerful consumer base in the country.'

Storm's deal with Bing came to an end in 2014, by which time the league had signed a significant sponsorship deal of its own. In 2011 – the WNBA's

15th year – they signed mobile phone operator Boost Mobile as the league's sole 'marquee' partner. It was the most lucrative contract in WNBA history (although the full financial terms were never fully disclosed), and certainly its most comprehensive. The partnership put Boost Mobile's logo on the front of all WNBA team jerseys barring two franchises that already had deals in place with similar companies (Phoenix Mercury with Verizon and San Antonio Silver Stars with AT&T). It also allowed the brand to have its logo on display on courts and become the title sponsor of the annual WNBA All-Star Game.

Boost Mobile believed the WNBA was the right partner for them because the league attracted the young, urban, multicultural fans that the company considers its core customers. 'With the WNBA we feel we hit the nail on the head', said Steve Gaffney, the Vice President for Corporate Marketing at Boost Mobile. 'When we looked at the all the assets of the deal, from the jersey visibility to the court visibility to the overall stature of the Boost Mobile brand, it is a great alignment. This is a cost-effective way to align with a premier women's sports brand.'

The WNBA has in many ways defied the odds by surviving for as long as it has. In May 2013, the website 24/7 Wall St, which every year bleakly identifies 10 American brands that they claim are on the brink of disaster, predicted that the WNBA would disappear before the end of 2014. They cited the impending retirement of powerful NBA Commissioner (and the man credited with being a major player in the creation of the WNBA), David Stern, as a major factor in their prediction, with 'awful' crowd numbers adding to the bleak outlook: 'Attendance for half of the teams dropped by double digits between 2011 and 2012. Owners have little financial reason to support the league. The *Chicago Sun Times* reported in 2011 that, 'The majority of WNBA teams are believed to have lost money each year, with the NBA subsidizing some of the losses.'

And yet the WNBA continues to survive, bolstered by a long-term broadcasting deal with ESPN that dates back to the league's inaugural season in 1997 and currently runs up to 2022. Its impressive longevity means the WNBA has become a model that other women's sports around the world look to emulate in the constant bid to thrive and survive.

Four years after the WNBA was founded, the world's first professional women's soccer league was launched. The Women's United Soccer Association (WUSA) emerged in a blaze of glory the year after the US Women's National Team's (USWNT) won the Women's World Cup in 1999. The final against China was played in front of 90,185 screaming fans in Pasadena, California (the largest crowd ever to watch a women's sports event), and saw the US emerge on top after a tense game that was decided by a penalty shootout.

The enduring image from that tournament is that of US player Brandi Chastain whipping off her shirt and falling to her knees with fists pumping in celebration after scoring the winning penalty. Chastain dismissed the incident as 'momentary insanity', but for her sport it was a moment of genius. The image of Chastain was splashed on the covers of *Newsweek* and *Sports Illustrated*, while *Time* magazine also made her a cover star. Chastain became probably the only person in the world to have a section on her Wikipedia page subtitled '*Sports bra episode*', while her sport revelled in the media hype that followed.

A total of $40million was committed to the launch of the Women's United Soccer Association in 2000. The money was invested by a group of deep-pocketed media moguls led by the chairman and chief executive officer of Discovery Communications, John S. Hendricks. He was convinced that the excitement around the World Cup showed there was huge potential in the women's game, saying, 'We think this is an exciting time, we think we have the right ingredients.'

But just three years later, and days before the US squad was about to begin the defence of their World Cup crown at the 2003 tournament, the league folded. By then, it was reported that it had burned through a grand total of $100million ($40million in its first year and $60million over the two that followed).

'I was intoxicated by what I witnessed in 1999, and I mistakenly believed that level of support would flow over into the league', said Hendricks. His words also ring true for the other investors who had made financial assumptions involving corporate sponsorship, debt, attendance and television exposure that proved to be overly optimistic.

'WUSA was a league built upon a national media model', wrote senior writer Bill King on the *Sports Business Daily* website. 'It sold multimillion-dollar sponsorships to large companies behind the promise that it would deliver TV ratings akin to regular-season baseball. It signed a sizable rights fee deal with the now-defunct Pax TV network, which few viewers could find. The cheque cleared, but production costs were high and promotion was zero.'

Throughout its three years of operation the league failed to secure a slot on network TV (Pax was a cable channel) for a single game. This meant the profile of the game slipped further away from its World Cup high, and, crucially, left the league struggling to draw the investment from the sponsors that it so badly needed to cover costs.

The hope had been that the league would attract eight corporate sponsors, each paying $2.5million per year, but only two – Hyundai and Johnson & Johnson – signed on at that level. With the league's financial troubles widely known going into what turned out to be its final season, many players, including Mia Hamm (who ranked third on the *Sports Business Daily*'s list of most marketable female athletes in the same year the WUSA folded), agreed to take pay cuts. Those on the highest wages saw their salaries drop from $80,000 to $60,000. Teams also trimmed squad sizes from 18 to 16 players, but ultimately neither of these belt-tightening measures could compensate for a severe lack of revenue in the face of corporate indifference.

Hendricks cut a frustrated figure, saying it would have taken 'only six or seven CEOs in America' to step forward to prevent the WUSA from folding: 'An independent women's professional league can survive', he insisted, 'if it has corporate support.'

It was six years before a successor to the WUSA emerged. Women's Professional Soccer (WPS) launched in March 2009 – in the midst of recession. Seven teams were committed to the inaugural season with the league's first commissioner, Tonya Antonucci, claiming lessons had been learned from the failure of its forerunner. 'We've really cut the cost back and set our expectations modestly', said Antonucci. With the recession starting to bite, she felt that women's soccer could capitalise on the fact that sports fans would be looking for cheaper ways to get their fix: 'We're an attractive and affordable alternative. Whereas in a good economy, we might have been perceived as a lower priority among sports fans, we might actually have some sports fans sample us who wouldn't have otherwise.'

While its predecessor had launched with grand plans for national domination, WPS focused on building from the bottom up, taking what Antonucci called a 'local, grassroots approach' that would hopefully elicit the type of slow and steady growth that leads to longevity.

But while costs were down (the average salary for a WPS player was $32,000 compared to $40,000 in WUSA and venues were more modest), making money remained a challenge. Fox Soccer Channel agreed to show a WPS 'Game of the Week', but there was no fee in it for the league, meaning it entered the fray without a television rights deal in place. That in turn meant less revenue and less publicity – a familiar sounding story.

WPS also launched with just two national sponsors on board: Puma and bottled-water brand Hint. The plan had been to have five in place before a ball was kicked. This shortfall was no surprise to leading sports management consultant, Donna A. Lopiano. She says: 'You have an American market where the big sponsorship money is tied to television deals because the advertisers will not do anything without television. The keys to the kingdom are not available to new sports, men's or women's.'

And so it proved. Round two of women's soccer's attempt at professionalisation failed in 2012. The league announced the suspension of the 2012 season in January before finally closing in May, just two months before the US women's soccer team were due to compete at the London Olympics. Jeff Kassouf, who founded US women's soccer website Equalizer Soccer estimates that while the scale of the league's debts was far smaller than those incurred by its predecessor, teams were still losing between three and five million dollars per year.

At the time of the league's collapse, Kassouf wrote: 'After two failed attempts at creating leagues – both of which have some striking similarities but on different economic scales – it should be clear at this point that there has to be help from US Soccer or MLS (Major League Soccer is the professional men's league in the USA and Canada) in making it work.'

Kassouf's call to arms clearly had some effect as the national governing body – US Soccer – stepped up to the plate, having finally recognised that without their dedicated input the fragility of any professional women's league would remain. Their aim was to create as strong a US women's soccer team as possible to challenge for the 2015 World Cup, which was to be held in Canada.

Just as the FA had been behind the launch of the Women's Super League in England two years earlier, the US Soccer Federation (USSF) unveiled the National Women's Soccer League (NWSL) in April 2013, aiming to succeed where others had twice failed. What immediately set the league apart from its forerunners was that the salaries of the best players were to be subsidised, helping teams to create world-class squads while staying within the salary cap.

The American federation joined forces with the Canadian Soccer Association and the Federation of Mexican Football to try and create as strong a league as possible. Each federation pledged to pay the salaries of their national team players, meaning the USSF would cover the wages of up to 24 national team players (three per team), Canada's association up to 16 and Mexico's up to 12 (teams are allowed up to two players from each of these nations).

For former captain of the US women's team Julie Foudy, this was a financial model that made perfect sense: 'The league has the American, Canadian and Mexican federations now taking the most expensive players off the league's balance sheet. These federations are paying for their respective national team players, not the league. That is a sizable chunk when you are talking about seven players, more than a third of your roster.'

Kassouf agrees when I get him on the phone to discuss the state of women's soccer in the US, telling me: 'I think this is the best model of the three. Whether it's the answer and long term sustainable is the question but of the three it has the least red flags.'

The league did not have a broadcasting deal in place at the time of its launch, however, setting alarm bells ringing almost immediately. But Executive Director of the league, Cheryl Bailey (who was the US women's team general manager from 2007–11), was quick to point out that a national television contract and a clothing deal were both close to being signed off.

Initially, games were streamed online via team websites and the league's YouTube channel. 'That's great for fans,' says Kassouf, 'but not great for taking it to a new audience that is less likely to actively seek games out.' A deal with Fox Soccer did come eventually, but it only covered nine matches at the tail end of the season, starting on 8 July. Until then, it was YouTube or nothing.

Ahead of the league's second season, a one-year deal with ESPN was signed which saw the network commit to showing three regular season matches, both semi-finals and the NWSL Championship match on ESPN2, while three other regular season matches would be aired on the network's online streaming service, ESPN3. 'All three playoff games were on TV (ESPN2) which was big for the league', Kassouf says. 'It was the most exposure to date to a mainstream audience.'

There is one particular area that still gives cause for anxiety though: that of national sponsorship. 'They really don't have anybody', says Kassouf, clearly perplexed at the continued absence of league sponsors. 'They have the Army National Guard as their Official Armed Forces Partner, but it's unclear what they actually do beyond putting their name on a couple of awards.

'They also have Nike. It's a Nike-sponsored league, but this is year three and there has never even been a press release stating that this is a Nike-sponsored league. I'm not sure why it was swept under the rug but it's almost a running joke that this never actually got announced. I remember being on the conference call of the league launch and saying: 'So you're wearing Nike', and the US Soccer president Sunil Gulati responded with something to the tune of: 'We can't say anything about that right now.'

'The whole league is Nike, just like Major League Soccer [MLS] has an Adidas deal. Every piece of NWSL material that is officially licenced has the Nike logo on it and there are some Nike field [advertising] boards around stadiums, but there has never even been an official press release to say: Hey, Nike is the official sponsor and supplier of NWSL. It's really weird.'

By contrast, in the UK the FA Women's Super League (FAWSL) makes plenty of noise when sponsors come on board. And why not? By shouting about such investment the league projects an image of itself as a thriving entity that is far more attractive to other potential backers.

I headed to the Wembley Stadium home of the FA to meet Sissel Hartley, the FA's Marketing Manager for Women's Football. She proudly told me that many countries are actually looking at what the FA has done to turn the Women's Super League into such a stable entity since it launched in 2011: 'They want to know how we have established a league in four seasons that has media share, broadcast share, marketing share. The WSL has the highest awareness of any women's sports league in this country.'

Some might argue that the competition is not all that strong. But not even the FA's strongest critics can deny that they did get some things right from the league's outset. While the first two US attempts at professionalising the women's game were crushed beneath the weight of ambitious salaries and large stadia, the Women's Super League launched with the view that starting smaller was the only way to get bigger.

The WSL was set up as a semi-professional league with clubs only allowed a maximum of four players earning a wage of more than £20,000 per year. For the rest, that meant supplementing their on-pitch earnings with part-time work, for the time being at least. The FA's stated ambition was to one day turn the league into a fully professional one, but to ensure it got there in one piece, a modest starting point was deemed necessary.

At time of writing, the league is approaching its sixth season and the FA's salary restrictions have moved on, with the four-player rule being replaced by an overall salary cap threshold that is determined by each club's individual budget (still with me?). What that means in practice is that the salaries of each club's players cannot total more than 40 per cent of that club's annual operating budget.

It has allowed the top players at some Super League clubs to train full time (these include 2014 WSL runners-up Chelsea, the champions Liverpool, 2015 FA Cup finalists Notts County and Manchester City, where the teams' international players are able to live off the combination of their club salary and their central contract). It's a confusing halfway-house between professionalism and semi-professional that's best summed up by Chelsea Ladies and England striker, Eni Aluko, who asks: 'Is football professional because teams are training every day? Yes. Is it professional when contracts aren't across the board? No. As long as the two don't match up, we've still got a way to go.'

For the FA's Director of the National Game and Women's Football, Kelly Simmons, the move to fully professionalise the women's game is one that can only come further down the line. 'To run a women's professional team or a women's professional league is expensive, because you're looking at a significant number of players who need to be full-time professionals', Simmons said in a 2014 interview with *Sports Pro* magazine. 'The challenge still is to, through the league and the clubs, generate new revenues to enable us to do that and to move from part-time to full-time, and to get more commercial partners investing and more fans through the turnstiles.'

It's a long-term ambition for the FA, then. But it also seems to be one without any apparent timeframe or ideal end-date. This makes it an ambition that's far too easy to overlook and put on the back burner – a position with which women's football has become all too familiar over the years.

One of football's major rivals for female participation in the UK is netball – a sport that might take issue with the claim of the FA's Sissel Hartley that the Women's Super League has the highest awareness of any women's sports league in this country. The Netball Super League is an annual domestic competition that has had a deal with Sky Sports since 2006. The latest extension started in 2013 and is due to last until the end of the 2016 season. This deal sees Sky commit to showing one game a week throughout all 12 rounds of the competition and includes all of England's home international fixtures, making Sky Sports the undeniable home of netball – a sport whose participation figures have risen rapidly in recent years, thanks in no small part to the Back to Netball scheme that was launched by England Netball in 2010. The project aims to bring women back to a sport they probably last played at school. It operates sessions all over the country and has been a big success, with some 60,000 taking part since Back to Netball first launched. It's a figure that no doubt contributed to the latest statistics from Sport England, which showed that 148,700 people played netball regularly between October 2013 and October 2014 – an increase from 122,200 the previous year.

It was perhaps seeing Sky's commitment to netball that encouraged BT Sport to secure the rights to show football matches from the FA Women's Super League as soon as it launched in 2013, although Head of BT Sport, Simon Green, insists there were other more decisive factors: 'We launched the year after women's sport had featured so strongly during London 2012. It was clear that women's sport did have the power to excite and drive audiences if it was of the right standard and staged in the right way. We are a commercial organisation and need to make a commercial return on our investment. In order to do that, we want to appeal to as wide an audience as possible.'

As well as becoming a broadcasting partner for the WSL, BT Sport also signed up to become a founding partner for a new commercial programme for women's football from 2014 to 2018, and acquired rights for the England Women's Senior Team and the FA Women's Cup. The channel has thus become an important part of the FA's marketing strategy when it comes to attracting commercial partners for the women's game.

While the 2014 report into sponsorship by Women in Sport showed that a huge gap remained between the funding of men's and women's sport, it did recognise this new attitude from broadcasters, welcoming it as a sign that changes on the sponsorship side could follow – a theory that is backed up by recent deals in the women's football and netball worlds.

England Netball signed their biggest ever deal ahead of the 2014 Super League season, with soft-drink company ZEO signing a contract worth an unprecedented six figure sum over 12 months. But that deal was trumped just before the Netball World Cup kicked off in 2015 when England Netball signed their most lucrative sponsorship deal ever, with the health and life insurer, Vitality. Add this brand to the others already on England Netball's list of sponsors, including sports company ASICS and car manufacturer FIAT, and it's clear that the sport is an attractive prospect for investors.

So, why netball? Sponsors see the sport as a relatively cheap way to reach a huge number of women and develop a valuable affinity with them. Ian Sykes managed ZEO's partnership with England Netball, and says that the brand were keen to "reach a female audience within an environment that promoted a healthy, active, balanced lifestyle, and netball delivers that." He also highlighted the family-focused audience at Super League games – another demographic that ZEO was keen to tap into.

With the game continuing to grow (membership of England Netball increased by five per cent to 92,000 in 2014) and the 2019 Netball World Cup to be held in the UK, the sport looks set to continue winning the sponsorship battles that get the better of so many other women's sports.

The longest-serving partnership the FA Women's Super League has is with Continental Tyres, a company that also has strong ties to the men's game internationally. But while the FA once packaged commercial deals for the women's game together with those for men's football, it now separates the two, giving women's football its own distinct commercial partner programme that is being sold separately to the men's game. It was a conscious decision, says the FA's Kelly Simmons, as they were finding that the partners they got who had also signed for men's football were not necessarily the right ones to help them grow the women's game.

Instead, the FA wanted partners who were truly dedicated and focused on helping them make women's football a professional sport. So far the FA has secured four major commercial sponsors to support women's football, with each one owning rights associated with a specific area of the game. BT Sport and Continental Tyres support the WSL, Vauxhall supports England Women and Nike is the exclusive kit sponsor. 'There are new revenues coming in that the women's game didn't have', says Simmons. 'Strong brands and partners are helping us move the game forward.'

Not only can partners of women's football in the UK benefit from an affiliation with the FA (whatever you think of the organisation it maintains one of the highest profiles of any sporting governing body in the UK), but with five of the eight teams in the WSL linked to Premier League clubs (Chelsea, Arsenal, Liverpool, Manchester City and Sunderland), they can also link up with some of the best known brands in football. During Manchester City Women's first season in the league (2014), they recorded the highest average attendance (949) in the division – an impressive figure when you consider that the average for the league as a whole that year was just below 730.

The FA's Marketing Manager, Sissel Hartley, is quick to tell me that being attached to a men's team is not the be all and end all for WSL clubs, saying: 'Bristol Academy aren't attached to a men's club at all and do incredibly well without that around them.' But Bristol were in fact the only team in the top tier of WSL without a male equivalent (and were relegated to WSL2 for 2016). Having a ready-made brand and at least to some extent, an already established fan base, are advantages that automatically make teams attached to men's clubs front runners in the fight for investment.

For those sports that can't lay claim to the same levels of media exposure or mass participation from women and girls at grass roots level, the challenge of attracting investors ramps up another notch. It was this kind of test that greeted the Rugby Football Union's (RFU) Chief Marketing Officer, Sophie Goldschmidt, in July 2012 when the governing body finalised its integration of the Women's Rugby Football Union – a move that the RFU said would help them achieve their ultimate aim of 'broadening the reach of the game to the widest possible audience'.

The Women's RFU had previously existed as a separate body that had governed women's rugby since 1994 (in the same way the Women's Football Association had overseen women's football until the FA took over the running of the game in 1993). When I meet Goldschmidt at Twickenham, the historic home of English rugby, she tells me that the integration of the women's game within the RFU has given it a huge boost: 'Now, everything we do from a development, grass roots, commercial and otherwise standpoint, is for both the men and the women. From a commercial perspective, as deals come up I think we'll be able to generate more revenue for the women, and in the interim our partners are now supporting them as well as the men's team.'

So while the FA has moved on from the point where they were packaging deals for men's and women's football together, the RFU lags some way behind. But this is just the beginning of a journey for women's rugby, and it's one that Goldschmidt and her colleagues hope will lead them to a position where they can follow the FA in negotiating deals for the women on their own terms.

One place where women's rugby can consider itself ahead of women's football in England, though, is on the field of play. While England's footballers are yet to win a major tournament, England's women won the Rugby World Cup in 2014, giving the sport's profile a tremendous boost. Images of the team in their moment of glory were splashed across the front pages of the national newspapers and months later they were still winning, collecting the prestigious Team of the Year trophy at the BBC's Sports Personality of the Year awards. But would this success translate into an increase in willing investors?

'It was great timing for us', says Goldschmidt of England's World Cup victory. 'We'd not long integrated the women and had a lot of our commercial contracts coming up for renewal. Those commercial deals had been heading the right way but it was quite a slow process. The World Cup turbocharged it. There is still a big disparity between what the men and women are able to generate commercially, but that victory was a real step change for us. We don't need that success so much on the men's side just because it's more established and a more mature product. For the women those moments make a massive difference.'

Goldschmidt says it could take between 10 and 15 years for the oval ball game to catch up with women's football, not only in commercial terms but also regarding participation and profile. She tells me that rugby for women is still a fairly immature sport – recalling her school days when playing football was an option for girls, while rugby wasn't. It means that football has had a head start on rugby when it comes to attracting female participants, while it's also helped by not having some of the barriers to participation that rugby has, bearing in mind the contact element of the game.

'Ultimately, to get the real commercial revenue that I think we would all want', says Goldschmidt, 'there needs to be more people playing rugby and more people engaged. Compared to the men's game at the moment there's a massive disparity in both of those things so you have to be realistic, it's not like we're suddenly going to generate hundreds of millions of pounds. At the end of the day you have to provide the value. While the women are great role models and as a product, per se, they're fantastic, the interest still isn't where we want it to be. But I think having the extra focus and resource that it does now from across the organisation [as opposed to when it was governed by a standalone body] will really help.'

The Six Nations tournament that followed England's World Cup success revealed that Goldschmidt was right to be pragmatic. Those wanting to watch the World Champions in action on television had to wait until England's fourth game of the tournament against Scotland, which was broadcast by Sky Sports. Until then, however, it was a matter of seek and ye might find, but only if ye seek hard enough.

England's opening match against Wales was streamed online by BBC Wales, after which their games against Italy and Ireland were streamed by the RFU and Irish RFU respectively. England's fifth and final game against France was live on the BBC, making it just two England matches from five that were available to television viewers. With neither the Six Nations nor BBC websites listing viewing options for anyone wanting to watch the Women's Six Nations (this is where specialist sites like scrumqueens.com come into their own), simply finding out where and when England's fixtures were being shown was a considerable challenge. If the RFU truly wants to grow the women's game, it simply must give potential viewers better options for seeing it in action.

Two other sports that make interesting studies in sponsorship – albeit for very different reasons – are rowing and cycling. For the former, Saturday 11 April 2015 heralded the start of an exciting new era when the Women's Boat Race contested by Oxford and Cambridge was held on the same day and over the same iconic 6.8km stretch of the River Thames as the world-famous men's Boat Race. It was the first time in the 88-year history of the race that the women had been permitted to do either of those things.

In previous years the women's race had taken place a week before the men's and on a different part of the River. While the men's race received mass media coverage and was televised live by the BBC every year without fail, the women's race existed well below the radar of the general public.

That was until Helena Morrissey, Chief Executive of Newton Investment Management, founder of the 30 per cent Club (which aims to encourage FTSE boards to recruit 30 per cent female members), and mother of nine (yep, 9), showed up. In 2010 Newton was considering different sponsorship options, but the company's ethos went against the idea of splashing the cash to see their name adorn the shirt of an already well-known sports team. 'We wanted to be actively involved as a sponsor and influence the evolution of an event', says Morrissey whose research uncovered what she believed to be a hidden gem: the Women's Boat Race.

Shocked to discover that the race had no money in it, Morrissey struck a deal. In 2011 Newton would sponsor the Women's Boat Race. The exact details of the deal aren't known but it's safe to assume that the initial lay out was relatively small – indeed, Morrissey has referred to it as a 'not-so princely sum'. The publicity that Newton received in return was anything but small, however. The day after the 2011 race, the front pages of national newspapers carried a picture of the Oxford crew, with Natalie Redgrave (daughter of legendary Sir Steve) celebrating triumphant, and 'Newton' written large across her shirt. 'On advertising alone', says Morrissey, 'our initial investment had more than paid off.'

While the extent of the coverage undoubtedly had more than a little something to do with the involvement of Redgrave junior (the British press love a sporting family success story), it was enough to show Morrissey the potential of the annual event. Her next ambition was to ensure that Newton's money was making a real difference. Morrissey decided to put the women's race where it belonged: on a level pegging with the men's.

Her proposal was that Newton would provide the funding to move the women's race to the Tideway, where the men's race is held. To Morrissey's surprise (traditions without a basis in any solid reasoning are rarely ended by anything as simple as common sense), the proposal was welcomed: 'It transpired that the Vice-Chancellors of Oxford and Cambridge had long believed there should be equality in the Boat Race', says Morrissey. 'Encouraged by our enthusiasm, they made the joint decision that the women would indeed go to the Tideway in 2015.'

At that time, there was still no guarantee that the women's race would be covered by the BBC but it was not long before the broadcaster embraced the idea (no doubt helped by the fact that both races would now take place on the same day and in the same place). Paul Davies, Executive Producer for the BBC's coverage, said: 'We will cover [the women's event] as a proper race, that's for sure. It's crucial now it has made the move, that we make the move with our coverage.'

Morrissey is in no doubt that Newton's sponsorship played a critical role in extracting this commitment from the BBC. Indeed she admits that, as funders of the women's race, Newton was able to 'apply a certain amount of pressure to ensure coverage', and thus make sure that the company received the maximum return on their investment.

This success, allied with the unequivocally positive PR and feedback Newton has received, legitimised the company's decision to go where few other corporate sponsors dare to venture: the world of women's sport. But Morrissey is convinced that others should follow her lead: 'Commercially this is something that's quite smart, it's not a charitable act. My message to companies would be to have the confidence to take that step. Decisions about whether to invest cannot be made on existing viewing figures, for example. Instead companies must consider what the viewing figures *could* be if there was investment and meaningful partnerships between all concerned. A lot of women's sports are economically viable, you're not looking at something that's established and priced up, plus it's a very exciting journey to embark on.'

From the inspirational words of Helena Morrissey we turn to some well-worn ones from Team Sky's Manager (and former British Cycling chief), Dave Brailsford. After watching young British rider Lucy Garner win her second consecutive World Junior Road Race title in 2012, just months after Britain's female cyclists had won five medals (three of them gold) at the London Olympics, he told the *Telegraph* he had been examining the best ways to support Britain's women on two wheels: 'We are on the case, recent comments have not been falling on deaf ears and we have been thinking hard about it.

'Rather than just dive in I'm trying to hold everybody back just a little bit, maybe just four or five weeks, so that we can review everything properly and make sure we get this right first time. We are very well aware that there is a stark inequality between women's professional cycling and men's, so British Cycling, along with Sky as its key partner, have been looking at some structures to see how best we can support and develop these girls. There has never been a better time to be a talented young British rider.'

Two years later, Brailsford was answering the same questions with similar responses, telling the BBC that the idea of a female Team Sky was something he had been 'talking about a lot', and that he was still 'very aware that there needs to be a greater parity'. Fortunately, Lucy Garner hadn't wasted her time waiting for Sky to act, and signed her first professional contract with Dutch team, Argos-Shimano, soon after her 2012 success.

The beginning of 2015 did indeed bring news of a new Team Sky venture, but it was not one that involved any female riders. Instead it was a development squad led by the winner of seven Olympic medals and the first British man to win the Tour de France, Bradley Wiggins. Called WIGGINS, the Sky-sponsored team was launched with the aim of helping its eponymous hero in his transition from road to track racing in time for the 2016 Olympics in Rio.

In the meantime, other British women's teams have emerged. Wiggle Honda launched in 2013 under the leadership of Australian rider Rochelle Gilmore, who secured financial backing from the Bradley Wiggins Foundation. She approached Wiggins after the 2012 Olympics in London and impressed him with her proposals for a professional women's team that was designed to give Britain's female cycling talent the chance to become as professional as their male counterparts.

It's not an easy ambition, considering the general state of professional women's road racing. While most women's sports are becoming more professional, competitive and sponsor-friendly than they ever have been before, cycling is something of an anomaly in that it has actually gone backwards. When Britain's 2008 Olympic road race champion Nicole Cooke was growing up (something she talks more about in her profile, that follows Chapter 5), she could look forward to a future racing in a women's Tour de France against a host of teams that were capable of putting out strong squads for a season of big races. But by the time she retired, Cooke was looking back at a women's professional cycling scene that had deteriorated.

The last time La Grande Boucle Feminine (the female version of the Tour de France) was held was in 2009, by which time the race that in its heyday had been between 10 and 15 stages long had become a four-day long event with just 66 riders on the start line. There are some stage races that remain significant events though, with the women's Giro d'Italia held over 10 stages in 2015 and Britain's own Women's Tour proving successful since its launch in 2014. In the main though, the women's cycling scene has regressed since the late 1990s.

Teams have struggled to survive as sponsors have decided to take their money elsewhere, put off by a women's cycling scene that lacks consistency and coverage. For the riders that has meant years of chopping and changing from one team to another as finances dry up and teams fold. It has also meant living off a wage that for most riders requires taking on part-time work, with only a small percentage of female cyclists able to live off their earnings on the bike (at present there is no minimum wage in place on the women's pro tour).

Consider then, the prospects for Britain's über-successful female track cyclists who might have ambitions to take their talents on to the road (and earn a decent wage by doing so) in between going for Olympic glory. For the likes of Laura Trott, Joanna Rowsell, Dani King and Elinor Barker – who between them have a mightily impressive haul of European, World and Olympic titles – there should be endless opportunities waiting. But instead they are limited by a women's road racing scene that pales in comparison to the men's, with few teams and even fewer that can afford to give them the life of a true professional (there's more to come on the wage issue for women in sport in Chapter 5, so save some ire for later).

Back to Rochelle Gilmore then, who along with taking advice from Sir Wiggins, has also benefitted from being able to pick the brains of Sir Brailsford. In an interview with the *Guardian* not long after her team Wiggle Honda launched in 2013, Gilmore revealed she was in close contact with Brailsford and the rest of the Sky team, relying on them for 'advice and guidance'. Her belief at that time was that Sky were waiting to see how her team progressed before making their own move into women's cycling. 'If everything goes well here, I wouldn't be surprised if they got involved', Gilmore told the *Guardian*. Some three years on, Gilmore is left wondering, like the rest of us, why Team Sky has not backed up Brailsford's words with some clear action.

When Britain's Nicole Cooke retired in 2013 she tells me she was convinced that British Cycling and Team Sky were planning to launch a women's team. Her brow furrows as she says: 'But they haven't done that and it's really sad.'

In a 2014 interview with *Cycling News* she went further, saying: 'There are riders that are huge medal potentials who deserve to be supported seriously (considering the budget that Sky has and British Cycling has) and I think we're at the point where they've got the know-how. If it's not happening, it's for other reasons.'

I asked renowned cycling journalist and author Richard Moore for his view on Team Sky's reluctance to get involved in women's cycling, as someone who has spent much time in the company of Brailsford and co. He tells me he is less surprised than most by the non-appearance of a women's Team Sky, asking: 'Why would they sponsor a women's team when there isn't, or hasn't been, a very healthy women's scene? If I was a sponsor getting into cycling, I wouldn't sponsor a women's team.

'Having said that, if Sky's mission is not just about winning the Tour [de France] but also about encouraging people to ride bikes and promoting the sport, then it's hard to understand why they *don't* have a women's team. They could run a women's team on what they pay one [male] rider, frankly. Someone like [Team Sky rider] Ben Swift is on about £500,000 a year. You can run an entire women's team for that, no doubt.'

Where Moore does see signs of positivity is in the creation of the Women's Tour, which was launched in Britain in 2014 by sports events and marketing company SweetSpot Group. The inaugural race secured sponsorship from Friends Life, was televised on ITV4 and Eurosport and was deemed an overwhelming success, with huge crowds turning out to line the route throughout the five-day Tour.

SweetSpot's Director, Guy Elliott, believes that elite women's cycling was a sport that had been 'neglected both domestically and internationally', and that having a standalone Women's Tour in the UK was a big step towards putting that right. He says: 'When you look at women's sport, from the minute women enter adolescence they are treated as second best. One of the agendas we want to wrap around our Women's Tour is that they're not second best, so they should be treated in their own right as athletes.'

Richard Moore agrees that the Women's Tour could be 'a real game changer' in terms of bringing in sponsors for teams, telling me: 'If it's televised every year and there continue to be the huge crowds that were there in 2014, then if I was a sponsor with half a million pounds, I would probably think it is worth doing for that. You need those flagship events first before you can get sponsors coming in wanting to be involved.

'I think this is the fundamental point when it comes to Team Sky: you can't expect sponsors to do it just because it's the right thing to do. Sponsors get involved in sport because there's something in it for them. Trying to persuade them to back a team because they *should* do it or for politically correct reasons are not very good ways of selling a sport. You have to give them a better commercial reason for doing it and I think that's slowly what is happening.'

Another race that launched in 2014 with the aim of getting women's cycling back on the map was *La Course*. A circuit race contested over 13 laps (91 kilometres), *La Course* takes place on the morning of the final stage of the men's Tour de France and on the same stretch of Paris tarmac where the men end their own race later that day. It was the result of a determined effort from a group of professional female cyclists calling themselves *Le Tour Entier* (meaning 'The Entire Tour'), who decided the time for change had come and launched a petition for the return of a women's Tour de France. While the UCI remained adamant that a full Tour remained a logistic impossibility, *La Course* was deemed a sign that their attitude to women's cycling was starting to change.

In an essay for the *Independent* newspaper ahead of the inaugural running of *La Course*, one of *Le Tour Entier's* members, Britain's own Emma Pooley, wrote that, 'A women's Tour next year would be an impossible leap: the media coverage, fan base, sponsorship and professionalism of the women's sport has to develop gradually. But *La Course* is a radical step change in that development.'

While the race isn't the most challenging circuit on the women's calendar (apart from in the pouring rain when the surface becomes dangerously slippery, as happened in 2015), and doesn't bring the winner anything as tangible as a jersey, a title, or a medal, it is of huge significance to female riders for one single reason: audience. The Tour de France is watched by millions worldwide, and thanks to its scheduling on the same day as the men's race arrives in Paris, *La Course* is televised in 157 countries, giving it a greater reach than any women's road race has ever had (except perhaps for the Olympic road race). For team sponsors, it's the sort of shop window they might never have expected women's cycling could offer.

Now two years old, the *La Course* effect is starting to take shape. In 2015 the second edition again featured one of the season's strongest line-ups of teams and riders, while the prize money (£4,250 to the winner and £16,000 overall) was one of the highest on offer in women's cycling. The success of the event is also starting to have a domino effect. In 2015 the men's Tour of Spain (the Vuelta) included its own *La Course* for the first time after race organisers Unipublic agreed to host *La Course* by La Vuelta on Madrid's central boulevard, the Paseo de la Castellana on the final day of the men's race. So it appears as though more eyes are being opened to the fact that women's cycling has as much to offer as men's. While there remains a long road ahead in terms of establishing equality – something the UCI could be far more proactive in doing – there is hope that one day the sport might again resemble the one that Nicole Cooke fell in love with as a child.

It isn't only in cycling that we can see reluctance from established brands or teams to broaden their scope in terms of gender. In football, the most glaring absence from a league that contains the likes of Chelsea, Arsenal, Liverpool and Manchester City is the name of Manchester United, who last had a women's side in 2005, when club bosses decided their funding was better spent on youth development. The club runs junior girls teams, but has shown no interest or desire to follow their fellow Premier League clubs in launching a women's side, despite coming under considerable pressure to do so. Following the Women's World Cup in 2015, the Sports Minister Tracey Crouch called it 'incredibly disappointing' that at a time when interest in women's football is on the rise, one of the biggest clubs in the world is continuing to ignore it. 'It is right that they should rectify that as soon as possible', said Crouch. United's response was to confirm that they still have no plans to re-introduce a women's team but that it's something that remains, as ever, 'under review'. File alongside: 'Employing a female manager' and 'telling players to wash their own kit' in the 'Things Unlikely to happen at Manchester United' drawer.

So while there are more brands that now understand women's sport can offer them tangible commercial benefits such as improved access to target markets, brand awareness and an association with positive role models (all for a fraction of the cost that men's sport can), there are many that still take the 'approach with caution' attitude to women's sport.

At the moment it is far too easy for those in the latter camp to point to a lack of media coverage as justification for their reluctance. Equally, it remains far too easy for those making broadcasting decisions – like the ones that relegated most of England's Six Nations games to the internet – to point to the absence of an engaged fan base and sponsor support.

The viewing figures for the FIFA Women's World Cup in 2015 were impressive (the final between USA and Japan was the most watched football match in US history, with a record 25.4 million viewers, while England's semi final match against Japan drew a peak audience of 2.4 million, despite starting at midnight). These numbers were largely thanks to England's successful run (after all, how often do we get to watch England football teams in the latter stages of a major tournament?). But whether they are yet attainable for other women's sports is doubtful. Many broadcasters (Sky among them) refuse to reveal viewing figures, arguing that as they offer such a variety of platforms on which viewers can engage it's too complex, but it would be fascinating to know how many people actually tune in to watch women's sport when it does make it to our screens.

Do women watch women's sports? In a survey of 1000 UK adults conducted by One Poll in 2014, 59 percent of women said that they were interested in women's sports (with 69 percent of men saying the same). And the numbers remained fairly impressive for those actually watching women's sport on TV with 69 percent of people (men and women) claiming to have previously tuned in to some form of women's sport.

In America, media researcher and Professor of Communications at University of Tennessee, Erin Whiteside, surveyed 19 married women on why they did or did not watch women's sport and found that for many, the biggest issue was time. "Women's sports consumption tends to be dictated by their responsibilities in the home," explained Whiteside. "What they watch is largely a function of what's on at the moment." And nine times out of ten, that is not women's sport, but men's.

Whiteside's study has obvious limitations – the tiny sample size and the fact that all the women were married, being the main ones. It does though provide food for thought about the reasons why for some women, sitting down to watch a 90 minute game of football might not be quite as straightforward as it is for many men.

Personally, given the choice between watching a game of netball, women's rugby, or women's cricket and a Premier League football match, I'd choose the latter every time. But that's not a gender issue, it's a sporting one. I prefer football to all those sports. If it was a choice between watching a Women's Super League match and a Premier League one, that would be tougher. If I'm honest, I'd probably flick between the two to establish which one is the better game before deciding which one to watch. Until recent years I could have counted the number of women's football matches I'd seen on one hand, but that had more to do with the scarcity of televised matches than my own preferences. For other female sports fans it's a similar story – most have become used to watching and engaging with men's sports above women's simply because that's what has always been there, both on TV and in the newspapers. But the young girls of today are growing up with more choice, and it's reasonable to hope that will lead to a growing audience for women's sport.

What about men? Are they inclined to watch women's sports? When it comes to tennis, athletics and possibly golf, too, most male fans of those sports seem happy to tune in whether it's men or women competing. But with team sports it seems to make more of a difference. I work in an office full of men who watch sport for a living (I work at *Sport* magazine), and the responses are markedly different when they are watching women's football or cricket to when they are watching the men's versions. While male players or teams might get singled out for criticism, when it comes to women's sport, such criticisms are often put in the context of women's sport as a whole. For example, when watching a female goalkeeper fail to make an 'easy' save, the comments are less likely to focus on her specific error than on the failings of female goalkeepers in general. But again, the young men of today are being exposed to women's sports more than ever. For them it won't be so unusual to see women throwing themselves into tackles, leaping across a goalmouth or taking wickets.

A key to improving the situation when it comes to the visibility of women's sport, says the Chief Executive of Women in Sport, Ruth Holdaway, is about creating a solid calendar of regular competitions and events for sportswomen: 'For women's sport, the Olympics and Paralympics are almost everything. For those few weeks every four years, our sportswomen receive the recognition from media, sponsors and the public that they deserve. However, at other times, the annual sporting calendar is dominated by a well-established series of, almost exclusively male, sporting events. In order for the situation to improve, our sportswomen need the regular opportunity to compete in events which make the sporting world sit up and take notice.

'An annual calendar of regular, high-quality competitions would generate an engaged fan base, providing broadcasters, journalists and potential sponsors with highly sought after content.'

This echoes the statement made so proudly by Stacey Allaster of the WTA that, 'we have five Olympics every year', in reference to the four Grand Slams and the year-end tournament between the world's top eight that showcase women's tennis through the season. Taking this into consideration, is it really any wonder that women's tennis is the most successful professional sport for women?

This is by no means a quick fix, however. For women's tennis, it is a process that started in the 1970s. It requires women's sport to have consistency and to ensure that when events are held, they are not held quietly. Fortunately, this is now easier – and cheaper – than ever before. The explosion of social media in recent years means that generating publicity and communicating with a potential fan base can be achieved using Facebook, Twitter or popular blogging sites – the most successful ones use all three.

The hope is that future years will see more women's sports join the likes of netball, football and basketball in providing top level competition for the nation's elite athletes week in, week out and year after year. And that this in turn will attract investment from brands who understand what women's sport can offer. There will always be those who don't – or won't – get it, but as they become outnumbered by those who do, the percentages will finally start to reflect the true value of women's sport.

Maggie Alphonsi

THE GAME CHANGER

The best-known figure in women's rugby is under pressure. 'Over here, Maggie', comes the shout from one side of the room, closely followed by a similar request from the opposite corner. The attention is welcomed, though. Indeed a huge smile is fixed across Maggie Alphonsi's face as she runs from one admirer to another with impressive pace, considering the kitten-heel shoes she's wearing in place of her rugby boots.

Alphonsi's smart attire and jovial mood are linked to the fact that for the first time in their relatively short history, the England women's rugby team are being properly recognised for their achievements. On the day that I meet her, for example, they are named Team of the Year (2014) at the Sports Journalists' Association's 65th annual British Sports Awards. And Alphonsi, as the team's best-known player, is very much in demand.

'This is quite a shock to us', Alphonsi tells me, puffing out her cheeks as she tries to absorb the countless plaudits and endless praise heaped upon both her and the rest of the England team. 'I spent a lot of my career just working hard and not necessarily always being recognised for it. At the time you do kind of wish people understood how hard you've worked to get to where you are, and that what you've achieved has taken a lot of effort. You just want to be recognised, really. But eventually you get to a point where you think, I'm not doing it for recognition. I'm not doing it for an award at the end of the year. I'm doing it because that medal means more to me than anything.'

'That medal' is the one that was hung around Alphonsi's neck on 17 August 2014, the day that England's women became champions of the world. 'Winning the World Cup was my final goal', says Alphonsi, who announced her retirement from international rugby shortly afterwards. 'It's great that we are getting these awards now and that finally the team is being recognised for its achievements, but at the same time the one thing we all wanted was that medal. So if we hadn't got any awards, I think we'd still be happy right now.'

England's women winning their first World Cup since 1994 not only brought Alphonsi and her teammates the success and recognition they had spent so many years fighting for, it also brought them to the start of a new era. Before the tournament almost the entire England squad were essentially amateurs who squeezed in training sessions and games around their day jobs. Among them police officers, plumbers, vets, teachers and students, most of whom took around three months' unpaid leave to play in the World

Cup. But following England's historic victory in Paris, the Rugby Football Union (RFU) announced that the country's top female rugby players would be paid for the first time, with 20 England players handed professional contracts.

'It's brilliant for them', beams Alphonsi. 'These girls now have a chance to train as hard as they need to train, rest when they need to rest and concentrate on getting themselves incredibly fit for a great sport. It has come at just the right time. The big window is the Olympics in 2016 [when rugby sevens will become an Olympic sport for the first time], and we've got huge potential in our team. I think they can come away with a medal.'

There is a bittersweet irony to the fact that Alphonsi has surrendered her England shirt at the very point when the women's game is picking up speed. Most of her career was spent pushing with all her might to try and get it out of first gear. She recalls having to fight for opportunities to train depending on when the men wanted to train (because the men had priority when it came to using the pitch), the struggle of promoting girls' rugby and finding facilities. But she also says she feels very fortunate to have always had good coaches and people around her who made her believe that anything was possible.

Liza Burgess was the first to make Alphonsi believe. A former captain of the Wales women's rugby team and one of the pioneers of the women's game, Burgess was a PE teacher at Salisbury Secondary School in Edmonton when she spotted a teenager whose exuberance in the classroom translated into eye-catching dynamism on the playing field.

'I got into trouble quite a lot at school', says Alphonsi, a touch sheepishly. 'My poor mum had to come in to defend me once when I almost got suspended. But in sport I was brilliant – the most well behaved student you could probably find.' Her PE teacher, Mrs Burgess, heard the reports from other teachers about Alphonsi's behaviour, and knowing about the teenager's enthusiasm for sport, suggested she give rugby a try.

'She thought it would help control my behaviour and give me skills like leadership, respect and discipline', says Alphonsi. 'Rugby's one of those sports where you can be multi-disciplined – I could run, throw and tackle. When I was growing up, just doing one event didn't feel as though I was being pushed very much. But in rugby, I could show off more of my strengths. At quite a young age I remember thinking I don't understand why a lot more girls don't play the sport. It didn't make sense to me.'

Before Burgess introduced her to the oval ball game, athletics had been Alphonsi's strength. She was such a promising discus thrower in fact that her local authority had given her funding to represent the borough of Enfield in competitions around the country. 'She had real potential in any sport', recalls Burgess when I ask about her star pupil. 'Whichever sport she put her mind to – athletics or rugby – she would have made it big time because she just had a real drive and passion for sport. She lived it. She breathed it. It meant everything to her.'

Alphonsi's mother was keen for her to stick with athletics. 'It was a sport you saw on TV', she explains, 'and there were women in it, whereas rugby union was never really seen as a sport for women.' But Maggie's mind was made up. After one summer break, she went back to school for the new term with some news that left her PE teacher both delighted and a little horrified. Burgess remembers Alphonsi returning after the holidays and telling her that she'd spent all the money given to her by her borough – the grant that was designed to help her succeed in athletics – on rugby kit. "That moment has always stuck in my mind,' recalls Burgess, 'because I knew then that she was hooked.'

While Alphonsi's mother might have initially been disappointed with her daughter's choice, she soon saw the bigger picture. Maggie was born with a club foot, and her mother knew that it could have left her barely able to function normally, let alone compete in any kind of sport. 'My right foot was turned all the way in', explains Alphonsi, 'but when I was quite young my mother made the decision to get it operated on and straightened. It's not something you can leave for too long because the bones fuse together more as you get older. It meant I spent a lot of my early years going in and out of hospital to make sure my foot was in the correct position.'

Many athletes compete in the Paralympics with a club foot, but Alphonsi's passion for rugby ruled out any Paralympic involvement, leaving her with only one option: To build a body that was as fit and strong as possible. That way she hoped to be able to minimise any issues her foot might cause. 'I never really acknowledged it', says Maggie. 'I just trained and worked really hard. I realised early on that it meant I was never going to be as quick as some of the other girls, but instead of seeing that as a barrier, I used it as an opportunity to try and be the best that I could be.'

Alphonsi's journey towards that end goal really began at the age of 14, when Burgess took her and a few other girls who had shown an interest along to Saracens rugby club (where Burgess herself played). There, they joined in with the team's junior sessions under the watchful eye of Saracens coach, Katie Ball. When the junior team swelled to about seven players, it meant they could get their first taste of competitive rugby at a festival (numbers were often reduced in those days says Alphonsi, because most girls' teams weren't able to scrape a full 15 together).

This was when everything fell into place for Alphonsi, says Burgess. Before long she was playing for her regional team and getting invited to development camps at Loughborough University where she would first meet Gary Street – the man who would go on to become her coach in the England women's team.

Street recalls once giving a talk to a group of girls who were part of a talent identification programme and ending with the requisite: Are there any questions? While most of the young teens were too shy to speak up, Alphonsi's hand immediately shot high into the air: 'Hi, I'm Maggie Alphonsi. I want to be the best player in the world and win the World Cup for England', she declared, before reeling off questions on a variety of topics from nutrition to training programmes and everything in between.

Alphonsi's burning desire to represent her country on the rugby field was first ignited by a trip to watch the England women play against Scotland at Worcester. 'It was organised by my coach at Saracens, Katie Ball', says Maggie. 'She knew a few of the players on the England women's team so I got to meet the captain at the time who was a lady called Paula George. I just thought, wow, she's amazing. I want to be like her. That was when I first really became aware there was an England women's team, and from then on I was just determined to represent it.'

She didn't have long to wait. In 1999, Alphonsi was picked to play for Great Britain in the Under 16 touch rugby squad – a selection she considers to be a big turning point in her career. The tournament was being hosted in Australia, with players' families asked to cover the cost of travel. Coming from a single-parent family, raising the funds was a struggle for Alphonsi and her mum: 'She took out a loan but it wasn't enough, so I went to my Head of PE who said that if I took a bucket around every class she would double the amount I made. I raised between £200 and £300, and she was good to her word. Another PE teacher also raised £500 doing a sponsored event. I realised that if they cared about me that much, I owed them and I'd better work hard for my GCSEs.'

Transferring her work ethic on the pitch to her work off it meant that Alphonsi left school with an impressive set of results. Alongside working on her rugby with Saracens and the England Women's Development squad, she went on to do a degree in Sport and Exercise Science. But in the midst of her studies, came the moment Alphonsi had been waiting for. In 2003 Maggie was called up to the national team, winning her first England cap at the age of 19. 'It really doesn't seem that long ago', she says, smiling at the memory of her England debut. It came against the USA whom England beat 15-8. 'I remember I wore the No. 12 shirt and scored my first try', says Maggie. 'It just capped a great day. I never thought that I would get the opportunity to represent my country, so to do it at the age of 19 was amazing.'

Balancing sport with university life was quite a challenge though, she admits. 'On Wednesdays everyone played university sport and then went out and had fun, but I didn't want to play for the university's rugby team in case I got injured. I didn't socialise or drink, either. I trained, studied, went to lectures and played rugby on the weekends. It was three years of boring, serious hard graft. I probably didn't live my university life as much as I could have, but I don't have any regrets. I got the degree I wanted and got to play the sport I love.'

The England team benefited from her commitment, too. Three years after Alphonsi won her first cap the women's team enjoyed a breakthrough 12 months, starting at the 2006 Six

Nations. France had dominated the tournament for the two previous years, winning the Grand Slam in 2004 and 2005, but in 2006 England ended that run in some style. Not only did they subject France to a 28-0 thrashing in Paris, but they also won the Grand Slam, scoring a massive total of 213 points and conceding just 33 over five matches.

Six months later England reached the World Cup final. It was to be a repeat of their final four years earlier against an indomitable New Zealand team who were searching for their third consecutive World Cup win. England, meanwhile, were seeking revenge for the 19-9 defeat they suffered against the Black Ferns in the 2002 final.

From the first whistle, the challengers took the game to defending champions. With less than three minutes on the clock, England were just three points behind the defending champions – the trophy still within their grasp. But right at the death, the inevitable happened: New Zealand scored the try that would ensure they retained the trophy and secured their third straight World Cup crown. England's battling performance was proof, however, of the significant steps forward made since their defeat four years earlier.

Even so, Alphonsi remembers feeling devastated by the defeat. 'After the game I was completely knackered, I had given my all to it. I felt like I had left every last drop of energy on the pitch. I just remember looking around at my teammates and seeing the sadness in their faces, too. I promised myself there and then that I would be back and that I wouldn't stop until we became world champions. I see that final as a pivotal point in my career, really. It gave me the direction and drive I needed to really know what I wanted to achieve.'

At the time, the 2006 World Cup final was considered to be the best game of women's rugby in history, with Alphonsi's 'inspirational' performance lauded by the British newspapers in their (albeit brief) match reports. Sky Sports commentators Dewi Morris and Stuart Barnes were so impressed by her ferocious tackling, they singled her out, nicknaming her Maggie 'The Machine'.

While players can often be too consumed with the end result to see the bigger picture, Alphonsi says that in the case of the 2006 World Cup final, the players knew it was something of a special match: 'I felt when we were out there that both teams were playing above what they'd done before', reflects Alphonsi, 'and it showed me that there do not have to be limits to your game.'

At the end of 2006 Alphonsi won the first award of many that would come her way during the course of her 11-year England career. She was named Player of the Year by the International Rugby Board (IRB) alongside the men's winner, Richie McCaw. Alphonsi was honoured to be recognised, but her acceptance speech left little doubt that England's second place would never satisfy her: 'The whole of the England team worked so hard to get where we are today, and it's a shame that we came so close in the final of the Rugby World Cup and didn't come away with the prize we desperately wanted. Hopefully this award will go some way, for all the members of the squad, towards knowing that what we achieved in Canada has been recognised.'

Another four years separated Alphonsi from her chance to go one better at the next World Cup which was to be held in England. But there was plenty for her to work towards in the meantime. There was her club, Saracens, and their defence of the Women's Premiership crown they had won in 2006. There was England's bid to stay on top of the Six Nations pile. And there was her job as a Club Coach Officer with the Rugby Football Union for Women (RFUW), which involved working with women and girls at rugby clubs across the Thames Valley.

Alphonsi's World Cup disappointment was temporarily eased as Saracens went through the entire season without losing a game, and England became Six Nations champions again, winning their second successive Grand Slam. They would win the next three as well (including two more Grand Slams), leaving Alphonsi and co. as one of the favourites going into the World Cup in 2010 – a tournament that they knew presented a massive opportunity to drive interest in the women's game.

England's preparation for their home World Cup involved four tough training camps around the country, one of which was an army camp. Four years on, the memories of it still bring a grimace to Alphonsi's face. 'The aim there was to make us work really hard under fatigue and sleep deprivation, but it was a good team bonding session, too. We went into the World Cup with a really tight squad.'

Although four years and plenty of victories had passed since Alphonsi played her part in England's near-miss in 2006, she says the painful memories were never far away as she prepared for another tilt at achieving her dream: 'Personally I still thought about losing in the World Cup final four years earlier. I even got feelings about it when we first arrived at Surrey Sports Park [where the opening rounds were being held].'

There were no signs of nerves on the pitch, though. England's first game against Ireland was a physical encounter – 'Ireland knew us inside and out, and vice versa' – recalls Alphonsi, but England's quality shone through and they started the tournament with an impressive 27-0 win. Another clean sheet followed in the game against Kazakhstan, when England added a mammoth 82 points to their tally.

'Our final group game was against USA,' says Alphonsi, 'which we knew would be a tough one as they are very good athletes and a very physical side. We knew we had to win and get a bonus point to progress further into the semis, and thankfully we won 37-10.'

And so England steamed into the semi-finals where they would take on Australia at the Twickenham Stoop. 'Some of our squad had played against them in the Rugby World Cup 7s in 2009, me included', says Alphonsi, 'and we had lost to them in the quarter-finals. We were gutted by that, so a lot of the girls were quite up for playing them again.'

Profile: Maggie Alphonsi

England made a good start and took a 12-0 lead in the first 23 minutes, but Australia soon hit back with a series of strong attacking moves that tested the home side's defence. England stood firm, taking their 12-0 lead into half time and clinging onto it throughout the early stages of the second half. Finally, a last-minute penalty moved England further ahead and ensured England's safe passage into what would be their third successive World Cup final against New Zealand.

'The tournament itself didn't have much media attention to start off with', recalls Alphonsi, 'but, as it progressed and we did well and got to the final, the media started to take note of us.' Alphonsi – and her performances – was central to much of the coverage. When the head coach of the Australian team England had beaten in the semi-finals was asked what the key to England beating New Zealand in the final would be, he smiled and said: 'They have to clone Maggie Alphonsi 15 times'.

'The Machine' was having as big an impact on those watching her play as she was on those who felt the force of her power on the pitch. Even those who knew what Alphonsi was capable of were in awe. Stephen Jones, the *Sunday Times* correspondent, who had seen every Women's World Cup since the first in 1991, called her display against Ireland in England's opener 'the greatest individual display I have seen by a female player, and not so far down my all-time list by either sex'.

With more eyes on her and the team than ever before, Alphonsi went into the final against New Zealand believing it was finally England's time. A crowd of 13,253 believed too, belting out a passionate rendition of 'Swing Low, Sweet Chariot', and cheering on England as they advanced in a line towards a New Zealand team roaring their way through the Haka.

The Black Ferns put England under intense pressure from the instant the whistle blew. At half time the home side were down 7-0, but forced a penalty early in the second half to narrow the deficit to 7-3. With 22 minutes left to play New Zealand's skipper, Melissa Ruscoe, became their third player to be sin binned and England went on the attack, levelling the score at 10-10. The hopes of the home crowd soared, but an England error soon allowed the Black Ferns to move ahead to 13-10 with 14 minutes left. Once in control, the champions did not relinquish it.

Alphonsi was crushed. Four years after promising herself she would get her hands on the World Cup trophy, it had escaped her again. In public she remained positive, telling the media: 'We'll just go away work on things. It was a tough game. It was a very even game. The whole tournament has been fantastic. We'll go away and work hard and I guarantee in four years' time we'll come back and we'll change the score.'

Looking back at the defeat now though, Alphonsi admits, 'I was devastated. It was a real low point and the start of some difficult years for me with injury.' Maggie's performances at the World Cup had caught the nation's attention in a big way, though.

So much so that in November 2010 Alphonsi won the *Sunday Times*' Sportswoman of the Year Award, beating off competition from the likes of Jessica Ennis (who had returned from injury to win a European heptathlon title) and Amy Williams, whose gold medal in the skeleton at the Winter Olympics had been Britain's first in an individual event at the Winter Games for 30 years.

In her acceptance speech, an overjoyed Alphonsi explained why the award meant so much to her: 'What makes this award so special is that it is decided by the public vote. It just shows what a fantastic rugby community is out there.' It also showed that she and her England teammates had achieved at least one of their aims at the 2010 World Cup, and taken their country's interest in the women's game to new heights.

Not only had Alphonsi won the admiration of the general public, she had also turned the heads of England's rugby writers – a group of men not easily impressed. In January 2011 she was awarded the prestigious Pat Marshall Award that is presented annually by the Rugby Union Writers' Club to the outstanding rugby personality of the previous year. Not once in the award's 50-year history had a woman ever won it. Previous years had seen Gareth Edwards, JPR Williams, Jean-Pierre Rives, David Campese and one of Alphonsi's own rugby heroes, Jonah Lomu, presented with the award, and now it was in her quivering hands.

'I really wasn't expecting it', says Alphonsi. 'I didn't even know I had been nominated. I just remember getting a standing ovation from all the guys in the room who were well-respected rugby writers. For me to win it was quite a unique thing – it was pretty special.'

With interest in women's rugby finally on the rise, England went into the 2011 Six Nations under more pressure than usual. The BBC was broadcasting England's game against Scotland at Twickenham with Sky Sports showing live coverage of their game against France. The change in attitudes went beyond the increased media coverage too, as Alphonsi told the *Guardian* ahead of the Scotland game: 'Before, if you went to a men's rugby club some of those guys would have been very against women's rugby. Now they want to support the game. People don't see those things because they are small, but for me that's a massive cultural difference. Some of the guys who wouldn't have talked to me a few years ago now actually want to support the programmes we're working on. That's exciting.'

England were so dominant during the tournament that they conceded just eight points en route to winning their sixth straight Six Nations crown and second consecutive Grand Slam. When England went on to get the better of New Zealand in a three-Test series at the end of 2011, it seemed as though they might finally be able to lay claim to being the world's best women's rugby team – despite not having a World Cup trophy to prove it.

By the turn of the year, thoughts were already turning towards the 2014 World Cup, with the chance to win a seventh consecutive Six Nations title in 2012 seen as a stepping stone towards that golden end goal. England did everything that was expected of them, throwing another Grand Slam into the bargain, but the games were becoming noticeably more competitive. With England having to work hard to beat France and Ireland in their final two fixtures, the belief grew that technically and tactically the women's game was making huge strides.

For Alphonsi, the Ireland game brings back some less positive memories. During the first half she was forced to leave the field with a knee injury that would keep her out of England's triumphs in the European Cup later that year, as well as Sevens tournaments in Hong Kong and at Twickenham. She needed surgery and months of rehabilitation work with a physiotherapist. The operation went well and Alphonsi expected to be back on the pitch in less than a year, but her body had other plans.

'It became very complicated', explained Alphonsi in an interview with *The Rugby Paper* in 2014. 'The injury and surgery and then the rehab set off a chain reaction of injuries down the right hand side of my body where I have my club foot – the foot points in more than usual – and the biomechanics down the right hand side of my body went a bit haywire. Until I got injured everything miraculously seemed to work in its own sweet way, but afterwards all the muscles and joints started reacting and overcompensating so as well as the knee I started getting big hamstring and lower back problems as well as pains in the foot.'

It was 20 months before Alphonsi was back playing again. During that time she questioned whether she would ever wear the England shirt again. 'I spoke to a lot of friends and people I trust and the message was pretty much the same from all of them. "Have you achieved what you set out to achieve in your rugby career?" they all asked. And the answer was always, "No". I hadn't become a world champion, that gold medal winner I always wanted to be. So once I acknowledged that to myself, all thoughts of retirement were banished.'

Her return to international rugby finally came in November 2013, in time for England's autumn internationals against France at Twickenham and Canada at Twickenham Stoop. 'It's made me a lot stronger', she said of her injury problems, before getting back on the pitch. 'Now I'm back I'm determined to work hard to get my shirt. It's been a long 20 months but it's great being around the girls again, and makes you realise what you've missed.'

England quickly realised what they had missed, too. The highlight of a 40-20 win over France was undoubtedly the wide smile on Alphonsi's face as her teammates congratulated her for scoring one of England's six tries. It was sweet revenge for England after the French had become the first team to beat them at Twickenham in the Six Nations earlier in the year, but Alphonsi was already focusing on the future and her long-term goal of winning a World Cup medal: 'This year is a big year', she said, 'this is officially the countdown to the World Cup.'

England did not go into the sport's showpiece event as Six Nations champions like they had done four years earlier, though. Instead it was the World Cup's host nation, France, who raised their country's hopes by winning the Grand Slam and consigning England to second spot. 'That was a bit of a wake-up call', says Alphonsi, 'it was a real motivation in training. There was a lot of frustration to be worked off and hunger to improve and go to the next level.'

England's frequent training camps left them feeling fitter and better prepared than they had ever been by the time the tournament came around in August 2014. When the team arrived in Marcoussis, where their pool games against Samoa, Spain and Canada would take place, Alphonsi was in bullish mood. 'I'm very confident that we are ready to win the World Cup', she told the BBC, explaining how the bitter defeat on home soil four years ago was driving the team on: 'Me and a few of the other players are living off of that pain, determined not to go through that again.'

In their opening game England faced the tough physical challenge of playing Samoa, but had too much pace and guile for their opponents to beat, particularly after the Samoan full-back was sent off after 12 minutes. A 65-3 victory sent England into their second game against Spain with plenty of confidence – so much that coach Gary Street felt comfortable enough to make 12 changes to his team.

Alphonsi was rested for the 45-5 win, but returned to the starting line-up for the group decider against Canada. 'We had played and beaten them twice the previous year', says Alphonsi 'but they pushed us to the very end and a draw was probably a fair reflection of the match.' With the match ending 13-13, England topped the group by virtue of their superior points difference.

The draw had devastating implications for the defending champions New Zealand however, who finished second in their pool. Having collected one point fewer than the Canadians, the Black Ferns were eliminated, meaning that instead of having to play their World Cup nemesis in the semi-finals, England instead faced Ireland. 'Ireland had shown just how good they were by beating New Zealand in the group stages', says Alphonsi, 'but thankfully we played our best rugby of the tournament and put 40 points on them.'

Alphonsi's performance in that game was crucial to England's victory. After their slightly lacklustre showing against Canada, Gary Street's side needed their big players to come to the fore, and, with 20 bruising tackles and a dominating performance at the breakdown, it was Alphonsi who led the way.

'Losing those two finals had driven me on for the last eight years', says Alphonsi who went into her third (and England's fourth) consecutive appearance in a World Cup final adamant that history would not be repeated. 'Our psychologist played an important role by helping us to mentally prepare for any scenario, but I and all the other players were determined not to let it happen again. We were going to do everything possible as a team to win it. We were not going to lose that game.'

The starting line-up for the final included 11 players who bore the scars of England's defeat on home soil four years earlier, with Alphonsi and three of her teammates having also played in the 2002 loss four years before that. The game started cagily, but England took a promising 11-3 lead into half time raising hopes that England's time had come. But when Canada scored a penalty four minutes after the restart, the flags of St George in the crowd started waving a touch more frantically. Midway through the second half, Canada moved to within two points of England, but the response from Alphonsi and co. was almost immediate – Emily Scarratt securing three points to put them five clear, with 20 minutes remaining. The final flourish came in the closing minutes when Scarratt cut through Canada's defence with a sensational run to seal the victory Alphonsi – and England – had craved for so very long.

'I struggled to find the words to describe my feelings after the final', says Alphonsi. 'Winning was simply massive. It was accompanied by a mixture of relief, having lost the last three finals, and happiness at having achieved something that as a team we had worked so hard for. It was such a great feeling. We all work hard for something but we don't always achieve it. To finally get across the line was amazing.'

Having gone into the tournament debating how many more years she should – and could – hang onto her England shirt for, Alphonsi joined in the post-match celebrations with her teammates knowing that her time was up. When the final whistle blew on her third World Cup final, she was bubbling with mixed emotions. There was the delight of winning, but also the painful realisation that she would never pull on the white shirt ever again.

'Having spent 11 years giving everything I could for England, I was gutted at the prospect of not playing for the team again, but I was also so happy with what I had done and what the team had achieved in that time. I dread to think what would have happened if we had lost. My body couldn't have taken much more, but I think I would have found a way of pushing myself on for another four years. Fortunately, I went out having achieved everything I wanted. Winning the World Cup was the perfect way to bow out.'

Reaching the summit of the sport she adopted as a teenager when it was unpopular, unfunded and largely unknown as a women's game, left Alphonsi seeking a new challenge. Her insatiable appetite for training, competing and ultimately for winning needed a new direction. It was one that Alphonsi found by going back to her youth and to the days before her PE teacher showed her that girls could play rugby, too.

She returned to the world of field athletics, specifically to the throwing disciplines to see where her discus and shot put technique could take her after the age of 30. 'The last time I checked, I held the Borough [of Haringey] record for the shot put for Year 8' she told the *Sunday Times* in December 2014. 'I would have been about 13. Then I picked up a rugby ball and stopped throwing.'

Alphonsi's main motivation for going back to athletics was the prospect of competing for Great Britain at the 2016 Olympic Games in Rio. So, why not aim to get there as part of Great Britain's rugby sevens squad? 'I could have', she says, 'but there were so many young players coming through. They're quick and strong and only 17 or 18 years old.'

One senses that Alphonsi also wanted to test her body and brain in a new way after dedicating more than half her life to learning and executing her craft on the rugby pitch. In the throwing circle there are no bone-shuddering tackles to make, nor any dangerous liaisons with flying boots, just Alphonsi and her missile of choice.

While no one who has seen Alphonsi's strength in the tackle – or been a victim of one – would doubt the power in her compact, 5'4" physique, Alphonsi knew there were no guarantees it would translate into Olympic-standard throws. 'I watched videos of the top throwers and really had to break the technique and footwork down because you look at it and initially you think, how on earth is he or she getting round that circle? All I saw at the end was the ball flying out of their hands.'

Her first few months went reasonably well and she managed to win a few competitions. But as the year (2015) went on, Alphonsi realised that qualifying for Rio 2016 would be too big a challenge. She also found herself spending too much of her time from August to October working with ITV on their coverage of the Rugby World Cup. It was an experience that made her realise how much she missed rugby. In November 2015 she decided that her future was not in shot-put but in rugby, as a pundit and commentator.

It will give her the perfect platform to prolong the 'Alphonsi effect' that has done so much already for women's rugby.

Most of her playing days were spent competing on clubs' back pitches and changing in the toilets, while her exploits with England garnered little media attention until the World Cup was held on home soil in 2010. It was that World Cup, says Alphonsi, which had a significant impact on how the game was viewed in England: 'What I loved about 2010 was how afterwards people came up to me and said, "That was a really great game of rugby", or "You're a really good rugby player". The "woman" bit they used to put in had gone. That was what we had been wanting for ages. It wasn't women's rugby, just rugby. It's taking time, but we're getting there.'

Alphonsi's role in achieving that and in taking the game to a new level, not only in her home country but internationally, cannot be overstated: 'I may have played a small role in changing a few perceptions through the way I played', she says modestly, 'showing that women hit equally as hard as guys, that the breakdown is equally competitive as the men's game, and that girls can relish the physical challenge as much as men do. But there are some fantastic players coming through now who will take it to another level. So if I started it off, someone else will come along and finish it.'

With that, Alphonsi says her goodbyes. With another award in hand she has a train to catch. This is a woman with little time for self-congratulation but all the time in the world for working towards her dreams and helping others to achieve theirs. Whoever those players are that finish the job Alphonsi started in rugby, they will know that without the 'Machine', their task would be a far more difficult one.

4: Culture clash

Sexism still exists in sport. That's hardly a surprise, because for as long as sexism still exists in wider society then it will always find a way to enter the sporting realm. It used to barge in through the front door all brash and bold, leaving no one in any doubt about its presence. But these days it makes more of an effort to avoid detection, sneaking in via a side gate or open window so no one notices its presence until it's too late. It's curled up on the sofa and refusing to budge.

For a long time, sexism in sport was accepted with a shrug. Maybe even a wry smile and a few words suggesting it's somehow 'to be expected'. In recent years though, the number of people speaking up against it has grown. The smiles are often still there (hiding a mouthful of gritted teeth), but now they are accompanied by reasoned questioning and valid arguments against its presence.

Four-time Ironman World Champion, Chrissie Wellington, has devoted a large amount of time and energy to encouraging equality in sport since retiring from competition in 2012. When we meet for a stroll through London's Hyde Park, she tells me that sexism in sport simply reflects a 'deeper seated inequality in society', highlighting such vastly differing worlds as the City of London and stand-up comedy as examples of environments that remain male dominated.

'A lot of it comes from deep-rooted cultural biases, but it's also about the structural biases that exist – the make-up of boards, for example. It even comes from the language that we use with kids and what we enable and allow them to do. I think we need a wider change.' While Wellington admits that change can't just come from 'one body, one organisation or one sector', she does believe that sport has a key role to play, saying: 'Sport can help to trigger that wider change and also a change in perception about what women can and can't do, not only on the sports field but more generally, too.'

How then is the sports world faring in tackling these deep-rooted cultural biases? Naturally it very much depends on where you focus your gaze. Wellington describes her sport of triathlon as 'very egalitarian', explaining that in terms of prize money, commercial opportunities, race distances and media opportunities, women are very much equal to their male counterparts. She puts it down to the relative newness of the sport (the first modern swim/bike/run event to be called a triathlon was held in 1974 in California and the sport's Olympic debut only came at the Sydney Games in 2000), and the fact that unlike many sports that date back much further, women took part in triathlon from the outset.

'We've also had women at the highest levels of governance', adds Wellington. 'The President and Vice President of the International Triathlon Union (ITU) are both women, and the head of British Triathlon was a woman – Dr Sarah Springman [who stepped down in 2012 after serving the maximum number of terms].'

Compare triathlon's gender parity with football and the so-called beautiful game does not come out of it well. Back in 1995 though, there was a sense of optimism around the future of women's football. It was then that Sepp Blatter (who at the time was General Secretary of football's international federation, FIFA) made his famous declaration that 'the future is feminine'. The Swiss leader was speaking not long after the second edition of the FIFA Women's World Cup had been held in Sweden, and while few believed that football was heading down a road that would take it anywhere near a place called 'femininity', there was a general swell of positivity around the women's game.

It was a shame then, when nine years after making his promising statement, Blatter added this provocative caveat in 2004: 'Let the women play in more feminine clothes like they do in volleyball. They could, for example, have tighter shorts. Female players are pretty, if you excuse me for saying so, and they already have some different rules to men – such as playing with a lighter ball. That decision was taken to create a more female aesthetic, so why not do it in fashion?'

Why not, eh Sepp? And while we're at it, why don't we just swap team shirts for sports bras and get players to strut one-by-one onto the pitch before kick-off, like models on a catwalk?

Needless to say, Blatter's comments left female footballers (and women in general) dismayed. Pauline Cope, who was then the England and Charlton goalkeeper, said: 'He doesn't know what he is talking about. We *don't* use a lighter ball for one thing, and to say we should play football in hotpants is plain ridiculous. It's completely irresponsible for a man in a powerful position to make comments like this.'

Skip ahead to 2010 and the world's best amateur female boxers were confronted by a similar suggestion from Dr Ching-Kuo Wu, the President of the International Boxing Association (AIBA). At the Women's World Championships in Barbados that year, Dr Wu gathered boxers and trainers together to announce that the AIBA was seriously considering making skirts a part of their uniform.

'I have heard many times, people say, "We can't tell the difference between the men and the women", especially on TV, since they're in the same uniforms and are wearing headgear', explained Dr Wu after hearing that the idea of boxing in skirts had not been a complete hit. 'The uniform was presented [in Barbados] as optional. After we hear about its comfort and how easy it is to compete in the uniform, it may be compulsory. But we are still working on it.'

A year and a half of deliberation followed, during which time an online petition opposing the new uniform collected more than 58,000 signatures. British boxer Nicola Adams (not yet an Olympic gold medallist, but at the time the European flyweight champion) also made her feelings clear, telling the BBC: 'I don't think it's fair to say female boxers should be in a skirt. You don't see female footballers going around in a skirt. Boxing has always been in shorts. I don't see why it should change to skirts just because you're a female.'

Her words did not fall on deaf ears. In February 2012, the AIBA announced that the wearing of skirts in the ring would not be compulsory, with Dr Wu conceding: 'Some women want to wear shorts and some others want to wear skirts, so the decision we have made is that we shall make it optional.' For the majority of the world's female boxers this means they are free to continue boxing in shorts, as they have always done. But boxing writer John Dennen tells me he has seen a few international female fighters wearing skirts in recent years, mentioning those from Poland in particular. He does admit, though, to not knowing whether that has been an individual choice made by the boxer or whether their national governing body has made that decision on their behalf – something that would muddy the waters a little when it comes to discerning whether having the option is a good or a bad thing.

While Blatter's call for female footballers to don tighter shorts left him battling barbs from women the world over, it was just a warm-up compared to the battle he found himself embroiled in years later, ahead of the 2015 Women's World Cup in Canada. The issue was FIFA's decision to play the entire tournament – including the World Cup final – on artificial turf as opposed to the real grass normally seen at major football tournaments.

It was a decision that left football's ruling body – and Blatter – accused of blatant sexism from all quarters. Even (somewhat bizarrely) from Hollywood superstars: 'Women's World Cup is the best Soccer of the year. Hey Fifa, they deserve real grass. Put in sod. Hanx.' This is a Tweet from Tom Hanks (yep, he of *Forrest Gump*, *Philadelphia* and *Saving Private Ryan* fame). And he wasn't the only star name speaking up for the world's female football players. One of basketball's biggest names, Kobe Bryant, joined in too, tweeting a photograph of the leg injuries suffered by US striker, Sydney Leroux, during a game played on artificial turf (one of the many arguments against playing football on artificial turf is the claim that it causes more injuries than playing on grass). Bryant signed off his Tweet with the hashtag #ProtectTheAthlete, for good measure.

The use of artificial turf was a part of Canada's original bid to host the tournament, based on their reasoning that it is better suited to year-round use in the harsh Canadian climate. When Canada's only competition (Zimbabwe) to host the 2015 World Cup withdrew their bid in March 2011, FIFA was left with little choice but to give Canada the nod.

For many players, the prospect of playing an entire tournament on the harsh, unforgiving artificial surface was far from satisfying: 'From the perspective of goalkeepers, we have to jump on this concrete', Germany goalkeeper, Nadine Angerer, told *Sports Illustrated*. 'We are landing all the time, and it's really bad. I played just a few weeks ago in Vancouver on this turf [in a Germany-Canada friendly]. Seriously, it's concrete.'

While injury prevention was a big concern for the players, so too was the effect the surface would have on the quality of football: 'The game is played differently [on turf]', said US striker Alex Morgan. 'The bounce on the surface is different, and a lot of players don't play the same way on turf as on grass, because they don't want to go down for a slide tackle or do a diving header.'

The England team, including former captain Casey Stoney, saw FIFA's decision as one they would simply have to swallow. 'It's not ideal', said Stoney when I spoke to her about it a few months before the tournament. 'Obviously we would all love to play on grass but the Canadian bid was the best one [not to mention the only one after Zimbabwe withdrew from the initial bidding process]. We're not going to be able to change it so all we can do is prepare ourselves the best we can to play on it.'

Not everyone accepted it so readily, though. In July 2014 a group of players, including US team members Abby Wambach, Alex Morgan and Heather O'Reilly, Germany goalkeeper and 2014 FIFA World Player of the Year Nadine Angerer, Spanish midfielder Veronica Boquete and five-time FIFA World Player of the Year Marta of Brazil, instructed legal representation to write to FIFA and the Canadian Soccer Association (CSA). In the letter they called for the six World Cup stadiums – in Vancouver, Edmonton, Winnipeg, Ottawa, Montreal and Moncton – to be converted to grass.

After two months of waiting, FIFA and the CSA had failed to provide any meaningful response to the letter. With the days to kick-off ticking by, the players released a statement reiterating their view that: 'Forcing the 2015 Women's World Cup to take place on artificial turf rather than grass was not only wrong but also constituted illegal sex discrimination. Men's World Cup tournament matches are played on natural grass, while CSA and FIFA are relegating female players to artificial turf. The difference matters: plastic pitches alter how the game is played, pose unique safety risks and are considered inferior for international competition.'

The statement added that the inaction of both organisations had left players with no choice but to take legal action: 'Whatever happens in court, CSA and FIFA have lost any claim to being good stewards of the women's game – until they correct their mistake ... Getting an equal playing field at the World Cup is a fight female players should not have to wage, but one from which they do not shrink. In the end, we trust that fairness and equality will prevail over sexism and stubbornness.'

The men's World Cup has *never* been played on artificial turf. In fact, for the 1994 tournament, FIFA spent $2million on installing natural grass over artificial turf in Detroit and New Jersey. If they could do it for the men, then why not for the women?

On the eve of the World Cup draw in December 2014, FIFA's General Secretary Jerome Valcke dismissed the claims of discrimination as 'nonsense'. He claimed it had nothing to do with the 'd-word' and expressed his utter disbelief that 'no one would recognize what FIFA has done for the development of women's football over the last 15 years.'

With the case dragging on and the CSA raising every procedural argument in the book to create more delays, including turning down the judge's suggestion of mediation with the players, time was running out. So, on 21 January 2015, the gender discrimination lawsuit against FIFA and the CSA was dropped, bringing a regrettably predictable end to the dispute.

Nevertheless, in a statement, US striker Abby Wambach said she hoped the players' actions had made some impact: 'Our legal action has ended. But I am hopeful that the players' willingness to contest the unequal playing fields – and the tremendous public support we received during the effort – marks the start of even greater activism to ensure fair treatment when it comes to women's sports.'

Valcke's response was arrogantly dismissive of the entire episode, his words whitewashing everything that had gone before: 'We – the participating teams and the organizers – can now all focus on the preparation and promotion of the biggest event in women's football this June in Canada.' How he kept a straight face while saying that, after spending months ensuring that the biggest event in women's football wouldn't provide the players with the opportunity to be at their best, is beyond me.

In February 2015, former professional soccer player Caitlin Davis Fisher wrote an article for Al Jazeera's American website expressing her belief that the saga was emblematic of an altogether bigger battle: 'By placing the Women's Cup on an inferior surface, soccer's governing body reinforced what we have been telling female athletes for decades: Their game is second-class. It is also the same subtle message we send to girls and women everywhere, every day: They deserve less.'

She highlights the fact that while FIFA's arguments in favour of using synthetic turf relate to its durability, consistency and simple maintenance, the players focus on the effect of the artificial turf on performance and their bodies. 'These opposing arguments', says Fisher, 'represent a significant albeit subtle distinction that can prompt us to think about where value is being placed. Accepting that women should play on substandard fields is the same as accepting a gender pay gap. The turf issue is not petty sports debate. It is about real rights.'

Fisher's final point is a crucial one. In the sports world, sexism is easily dismissed by both perpetrators and victims, as nothing more than 'a bit of fun,' or 'banter', meaning it is rarely treated with the same seriousness as other forms of discrimination. The FA doesn't even bother to mention it directly in their own Ground Regulations, which state that 'abuse of a racist, homophobic or discriminatory nature will result in arrest and/or ejection from the ground'. It's little wonder then that not one club has ever been punished by the FA, UEFA or FIFA for sexist abuse in a stadium.

Should fans be thrown out of a stadium for shouting 'Get your tits out' at a female physio as she runs onto the pitch to attend to an injured player? (As happened at Manchester City vs. Chelsea in September 2014.) What about for making fun of sexual violence, like the Arsenal fans who expressed their displeasure with Robin van Persie after he left for Manchester United by singing: 'Van Per-sie, when a girl says no moleeest her'? (Van Persie was arrested on suspicion of rape in 2005, although the case was later dismissed.)

Anna Kessel is a sports journalist and the chair of networking group Women in Football, which was set up in 2007 and now represents over 1,200 women working in the football industry. She says that neither of the instances above were likely to generate any response from the authorities: 'And yet, if fans were to sing comparable songs of a racist or homophobic nature, football authorities would at least be compelled to take action.'

While 25 per cent of the Premier League's match day revenue now comes from female fans, Kessel says there is still 'little protection in place, either for women who work in the football industry, or for women and girls who attend matches as fans.'

For those wondering why sexism continues to be so overlooked, the Chief Executive of the Premier League, Richard Scudamore, provided some depressing answers in May 2014 when he was exposed for sending sexist emails. Scudamore's temporary personal assistant, Rami Abraham, found the messages, which were sent from her boss's work account to senior colleagues. In them, he made crude, sexist remarks about a female colleague, mocked 'female irrationality' and referred to females as 'gash'. Charming.

While Scudamore operates in a predominantly male sport, he has often presented himself as leading the way in promoting the growth of women's football, and once claimed that the Premier League he oversees strives to be 'at the leading edge' of the 'whole equality agenda'. Neither of which tally particularly well with the content of his emails.

In the days after the contents of Scudamore's inbox were revealed, the England women's goalkeeper Rachel Brown-Finnis (who has since retired) labelled the emails 'an insult to all women'. Women in Football also responded swiftly, releasing a statement calling for the Premier League and the FA to 'conduct a full and proper investigation and to strengthen their commitment to ensuring gender equality across the game'.

Strong words also came from the FA's only female director and Chair of its inclusion board, Heather Rabbatts, who said there was 'growing evidence of a closed culture of sexism' at the Premier League. 'It is increasingly clear', said Rabbatts, 'that steps are needed as a matter of urgency to review governance at the Premier League with a view to improving accountability and tackling head on a culture that demeans women and seems to discourage their involvement in the game's administration.'

Rabbatts added her belief that 'these challenges go beyond the current situation of Chief Executive Richard Scudamore', but said that if the league was to move forward in a positive way, then 'he and they should give serious consideration to his position in the coming days'.

Instead of taking Rabbatt's sage advice, the league announced just two days later that Scudamore would keep his job and that 'no further disciplinary action is required or justified'. Their statement claimed that an 'examination of a very large quantity of emails and other documents, including those copied without authorisation by the former employee, indicate that there is no evidence of wider discriminatory attitudes or inappropriate language or a general attitude of disrespect to women.' How interesting that in the same breath as their defence of Scudamore the League also found room to blame his PA for daring to find the emails that so damaged his reputation.

Those holding on to any slim hope that the FA might step in and take firm action were let down just 24 hours later when the chairman of the national governing body, Greg Dyke, said: 'The FA does not as a matter of policy consider private communications sent with a legitimate expectation of privacy to amount to professional misconduct.' His view was that as Scudamore was not an employee of the FA, the organisation 'had no position in terms of employment policy or taking disciplinary action'.

And that, largely, was that. Scudamore released a statement apologising for what he called the 'inappropriate content' of his emails (although he too, found space within his apology to admonish his former PA for looking where he claims she should not have been), and the football world moved on.

For Dr Carrie Dunn, who is a sports researcher at the University of East London, Scudamore's emails are an example of the kind of 'unthinking, automatic sexism' that is pervasive within the sport. In a blog published on feminist website, The F word, Dunn wrote: 'Clubs and authorities continue to pay lip service to the idea that football is for everyone, but sexism is deeply embedded in the game and its structures, meaning that sexist attitudes and actions continue even if individuals and groups are not consciously aware of them (and so you get people claiming their words are "just a joke" or "banter" and of course they "love women").'

In her own book, *Female Football Fans: Community, Identity and Sexism*, Dunn reports one FA employee telling her: 'I think if you were to say to people, "What's racism in football?", they would generally understand it's probably black, white, Asian abuse. But if you say, "What's sexism?" I don't think anyone could answer that.'

The structure of the English game is controlled by an FA that Dunn says is led 'pretty much by a bunch of middle-aged to old white, fairly well-off men and it is reflected throughout the game. Look at the people they're representing: the fan bases, the participants. Whether it's officials or players, how can you possibly represent them when you've only got one demographic reflected in a governing body? I think the FA needs to get its own house in order before things can change.'

The FA and the Premier League might still be conflicted over how to deal with the culture of sexism that pervades football, but in 2011 Sky Sports showed that at least the people responsible for bringing football into our living rooms aren't afraid to take action when a line has been crossed.

When Richard Keys and Andy Gray, two of the broadcaster's longest serving and most popular presenters, were recorded making disparaging comments off-air about female assistant referee Sian Massey, ahead of a Premier League match in January 2011, it sparked widespread outrage. Although they weren't on air, the pair were still mic-d up when they were heard in a leaked recording agreeing that female officials 'don't know the offside rule' before Keys went on to mock claims made in the *Sun* newspaper by the West Ham vice-chairman Karren Brady regarding the level of sexism in football: 'See charming Karren Brady this morning complaining about sexism? Yeah. Do me a favour, love.'

The managing director of Sky Sports, Barney Francis, initially suspended both men and suggested they would also be disciplined internally. Their comments, said Francis, were 'totally unacceptable' and 'inexcusable from anyone at Sky regardless of their role or seniority'.

A day later another clip emerged, this time showing Gray engaging in what his employers later deemed to be 'offensive' and 'unacceptable' behaviour (he was filmed asking a female presenter whether she would like to 'tuck him in', as he finished preparing his outfit to go on air). Francis sacked him. Keys went next, handing in his notice after giving a radio interview in which he suggested 'dark forces' had been responsible for leaking the damning footage. He did also admit, however, that his and Gray's 'prehistoric banter' was 'not acceptable in a modern world. We were wrong.'

The *Guardian* newspaper spoke to several current and former Sky Sports employees who had worked alongside Keys and Gray and delivered the following conclusion: 'Keys and Gray were a double act that was emblematic of a Sky Sports culture that characterised the broadcaster's buccaneering early days, but which had failed to move with the rest of the company as it grew.'

This is certainly the view of Andy Cairns, who has been at the company for 25 years and now heads up the Sky Sports News channel. When I meet him at the broadcaster's west London headquarters he is bullish about the fact that Sky Sports is no longer seen as what he calls, 'the blokey channel' (just to reinforce the fact, the PR person from Sky who arranged the chat has ensured that the female producer of Sky's weekly Sportswomen show, Anna Edwards, is also present).

Cairns tells me how shocked he is by the scarcity of females entering sports journalism. While 54 per cent of journalism students are women, only one in nine sports journalism students are female – something Cairns says he is passionate about changing. Not least because it would make the hiring process easier at Sky Sports, where Cairns says it is imperative to have different views in the newsroom, boasting that their 70-30 gender split is 'so much better than most sports newsrooms'.

For Cairns, a diverse newsroom is particularly key in today's era of 24/7 rolling news. 'We want to be able to keep a story going so we need different angles on it. We want to represent all the views, which is why it's so important that we have people from diverse backgrounds. It makes it a much better product.

'When we set up Sky Sports News we were very clear on the type of culture we wanted here. We wanted it inclusive. We wanted the women to feel comfortable when they came to work. There have been a few uncomfortable incidents over Sky's career but I'd like to think that's never been anything that has come into Sky Sports News. We were starting with a blank sheet of paper, so we weren't stuck with any old traditions like newspapers that have been traditionally male.'

While Cairns is correct in saying that the channel has a wealth of female broadcasting talent, some question whether these women are given the same opportunities as their male counterparts. I spoke to one agent who looks after a number of female presenters that have worked for the channel and says that in terms of chances to progress their careers, the women at Sky are restricted – there is no system or structure for advancement.

In the channel's early days the agent recalls that female presenters were told it was the job of the male presenter to ask questions when studio guests were on air. The agent also claims that for many years you simply wouldn't see Sky's female presenters involved in any of the channel's many live football broadcasts (although this has started to change recently with Natalie Sawyer and Kate Abdo bucking the trend on occasion). When the agent had previously pointed out this dearth of female presence in live football to those in charge, they were told that 'the talent simply isn't there'.

Well-renowned sports broadcaster Gabby Logan worked at Sky Sports from 1996 until 1998, and says she was left with little option but to go elsewhere if she wanted to continue to develop as a broadcaster: 'When I was at Sky in 1998 I felt I had to go to ITV to progress my career, they were giving me the opportunity to present live football, which at the time Sky weren't.'

In recent years, however, there has been a renewed commitment from the likes of Sky Sports and the BBC to ensure there is more of a female presence in their sports programmes. For example, Sky Sports often have a female presenter hosting their Saturday night Premier League highlights programme, while Logan has presented *Match of the Day* on numerous occasions when regular host Gary Lineker has been absent.

Football broadcaster Jacqui Oatley was the first female commentator to appear on *Match of the Day* in 2007, at a time very few female broadcasters specialised in football. When I caught up with her on the phone (while she was en route to a football stadium, naturally), Oatley told me she feels as though there has been a 'motion towards having more representative broadcasters in recent years'. Oatley says this is a crucial step: 'It means that women don't feel like it's a closed shop anymore. You can switch on the TV or radio and it's not just men talking about football. I think the word "representative" is important because it's not tokenism, it's about providing a fair representation. The key thing is making sure that it's not someone who is brought through prematurely just so a box can be ticked saying that there is a female on. The good thing is there are a lot more good female broadcasters out there now because they're being given opportunities at a lower level.'

What is taking longer to achieve though, says Oatley, is a real acceptance of female commentators in football. It's something she knows all too well, having endured a barrage of criticism after making her *Match of the Day* debut. 'I still feel that commentary is another world apart from any other type of sports broadcasting and particularly in football because the sport is so male dominated. It's very different to tennis or athletics.

'People are used to seeing a woman ask questions about football now, and they seem ok about that. But they're not so convinced about women answering questions about football. So they don't mind you doing radio updates saying: "West Ham nil, Stoke nil, no chances for either side but so and so missed a penalty." People are ok with that but some do struggle when it's a woman who is there to talk them through the game and give an opinion on it.'

Hearing a female voice coming through the airwaves is also something that can make listeners jolt, says Oatley, purely because 'people aren't conditioned to hearing a woman commentate. That's still something that needs to be broken down. I'm convinced it's down to conditioning. I don't think people are born prejudiced, I think it stems from the way people are brought up. They might only hear dads and brothers talking about football and then hear men on the TV and radio so they get conditioned to trust the male voice.

'If you then hear a woman in that environment, it's a change from the norm. All those thoughts of sisters and mums asking, "which way are they kicking?" and making comments from a base of a lack of interest become ingrained in some people's psyche. They then relate the female broadcaster, who is perfectly qualified to talk about football, to the person they know also with a female voice, who doesn't know about football. That's only going to be broken down with time and hearing more women who clearly do know what they're talking about.'

A similar story has unfolded in the USA, where female broadcasters have been a part of the sports landscape for decades, but have rarely been given leading roles. 'Women in sports television are allowed to read headlines, patrol sidelines and generally facilitate conversation for their male colleagues', says Fox Sports host Katie Nolan. 'Sometimes, they even let us monitor the internet from a couch. And while the Stephen A. Smiths, Mike Francesas, Dan Patricks and Keith Olbermanns of the world get to weigh in on the issues of the day, we just smile and throw to commercial.

'It's time for women to have a seat at the Big Boy table, and not where their presence is a gimmick or a concept, just a person who happens to have breasts offering their opinion on the sports they love and the topics they know.'

Nolan said the above during her show on Fox Sports' digital channel in September 2014. At the time, America was glued to a domestic violence case that had left its flagship sport, the NFL, under scrutiny like never before. Nolan's point was that the NFL would 'never respect women and their opinions as long as the media it answers to doesn't'.

The league's problems started when they suspended Baltimore Ravens running back Ray Rice for the first two games of the 2014–15 season after he was indicted for striking his fiancée, Janay Palmer, unconscious in a hotel lift in February 2014. For many people – including Congress who criticised the NFL for taking the case too lightly – the two-game ban was far from satisfactory.

One month after handing out Rice's two-match ban, the NFL's much-criticised Commissioner Roger Goodell announced the league was introducing a new, harsher policy for domestic violence. First-time offenders would be subject to a six-week suspension, while anyone who committed a second offence would be banned for life. The commissioner also sent a letter to all 32 team owners admitting that he 'did not get it right' in relation to Rice's punishment.

The 2014 season was just four days old when disturbing video footage emerged from the night Rice's altercation with his fiancée (now wife) took place. It showed the NFL star punching Palmer (his partner) in the face, sending her crashing into the side of the lift and leaving her slumped on the floor. Hours after the video was released, the Ravens terminated Rice's contract and Goodell announced that he was now suspended indefinitely from the NFL (Rice later won his appeal against the suspension in November 2014 meaning he is eligible to play again, but at time of writing, he remains an unsigned player).

The episode raised serious questions about the way in which America's most popular sport views violence towards women, and in turn, what messages that is sending out to players and fans. Indeed, the Rice case is just the latest (and the most prominent) example in a long line of domestic abuse cases for the league. According to a database compiled by *USA Today*, 85 of the 713 arrests of NFL players since 2000 were for domestic abuse incidents.

'It has long been clear that the NFL is indifferent to violence against women', wrote Katie McDonough on US news website Salon. 'This incident was just too much of a media headache to ignore, so the NFL acted – belatedly, inadequately, cynically.'

The NFL's incompetence did have one positive outcome: It brought the women who had spent so long on the sidelines of sports broadcasting into the mainstream. In September 2014, the *New York Times*' Jonathan Mahler wrote a piece headlined 'In Coverage of NFL Scandals, Female Voices Puncture the Din', in which he said that female broadcasters had been providing a perspective on the Ray Rice story that their male counterparts simply couldn't. This was a moment, wrote Mahler, that female sports broadcasters saw as a potential watershed one for their profession, 'a turning point that could bring them more fully into the conversation.'

One such broadcaster was ESPN's Hannah Storm who, for the first time in her 30-year career, was asked to deliver a first-person commentary on the air about the NFL and domestic violence. While she agreed that the events had been a 'catalyst for new voices', she warned that those voices would have to stay 'front and centre if we are going to provide a really rich and intelligent dialogue about sports'.

Ironically, the NFL would likely welcome more female voices into the game. In recent years the league has made a concerted effort to increase its female fan base, and in 2012 it looked as though it was succeeding with a reported 44 per cent of all football fans said to be female – a prized demographic for the value they represent to advertisers.

But the league's image has been severely damaged. Not only by the Rice case, but others including that of Minnesota Vikings running back, Adrian Peterson, who was suspended indefinitely in November 2014 over allegations of child abuse against his four-year-old son (Peterson was reinstated in April 2015 after his appeal was upheld by a US District Judge). Considering the cumulative effects of these incidents, it would be no surprise if that percentage dropped off.

A case that did not make as many headlines as that of Rice but reflected equally badly upon the NFL was that of the Buffalo Bills cheerleaders, otherwise known as the Buffalo Jills. In April 2014 it was announced that the Bills would no longer enjoy the morale-boosting presence of their chief support act at NFL games because of a lawsuit filed by five former Jills.

The cheerleaders alleged flagrant violations of state minimum wage laws, claiming they had not received a single penny in wages in return for hundreds of hours of work and practices. The most they could hope for, they told the *New York Times* in December 2014, were 'a few small tips and appearance fees here and there'. One of the women was quoted as having made $420 for more than 800 hours of work, while another collected just $105.

The money was only one part of a bigger and wholly rotten picture. 'Supervisors ordered the cheerleaders to warm up in a frigid, grubby stadium storeroom that smelled of gasoline', reported Michael Powell in the *New York Times*. 'They demanded that cheerleaders pay $650 for uniforms. They told the cheerleaders to do jumping jacks to see if flesh jiggled.'

The contracts signed by the Jills dictated everything from the colour of their hair and nails to how they handled their menstrual cycle. In the thick handbook given to all Jills, there is a section titled 'General hygiene and lady body maintenance', in which they are told to 'use a product that [sic] right for your menstrual flow. A tampon too big can irritate and develop fungus. A product left in too long can cause bacteria or fungus build-up.' They're also told to wash their feet daily and keep toenails 'tightly trimmed and clean'.

All this for the 'honour' of performing on the field of their home team – one that denied it even employed cheerleaders: 'For decades the Buffalo Jills trademark has been licensed to independent third parties who have assumed the responsibility for the selection, management, training, scheduling and compensation of the cheerleaders', said a statement on the Bills website in response to the lawsuit. 'We are aware of public statements and allegations that have surfaced since the start of the recent litigation which attempt to give the impression that our organization employs cheerleaders. Such statements are inaccurate and misleading.'

It is true that the Jills were managed by Stejon Productions Corp., but unfortunately for the Bills, the subcontractor openly admitted it acted on the teams' behalf, with Stejon's lawyer, Dennis Vacco claiming 'the Bills control everything, from the moves to the uniforms to the dances'. The state judge agreed, ruling that the team set the terms and approved the contracts for the Jills. There's yet to be any decisive outcome in terms of compensation but the Jills have succeeded in prompting proposed changes to New York's labour laws that, if passed, would ensure better working conditions for cheer and dance teams in professional sport.

The NFL itself has had little to say on the matter (predictably). This is not the first time a team has been sued by its cheerleaders – teams including the Oakland Raiders, Tampa Bay Buccaneers, Cincinnati Bengals and New York Jets have all been faced with lawsuits – but each time it happens the league just shrugs and tells its teams: You sort it out.

In an affidavit, the NFL Commissioner, Roger Goodell wrote that he had 'no knowledge' of the Jills' 'selection, training, compensation and/or pay practices'. Even if this is true, Goodell's willingness to turn a blind eye to the bad practice continuing under his watch is just one more example of how the NFL values women – or doesn't, as the case may be.

Away from the overtly male-dominated worlds of football (UK) and American football there are the more surprising (and perhaps less clear cut) cases, such as that of British Cycling. If there is one national governing body that one would not expect to find fending off accusations of sexism, it is one that can point to the immense success of riders like Beijing Olympic road race champion Nicole Cooke, two-time Olympic champion Victoria Pendleton, double Olympic gold medallist Laura Trott, and Olympic silver medallist and World Champion Lizzie Armitstead.

But in the autobiographies written by Pendleton (in 2012) and Cooke (2014), the system that has produced so many gold medal moments in the last three Olympic Games takes quite a bashing. Pendleton claims that the way in which her relationship with British Cycling sports scientist Scott Gardner was handled, after it became public knowledge in 2008, left her feeling cut adrift and rejected, writing: 'The entire backroom staff at GB Cycling was held up as an ideal model of excellence. British cyclists, we were told, were the most skilfully and sensitively managed group of sportsmen and sportswomen in the country … if only they knew how different my experiences at work were in reality … Training became a solitary trial. I cycled alone. I sat alone. I ate alone.'

Cooke's issues with British Cycling began far earlier in her career than Pendleton's, and were a continuing feature throughout her 11-year career. While she does also point the finger at cycling's international governing body, the UCI, for overseeing a sport that she says prioritised male competitors over female, Cooke's most vehement criticisms relate to her treatment – and that of women's cycling as a whole – by her national governing body.

She was just 14 when she discovered there was no national competition for a girl her age to enter and, from then on, her feeling that she and other female riders were forever bottom of British Cycling's list of priorities only intensified. 'While I was coming along – very successful, very young and doing everything by myself – it obviously didn't fit in with the "importance of the coach" and all those dynamics', Cooke said in an interview with *Cycling News* in 2014. 'It really was a clash of cultures'.

It has been claimed by some that the individual characters of Pendleton and Cooke were contributing factors in the problems they had with British Cycling. Pendleton has often described herself as being 'psychologically fragile', which has been used as proof that she was simply not suited to the extreme pressures of elite sport. Cooke, meanwhile has long been described as an 'outsider', the rider who preferred to work alone, enabling her to do things 'her way'.

More recently, Olympic silver medallist Lizzie Armitstead has been described in similar terms by British Cycling's head coach (and a man with whom both Cooke and Pendleton had their run-ins), Shane Sutton. 'This is elite sport and the coalface of it isn't nice', he said in an interview on the Telegraph's Cycling Podcast in November 2014. 'It's a tough place to be, and it doesn't suit everybody. Look at Lizzie [Armitstead]. The programme doesn't suit Lizzie … she doesn't buy into the programme fully and we don't expect her to.'

Armitstead is currently riding for the Dutch team Boels Dolmans and thriving, despite not being involved in the British set up. In 2014 she added Commonwealth Games gold to her Olympic silver and won the Women's World Cup (a season-long series of races that take place around the world). She repeated her World Cup feat in 2015 and fulfilled her long-held dream of winning the World Road Race Championships too, thus establishing herself as one of the world's best riders on the women's professional scene.

When Armitstead won Team GB's first medal of the 2012 Olympics, she took full advantage of the media platform it gave her, telling reporters: 'The sexism I have encountered in my career can get quite overwhelming'. It was widely assumed she was referring to the sport as a whole, rather than to her dealings with British Cycling (and while wearing the Team GB kit, she most probably was). But that's not to say she's entirely satisfied with the governing body's provisions for its female road riders.

At the 2014 World Road Racing Championships, British Cycling came under fire for not sending a single female rider to compete in the time trial, and including two mountain bike riders in the six-woman team for the elite road race. Defending their selection policy, British Cycling claimed there was not a single medal contender among their prospects for the time trial.

It led to vehement criticism from some quarters. When I asked Nicole Cooke about it, she said it showed that British Cycling was effectively 'ignoring' the women's road and time trial. 'The British Cycling World Class Performance Plan has all the money it could ever need', says Cooke. 'Why didn't they enter anyone? Possibly because if they actually supported the women, they might do better than the men, and then they can't justify spending millions on the men's team because then the women are more deserving.'

When asked about British Cycling's decision on the eve of the Championships, Armitstead was initially reluctant to join in the criticism, but as the questions kept coming she found it increasingly difficult to defend their stance, saying: 'There is no women's road programme [within British Cycling]. That is the reason why there is no one else to choose from. So yeah, it could be a lot better, but from my perspective, if you want to be the best in the world, you have to go out and search for yourself. It's not that things should be given to you on a plate.'

Going out and searching for it is exactly what Armitstead had done of course, in joining Dutch team Boels Dolmans where she said, 'I've found that support I need'. Armitstead signed off by claiming she believed that same support would be forthcoming if she went to British Cycling having proved she was one of the best in the world. But with no women's road programme yet in place (although in June 2015, British Cycling announced their intention to establish one as part of a shake-up of its system heading towards the 2020 Olympics in Tokyo), it remains unclear and untested whether that would be the case.

Respected cycling writer Richard Moore has covered British Cycling's relationships with female riders with interest over the years, and says: 'There have been a lot more personality issues between the women riders [than the men]. There have been with some male riders as well but they've been able to manage them, somehow.'

'It's a chicken and egg thing', he says of the fallouts that have punctuated British Cycling's years of success. 'The female riders have felt discriminated against to some extent, but their responses and reactions to that have made the situation even worse and harder to manage. I think it has left [Dave] Brailsford thinking "why the hell would I want to run a team with this lot?" He's had a lot of problems with women. I don't know if that reflects on him or if he's just been unlucky.'

It is impossible to know whether British Cycling's 'women issues' are based purely on personality clashes or if there are deeper, cultural reasons why some female riders have found it difficult to be a part of the elite set up. Indeed, it could be a combination of the two. Cycling author Feargal Mckay sums the conundrum up particularly well: 'For an organisation that pats itself on the back for its attention to detail, it would seem they have yet to master emotional intelligence.'

The fact remains though, that in terms of success Britain's female riders have not done badly. 'We've had a lot more success on the road at the Olympics with the women than with the men', points out Moore, correctly. Unless that success comes to a halt, one suspects British Cycling's methods and attitudes will remain the same. And as a result, some of Britain's female cyclists will continue to feel the need to do it their own way.

For many sports and for the media that covers them, it has taken time to adjust to the growing presence and influence of women. For the sports discussed in this chapter, the adjustment has proven to be particularly complex, with the structures governing them struggling to understand exactly what they could be doing to improve matters. This has led to a lack of positive, decisive action being taken to help rid the sports of a culture that has become ingrained so deeply that some fans have come to accept it as 'part of the game'.

While cycling does not fit the same mould as football – you don't tend to hear shouts of 'get your tits out' at the Velodrome or roadside (thankfully), it seems British Cycling has some work to do in order to ensure it can meet the physical and emotional needs of all its riders. The former head of British Cycling (and now Team Sky supremo), Dave Brailsford defined his theory of marginal gains as the idea that 'if you broke down everything you could think of that goes into riding a bike, and then improved it by 1%, you will get a significant increase when you put them all together'. Surely that should include doing whatever is necessary to create a national governing body that is capable of adapting its methods to provide the same support for all of its riders, no matter what their character traits – or gender – might be.

Kelly Smith

In December 2009, England footballer Kelly Smith decided she could no longer hide from the truth. Beneath the headline 'How I beat the drink and turned into England's best player', Smith talked openly to a national newspaper about how a series of major injuries had left her depressed and unable to stop drinking. 'When you're older, you have more in your locker to cope with the emotions' she told the *Daily Mail*. 'But when I was younger, when I couldn't play through a broken leg, through knee surgery, I'd be drinking, I'd be depressed, I'd be having negative thoughts all the time like, "I might not ever play again". So my psyche was wrong, all messed up.'

As the headline suggests, Smith had emerged from these dark times to resume her career as one of the best footballers in the women's game. When we meet, some six years have passed since she let the world in on her secret struggles. She has gone on to become England's all-time record goal scorer and helped her nation to reach the quarter-finals of the 2011 World Cup and a home Olympic Games.

Days before we meet, however, Smith has announced her decision to retire from international football. From the outside, the timing seems odd. The 2015 Women's World Cup is just months away. Why not aim to play a part in one more major tournament before handing back your England shirt for good? 'I feel like I've been very distant from the England set-up for the last two years, really. I haven't played a full 90 minutes in that whole time. So I just felt like it was the right time to pull away.'

Her emotions remain close to the surface when she dwells on what she calls the 'toughest decision' of her career. During an interview with Sky Sports' Sportswomen programme a few days after we meet, Smith is asked to look back on her England career. Halfway through, she stops the filming, unable to hold back her tears. Her depth of feeling is not surprising when one considers that Smith's international career spans 20 years of her life, her first England call-up coming at the tender age of just 16.

At the time, Smith was playing for Wembley Ladies in the Women's Premier League. Since her days of kicking a ball around with the boys in the school playground, playing football was the only thing Smith had wanted to do. Finding opportunities to play had not been easy though. 'There were no girls' teams then', she says, explaining why she spent her childhood playing alongside boys, starting off in the school team where she was 'just one of the lads' before joining her first Sunday league team, Garston Boys FC.

'I was the only girl but I looked like a little tomboy at the time so I fitted right in. To the boys on my team it didn't matter that I was a girl, but it started to be an issue when I scored three, four or five goals per game. Then parents from opposition teams would get irate with me. It was never the boys who got upset, they would just get on with it, but the parents would be angry and jealous about this girl who was beating up on their boys.

'There was uproar. I was even shouted at by adults on the touchline at matches. It was an awful experience to go through.' When opposition teams started refusing to play against Garston while they still had Smith in their ranks, she was told the team had no other option than to let her go. Smith moved on, joining another local boys' team, only for a similar scenario to play out there.

Realising that she would never be truly welcome in a boys' team, Smith turned to her local women's club, Watford Ladies. They had no youth set-up but said she could play in their five-a-side team where she became the 'kid' among four full-grown women competing in a local league. She chuckles as she remembers: 'They stuck me in goal because I was too small to be out on the pitch.'

At that age Smith wasn't even aware there was an England women's football team. It was only later, when her dad – having 'spotted a little insert in the paper about it' – took her to see England women play against Germany at Watford that she saw the possibilities ahead. 'I knew right away that it was what I wanted to do', she says. 'I had always wanted to be a professional footballer when I was growing up, but I didn't have any league to aspire to be in because there was no professional league. There was the Women's Premier League, but you had to pay your subs each week to play in that, so you weren't a professional footballer.'

The men's Premier League arrived in 1992, sending football in England soaring to new heights of popularity, media coverage and money. A young Smith watched on, soaking it all in. 'I used to record *Match of the Day* and emulate moves I'd seen using a little ball or a balloon, whatever I could find. I just wanted to score goals, dribble, take players on, create goals and celebrate goals. I've always had that creative instinct and vision; I guess I was born with it.'

Smith's first real football home was a girls' team called Pinner Park for which she left Watford Ladies, relieved to be able to play with and against girls of her own age. The team swiftly became one of the best around, winning five-a-side and 11-a-side competitions across a number of years. When Smith was 15, Pinner Park merged with Wembley Ladies and she was immediately earmarked as someone capable of stepping straight into Wembley's first team.

'We played every Sunday and trained two nights a week out in the cold behind the main football pitch', recalls Smith. 'Looking back at it now, those conditions were awful. But at the time I thought this was as good as it got in women's football. The game was not what I had hoped or imagined it could be when I was a young girl. It certainly wasn't the sort of life my heroes like Ian Wright were having.'

Nevertheless, Smith's talent was starting to turn heads. Ahead of the 1995–96 season, an article in *The Independent* tipped Wembley Ladies for the title, describing them as 'a strong, well-organised outfit', and identifying 16-year-old Kelly Smith as 'the outstanding prospect in the women's game today. She's lethally quick and bountifully gifted.'

Smith's eye-catching ability soon led to a dream opportunity that would alter the course of her entire career. In 1995 she was playing for Pinner Park (the team still had a five-a-side presence) in the Watford Football Festival – an annual tournament featuring teams from the USA, Denmark, Germany and Sweden. Smith didn't know it, but there was an American college scout watching among the parents and friends. Unwittingly sparking up a conversation with her dad on the touchline, the scout pointed to his new acquaintance's daughter and said: 'That Pinner player's a special talent. She could probably get a scholarship to play in the States.'

'I already knew that soccer scholarships were a big thing,' says Smith, 'but after the match I spoke with the scout and he sold the whole dream package to me: Scholarship, education, housing and football. He told me I could play football every day! He had contacts with two colleges in New Jersey, one to Seton Hall and one to their rival school, Rutgers. Another school – George Mason in Virginia was also interested in me.'

Smith made contact with all three schools, but faced a dilemma that went beyond choosing between this trio. While she was desperate to chase her dream, Smith was also mindful of the fact she was only halfway through studying for a BTEC National Diploma in sports science that would ensure she had something to fall back on if it all went wrong. She was also nervous about leaving home at such a young age: 'I remember wishing more than anything that I could have this opportunity in England, but it just wasn't possible then for a woman to be a professional footballer in my home country.'

Even so, Smith remained determined to pursue her dreams, accepting that she would have to leave her family and home behind to do so. She did refuse to ditch her 'Plan B', though. After settling on Seton Hall as the college where she would begin her American soccer adventure, Smith informed the head coach there that if they really wanted her, they would have to wait until she had finished her studies for her arrival.

By the time of her eventual departure in 1997, much in Smith's life had already changed. For a start, she had become an England international. 'I got a letter through the door telling me I was being called up for England', she recalls. 'I was ecstatic.'

Smith was 16 when the summons came from the England manager, Ted Copeland. But her excitement at winning her first cap was quickly tempered by a less than welcoming atmosphere at England's pre-match training camp. 'I was so nervous on that first camp. I had come up against a number of the England players when playing for Wembley so I kind of knew who they were, but it was a really intimidating environment to go into as a 16 year old with these older, bigger women.

'No one really spoke to me. I was really shy back then, too, so I wasn't able to strike up a major conversation with anyone. The group was very cliquey at the time, people kind of stuck with their own comfortable units, so it was really hard. It wasn't enjoyable to be a part of it at that time.'

Later in her career, as one of the more experienced players in the England set up, Smith made sure that young players coming into the squad were presented with a far more welcoming atmosphere than the one she found: 'I've experienced that feeling so I always put an arm around them and made them feel more comfortable. It has massively changed since the days I first started playing with England – it's not like that at all now.'

One notable teammate on Smith's first England squad was Hope Powell, who would go on to become England's first ever full-time coach in 1998, managing Smith at international level for the next 15 years, before she was sacked in 2013. The pair would grow close over the years, but their initial meetings left Smith wary of her England colleague.

'Scary' is Smith's immediate response when asked for her initial impressions of Powell. 'She still is', she says, laughing. 'She was a really great player though. I don't think Hope got enough accolades for the level of player she was. But if you didn't pass her the ball in certain situations she'd certainly tell you about it. She was really intimidating.'

A few weeks later, Smith scored her first goal for England in a 5-0 win against Croatia at Charlton Athletic's home ground, The Valley. Her international career was up and running but back at her club, Smith felt she was stagnating. 'I had become disillusioned at Wembley', she says. 'As I got older and I grew in confidence I found I always wanted the ball – and I didn't always get the ball.'

She also grew increasingly frustrated with the approach of the coach, John Jones, whose sessions focused largely on improving players' physical fitness, meaning there was little opportunity for Smith to work on her technique and skills: 'I wanted to play on the ball as much as possible. I thought he had his priorities the wrong way round.'

Desperate to leave, Smith told her dad she'd had enough. She wanted out, and she had found the perfect place to go after talking to Arsenal Ladies manager, Vic Akers. An Arsenal fan since she was taken to her first ever football match at the Gunners'

Highbury home, Smith had always harboured hopes that she would one day be spotted by Akers and get the chance to play in the same kit as her Arsenal heroes. And now it had happened.

'I felt like I had really made it. Vic showed me the marble hall at Highbury and took me out on to the pitch. I was in my element. He took me upstairs and I saw all the trophies from the glory days. I went into the changing rooms too and saw all the bathtubs that the greats had used. Having supported them from such a young age, it was a truly amazing experience.'

Smith signed her first Arsenal contract in the Highbury boardroom towards the end of 1996 and could hardly wait to put on the iconic red and white kit, despite the fact it wasn't exactly made to fit: 'It was oversized men's kit and tracksuits in those days, so looking back they weren't too flattering. Back then we didn't have any female fitted items of clothing like we do now, but wearing an Arsenal shirt meant everything to me anyway. It still does, really.'

Smith helped Arsenal to win their third Women's Premier League title that season, scoring twice and assisting a third goal in a 3-0 win over Liverpool that secured them the trophy. As quickly as it had started though, Smith's Arsenal career was over. With her studies completed, she made the tough decision to leave in order to take up the offer of a place at Seton Hall University in New Jersey.

'It was hard', she says 'but Arsenal and England wasn't the whole dream. Deep down I knew I owed it to myself to go. I didn't have a job when I was at Arsenal and I wasn't getting paid to play.' At that time in the 1990s, women's football was entirely amateur, with most players holding down jobs and fitting in training sessions a couple of nights a week. These days the top level of women's football is semi-professional, with most players earning a wage. For some top players this is enough to live on, but others still need to supplement it with part-time work.

Smith was also frustrated because she wanted to be training more: 'Across the board in England at that time, most clubs were only training two nights a week. It wasn't enough. I wanted to be training every day. That was my view of being a professional: Playing every day, being in the gym, getting stronger and constantly improving. Having the ball at your feet every day – that's what sold going to America for me. I went there to be, in my eyes, a full-time professional.'

Within 24 hours of her arrival on US shores however, Smith felt like she had made the biggest mistake of her life. 'Looking back on it now', she says, 'it was probably down to the fact I had all these expectations of how my arrival would be, and they weren't met. I thought the whole team would be there, but, because it was during the summer, the campus was dead.

Roberta Gibb in action during the Boston marathon, 1966. (Photo by Fred Kaplan/ Sports Illustrated/Getty Images)

Jock Semple attempts to remove Kathy Switzer from the course during Boston Marathon in 1967. (Photo by Paul J. Connell/ The Boston Globe via Getty Images)

Eighteen year-old English boxer Barbara Buttrick (right) in training with a male sparring partner, 1949. Buttrick later founded the Women's International Boxing Federation (WIBF).

(Photo by Keystone/Hulton Archive/Getty Images)

Austrian ski-jumper Paula Lamburg, who set the world record of 22 metres for ski jumping in 1911. (Photo courtesy of the US Ski Jumping Association)

Billie Jean King and Bobby Riggs during the Battle of the Sexes Challenge Match at the Astrodome on September 20, 1973 in Houston, Texas. (Focus on Sport/Getty Images)

Billie Jean King at the Battle of the Sexes Challenge Match against Bobby Riggs at the Astrodome on September 20, 1973 in Houston, Texas. (Focus on Sport/Getty Images)

Nicola Adams of Great Britain celebrates victory after the Women's Fly (51kg) Boxing final at the 2012 Olympic Games. (Photo by Popperfoto/Getty Images)

Jessica Ennis celebrates winning gold in the Women's Heptathlon at the London 2012 Olympic Games. (Photo by Popperfoto/Getty Images)

Jo Pavey of Great Britain and Northern Ireland crosses the line to win gold in the Women's 10,000 metres final during day one of the 22nd European Athletics Championships at Stadium Letzigrund on August 12, 2014 in Zurich, Switzerland. (Photo by Michael Steele/Getty Images)

Dick Kerr International Ladies FC, undefeated British champions in 1920-1921. (Photo by Bob Thomas/Popperfoto/Getty Images)

England celebrate as they win the IRB Women's Rugby World Cup 2014 Final between England and Canada on August 17, 2014 in Paris, France. (Photo by Jordan Mansfield/ Getty Images)

Maggie Alphonsi breaks with the ball during the Women's Six Nations semi-final between England and Ireland at Twickenham Stadium on February 22, 2014. (Photo by David Rogers – RFU/Getty Images)

Katherine Grainger and Anna Watkins of Great Britain celebrate with their gold medals draped in a Union Jack during the medal ceremony for the Women's Double Sculls final of the London 2012 Olympic Games at Eton Dorney on August 3, 2012.
(Photo by Ian MacNicol/Getty Images)

Chrissie Wellington on stage during the 26th Annual Nautica Malibu Triathlon on September 16, 2012 in Malibu, California.
(Photo by Christopher Polk/WireImage)

Oxford (front) and Cambridge women's crew race at the start of the boat race between Oxford and Cambridge on April 11, 2015 in London. This was the first time the women's crews attacked the same course as the men's Boat Race.
(Photo from Justin Tallis/AFP/Getty Images)

Michelle Wie sends a tee flying on the 16th hole at the 2014 Sony Open in Hawaii, USA. (Photo by A. Messerschmidt/Getty Images)

The Buffalo Jills cheerleaders of the Buffalo Bills dance during an NFL game against the Oakland Raiders. (Photo by Tom Szczerbowski/Getty Images)

Brandi Chastain of Team USA celebrates during the Women's World Cup against Team China at The Rose Bowl on July 10, 1999. (Photo by Jed Jacobsohn/Getty Images)

Kelly Smith of England kisses her boot after scoring her first of two goals against Japan during their opening game of the 2007 FIFA Women's World Cup football tournament on September 11, 2007. (Photo by MARK RALSTON/AFP/Getty Images)

England captain Stephanie Houghton during the Women's Football first round Group E Match between Great Britain and Brazil, during the London 2012 Olympic Games. (Photo by Jamie McDonald - FIFA/FIFA via Getty Images)

England celebrates after winning the FIFA Women's World Cup 2015 Third Place Play-off match between Germany and England, 2015. (Photo by Lars Baron – FIFA/FIFA via Getty Images)

Nicole Cooke of Great Britain in action during training for the UCI Road World Championships on September 20, 2012 in Valkenburg, Netherlands. (Photo by Bryn Lennon/Getty Images)

The peloton heads up the Champs-Elysees during the La Course on July 26, 2015 in Paris, France. (Photo by Doug Pensinger/ Getty Images)

'The assistant coach picked me up from the airport and dropped me off at the dorm. It was late in the evening and when I got in my room there was no bedding, no electricity or anything, and I thought, what have I done? I didn't have any money for food or even know where to go on campus to get food. I felt stuck and had no mobile phone then so I had no way of calling home. I just put a towel on the mattress, covered myself in jumpers and cried myself to sleep.'

The following day was not much better. Although Smith met up with her teammates who were on New Jersey shore for pre-season training, she was not allowed to put her boots on and join them because her international clearance had not been arranged. 'My BTEC grades had to be transferred over to the American points system before I had the amount of credits required to study for a degree at Seton Hall. Until I had that credit I couldn't even train with the team.'

Smith was a shy, introverted teenager who found it difficult to make the first move when making friends. She had always found it easier to do so with a ball at her feet, when she could express herself freely. Take that away from her, and she would retreat even further into her shell. So while Smith's boots were locked away for almost a month while she waited for the administration process to be complete, she struggled to fit in with her new teammates. 'I hated it', she says bluntly. 'I wanted to go home.'

It was only thanks to her mother that she stayed. 'I'd be crying down the phone to her every weekend, saying: "I fucking hate it, I want to come home." And she'd say: "Just stick it out for another week and let's see how you feel next Sunday." Gradually it got easier. Once I started playing, the phone calls weren't every week but every two or three weeks. When mum eventually asked: "Are you going to stay now?" I was like, "yeah, I love it".'

In her first five games for the Seton Hall Pirates, Smith scored nine goals and made two assists. She became one of the best-known names and faces on campus, ending the season with the accolades of both Player of the Year and Newcomer of the Year. Everywhere Smith went she was 'that English girl, the star soccer player'. Suddenly all eyes were on her, and she had no idea how to handle it. 'I wasn't expecting that and it made me really uncomfortable. I hated giving interviews or anything like that because I'd never experienced it before. Now I was being asked to give interviews all over the place and even do a few bits for television. I felt like I'd been thrown into this big social circus and was just overwhelmed by it all.'

The American college season lasted for just three months, starting in early August and running until the end of October. While she was busy playing and training, Smith was happy. She could be herself and enjoy the feeling of confidence that playing football gave her. But the off-season came round too quickly and lasted for too long, in Smith's eyes.

'Off the field I was a completely different person. I was unable to cope with any of the extracurricular stuff that was being thrown at me. I needed to find a solution. Without realising it, I began to find solace in alcohol … I just found that drinking made me a much more confident and fun person to be around – and someone I liked.'

Back home in England, Smith had never been a big drinker, she was too focused on her football. But at Seton Hall she made friends, and there always seemed to be a party going on somewhere. 'It started off as a bit of fun', she says, 'I was away from my parents, I was young and there was an opportunity to drink every night if you wanted to take it. So it slowly got into a habit for me.'

It was not long before the 'fun' and social aspect of Smith's drinking disappeared. Instead of saving her boozing for parties, Smith started delving into the stocks of cheap beer in her dormitory fridge as soon as her classes were finished for the day, sinking can after can as fast as she could. She'd drink from late afternoon through to the evening, when she would either accompany others to a bar or stay in the dorm, drinking. In her 2012 autobiography, Smith wrote: 'It could go on for six or seven hours a night … The whole thing became a routine. I didn't know any different than to wake up at college with a hangover. I would simply drink a pint of water and go about my business.'

Somehow, she managed to keep her training going and stay in reasonable shape, and when the season started up once again Smith was able to curb her drinking, for the most part. As long as playing football was fuelling her confidence she did not feel the same need to go searching for the relaxed, outgoing Kelly who emerged after a few beers.

The following two seasons saw Smith top the scoring tables in the Big East conference and all of the NCAA (the National College Athletic Association, which oversees sports and athletic championships at colleges and universities across the United States), with tallies of 25 and 22 goals respectively. The accolades flooded in: Smith was twice named the Big East Offensive Player of the Year. In her first season she was NCAA Rookie of the Year and NCAA Offensive Player of the Year in her third.

Seton Hall Pirates' results improved too, with the team finishing higher up the table than they ever had done before the arrival of the 'English soccer star'. By the time Smith's university days were over, she had made such an impression that her number 6 shirt was retired in her name – no other female footballer at Seton Hall had ever received the same honour. Smith calls it one of her proudest accomplishments: 'Only two other women in the history of Seton Hall have ever had their numbers retired and I am the first one not to play basketball … My number 6 banner which says 'Kelly Smith – Soccer' hangs in the basketball arena at the university and will be there forever.'

Smith had reached another crossroads in her career. Should she stay in the US, and hope that whispers she'd heard about the planned launch of a professional league for women turned into something concrete? Or should she return to England, where she had a verbal agreement with Vic Akers that there would always be a place for her in the Arsenal Ladies team?

For Smith, the answer was simple. She only needed to look at the relative strengths of the England and USA national sides to know where she stood a better chance of making a living from the sport she loved. If a professional women's league was ever going to happen, then the odds were massively in favour of it happening on that side of the Atlantic, and Smith wanted to ensure she would be in prime position to be a part of it.

For the time being, Smith made a living as the assistant coach at Seton Hall, and played football part time for the New Jersey Lady Stallions. Staying in the USA meant that Smith had a front-row seat (figuratively speaking) to the 1999 Women's World Cup which took place across the country that summer, and which the home team won, after an intense final against China. At the Pasadena Rose Bowl in California, some 90,185 fans watched, enthralled by the drama as the World Cup Final was decided via a penalty shoot-out.

When the USA team emerged victorious, scoring five penalties to China's four, the nation went women's soccer crazy. 'I enjoyed watching how much the US public took to the women's team', says Smith. 'I saw these women become household names overnight'. She had been in the stands for the opening game of that World Cup between USA and Denmark, and could not help feeling frustrated at the fact England had not qualified (they had reached the quarter finals in 1995 when Smith was on the fringes of the squad, but would not qualify again until the 2007 tournament).

'I was sitting there with gritted teeth thinking, this could be us. I could be on that pitch playing against these teams. I guess there was a bit of angst that we weren't good enough to qualify at that stage.' Nevertheless, in a stadium that was full of 80,000 people, Smith knew that right in front of her eyes, something special was happening to the women's game.

When the world's first professional soccer league for women – the Women's United Soccer Association (WUSA) – was founded in February of the following year, Smith felt proud that her nervous, 18-year-old self had made the right decision to leave home. 'I was in the right place at the right time. I had put myself in that situation by going to college and making a name for myself out there. Everyone knew Kelly Smith, the England player from Seton Hall.'

She was one of many top players from all over the world to be approached by the new league and asked if she wanted to put her name forward for the draft. Obviously, she said yes: 'I wanted to be a part of it. It was what I had always wanted.'

KICKING OFF

Smith was picked up by her first-choice team, Philadelphia Charge. She'd chosen them because it was the closest club to New Jersey where she had made a few close friends, and she wanted to stay on the East coast because it meant a short flight back to the UK when she needed it.

When the league launched in 2001 it was made up of eight teams featuring 160 of the world's best players, all of whom were being paid to play football. It was a $100 million set up that was unprecedented in women's sports with Smith the only representative from England in the league for its inaugural season. Not that she cared. Life at Philadelphia Charge was exactly what Smith had dreamed of: 'Waking up, going to training in the morning, not having to do college work or a job. I was loving life out there.'

A sell-out crowd of 15,000 gathered for the team's first game in April 2001. As Smith stood on the pitch alongside her teammates listening to the American national anthem blast out of the stadium speakers, she felt herself welling up. 'It was my debut as a professional athlete and I couldn't stop myself from thinking, "Wow, my dream has come true" … it all meant so much to me.'

The dream continued as Philadelphia went on to win the game 2-0, with Smith involved in both goals. She was brought down for the penalty that led to the first and scored the second, all of which was broadcast live on television. It was so far removed from anything Smith had ever experienced playing in England. She was playing on a huge stage, in a professional environment and she was getting paid for the pleasure.

Throughout that first season the crowds remained large, levelling out at 10–12,000 per game. The players became well known, finding themselves stopped in the streets and at the supermarket by fans wanting an autograph or a chat. The gap between women's football in England and women's soccer in America was increasing – and it left Smith burning with frustration whenever she flew home to fulfil her international duties.

'I would come back and want to experience what I had in America – the attention, the exposure, the limelight. But it was flipped. What was happening in England was the reverse of what was happening in America. I would play for my country and there would hardly be anybody at the game.'

It wasn't just her diminished profile that fuelled Smith's despondency with the English game. While the national team was showing signs of marginal improvement, having qualified for the 2001 European Championships – their first major tournament since 1995 – Smith was painfully aware of the differences between her England teammates and those in Philadelphia. 'Our training sessions at Philadelphia were so intense. Every day, everyone was giving 110 per cent on the field and I had picked up that mentality too, to always give it my all in training. I didn't see the same with England. In terms of attitude, training methods and application, there was a real gulf between the two.

'Some players in training with England weren't putting it all in or just weren't concentrating. It was little things, like as soon as you'd finished drinking from your water bottle [with Philadelphia] it was expected you would run straight onto the pitch, but in England some players would stand there talking. Those things are about adding professionalism to the game, and England was lacking that because the players hadn't had it with their clubs. I had seen that side of the game and tried to bring it into my situation with England, but it really wasn't working.'

At the European Championships in Germany in 2001, England faced a tough task just to get out of their group. Up against Germany, Sweden and Russia, Hope Powell's side opened their tournament with a hard-fought 1-1 draw against Russia, but were then well beaten by Sweden and Germany, conceding a total of seven goals without reply. Smith's impact on the global stage would have to wait.

Back in Philadelphia, her first season ended with a place on the Women's United Soccer Association Global Eleven All Star Team. Proof, if needed that despite her country's own failings at elite level, Smith belonged among the world's best footballers. Further evidence came when she was named as captain for the 2002 season – a responsibility she relished, scoring four goals and contributing three assists in the first seven games of the season.

These highs made it all so much harder for Smith to deal with when the low suddenly hit. It happened during a match against the Bay Area CyberRays when, with the ball at her feet, Smith twisted her body to put a cross into the box. But while her body moved, her knee stayed where it was. A loud 'pop' followed by excruciating pain in her right knee was all the evidence Smith needed to know that she had suffered a serious injury.

Her anterior cruciate ligament was completely torn: 'It was flapping around in there', she says of what was her first serious injury. After surgery to repair the ligament, Smith faced two more new experiences. First there was the recovery period – when she was hobbling around on crutches and lying in bed with her leg strapped into a machine that would slowly move her leg as she tried to sleep. This was followed by months of rehabilitation, when Smith worked on building the muscles in her right leg back up to the level needed to play professional football.

'Everyone knows an ACL injury means you're out for 6-9 months', says Smith. 'It was devastating. I would watch the Philadelphia games on crutches. That was tough to deal with mentally. One minute I was a big part of the team, the next I was out of the game and out of the team's plans.

'But I was determined to come back in a record amount of time and I was prepared to do anything possible to do that. I was working with the physiotherapist three times a day, and after five months I got myself back running. I was proud of that. I didn't have football, all I had was rehab so I was going to give everything to that.'

After a long, hard summer of fitness and rehabilitation work in Philadelphia, Smith felt in prime condition for the start of the 2003 season – one she believed was going to be a big one for her. 'I was in really good shape, probably the fittest I had ever been in the US … Here was my opportunity to prove myself as the footballer I knew I could be, in the best and biggest women's football league in the world.'

Her return lasted all of one and a half matches. During the second match of the campaign against New York Power, Smith went up for a header with New York player Shannon Boxx. As she came down, Boxx accidentally swiped at Smith's right knee, and she knew it was bad straight away. A scan later confirmed it – she had a torn cartilage and bruising on the bone. When the surgeon told Smith it would be five months before she could play again, a gaping chasm suddenly opened up in front of her. Five more months without football. Five more months of long, lonely hours in rehab. Five more months of watching her teammates get on with life without her.

'It affected me badly', says Smith. 'Mentally it was so tough to be out again. It's a hard thing for people on the outside to comprehend what it's like, being on the sidelines by yourself, doing everything by yourself, seeing your teammates together and not feeling a part of that. All the strength I had shown during the months of rehabilitation after my ACL injury now seemed to evaporate.'

Without football, Smith found herself turning to alcohol once again, both as a means of filling the void and of numbing the physical and mental pain she was in. Most of the time she was drinking on her own, replacing the cheap cans of beer from her university days with the harder stuff that went down even quicker. At this stage Smith says she retained a semblance of control over her drinking, but it was the beginning of a dark and dangerous road.

In the summer of 2003, the Women's World Cup returned to America (China had been the planned hosts but the outbreak of the SARS virus caused the tournament to be moved). England had failed to qualify yet again, but Smith was asked to be involved as part of the BBC's coverage, interviewing players and presenting some of the programming. It was a positive break for her as she left Philadelphia and the monotony of rehab behind her for a trip to California where the USA team was in a training camp.

While she was there, news filtered through that the WUSA was in serious financial strife and in danger of closing down. 'It was a total shock', says Smith, 'especially as it folded just before the World Cup. There had been no hint whatsoever this was going to happen. Then once the rumours started it was all over very quickly.

'I woke up one morning and it was there, and I went to bed at night and it was all gone. I couldn't comprehend that. The day had started with me as a professional footballer and ended with my dream job gone and me out of work.'

After three seasons the WUSA had made reported losses of $100million – money they were never going to make back. They were left with only one option: To pull the plug. The hope was that another World Cup success might help to salvage something, but the USA finished third behind Germany and Sweden. The majority of the country shrugged and moved on with their lives.

For the players, there was little choice but to do the same. Smith and many of her WUSA colleagues opted to play in the semi-professional W League, with England's finest export joining the New Jersey Wildcats. The season started perfectly, with the Wildcats winning all of their first eight games. And then lightning struck, for a third time. In the ninth game of the season against Western Mass Lady Pioneers, Smith was caught by a reckless tackle from opposition defender Cindi Walsh. 'She came straight in on my standing leg two-footed', recalls Smith. 'The crack on impact told me everything.' Smith's leg was broken. Hot tears flowed down her face as she confronted the thought of yet another season on the sidelines.

She did her rehab work for a couple of hours a day, but after that Smith would return to an empty house and drink away her pain. 'I was getting drunk to block out the reality of a situation I could not deal with', she wrote in her autobiography. 'I used vodka to obliterate my sad life. But my life got sadder as a result. It quickly spiralled out of all control.'

This time the drinking continued even when she got back to training and was feeling the endorphins starting to buzz around her body once again. This time she felt a desperate need to drink. Without alcohol she became anxious, and the cravings took hold so badly that she would give in and get drunk. The self-hatred that followed the next morning was all part of a vicious circle in which Smith found herself trapped, with no idea how to escape.

Her saving grace came when she broke down during one of her telephone calls home with her dad. He flew out to Philadelphia and took her home, ending a seven-year stay that had yielded so much promise, but delivered one too many knock-out blows. At 25 years old, Smith moved back in with her parents, adamant that her days of playing football were over: 'I was done with football. I didn't want to play again. Didn't want to kick a ball again. I had got myself so far in a funk I didn't know how to get out of it. I hated football.

'It was the lowest point of my life. At times I didn't really want to be here. I thought about committing suicide. I hated my life.'

Smith continued drinking even after moving home, hiding the true extent of it from her parents. But there was one person from whom she could not hide it – England manager, Hope Powell. Not long after her return from America, Smith was due to meet up with the England medical team in Loughborough so they could assess her recovery. She arrived at the camp 'pissed out of her face', after stopping off at a bar for a few vodkas en route, and it did not take long for the news of her sozzled state to filter through to the England manager.

'I think Hope had a history with alcohol addiction in her family so she knew the signs', says Smith. 'I told her how I was feeling and how much I was drinking and she said: "If you want help, we'll get you the help you need." If it hadn't been for her, my football career would probably have ended in 2004. I may not even be here today without Hope. That's how bad things had got.'

Facing up to Powell was the wake-up call Smith needed. Suddenly she realised that yes, she did need help. Two stints in rehab followed, first at The Priory, where after two and a half painful weeks she decided it was not the right place for her, and then at the Sporting Chance clinic founded by former Arsenal and England captain, Tony Adams. It was here that Smith started to find her way back, and with the addition of regular attendance at AA meetings, life gradually became easier to handle without the need for alcohol.

It was towards the end of 2004 that Smith picked up the phone to hear Vik Akers on the other end of the line. She was out of rehab but he knew that she was some way off returning to the game. As Smith says: 'I had no desire even to watch football at that point.' Even so, the Arsenal Ladies boss would call her regularly, just for a chat at first. Gradually, Akers started to gently nudge Smith towards playing, suggesting she come along to a training session: 'Just come down, bring your boots and have a kickabout.'

Akers' gentle persistence gradually wore away at Smith's reluctance. Eventually, she succumbed and re-joined her old Arsenal teammates for some of their training sessions. 'That's how I fell back in love with the game again. Just running around and getting the endorphins going, chasing a ball and playing again. It took a while, but after a few weeks of joining in with training my fitness had improved and I felt like I was actually ready to do this again.'

Having suffered three major injuries in swift succession, Smith admits that the fear of picking up another was 'always there, in the back of my mind. It's hard to get away from it. But once I got out there and started enjoying myself again – scoring goals and helping the team win – I would just get lost in that moment.'

Smith re-signed with Arsenal in early 2005. Over the next four years she made 112 appearances and scored 100 goals (in all competitions), helping the team to reinforce their dominance of the women's game in England. In her second season back, the club achieved something no other British team had managed when they added the UEFA Women's Cup trophy to their collection. 'It was amazing for Arsenal', says Smith, looking back at the 2006–7 season that remains the most successful in the club's history (they were unbeaten in the league and also won the FA Women's Cup and the FA Women's Premier League Cup that year). 'The average age of the squad was quite young, but a lot of the players were high-level internationals that really wanted to work hard.

'We played some really good football at that time. Vic [Akers] put the belief into us that we were world beaters and we went into pretty much every game knowing we'd win because of the talent we had in the squad.'

If there was one negative point to emerge from that season, it was that Smith could not play in the UEFA Cup final. This time it was not injury that kept her off the pitch but a suspension, earned in the first leg of the semi-final against Danish side, Brondby. Smith had put Arsenal 1-0 up when she was booked during the second half for kicking the ball away, and scored her second after Brondby equalised, putting Arsenal 2-1 ahead. On 60 minutes, the Danes levelled the score again, however. Then, with 12 minutes left to play, Smith made a strong challenge in Arsenal's own half and was sent off, meaning she would miss the second leg of the semi-final and the first leg of the final, if Arsenal made it.

Facing a chorus of boos from the home fans as she trudged off the pitch, Smith instinctively stuck a middle finger up at them – a gesture noted by the fourth official in his match report. It meant that Smith received an additional one-game ban to the two games she would already miss for the sending off, effectively ruling her out for the whole of the final – a match that would have been the biggest club game she had ever played in.

She insists it's not a moment she reflects on with regret, however. 'I felt like I helped the team get to the final so that was a proud moment for me. But obviously my behaviour then wasn't very good. I was quite angry at the referee for sending me off when I didn't think I deserved it. I probably should have controlled my emotions, but me being the hothead that I am on the pitch, I couldn't.'

With Arsenal doing so well on the global stage during that period, it's hardly surprising that the England team started to climb up the world rankings. With the majority of the Arsenal team also playing in Hope Powell's side, the club's success had a knock-on effect that helped lead to England's qualification for the 2007 World Cup – their first appearance at the tournament since 1995.

'We had been trying to qualify for over 10 years and it had become disheartening', says Smith. 'We had come close but would always get two or three injuries to key players which would hinder the team in those qualification games – the squad at that time wasn't very big. The real low point for me was when France beat us in the playoffs for the 2003 World Cup. At that point it felt like we'd never get there as this group of players.

'But in 2006–7 we were on a really good path. In order to qualify automatically [without the need for a playoff] we simply needed to avoid defeat in our last qualification game.' That game happened to be against France again, a team England hadn't beaten since 1974 and who were the favourites to qualify as group winners.

It was a match with added 'bite' given that France had been the team that prevented England from reaching the previous finals in 2003. For Smith, that was an experience that helped the team on this occasion. 'I think all the hurt and disappointment that we'd experienced in the past meant we were a lot more together as a team. We had all experienced that hurt of losing in those big games.

'Standing in the tunnel before we went out on to the pitch and looking in peoples' eyes, you could see they were so focused and determined. I knew then that we would get the result we needed.' A 1-1 draw was indeed enough. 'As the final whistle blew, we felt like we had won the game because we had qualified. We were finally going to a World Cup.'

It was another dream that had come true for Smith, and one that, just a couple of years earlier, she could never have imagined happening. At the tournament in China, England were drawn into Group A alongside Japan, Argentina and the favourites for the trophy, Germany. 'I felt it was my time', says Smith, who arrived in China injury-free and 'absolutely buzzing' about the opportunity to play on the biggest stage in women's football.

England's opening game was against Japan, a team ranked above them and that had been an ever-present at World Cup finals. The pressure was on their opponents to win, then and when Japan took the lead 10 minutes into the second half it seemed that was the likely outcome. With 15 minutes remaining, Smith was moved to centre forward. England needed a goal. Pretty soon, they had it after Smith slotted the ball coolly away into the bottom left-hand corner of the net to level the score.

'My mind went blank. It was a pretty euphoric moment for me. I had just scored my first ever goal at a World Cup and I really didn't know what to do or how to feel.' Filled with elation, Smith took off her left boot that had struck the ball so sweetly and planted a kiss on it before running to the corner of the pitch with it held high. The image of her putting lips to boot was captured by the world's photographers and would lead all the match reports in the international press the following day.

Two minutes after putting her left boot back on, Smith whipped both off after scoring again, giving England a 2-1 lead with seven minutes remaining. England were seconds away from securing three precious points when Japan scored from a free kick, five minutes into injury time. It was, says Smith, a 'heart-wrenching' finish to the game.

Back at the team hotel, Smith's goal-scoring joy would be further diminished when Hope Powell pulled her aside to tell her she was not impressed with the boot-kissing celebrations. 'None of the players had thought anything of it, but apparently the German coach Silvia Neid stirred it up by telling the press I should have been booked because I had taken a piece of kit off, which was a load of crap.

'Hope just told me: "People are going to target you anyway because you're a fantastic player, but doing what you did shows a bit of arrogance and they're going to want to kick you even more." I took her words and said I wouldn't do it again in any other game out of respect for her, but I don't regret doing it. No one has ever done it before and it has left me with great memories.'

England went on to reach the quarter finals where they faced the USA, meaning Smith was facing many of the players she had played both with and against during her time in the States. After holding their own in the first half, Powell's side were well beaten in the second, losing 3-0 to the 1999 champions. It was a disappointment for England but there had been plenty of positive signs – not least the 0-0 draw with Germany in the group stage that meant England had been the only team in the tournament to take any points from the eventual champions, and prevent them from scoring too.

Smith will always think of the 2007 World Cup as her 'best tournament'. She scored four goals and had shown the world that she possessed the skill, pace, movement and power to be considered one of the very best. 'It was the tournament that made me', she says, with a nostalgic smile.

The World Cup boosted the profile of women's football and elevated Smith's too. By 2009 she had been nominated for FIFA's World Player of the Year award four times. That year she achieved her highest placing, finishing third behind Brazil's Marta and Birgit Prinz of Germany – an achievement she labels as one of the proudest of her career.

By the time that glitzy awards gala took place in Zurich, however, Smith was no longer an Arsenal player. In February 2009 she made the decision to return to America after the launch of a second professional league – Women's Professional Soccer (WPS). 'When I came back from Philadelphia I said I would never go back because of my experiences there. I hated America for the way I felt leaving the country, so at first I had no intention of joining the WPS.'

But then things changed. A number of Smith's England teammates were considering making the move, and the more Smith heard about the quality of players who were signing up – including Brazil's Marta (who's considered by many to be the best player the women's game has ever seen), and the USA's Abby Wambach – the more she was tempted. And then there was the money. When her agent followed up the enquiries for Smith from two teams – Boston and Chicago – asking about salaries, the numbers coming back were hard to ignore. In relation to what she was earning at Arsenal, the money was massive.

'It was the chance to be a professional athlete again. Arsenal were still training just two or three times a week. The level of players had changed but in terms of opposition in the league it was still very mismatched. We were still the team winning the league and the FA Cup, and doing it with ease at times. It wasn't as challenging as I'd hoped it would be.'

Smith signed for Boston Breakers, as did her Arsenal teammate Alex Scott, meaning the two of them had a ready-made support network. 'I don't think I would have made the trip to Boston had Alex not been there', says Smith. 'She knew everything that had gone on in my past so she was a big factor in my decision to say yes.'

In her first two seasons in Boston, Smith was named in the WPS All-Star team, finishing fifth and fourth in the league's overall scoring charts at the end of each season. She loved the city too, calling it one of the best places she's ever lived in. But Smith's third season in 2011 was disrupted by injury and then all of a sudden it was over. Once again the league had hit a financial sticking point and in January 2012 it folded, just like its predecessor had done.

'I had figured that the league would learn from the mismanagement of the first league', says Smith. 'They said they had. So when it happened it was a complete shock again. We all thought they had the model, business plan and structure right this time. But again, teams were struggling financially. Some of the players had taken pay cuts in 2011, which should have given us a clue. I just couldn't believe it had happened again. How does this happen twice?'

By this time, Smith had played her part in two more major tournaments. At the 2009 European Championships, England reached their first major final of Hope Powell's tenure but came up against the world champions, Germany. The 6-2 scoreline sounds wider than the game actually was, and, for Smith, the tournament was one that yielded 'delight and disappointment in equal measure'.

At the 2011 World Cup in Germany, England were a far more experienced side than the one had competed on the game's grandest stage in 2007, and to Smith the squad looked even better than the one that had competed at the Euros two years earlier. Hope Powell's side qualified top of their group after recording two wins and one draw from matches against Mexico, Japan and New Zealand. But in the quarter finals they found themselves facing a familiar foe: France.

Smith went into the game nursing an inflamed Achilles after rolling her ankle in the group game against New Zealand. 'It meant I couldn't really train from then on because the more I played the worse it got. The best thing for Achilles injuries is rest, but there really isn't time for that during a tournament.'

In the back of her mind, Smith knew this could be her last World Cup. She was 32 years old and her body had already been through more trauma than most see in a lifetime. There was no way she was going to miss this match for a sore Achilles. England scored first and led for almost half an hour, during which time the pain in Smith's ankle intensified. Before she could do anything about it, however, Powell made England's third and final substitution. It was followed by a French equaliser, meaning Smith would have to play on for at least 30 minutes more.

She spent much of extra time wishing for penalties, believing it to be England's best chance of progressing as France took the momentum in that closing period. She would get her wish. Despite the pain in her ankle – 'I literally couldn't run on it. I felt like I couldn't push off my toe' – Smith had no qualms about stepping up to take the team's first penalty.

'I remember walking up there and seeing all the England fans to the right. It was quite a hostile crowd that day. Everyone was against us. Even the German locals were rooting for France. Normally I like to place the kick but this time I thought, I'm just gonna run up and lace it. Keep my head down and hit the target. Once the ball went in it was pure elation. I knew I hadn't played well in the game with my injury, so I needed to score to help the team.'

England went on to lose the penalty shootout 3-4, with team captain Faye White missing their decisive fifth kick. Despite being unbeaten in the tournament, England were going home. 'It took a good few months to get over it', says Smith. 'After the game a lot of us stayed up to the early hours of the morning. Faye was bawling her eyes out. I just felt sick. As much as we tried not to talk about the game it was hard to avoid it. The next few months were really hard. It was such a low point going out that way. You never really know when you're going to play in another tournament again.'

It wasn't too long though before confirmation came that Great Britain would be allowed to field men's and women's football teams at the London 2012 Olympics. It was a boost, but it also meant that when WPS folded at the start of the Olympic year, Smith knew she had little time to waste in finding a new team. Considering she had been training through the winter at Arsenal in preparation for the 2012 WPS season, it made sense for Smith to re-join the club where she had enjoyed so much success – and one that would give her the chance to play in the recently launched FA Women's Super League.

Just before her return was made official, Smith was part of the England squad that played in the annual friendly tournament, the Cyprus Cup in February 2012. In their semi-final against France she picked up a nasty injury that was initially thought to be bad bone bruising, but when she returned to Arsenal still limping, an X-ray revealed a fracture on the inside of her fibula (the bone that runs alongside your shin bone). When the doctors put her in a walking boot and said she would be back playing in six weeks, Smith breathed a sigh of relief that her season was not over before it had even begun.

But then she made it worse. At a photo shoot to help promote the new FAWSL season a few days after her X-ray, Smith was put in full Arsenal kit and told she would just be doing headers for the camera. Feeling no pain in her leg, Smith decided to take the boot off and have a little kick. 'As soon as I hit that ball I was in so much pain. I knew I had done more damage. The bone was fusing together while it was in the boot, but that motion of turning and striking the ball just cracked the bone even more – it wasn't even a proper football, it was made of foam.

'That put me out for just over three months. Vic Akers was not happy with me, and the fact it was my own doing made it emotionally hard to come to terms with – I had nearly fucked up my chances of making an Olympic team.'

Nearly, but not quite. Smith's name was included in the GB women's football squad when it was announced at the end of June and while she admits that, for her, the Olympic stage will never be as big for women's football as the World Cup, she was excited by the prospect of playing a tournament on home soil.

Her role was limited during London 2012 (because she was not yet fully fit), but Smith cherishes her memories of the tournament. Particularly those from England's match against Brazil in a Wembley Stadium filled with 75,000 fans. 'It's not something I ever imagined I'd get to do. It was amazing to know all those people were there to watch you. It wasn't like there was a men's game on before or after. These people had paid for tickets to watch GB play against Brazil.

'I remember walking out and seeing all the red white and blue colours, people with their faces painted and flags flying, horns blowing. It was quite an overwhelming, emotional thing singing the national anthem and looking up at all those faces – it really was special.'

But the high of that game and the 1-0 victory against Brazil was followed by disappointment just three days later when Team GB lost to Canada in the quarter finals. 'In hindsight I think that game [against Brazil] drained everyone', says Smith. 'I think our players were shot mentally and tired physically going into the game against Canada because certain players hadn't been rested to make sure they were fresh. It's easy to say it now, but if I was Hope Powell doing the Olympics again, I'd rest key players from the Brazil game which we didn't need to win. Yes, they would have been disappointed but it's about winning medals. You can be disappointed that you didn't play but ultimately you'll forget that disappointment if you win a gold medal.'

Powell would come under more scrutiny following England's performance at Smith's final major tournament – the 2013 European Championships in Sweden. 'It was a weird tournament to be a part of,' says Smith 'because it was very disjointed and disconnected. At the time a lot of players felt they should have been playing when they weren't, and there was a lot of bitchiness going on.

'You can never be successful like that if you know that your teammates are angry and thinking they should be playing instead of you. Everyone should be together and united – pulling in the same direction. But it wasn't like that. It felt very cliquey again.'

Asked how that situation had been allowed to develop, Smith says: 'I think across the board it wasn't managed in the right way. A lot of the players felt like it was players versus staff. There was a lot of unhappiness in camp, and you're not going to perform well if you're not happy and enjoying the trip. Our performances showed that.'

England finished bottom of their group, without a single win to their name. 'I think a lot of players couldn't wait to get home', says Smith. While Smith returned to Arsenal to take up a new role as player-coach, Powell's time in the English game was halted abruptly. The FA sacked her the month after the Euro 2013 debacle. 'It was a shock', says Smith, who has remained in touch with the coach she credits with helping her through one of the toughest times of her life. 'She had done so much for the women's game – she was responsible for taking it from nothing to the stage it's at now, really. So I always thought she'd get to leave on her own terms. But that's football though, I suppose.'

Smith would take another 18 months or so to mull over her own England future before deciding to end her 20-year relationship with international football. It had brought her immense pride, it had helped her to overcome obstacles that had seemed insurmountable, and it had ensured her legacy as one of the greatest female footballers of all time.

Smith remains at Arsenal where she is studying for her coaching badges, with the plan to remain involved with football for as long as she can: 'Whether that's coaching, management or whatever – I just want to stay in the game.' It's a game that she has seen make massive strides in the time since she was kicking a ball around with a team of boys, but it's one that she believes can still get better, with the right structure and support: 'I would love to see every team become pretty much full time. At the minute, there are players and teams in the FAWSL who are still working in jobs and are playing semi-professionally while Manchester City players are full time and most of our [Arsenal] players are full-time. So, there is a bit of a mismatch in terms of professionalism.'

Smith also says that teams in the Women's Super League could be playing in bigger stadiums and on better quality pitches that they currently are. Having watched closely throughout much of her career as Hope Powell battled to take women's football forward one painfully small step at a time in England, it's clear that Kelly Smith is primed – and almost ready – to continue the fight.

5: Just rewards?

When a 2014 survey by BBC Sport revealed that men receive more prize money than women in 30 per cent of sports, it was hardly a surprise. In fact for many, the most shocking aspect of the survey will have been that 70 per cent of sports *are* providing parity.

Facts and figures aside, the report achieved an important outcome: It encouraged people to think and talk about what sports women earn – or in some cases do not earn – for competing at elite level. It led to debates between columnists in national newspapers and was discussed on television, but it always ended with the same simple conclusion: It's complicated.

Of course, prize money is just one part of the intricate jigsaw that makes up women's sport, but along with salary, it is a revealing measure in the fight for equality. When Billie Jean King secured equal prize money for female tennis players at the US Open in 1973, she gave women's tennis a head start of many years on other women's sports. Most sportswomen wouldn't have dared to dream they could earn the same amount of money as their male colleagues at that time.

'Billie Jean just pushed the clock forward, she sped up the process', explains Martina Navratilova – herself a winner of 18 Grand Slam singles titles. 'Any progress is measured by jumps, and that [securing equal prize money at the US Open] was one of those jumps that allowed us to move forward as women athletes and to make a career out of it so it wasn't just a hobby.'

Even so, it took another 34 years before the fight for equality that King started was eventually finished. 'It took decades of effort', says former WTA chairman Stacey Allaster, who was President of the women's tour in 2007, when the French Open and Wimbledon joined the Australian and US Opens in offering equal prize money.

'We launched a public opinion campaign in France and Britain. We presented the data that showed our sponsorship revenues were very strong. We had a strong political campaign in business leaders like Richard Branson. Tessa Jowell, the Minister of Sport in Britain, was able to get Tony Blair on the House of Commons floor to say that Wimbledon should pay equal prize money. But our ace was Venus Williams.'

On Friday 1 July 2005, Venus Williams should have been preparing to take on the world Number 1, Lindsay Davenport, in the following day's Wimbledon final. Instead, the American was sitting in the boardroom at the All England Club alongside the women's tennis chief, Larry Scott and members of the Grand Slam Committee. The group of all-male businessmen, and one woman, was gathered for their customary annual meeting. But the presence of one of the world's top players in the room – particularly one that was due to play for her third Wimbledon title in 24 hours' time – suggested this was going to be an annual gathering with a difference.

The topic up for discussion was no secret. Williams had been leading the fight for equal pay in women's tennis at the Grand Slam events since she was 18, making her first statement at Wimbledon in 1998 when she said: 'I think in the Grand Slam events, it should be equal pay, and I think the ladies should do something about it instead of just accepting it for years to come.'

Back in the All England Club boardroom though, no one knew what Venus Williams was going to say that they hadn't already heard before. Williams sat tall and poised in her chair, composed herself and asked everybody in the room to close their eyes.

'Imagine you're a little girl', Williams began. 'You're growing up. You practise as hard as you can, with girls, with boys. You have a dream. You fight, you work, you sacrifice to get to this stage. You work as hard as anyone you know. And then you get to this stage, and you're told you're not the same as a boy. Almost as good, but not quite the same. Think how devastating and demoralising that could be.'

The room was captivated and listened intently as Williams spoke. 'It was one of the most stunning, poignant, powerful moments I've ever experienced in a business meeting', said the WTA Chairman, Scott. But it wasn't enough. The following February, Scott received a phone call from the powers that be at Wimbledon telling him that while the women's prize fund would be increased for that year's Championships, it would still not be as much as the men's.

With the women now 93 per cent of the way towards earning the same as the men, senior leaders in the WTA and Williams decided it was time to turn up the heat on the All England Club. On the eve of Williams's first match at the 2006 tournament, when she would begin her fight to win a fourth Wimbledon singles title, Williams published an essay in *The Times* under the headline: 'Wimbledon has sent me a message: I'm only a second-class champion.'

After opening with a provocative question, 'Have you ever been let down by someone that you had long admired, respected and looked up to?', Williams expressed her disappointment that the home of tennis was sending a message to women across the world that they are inferior.

'I believe that athletes – especially female athletes in the world's leading sport for women – should serve as role models. The message I like to convey to women and girls across the globe is that there is no glass ceiling. My fear is that Wimbledon is loudly and clearly sending the opposite message … It diminishes the stature and credibility of such a great event in the eyes of all women.'

Williams recalled and then dispelled every reason that the All England Club had put forward for maintaining the discrepancy, starting with the most commonly uttered reason why women should earn less than men: Men play a best-of-five-sets game, and therefore work harder for their money than women, who only play three sets.

It's a perk of the scoring system that dates back to the earliest days of Grand Slam tennis in the late 1800s. While the first Wimbledon tournament took place in 1877 (it's the oldest slam of the four), there was no women's event until 1884, when Maud Watson beat her older sister Lilian in three sets. At that time, it was considered too physically taxing for women to play a best-of-five-sets match, as the men did. But Audrey Snell, a librarian at the All England Club, remarks that even then this was a dubious claim, given that Maud Watson had won the Irish Ladies' Championship in a best-of-five-sets match in the very same year that she became Wimbledon Champion.

Wimbledon's precedent didn't stop the US women's singles championships from being played to five sets between 1891 and 1901. But that came to an abrupt halt in 1902, when the United States Lawn Tennis Association (led by an all-male team), decided that the five-set format was too strenuous for women. Despite protests from the leading players of the day, the women's US championships (now the US Open) and the other Grand Slams have been best of three ever since.

The WTA did introduce five set matches back into the women's game in 1984 though, when they made the finals of the end-of-year Championships a five-set affair. The theory at the time was that the extra sets would give fans more time to see Martina Navratilova – who at the time was blasting opponents off the court in less than an hour. But it had a different effect: 'Making the matches longer didn't increase excitement', wrote Chris Chase in the *New York Times* in 2013. 'When the matches were blowouts, the additional set was like adding 30 minutes to a bad movie. When the matches are close, the importance of early points is diminished.' I'd argue that's a statement that's as applicable to the men's game as it is to the women's, but the WTA clearly agreed, reverting to the best-of-three format in 1999.

In her *Times* article, Venus Williams explained that the women would be happy to play five-set matches at Grand Slam events ('Tim Phillips, the chairman of the All England Club, knows this and even acknowledged that women players are physically capable of this'). She also pointed to the set-up of Grand Slam tournaments which means that men and women are competing on the same stage, at the same time: 'So in the eyes of the general public', wrote Williams, 'the men's and women's games have the same value.'

Williams's final counter to the five-set argument is that the money athletes earn doesn't depend on the amount of time they spend competing (if it did, that might be the only time you'd ever see Usain Bolt run further than 200m). 'Athletes are also entertainers', says Williams, 'we enjoy huge and equal celebrity, and are paid for the value we deliver to broadcasters and spectators, not the amount of time we spend on the stage. And, for the record, the ladies' final at Wimbledon in 2005 lasted 45 minutes longer than the men's. No extra charge.'

The difference in prize money at the previous year's Wimbledon tournament had amounted to £456,000 – 'less than was spent on ice cream and strawberries in the first week'. For an event that made £25 million profit in the same year, the refusal to create equal prize funds could hardly be about cash, wrote Williams: 'It can only be trying to make a social and political point, one that is out of step with modern society.'

If the chairman of the All England Club (AELTC) wasn't cringing by this point, he will have been after reading Williams's final sentence: 'It's a shame that the name of the greatest tournament in tennis, an event that should be a positive symbol for the sport, is tarnished.' Ouch.

Williams failed to make an impact on the court at Wimbledon that year, losing in the third round to Serbia's Jelena Jankovic, but her words in *The Times* left a lasting impression. Tessa Jowell, then-Secretary of State for Culture, Media and Sport, wrote to the All England Club to express her dismay with their stance and the issue was raised in Parliament where then-Prime Minister Tony Blair said that he 'fully endorsed' equal pay.

'Nobody knew the piece would be so powerful', reflects Williams. 'It was just about really trying to express what it felt like to be treated unequally', she said. 'It just took on its own life.'

A few months before the 2007 Wimbledon tournament, Williams picked up the phone to hear the plummy tones of All England Club Chairman Tim

Phillips on the line. When he informed her that the women's singles champion at Wimbledon that year would receive the same prize money as her male counterpart, she let out a victorious scream. Perhaps she had a sneaky feeling even then that she would be the one picking up the cheque after winning her fourth singles title at SW19. But personal victories aside, Williams was simply happy that a discrepancy she believed was 'diminishing the years of hard work that women on the tour have put into becoming professional tennis players' had finally been erased.

That was not the end of the debate, though. Really, it was only the beginning. Ever since women's tennis established itself as a pioneer in terms of sporting equality, it has needed to defend that stance over and over again, particularly as the men's game entered what many believe to be a 'golden era'.

Roger Federer, Rafael Nadal, Novak Djokovic, and Britain's Andy Murray have taken men's tennis to levels never seen before – at least, not so consistently over such a lengthy period of time. There have been many 'greats' in men's tennis before, but to have four of them dominating the men's tour at the same time for so long is something truly exceptional. Consider this: prior to the men's singles final at the 2014 US Open, at least one member of the 'big four' had contested every Grand Slam final for the previous nine years.

By comparison, the women's game has often appeared like a flimsier link in the sport's armoury. It was a point French player Gilles Simon attempted to make in 2012, when he told a French radio station that the men deserved to earn more prize money than the women. 'I think that men's tennis is really ahead of women's tennis at this stage', said the newly elected ATP player council member, and a veteran of 10 years on the men's tour. 'Once more, the men spent surely twice as much time on the court at the women at the French Open ... Meanwhile, men's tennis remains more attractive than women's tennis at this moment.'

His comments provoked an immediate backlash from the likes of (then world number one) Maria Sharapova and Serena Williams, with the former saying: 'I'm sure there are a few more people that watch my matches than his', and Williams agreeing, in her own unique way: 'She's way hotter than he is, so more people will watch Maria.'

When asked to clarify his thoughts in a press conference a few days later, Simon stood firm, claiming that equal pay 'just doesn't work in the entertainment [business], because entertainment is not about being a man or a woman. It's just about the public coming to watch you or not.

'If women's tennis is more interesting than men's tennis, if the price of the women's final is higher than the price of the men's final, they will deserve to win more money than us.'

Simon's arguments had been made before, but rarely by a current, high-profile male player and almost never in front of a pack of reporters hungry for headlines. The Frenchman's initial comment about the length of time the male players spent on court at the French Open compared to the female players is the same one that Venus Williams addressed in her article in *The Times*. Players aren't, and have never been, paid by the hour. If they were, it would merely punish those who wrap up their victories in straight sets.

As Venus Williams also pointed out, many players on the women's tour have said they have no problem with playing five-set matches in Grand Slams, like their male counterparts. But the fact is that it's unlikely to ever actually happen. Why? 'You would have to ask them', said WTA chief, Stacey Allaster, referring to the governing body of world tennis, the International Tennis Federation, which sanctions the four slams.

In 2013 it was Britain's own Andy Murray who became the latest player to call for equal match lengths for men and women. When Allaster was asked to comment on his views she told the media that players on the women's tour were 'ready, willing and able' to play five-set matches. The problem, she said was that doing so would create a logistical nightmare for tournaments: 'It's already challenging [scheduling] the Grand Slams with [men's] five-set matches. For us, we think three sets works well for our fans, and as we look at the consumption of sport it's being done in shorter form.'

Indeed, in an interesting twist on the debate, tennis legend Martina Navratilova has often called for men's matches to be reduced. The best-of-three format, says Navratilova would help guard against injuries and prolong the careers of players like Nadal and Djokovic, highlighting the fact that most matches are now played on hard, unforgiving surfaces (the clay and grass court seasons amount to a tiny proportion of the entire tennis season), and that players put 'a lot more hours in' than they used to.

'Everybody hits the ball harder, you have to run harder, plus the courts are slower so the rallies take longer. This has to take its toll on the body. You play a long match and it takes you months to recover. It's like running a marathon in sprints, but then sometimes you have to go out and play a match the next day or two days later.'

Where Simon's argument becomes more complex is when economics are brought into play. Television rights and gate receipts for Grand Slam tournaments are driven by the combined attraction of seeing the world's best men and women compete for major honours. So, how can one say with any certainty how much of that revenue is driven by the men and how much by the women?

At Wimbledon for example, tickets are allocated via a ballot, so you have no choice in which matches you'll be watching or even what court you'll be on. Even once you have your ticket, you don't know which players you'll get to see until the order of play is released the day before you attend. It's similar at the other three slams, where you buy tickets to a particular court on a particular day – beyond that, the matches you see are mostly in the lap of the scheduling gods.

There are exceptions to this though, as once the tournament reaches the latter stages, tickets are designated as men's or women's semi-finals and finals. In these cases the prices of the men's matches are always higher than for the women's.

This is evidence of the additional commercial clout of men's tennis, says *The Times* journalist and author, Matthew Syed, who wrote about the topic the day after the BBC's survey on equal prize money was published. He went on to call the awarding of equal pay across all four slams 'illogical', claiming: 'It is no more coherent than paying Steph Houghton, the captain of Manchester City's Women's team, the same as Sergio Aguero [top striker for the Manchester City men's team].'

It is a tad disingenuous to compare the sports of tennis and football, given that women's football was played entirely by amateurs until a few years ago, while the men's game is a multi-million-pound monster of an industry. But this misjudgement aside, does Syed have a point when he says that 'depriving Roger Federer of income by handing it to female players is not far from daylight robbery'?

Tennis writer Ian Dorward compares tennis to golf, a sport that holds the major men's and women's events separately. 'The major men's championships in golf generate significantly higher revenue than the equivalent major women's championships. As a result, there is significantly higher prize money for the men compared with the women. It is simple economics – if you generate more revenue, there is greater scope for prize money.'

That heightened prize money in men's golf championships filters right the way down, too. It means that while tennis player Tomas Berdych earned $3,899,534 for his efforts in 2014 – a year in which his ranking never dropped lower than seventh in the world – that same amount of prize money would only have ranked him as the 16th highest earner on golf's PGA Tour that year. So it seems that keeping the men's and women's events separate means that male golfers get to share around a bigger pot of money than their racket-wielding equivalents.

The difference is also reflected in Forbes' annual list of the highest earners in sport. While a whopping seven of the 10 highest-paid female athletes in the world in 2015 were tennis players (including the top three), only Federer featured on the equivalent men's list from the men's tennis fraternity.

Syed's suggestion of 'daylight robbery' remains difficult to tally with a player who earned more than nine million dollars in prize money in 2014 alone. But his assertion that regular events on the men's tour attract more commercial revenue and bigger audiences than WTA events of a similar standing is one most people would readily accept.

And according to Dorward, it holds true: 'At men's only events' he writes, 'almost every revenue stream is higher than at women's only events. There are significantly more spectators at the men's events than there are at the women's events. To ensure that there is no bias due to location, if we compare the tournaments where men's and women's events are held, but in separate weeks, the same outcome is present. Similarly, the TV rights and overall coverage for men's tournaments are more expensive and extensive than for women's tournaments, and the sponsorship shows the same trend.'

All of the above seems to support Gilles Simon's argument that at present, men's tennis is driving bigger audiences and revenues than women's tennis, and thus it should be the male players who receive more prize money, even at events where the men and women compete alongside one another. Separate out the men's and women's tournaments at Wimbledon, for example, says Dorward, and 'it would be highly unlikely that the women's tournament would generate sufficient revenue to cover the prize money that is currently on offer. On the flip side, based on scaling up similar figures at other men's only tournaments, the men's tournament would almost certainly be able to cover the cost.'

What this argument overlooks, though, is that sport operates in cycles. Ask any football fan who witnessed the Spanish national team turn from all-conquering heroes into relative has-beens in the time it took to move from one World Cup (2010: champions) to the next (2014: exited at the group stage after winning just one match).

At present, a Grand Slam final between two of the so-called 'big four' is one of the hottest tickets in sport, let alone in tennis. But it won't always be so. At the turn of the century the women's game was leading the way entertainment-wise. The Williams sisters, Martina Hingis, Lindsay Davenport and Monica

Seles offered what many considered to be a more enjoyable alternative to the serve-and-volley game deployed by many of the top men at the time.

In recent years the WTA has suffered from an absence of the star names that littered the top 10 in the late 1990s and early 2000s, while the men's game has benefited from the prolonged dominance of four special players. Their almost constant presence in the closing stages of Grand Slams means that even the most casual of tennis observers is willing to pay for the opportunity to watch them compete. And with spectators certain of seeing at least one – and usually two – of the sport's biggest names play live, ticket prices for men's finals at the biggest events have sky-rocketed.

This can be seen in the resale prices of debentures at Wimbledon. Those who pay for Centre Court debentures at Wimbledon receive a ticket for a seat on Centre Court for each day of the Championships, but these are freely transferrable so holders can sell them on, making them a good indicator of how much people are willing to pay to watch certain matches.

The 2011 Wimbledon tournament saw two new champions crowned in Petra Kvitova and Novak Djokovic. Debenture tickets for the women's final between Petra Kvitova (playing in her first ever Grand Slam final) and Maria Sharapova (a three-time Grand Slam champion, including once at Wimbledon) were selling for £650. For the men's final between Djokovic (already a two-time Grand Slam champion) and Rafael Nadal (winner of 10 major titles at that time, including two at Wimbledon), debenture tickets were going for £2,900.

If the WTA was making its case for equal prize money in the current climate, with Serena and Venus Williams closer to the end of their careers than the beginning, and Sharapova the only other bona fide superstar name in the game (at present), their arguments for equal prize money might not possess the same clout. But the WTA isn't fighting that battle now, because it already won it in 2007. Can you imagine the lengthy discussion and debate that would be required if the levels of prize money between men and women needed to be adjusted with every 'changing of the guard' in the sport?

It was smart negotiating on the part of the WTA. As Allaster said, they had their 'ace' in Venus Williams and she fulfilled that role brilliantly, meaning that rightly or wrongly, equal pay at the biggest events in tennis will endure. Not everyone will agree with it: 'It is anathema to any concept of fairness', wrote Matthew Syed in *The Times*. But for those who see beyond the facts and figures and understand that the 'market forces' and 'free-market economics' used to argue against equal pay are themselves part of the vicious cycle that is preventing most women's sports from achieving parity, equal pay will always constitute the epitome of fairness.

Tennis occupies a rare space in terms of women's sports, however, and while equal pay is feasible for a sport that has allowed female athletes to compete as professionals since the 1970s, it is not necessarily right for one that is only just beginning the journey.

Cricket considers itself to be one such sport. The BBC's survey revealed that the winning team in the men's Cricket World Cup (2011) earned £2,500,000 while the champions of the female equivalent (which was Australia in 2013) pocketed just £47,000. On the surface, this seems to be yet another example of women's sport being told it is 'second class', in the words of Venus Williams. But others believe it is common sense for a sport that is still in its infancy. 'An absurd proposition' is how Clare Connor, Head of Women's Cricket for the England and Wales Cricket Board (ECB), described the idea of introducing equal prize money to cricket when the BBC report emerged in 2014.

In a blog on the *Guardian*'s website, Connor, who was the England Women's cricket captain from 2000 until 2006, pointed out the large strides made by women's cricket since 2005 – when the International Cricket Council (ICC) became 'responsible' for the women's game. She described how, from a standing start, the sport has been transformed on a global scale in eight and a half years. 'It's a sport that has professional players in some countries, clear pathways for global event qualification, a joint global event with the men [the ICC World Twenty20 tournament], one million participants globally and is fully integrated in terms of governance and strategy at ICC level', wrote Connor.

Despite this progress, Connor says that if the ICC suddenly decided to throw $2million at the women's game to equalise prize money, she would do everything in her power to redirect that money from players' pockets elsewhere. Instead, Connor suggests using it to 'continue to accelerate change, growth, sustainability and driving the profile of women's cricket so that the opportunities in cricket are well and truly equal.'

Connor points out the need for the international schedule to be expanded so that 'teams play more, performance standards rise and the best players become more visible'. She also says that any extra funds could be used to pay those players around the world who at present aren't paid a single penny to represent their country. While England's women became what the ECB proudly claimed was England's 'first group of full-time women's professional cricketers' in February 2014, other countries aren't quite there yet.

Even Australia, whose women's team is considered to be one of the world's best, aren't labelled as fully professional. Although as England pace bowler Anya Shrubsole told the BBC in 2015, that doesn't necessarily mean they aren't playing as though they are: 'Other international teams may not be professional by name, but they train full time, just as we did before we turned professional ... For those first series against India and South Africa after we turned professional, there was greater expectation from the media and from outside that suddenly we were going to blow everyone away, but realistically it's not like that.'

Connor's view on the equal-prize-money debate is echoed by Izzy Westbury, who is Middlesex Women's captain and a contributor to the UK's biggest cricket magazine, *All Out Cricket*. In an article for the magazine's website in 2015, Westbury considered whether the fact that female cricketers at the top level are now fully professional should mean they reap the same rewards as their male counterparts.

'Equal prize money is the final touch to a much bigger argument that needs to be won first', wrote Westbury. 'Targeting this as an area for improvement is a top–down approach. I want to earn the right to that prize money. As far as I know, so do all the other women playing the game.'

Connor and Westbury agree that equal prize money should be one of the final pieces that complete the jigsaw puzzle of women's sport. Introducing it to a sport that is only a quarter of the way there will certainly add to the picture, but it doesn't make structural sense and will likely end badly – with the whole thing having to be taken apart and started again from scratch (when the money runs out).

For renowned sports presenter Clare Balding, the issue of equal prize money actually detracts from the more pressing issue of salaries in women's sport. 'Before we talk about equal prize money I think we should talk about salaries that are worth living on', she says. Unlike equal prize money, this is an area in which the England Women's cricket team are leading the way, with 18 of the country's top players being rewarded with central contracts in May 2014. In the same way as with the men, these contracts are graded in three bands with reports that the top earners are making more than £50,000 a year.

Earning a 'salary worth living on' is a crucial step towards making sure these sportswomen, who are trusted with representing their country, have the support they need to do that as well as they possibly can. They can devote every ounce of their energy to training without having to worry about getting up for a nine to five the next morning. They can throw themselves into their gym sessions without fearing that one muscle strain will mean they won't get paid at the end of the month. They can pack their bags for a warm-weather training trip without having to lose money for taking time off from their 'day job'. It's a luxury enjoyed by a minority of sportswomen.

The ECB Chairman, Giles Clarke (who stepped down in 2015), said it was his wish that the England Women's cricket team would become 'some of the best paid sportswomen in Britain – certainly the best in British women's team sports'. They are certainly up there, but certain members of the England Women's football team can command more, thanks to their ability to top up their national team salary (which can go up to £26,000), with a salary from their club team (which can go up to £35,000).

For England captain Steph Houghton this means she can earn £61,000 a year, without taking into consideration any individual sponsorships she might also be able to command (though at present that's only reported to add another £4,000). But Houghton is one of a very small number of female footballers in England capable of earning such a wage, according to Matthew Buck, an agent who works for the Professional Footballers' Association and represents many of the England squad. 'The majority of centrally contracted players earn about £20,000 from their clubs', he told the BBC, 'but there are players in the Women's Super League who are on as little as £50 a week. Some younger players get their university costs paid for by teams, but many older players need to work second jobs or are also employed in other areas of their clubs.'

In the US, the National Women's Soccer League (NWSL) has been conservative with player salaries – understandably so, given that both previous attempts at establishing a professional women's soccer league failed to achieve any semblance of economic stability. But while female footballers in the UK have struggled to attract major sponsorship deals, some of the USA's star players have been able to attract serious money. Striker Alex Morgan, who was part of the USA's World Cup winning team in 2011 and 2015 (and in between helped them to secure Olympic gold in 2012), reportedly earns $2.8million (£1.8million) from sponsors and endorsements alone. Since bursting onto the international scene in 2011, Morgan's list of sponsors have included Nike, Bank of America, GNC, Mueller, AT&T, GE, Panasonic, and Coca Cola – a list to rival that of GB's athletics golden girl, Jessica Ennis-Hill.

Personal endorsements aside, the salary range for players in America's domestic soccer league has been quoted as varying from $6,000 to $30,000 per year (hardly worth Morgan rolling out of bed for). But when I speak to Jeff

Kassouf, the founder of women's soccer website The Equalizer, he says that most players in the NWSL will never earn anything close to that top figure.

'The $30,000 figure is a little bit deceiving,' says Kassouf, 'because that only applies to a very select few who are national team players and are making that in addition to their national team salaries. The $6,000 figure is obviously very low and unsustainable. But because the season only lasts for five months, the players in that lower bracket will try to take on off-season coaching jobs or run soccer camps or do individual [personal] training. The higher-paid players don't need to do that.'

Kassouf says that while this is not ideal, there is no other option if the league is to survive: 'The NWSL is a start-up focused on controlling costs – something [the first league] WUSA failed miserably at and [the second league] WPS, despite being hyper aware of WUSA's failures, also couldn't master. Player salaries are a massive expense. For now, these are the realities that women's pro soccer players face.'

The realities were similar for the England rugby players who lifted the Women's Rugby World Cup trophy in 2014. In the days following their victory, national newspapers revealed how England's women had juggled their World Cup preparations with working as plumbers, vets, lifeguards and teachers. Less than a week after playing a key role in the triumph, flanker Marlie Packer was filmed by the BBC returning to her day job as a plumber after taking seven weeks of unpaid leave to prepare for the tournament (though some players took as much as three months).

When asked if she would want the option of giving up her job to be a full-time rugby player, Packer told the BBC: 'Of course I would. I'd be stupid not to. I don't think I'd completely give up plumbing but I would like to put it down for a couple of years and be a full-time athlete.'

For Packer, and a further 19 England women rugby players, things were about to change. At the end of August 2014 the RFU announced they were giving full-time contracts to 20 players, including 12 members of the squad that won the World Cup. With rugby sevens included in the Olympics for the first time in 2016, the RFU believed the professional set up would give those England players who made it onto the British team for Rio the best chance of Olympic success.

On the surface, this is excellent progress for women's rugby. But with the RFU refusing to disclose salaries, it is hard to know whether the likes of Packer and her teammates have given up their jobs for something that will leave them financially worse off. The RFU's Head of Women's Performance,

Nicola Ponsford, promised they would 'work with every player to make sure everyone is sorted out financially and can focus on training' and that they want players to 'be able to commit to this without having to worry that they're not going to make ends meet'.

But according to one rugby writer I spoke to, most of the players are earning less than £20,000 per year, which for the majority is certainly less than in their previous jobs. Their contracts are also reviewed on a yearly basis. This fragility means that some have chosen to keep working as and when they can (i.e. when it does not interfere with training and playing commitments) to ensure they have something to fall back on.

This is where the 'real disparity lies', says Balding. 'They've given up jobs as teachers or plumbers to take on a full-time rugby contract that's worth less. They're playing for England – we're not talking about club sport.' The expectation on these players is now immense. England are World Cup winners, and so any time the team plays they are expected to perform to a certain level. Fail to perform and it's the players who will be subject to serious scrutiny, even if the level of support they have been given falls short of what world champions should expect.

Balding believes the important questions when it comes to women's sport are: 'Can you look at it as a professional career? Can you make a living playing elite sport?' Until the answer to these questions is a definitive 'yes', and professional sports women are afforded the opportunity to fulfil their potential without having to squeeze training sessions in around a nine to five, then equal prize money must surely remain of secondary importance to a liveable salary.

While young female athletes entering the worlds of rugby, football and cricket can now at least see that there is the potential for a career in their sport if they reach a certain level, women's cycling (road racing, to be specific) remains a somewhat less attractive prospect. When Britain's 2008 Olympic road race champion Nicole Cooke announced her retirement from cycling in January 2013, she released a powerful statement recounting the highs and lows that punctuated her 17 years on the bike. Under the heading 'Protection for women riders', Cooke expressed her dismay that a women's road racing scene that 'looked so promising when I turned pro in 2002' had 'crumbled' before her eyes.

Female riders are, wrote Cooke, 'exposed and vulnerable'. And she should know. Throughout her own career, Cooke claims that four teams tried not to pay her, leaving her with no other option than to take them to court in order to achieve settlement against a straightforward contract to get the wages she was owed. 'Sometimes you can recoup all of it', Cooke tells me when we meet in

London in late 2014, 'and sometimes it's a percentage. But this was four teams, to a rider who was doing quite well and winning races for those teams'.

In many ways though, Cooke was actually one of the lucky ones. With no minimum wage in place for professional female riders, there are plenty for whom racing can be nothing more than an expensive hobby – even if from the outside they appear to be professional riders, competing for professional teams on a professional tour.

'At a recent development camp in the United States', wrote cycling journalist Matthew Beaudin in January 2015, 'a potential professional racer was told she could expect to make more money as a middling employee at a fast food restaurant. She did not choose to leave her job to race.'

The minimum wage for male UCI World Tour cyclists is set at €35,000 (£27,800/$44,000 approx) per year, but most earn much more than that, with the average salary reported to be €265,000 (£210,500/$323,191 approx) in 2012, according to Ernst & Young. By comparison, the average salary for top-level female pro-riders is reportedly €20,000 (£16,000/$24,565) per year.

'Since there is no minimum,' writes Beaudin, 'it's not uncommon to hear about women racing for airline tickets, team kits, and a few bikes.'

The UCI has come up with various reasons for not enforcing a minimum wage in women's racing over the years. Asked about it in 2011, Pat McQuaid (who at the time was UCI President) said, 'We have an agreement in men's sport, but women's cycling has not developed enough that we are at that level yet.' In a 2014 article for *Cycling News*, Steve Beckett, who is the former Head of Cycling at British Sky Broadcasting, wrote that while McQuaid was 'probably correct in his observations', they shouldn't discount the UCI's role: 'To develop a sporting framework for female pro cyclists that remedies this situation.' Beckett added that, 'in this respect the UCI have been guilty of prioritising plans for men's road cycling'.

McQuaid's successor, Brian Cookson, was pressed on the topic even before he took office. In fact, in his pre-election manifesto in June 2013, he pledged to bring in a minimum wage for female riders in his first year as UCI President. 'If the UCI is to become a modern and progressive International Federation', wrote Cookson, 'then we must ensure there are rules specifying teams guarantee a minimum wage for women pro riders and proper, modern terms of employment.'

Cookson was elected the following September. By November 2014, questions were being asked. Where was this modern and progressive federation Cookson had promised? The UCI president repeated the claims of his predecessor, McQuaid – it was still too early. The result of introducing a minimum wage, Cookson told the *Guardian* 'would not be 500 women suddenly being paid the minimum wage'. Instead, the financially precarious position of most teams on the women's tour would mean that 'most would fold or re-register as amateur teams, so they wouldn't end up paying those women [riders] anything at all anyway'.

He has since softened his stance a little. Seeing signs of progress in the second running of the La Course event, held on the same day as the final stage of the Tour de France, and in increased levels of interest in putting on women's events from around the world, Cookson told Australian cycling website CyclingTips that he felt the time was coming when a minimum wage would be feasible. 'Next year we will see a major step forward in the creation of the UCI Women's World Tour', said Cookson in August 2015, referencing the new system that is being brought in for 2016 as a replacement for the World Cup Series (this new, two-division tour will include stage races as well as one-day races, while the World Cup had only offered the latter).

Cookson continued to say that he believed the UCI would be in a position to have rules about minimum wage 'within a short period of time', adding: 'I will take advice from the women's commission, from women who are involved in the teams and the riders' associations, and so on, as to when the right time for that is.'

The UCI's vice-president, Tracey Gaudry – often referred to as the most powerful woman in cycling – has made her views clear on the topic telling the website, Cycling News in February 2015 that she is "appalled" by some of the arrangements female cyclists have to put up with: "In some cases it's no better off than a decade or 15 years ago." But she also admits that a minimum wage is just one part of a bigger battle she and the UCI are facing – and that for this reason, we might have to wait until after 2016 to see a solution. "The UCI are drawing from owners and managers of women's professional teams, event organisers and directors to build the model that will establish the baseline set of criteria for any team to register as a UCI team. Minimum salary will be part of the equation but it's not the only part."

Nicole Cooke is in no doubt as to the damage the absence of a minimum wage can have on female riders, telling me how it can leave them at the mercy of team managers who are in the sport for all the wrong reasons: 'While there are some managers who are coming at it for the right reasons, for every one of those there are probably nine who are trying to live off the riders, get money out of sponsors and just take advantage of a women's road scene that isn't regulated.

'In 2014 the Estado de Mexico-Faren team didn't pay a lot of their riders from May onwards, one of which was [British rider] Lucy Martin [she left the team in September 2014]. Another one was Italian rider Giada Borgato, who was the Italian champion in 2012. She retired in November 2014 and wrote in an Italian article that there are parasites living off female riders and that she had ended her career very unhappy, not how she ever dreamed she would end up in cycling. That was 2014, almost two years after I asked in my retirement statement why women weren't worthy of protection.'

Young British rider Lucy Garner has become one of Britain's brightest prospects on the road since Cooke retired. She won the Junior World Road Racing Championships two years running (2011 and 2012) before signing her first professional contract with Dutch team Argos-Shimano in time for the start of the 2013 season. As of 2016 she is riding for Wiggle Honda. When I spoke to her at the end of 2014, with her third season as a pro in sight, it was clear she only saw one way forward for women's cycling: 'I'm on one of the most professional teams there are for women, and there are still girls in my team who are having to work alongside trying to be the best in the world. It doesn't make sense. It's really sad because they have that expectation on them from being on such a professional team and they're trying to achieve, but financially they have to try and get there themselves.

'Introducing a minimum wage would definitely help. I don't see why they don't have it. If you want to achieve the best then you have to be able to focus completely on what you have to do.' Garner's views echoed what 2012 Olympic road race silver medallist, Lizzie Armitstead, told Sky Sports News earlier in 2014 when she was asked about the feasibility of introducing a full-length women's Tour: 'Before we talk about having a three-week Tour de France ... we need to talk about the professionalism of it. You can't expect a woman who's holding down a part-time job to train for the biggest race in the world. She has to have a minimum wage, and I think it's pretty crazy that we don't have that.'

Referring to Cookson's claim that introducing a minimum wage too early would cause too many teams to fold, Nicole Cooke tells me that she doesn't see a problem with that result: 'Putting in a minimum wage will get rid of the teams whom nobody will be sorry to see go', she says. 'These fears about teams going out of business are stopping the sport from progressing because if you bring in a minimum wage then you regulate women's road racing. It will then become more attractive for sponsors who want to be associated with a credible structure and a credible racing scene.'

As well as giving female riders more protection, Cooke says that a minimum wage would have the knock-on effect of improving the quality and strength of women's road racing, because 'the teams will ask more of the riders'.

'At the moment there are a group of female riders who see road racing as a lifestyle choice. They can travel the world for a couple of years and get to ride their bikes, which they enjoy. They don't have to worry about making money for a few years, because they are supported by parents or whoever. That isn't helping the sport. We want teams that are being demanding of their riders, that are going to say: we're going to pay you a minimum wage and expect 100 per cent commitment from you in return.

'It would give such a boost to the whole women's road scene and you would see a big change. A lot of riders would ask themselves: am I going to commit the effort to this? You'd probably see some drop away, but then you would be left with the ones who have the drive and the passion and who want it to be a career. As it stands now, how can you dedicate yourself to a life of sport? At the end of it what have you got? Financially, nothing.'

In Britain, the sport's national governing body made a pledge of its own in March 2013: To get one million more women cycling by 2020. One year later, British Cycling President Bob Howden said their strategy was paying off: 'It truly feels like momentum is now building and we're starting to successfully tackle the historical gender imbalance. This work is transforming the culture and driving structural change across the sport.' In a report published on the British Cycling website, Howden talked of the equal prize money on offer at the UCI BMX Supercross event held in Manchester in April 2014 where all riders finishing in the top eight received the same prize money across both male and female categories.

'This move comes a year ahead of other rounds in the BMX Supercross series and ahead of many other countries hosting major events', boasted Howden, adding that British Cycling was 'leading the charge to bring in equal prize money across all disciplines'.

During Nicole Cooke's own career she fought hard for equal prize money. At the British Road Race Championships in 2003 after becoming national champion for a third time, Cooke asked for equal prize money to be introduced for the top three finishers in the men's and women's race in time for the 2004 event. At the time, Cooke tells me that British Cycling 'came up with a whole load of excuses why they couldn't offer equal prize money for the top three women'.

Given that British Cycling claim to be focused on 'transforming the culture' of the sport, I was disappointed to discover that at the National Junior Road

Race Championships held in July 2014, the winner of the junior boys race took home £220, while his female counterpart won less than half that amount at £100. 'It's very sad to see this kind of inequality exists at junior level', British Cycling level three coach Huw Williams told me.

He says that if it's based on the distance ridden (the boys rode 63 miles at the national junior championships while the girls did 40 miles), then British Cycling should simply get them to ride the same courses. Williams points out that at a race in Essex the weekend before the nationals, the main contenders for the junior girls national title raced 72 miles and loved it. 'For me, the prize money is less of an issue than whatever the motive is behind making the girls' race second class. But if distance is the reason, then give them equal distance (they would prefer it) and give them equal prize money. Parity has to start with the juniors. If they get lesser race distances and lesser prize money than the boys from an early age, they develop in an environment where women's racing is perceived as somehow second class.' And that surely is only going to keep the old culture – the one that British Cycling is supposedly trying to 'transform' – firmly in place.

Cooke believes that this old culture is so ingrained in British Cycling's make-up that they don't even realise that what they are doing is wrong: 'What message does that send to the girls?' She asks. 'They must think, why bother? You're going to get treated like shit no matter what you do. No wonder girls are not really looking at sport for a career.'

Cooke's closing barb hits upon a critical point. If girls grow up seeing and believing that sport will never offer them the same opportunities as it offers to boys, then why should we expect them to choose to dedicate their lives to it? It's true that equal prize money might not be 'realistic' or even sensible for all sports at this point in time, but there are many cases, particularly away from the elite senior level, where there really is no valid reason for rewarding male and female athletes differently.

In other cases, as with cricket, football and rugby at their highest levels, the focus should be on achieving equality of opportunity first and foremost, with equal pay and prize money a target once this has been achieved. Yes, this means that a decade after Venus Williams conveyed her wish that 'women and girls across the globe' could believe that 'there is no glass ceiling', it remains a wish unfulfilled. But little by little, sport by sport, the cracks are definitely starting to appear.

Nicole Cooke

THE LONE RIDER

'This is no saccharine fairy story', says Nicole Cooke of her 11 years as a professional cyclist, 'It couldn't be. I was a woman in macho man territory'. The headline moments of Cooke's career read like a familiar story: Talented sportswoman dedicates her life to becoming the best in the world and, despite injuries and tough times along the way, ultimately achieves her aim. By the time of Cooke's retirement in January 2013 she had won everything on offer including: Commonwealth, World and Olympic titles, the women's Tour de France (twice), the Giro Rosa (Tour of Italy) and the prestigious World Cup Series.

But the triumphs masked myriad murky sub plots that remained largely unreported by the cycling press until Cooke's retirement, when she took it upon herself to reveal all. In a 20-minute speech calmly delivered to a room full of journalists, Cooke talked of a young girl who, at the age of 12, looked a BBC reporter square in the eye and said: 'I want to win the Tour de France and win the Olympic Road Race.'

'At 12 I dreamed like every child. I hoped that some of my dreams could come true.' Cooke's face broke into a wry smile. At that age, she continued, 'one is unaware of the problems ahead'.

When we arrange to meet in the lobby café of the St Pancras Hotel in London, almost two years have passed since Cooke lifted the lid on a career's worth of repressed frustrations. She has come to London not only to speak to me, but also for a job interview, for Cooke is now a smartly attired 31-year-old retired sportswoman in search of her next career move. 'It will be nothing to do with British Cycling', she says firmly. 'I made a decision that I don't want to be involved too much in cycling for the near future because there are still too many raw ends on both sides with some of the personalities still at British Cycling and the lack of an apology, or even any recognition of the need for one ...'

The lid might have been lifted, but Cooke has clearly held on to her frustrations with a governing body that she believes repeatedly failed not only her but generations of female riders. She does not rule out an eventual return to the sport though, saying: 'Perhaps in five or 10 years' time I will come back to cycling or to WADA [the World Anti-Doping Agency], and hopefully put more world experience into making the sport better.' For now, Cooke believes cycling has too many ills.

She believes it because she has seen it. And because for years, no one wanted to hear her talk about it. 'It was quite hard for me to have a voice and draw attention to some of the issues', Cooke tells me. 'When I started cycling it was such a niche sport in Britain that the coverage was shallow. The big races didn't happen here, and British cyclists weren't very good, so there wasn't that history of coverage in place. There was one weekly cycling magazine and odd little snippets in the newspapers, but cycling journalists didn't write major articles.

'The cycling media was also very male orientated. When I came along I don't think they really wanted to write about a woman who was at the top of what they felt was their little sport, even if I was British. They were attached to the "heroic" nature of the sport on the road, and very much wanted a male hero. Most of the writers had turned what was their hobby into their work [in becoming a journalist]. They wrote about a world where the macho-man survives harsh odds to triumph over his rivals and is met at the finish by the podium girls, kissing them on each cheek.'

It was into this world that Cooke first entered as a young female cyclist. It was a world, says Cooke, where 'there was no female emancipation; the role of women was clearly defined as subsidiary'. She adds her story was hardly in the interest of the all-male team of journalists who were covering the sport: 'A young girl achieving where so many British men were obviously failing did not sit comfortably with them. It also didn't help that their professional horizon wasn't broad enough to take in the burgeoning international women's cycling scene.'

The consequence of this narrow view, says Cooke, was that the cycling press weren't familiar with the events or main protagonist on the women's circuit. 'It resulted in some strange interviews whenever they did speak to me. These journalists were a long way out of their comfort zones.' It also meant that for Cooke to get coverage for her results in the early years of her career was virtually impossible via the British cycling media. In those days it was Lance Armstrong or nothing if they wanted column inches or magazine sales.

Even earlier in her career though, simply finding the opportunities to race was 'virtually impossible'. Under UK law, cyclists under the age of 16 are not allowed to ride on the road in massed start events. When Cooke was young enough for that law to apply there was only one closed-road cycling circuit in the UK, and very few closed-road racing events organised throughout the year, so she had to look for other ways of developing her racing brain.

She discovered a youth camp in Holland based around road racing, and went there for the first time as a 12 year old. Each day the young riders would tackle a stage, with jerseys handed out at the end, just like a mini Tour de France. On the final Saturday the town centre was closed off and the youngsters treated to a full race with motorcycle outriders, following cars and commentators. On her first trip to the camp, Cooke won a polka dot jersey (awarded to the best climber) and returned home set on honing her talents to go back the next year as a better all-round rider.

In Holland, Cooke's eyes had been opened. She'd seen a group of female riders that was large enough to divide into two different age groups. Back in the UK, the British Cycling Federation (BCF, which would later become British Cycling) did not promote a single race just for females. In 1996 Cooke's parents wrote to the BCF suggesting they could encourage female participation by at least offering a national championship for girls. But that wasn't enough for the BCF. They were unable to look at the long-term gain, instead focusing only on what was right in front of them. They told the Cooke family that the demand for a girls' championship simply wasn't there.

In 1997, two years after she first attended, Nicole became the first ever British winner of the Helmond Youth Tour in Holland. Back home in the UK though, things were no better. With no girls' championship forthcoming, Cooke's only option if she wanted to race was to compete against boys that were up to two years her senior. Exasperated, a 14-year-old Cooke (with her dad's help) approached the BCF for a second time, this time to ask about the possibility of entering the British Women's Open 800m Championship. In response, she received a three-page letter from the BCF 'expressly forbidding' her from riding in the event. Their reasons, Cooke explains, were that 'I was not as fast as the adult women', so 'it was not "safe" to ride against them – and anyway, I did not stand a chance in the race, as if that was somehow a valid reason for not competing.'

Existing BCF rules did, though, allow Cooke to ride in the non-championship women's omnium (an event that featured an 800m handicap race), that took place at the same meeting and on the same day as the race she was deemed too slow to enter. The handicapper knew of Cooke and her ability, and placed her on the scratch mark (behind the rest of the field), alongside Helen MacGregor who had earlier become the British 800m champion. Among the riders ahead of them was a young Victoria Pendleton (who is three years Cooke's senior). Cooke knew exactly what she was up against and what she wanted to prove and raced accordingly, determined to leave no one in any doubt about her ability. As she crossed the finish line in first place, Cooke knew she had proven beyond any doubt that she deserved the chance to compete. And the BCF did too. The following year they introduced the first ever set of British Youth Track Championships for girls, with Cooke taking a clean sweep of all four titles on offer: pursuit, sprint, 500m and points race.

'Looking back, I'm proud of the 14-year-old me', says Cooke. 'Together with dad and the BCF official, we produced a change so that now British Cycling holds championship titles equally for boys and girls, on both track and road, for all youth and junior age groups.

'Meanwhile, some were asking how I could ride like that when I was just 14 … the truth is, I just rode my bike, a lot, because I liked it and wanted to become good. I have a work ethic that tells me, the more you do the better you are likely to become.'

Cooke also had a family that ensured she grew up believing in equality and that there was nothing beyond her reach. 'My mum and dad treated my brother and me the same', she says. 'We both had lots of opportunities and the way that sport was presented to us was that it was something for both of us to do – we were equal. Growing up in that environment where my parents were so supportive and always said you can do anything really helped me to progress with cycling. But I was also very driven. For me, the question was always: *How* am I going to get there? Not: *Can* I?'

Despite the relatively low profile of the sport throughout Cooke's youth, she recalls taking inspiration from fellow Welsh cyclists, Louise Jones, who won Commonwealth Games gold on the track in 1990, and Sally Hodge who won the demonstration event points race at the World Track Championships in 1988. 'I had two riders who had won gold medals in cycling at a world level that had come from my area. I saw them and thought ok, now I know it can be done.'

She also sought out the sights and sounds of women's cycling in any way she could. Every summer the Cooke family asked their local newsagent to arrange for the daily delivery of *L'Équipe*, the French newspaper dedicated to sport, so that they could stay up to date with the goings on in the Tour de France. 'I'm not sure how many households in Wales took delivery of *L'Équipe*', she says, 'but waiting a week for *Cycling Weekly* [magazine] wasn't much fun when the Tour was on.

'Reading [*L'Équipe*] also helped me with my French GCSE studies. There was the odd little snippet on women's cycling in there and even though it was only a little bit, it was those glimmers that showed me women's cycling was out there, and I hung on to these little straws of hope.'

Those straws of hope were reinforced during summer holidays to the Alps, where Cooke and her brother 'fought every centimetre up every mountain … wheel to wheel past every kilometre post to the summit'. Conquering these climbs – which included the 2,802 m of the Col de la Bonette, the highest road in Europe – left Cooke in no doubt that one day she would be competing in the women's Tour de France.

It was a race she first caught sight of during that in Cooke family holiday in 1999. The day started with Nicole leading her brother and parents in a ride up the Alpe d'Huez, before the four of them headed to Vaujany, where a 16-year-old Nicole got her first opportunity to see at first hand those she could one day be joining. 'It was the first time I had seen such a mass of elite women riders,' says Cooke, 'and the noise, colour and sense of excitement were overwhelming. I couldn't wait until I got in there, racing with them.'

But before she could do that, Cooke had races closer to home to focus on, namely the British Road Race Championships. With no event scheduled for junior women (although there was of course one for the junior men), Cooke utilised a rule that allowed a youth age competitor who had reached the age of 16 to ride in the senior event when there was no alternative. Lining up against a host of senior women who were a part of British Cycling's World Class Performance Programme (WCPP), and who benefited from all the funding, facilities and coaching that went with it, Cooke knew she had little to lose.

Despite wielding a bike costing no more than £200 (the WCPP spent around £3,000 per top bike per rider), Cooke knew that a summer of gruelling riding in the Alps had left her hardened both physically and mentally. 'Bring it on', she thought, '110km with these girls was not going to be as hard as some of the rides we had just done in the Alps.'

And so it proved. The schoolgirl who had just finished her GCSEs emerged victorious, winning her first national road race title (by the time of her retirement she would have nine more). 'Winning that senior title astounded a lot of people', reflects Cooke, describing the victory as one of the standout moments of her career.

Cooke's pride in what she achieved that day goes beyond any sense of personal triumph, though. In her retirement statement she claimed it as a victory that ensured the BCF introduced more racing options for younger female riders, including a junior category road race championship and series. 'They could not have done a better job', says Cooke. 'They stepped up and solved the problem I had brought to light in exactly the right way.

'Now I can attend local youth age events and see 45 riders, all locally based, and there are 18 or so girls competing in their own race. This is a huge movement … Previously, there were no events put on by the BCF for girls, and no support for girls. That all changed following my success as a Youth in the British Senior Championships. Now the likes of Dani King and Laura Trott have a shop window to display their exceptional talents. There is an infrastructure that supports them and nurtures their talent. I am just as proud of my part in bringing about those permanent changes as I am of being the first ever British winner of the Olympic Road Race or a major tour.'

While the administrative side of the sport in the UK changed in response to the pressure of Cooke's victory, not everyone at British Cycling was won over. The coaching staff, who were responsible for selection and training of the Elite Women's programme and for allocating Lottery funds to selected riders responded by cancelling the funding available to junior female riders in 2000, and stating that Cooke was too young to be supported on the senior women's programme. 'All the coaches were male and their pride stood in the way of them making the logical decisions', says Cooke. 'I had just beaten all the women they trained and supported, and they responded by freezing me out and changing the rules regarding support for the next year.'

Cooke adds another detail that she feels was a key part of the problem when it came to her relationship with British Cycling. Peter Keen, who at the time was the World Class Performance Programme Director at the governing body, was the personal coach of the rider who had come second to Nicole in the 1999 National Championships. He had coached her for many years, and had obviously felt rather put out when she had been beaten into second place by Cooke.

When it came to the 2000 Olympics, the UCI saved British Cycling from having to make another decision regarding Cooke's selection by introducing a new rule. In November 1999, the UCI stated that all female competitors in the road race had to be 19 years old or over. Realising what this meant for Cooke (who would only be 17 at the time of the Sydney Olympic Games), the Welsh BBC asked the British Cycling press office whether they were going to challenge the rule.

Cooke claims that the manager there, Philip Ingham, said that no, they weren't going to challenge the UCI's rule because her win at the nationals had been a 'fluke'. 'Legal experts read the story and offered me free support', recalls Cooke, noting that the Olympic Charter itself states that 'age shall not be a barrier to competing'. Despite the best efforts of these legal experts though, Cooke's appeal came to nothing.

The Olympic year would be a frustrating one for Cooke then, as she continued to prove herself worthy of a place in Britain's Olympic cycling team. In April she destroyed the 'fluke' myth by beating the Lottery-supported Olympic squad at a round of the National Series. But later that year, at the National Championships in June, Cooke was beaten. Although the rules governing the race state that riders must race individually, and not in teams, Cooke believed the other riders had decided they'd had enough of losing to her and teamed up to attack her, ensuring she was beaten.

Cooke's first mark on the world stage came at the World Junior Road Race Championships in France in October 2000. At that time, Britain's cyclists had been largely anonymous at World Road Race championships, with no winners since Mandy Jones took the senior women's title in 1982. 'You cannot look at it with the perspective of the current well-oiled British Cycling machine', says Cooke of that period. 'Year after year, GB had simply entered riders who mostly didn't even finish, let alone ride with any thought of victory.'

'To say that I was pumped up for the road race would be an understatement', she says of the World Junior event in Plouay. 'If anyone else had ideas about winning, they would have to deal with me first.' Cooke's GB teammates were wiped out in a crash early in the race, but she battled on, letting out a huge roar of triumph as she crossed the finish line in first place. 'I had fought the whole year through a system in which very few seemed to want to help me, and many more appeared to want to block me … it was only one gold medal, and a junior one at that, but nearly 20 years without any road race medals of any form was a very long time. At least some people at British Cycling were now paying attention.'

Despite her victory, Cooke describes the support system from British Cycling during those championships as woeful. She recalls one particular incident where the team were driven to the time trial course, 40km from where they were staying. Some four hours after they left, Nicole and her teammates were still in the car and when they did eventually arrive the weather had turned nasty, making the course virtually un-rideable. 'The system was employing the wrong type of people', says Cooke. After the race, her father got together with a number of other knowledgeable figures and put together a 29-page report on how to organise the support systems at a World Championships. 'He sent it to Peter Keen [then CEO at British Cycling] who read it and took on board a lot of its messages.' First up: The need to hire a world-class women's road racing coach.

The experienced Canadian cycling coach, Peg Labiuk (then Peg Hill), spotted the job advertisement from British Cycling in a trade magazine, and her impressive CV was enough to secure her the role.

Labiuk told me about what was for her a 'dream position'. 'I was overwhelmed by how much support they had', she says of the governing body. 'They had so much funding, they had the Velodrome [in Manchester], vehicles, and they decided to not go with sponsorship for equipment and buy what they wanted.' Taking all this into account, Labiuk says she was 'surprised' by the level of the athletes: 'There were a few who were doing very well, but they just didn't have the depth.

'They wanted to produce athletes that were going to medal in the Olympics and they only had maybe three that could do that. One was quite young in Nicole, one was being diverted to the track, and another one was struggling – she was extremely talented but her motivation wasn't as strong.'

Labiuk's first meeting with Cooke came at the 2001 British Road Race Championships, where the coach had been warned to expect a 'difficult' athlete: 'It was presented to me that she was demanding and a problem', says Labiuk. 'Perhaps they weren't prepared for an athlete that young who was so ambitious. But she and I understood each other extremely well, because I had been that ambitious when I was a young athlete.

'I wanted them [British Cycling] to see the potential there. I couldn't understand why there was resistance. She was an athlete who knew what she wanted and needed and produced results. What more could you ask for? She was viewed as being demanding, but I didn't see it that way at all.'

Cooke's potential became even harder to ignore later that year as she defended her World Junior Road Race title in Lisbon. 'Looking back, I never felt as much pressure in my career as I did for this race', she says. 'The other teams knew me from the previous year, they knew my style and they could base their strategies on me.'

And yet they still could not stop her from prevailing. Cooke's victory in the road race gave her an unprecedented hat trick of world junior titles in 2001, adding to her win in the time trial a few days before and the mountain bike world title she had secured in Colorado that September. Such a display of all-around strength left few doubting that there was a bright future ahead for the 18 year old who had only just finished her A-levels.

'She can be the greatest woman cyclist ever', said Shane Sutton, the tough Aussie who worked as a coach with Welsh Cycling before moving to British Cycling in 2002.

With a trio of world junior titles behind her, Cooke prepared to enter the world of women's professional road racing full of excitement about what the future might hold. But before she settled into her first home with the Italian arm of the Deia-Pragma-Colnago team, she received the surprising news that British Cycling had dismissed Peg Labiuk from her coaching position. Labiuk had been replaced by Richard Wooles – a man Cooke describes as 'a novice male coach, with no experience of riding on the continent, no experience as a professional, and no experience of the female scene or coaching female riders.'

'It was crushing', Labiuk says of her dismissal, telling me that Peter Keen (then Performance Director at British Cycling) had never fulfilled his promise to provide her with a formal, written explanation for why she was sacked. 'I knew what I could do with those athletes, so it was confusing because they said all the right things and I certainly seemed like a good fit. Some people said it was because I connected with Nicole so well, but I'm really not sure why.'

Cooke believes it was a case of British Cycling expelling someone who they felt was posing too much of a challenge to the status quo: 'It was about choosing people that fit the mentality and the culture – a "yes man" who's just going to say yes to everything they want, rather than someone who says, "you're giving me a job and I'm going to do it." It didn't take long to see the true colours of BC management at that time.'

Labiuk's dismissal left another dent in the already damaged relationship between Cooke and British Cycling. She refused to sign the Team Agreement that asserted any rider belonging to the WCPP had to 'obey every instruction of the coach', on the basis that she would have no control over choosing said coach: 'Why should I be forced to take instructions from someone who didn't know me and I didn't know?'

Her refusal to accept British Cycling's laws meant that Cooke – now indisputably the best female road racer in Britain – continued her career without any Lottery funding.

As of 2002 though, she would be earning her first wage as a senior rider, having accepted an offer of €8,000 for the season from Spanish-Ukrainian team, Deia-Pragma-Colnago. 'The reason I picked Deia', explains Cooke, 'was the presence of Spanish rider Joane Somarriba who had won the last two editions of the women's Tour de France … it meant we would be doing the top-level races and I would have a fantastic champion to learn from.'

Somarriba herself was looking forward to welcoming such a prodigious talent, saying: 'We've heard a great deal about Nicole and are delighted to have her with us … Making the move from junior cycling to the seniors is a big step and we'll have to see how she responds.'

The Spaniard did not have to wait long. Cooke's first win came in just her second race, at the Trofeo Citta di Rosignano, and she followed it up with another win in her fourth start at the Memorial Pasquale de Carlo. In total, Cooke racked up seven wins in her first season in the elite ranks proving that for some riders, the gap between junior and senior cycling is easily navigated.

Her determination to sweep all before her almost proved her undoing though, as she entered the 2002 Commonwealth Games in Manchester in a state of near exhaustion. With Wales expecting three medals from a rider they had taken so much pride in as she dominated the junior ranks, Cooke was left distraught after failing to deliver in her first two races of the Games – the time trial on the road and the points race on the track.

'She was in bits, emotionally shattered – she was in tears in the back of the team van', revealed the team manager, Shane Sutton. 'She was suffering from chronic fatigue and her carbohydrate stores were completely depleted.'

Cooke had six days to turn things around in time for the road race, going into what she called 'ultimate recovery mode'. On the eve of the race, Sutton called an impromptu team meeting with Cooke and her two Welsh teammates, informing them that instead of riding as a team, they should ride as individuals. 'He gave us the impression we were beyond any help he could offer', says Cooke of Sutton's implication that they had more chance of picking up a medal if they rode for themselves, rather than as a team led by Cooke. It was a tactic that ensured Cooke would once again be forced to go it alone against other riders who would be supported and protected by their teammates. 'We all knew that Shane wasn't right,' says Cooke, 'but I didn't rise to it.'

Defying all the odds and the formbook, a 19-year-old Cooke secured a stunning triumph in front of an ecstatic Manchester crowd. It was a display of tactical nous and sheer grit that left Sutton almost at a loss for words. All the Aussie could say was that it was 'a triumph of guts and class'.

The biggest race of her professional career so far, the Tour de France, followed hot on the heels of the Commonwealth Games. A drained Cooke struggled through the first six stages before she had to withdraw, but form was not her only concern. She and her French teammate Fany Lecourtois had not received their salaries for months and were becoming increasingly perturbed by the offers of blood tests and 'help' from their Directeur Sportif, William Dazzani, who was suspected of being involved in doping.

In Cooke's retirement statement, she revealed that the spectre of doping turned from whispers and shadows into something more tangible, early on in her professional career. She described finding 'bottles and vials with diaphragms on top for extracting the contents via syringes' inside the fridge of a team house she was staying in. 'I rang dad and asked what I should do. We chatted it through and came to the conclusion that even condoning the presence of "medicines" in the house I was staying could lead to pressure being put on me … So, I emptied the fridge and put the lot out in the front garden and [said] either it went or I went. It went."

The pressures to dope that Cooke experienced might not have been as intense as in the men's peloton (where the higher rewards combined with longer races created a doping culture for many years), but many female riders were still not strong enough to say no, including Canada's star rider, Genevieve Jeanson, who was a great rival to Cooke until her retirement in 2006. Jeanson never actually tested positive, but the clues were there. She missed a drugs test early in her career (receiving a trivial fine by way of punishment) and recorded unusually high levels of hematocrit (a measure of red blood cells) in 2003, for which she received exactly what the UCI rules required – a two-week enforced rest from racing but no censure.

'Throughout her career Jeanson repeatedly lied', says Cooke, comparing the Canadian's actions to those of Lance Armstrong. 'And yet now, she confesses that she had been on an extensive doping program since she was 16.' Jeanson admitted to her doping past in 2007, placing much of the blame on her coach, Andre Aubut, with whom she had worked since the age of 15. He was banned from the sport for life in 2009, but the damage to the world of women's professional cycling had already been done.

Every scandal that hit the sport – particularly those on the men's side – hurt the most vulnerable part of women's cycling: its finances. The start of Cooke's career coincided with the period during which cycling was still coming to terms with the aftermath of the Festina affair – the doping scandal that started when the entire Festina team from Spain was kicked out of the 1998 Tour de France. Their team masseuse was arrested at the French border with 400 vials of the blood-boosting drug EPO in his vehicle, and the team was left with little choice other than to admit their part in the obvious doping regime. The ensuing investigation and trial would go on until late 2000, but the impact on cycling (and the world of elite sport as a whole) would last far longer.

'Festina changed the course of cycling', wrote *Guardian* journalist William Fotheringham, in a piece reflecting on the decade that had passed since it occurred. 'But the ramifications outside of the two-wheeled world were also immense. For the first time in a single major sport, systematic doping at the highest level had been exposed. For the first time, it became evident that doping led not merely to positive tests but potentially to the collapse of an entire event.'

With the sport severely shaken for a number of years afterwards, sponsors of women's teams took their money and ran as far from controversy as possible, forcing teams' already small budgets to shrink even further (money also came out of the men's tour, but with stronger finances in the first place, they were better positioned to take a hit). Cooke's determination to remain honest might have preserved her own conscience, but it could do nothing to prevent her sport from regressing.

In the early stages of her career though, Cooke tried to put these things to one side and focus on her own goals. Her first season as a professional might have ended on a sour note, with her wages unpaid after her refusal to accept any extra 'help' to finish the Tour, but Cooke went into 2003 eager to move on.

She signed a two-year contract with top Italian team, Acca Due O, but only after receiving assurances from the manager that she would not be living with anyone who was taking drugs or using any 'preparations' that were taken intravenously. Cooke's annual salary would be €23,000, with no additional support from British Cycling after she was told that riding for a professional team meant she would not be eligible for a grant. 'Ultimately, I wanted support', says Cooke, 'the issue was not about the money … British Cycling either wouldn't or couldn't seem to accept what was required to become a successful rider.'

Cooke, though, knew exactly what she needed to do. Her 2003 season started relatively slowly – after three rounds of the World Cup (the UCI's season-long series of one-day races that awards points to riders depending on their placement), Cooke had just seven points. Frustrated that her form was not translating into results, she went into the fourth round – the Amstel Gold Race in Holland – determined to put things right.

The Amstel was one of the prestigious spring classics, with the women's race held on the same day as the men's version (although only the men's race still exists, with the women's event scratched after 2003). As Cooke watched the men line up, her mind was already in race mode, running through her tactics for the 75 miles of racing ahead. After a fairly quiet first 50 miles, she followed as Australian rider Oenone Wood attacked off the penultimate hill, and with 800m to go Cooke accelerated hard to the finish line to win by two seconds.

'No Brit had ever won a World Cup race', says Cooke, reflecting on the significance of her victory, aside from the fact it moved her to fifth place in the standings. 'It was an incredible win – right up there. But at the time no one was taking an interest. Ok, there was no internet and it was hard to know when the women's races were going on because there was so little information, but my dad would write a press release and send it out to all the newspapers.

'In one paper my brother's third place in a local race was recorded ahead of my World Cup win, which just made the results listings. You just wonder what was going through their brain that they can order it in such a way: Men's international, men's national, men's local and finally – if any space is left – women's. Even when that women's World Cup result supersedes the other things by a mile.'

Cooke had three days to recover before the next World Cup event, the Flèche Wallonne in Belgium. Her Amstel win ensured she was a marked woman throughout the 97.5km race, but Cooke was more than up to the challenge, winning by four seconds.

For the second time in three days, Cooke stood atop the podium of an elite women's road race. She also now found herself at the top of the World Cup standings and inside the top 10 of the world rankings for the first time. Even the 11-hour, 1000km campervan trip back to the team's Italian base could not dampen her mood as she reflected on achieving everything she had 'ever dreamed of as a 10 year old, charging up and down the hills on my little pink bike'.

A nightmare was to follow, however. Cooke was involved in a crash two months later that would impact upon the rest of her sporting career. It came during the third stage of Le Tour de Grande Montreal in Canada when Cooke collided with a stationary motorbike at 50kph. She was taken to hospital with her knee resembling 'a bloody pulp' poking out from her cycling shorts and her arm swollen 'like a football had been inflated under the skin'.

Stitched up and sent home to recover, Cooke was fortunate that the next round of the World Cup in Plouay was not for three months, giving her time to fully recover from the crash. The Plouay course was one of Cooke's favourites, with plenty of climbs and technical descents providing prime opportunities for attacks. Despite anxieties over her form and fitness she proved too strong for her opposition and took her third win of the series. 'It's a dream', she said after the finish. 'I had to have the whole month of July without riding my bike … I was very scared because last time I raced was a very long time ago.'

The victory left Cooke 118 points clear at the top of the World Cup standings with two races to go. She only needed one though, securing the series at the penultimate round in Nuremberg. In doing so she wrote her name in the history books as the first

Briton to win the World Cup and the youngest ever winner – male or female – at the age of 20.

Her next big target was the World Championships in Canada the following month, where despite the fact she would effectively be riding alone against nations fielding strong teams who could use their strength in numbers against her, Cooke started as the favourite to win. In the event, she finished third, adding a first senior medal to her four junior world titles. On the podium though, she fought back tears of frustration as she mulled over the 'tactical errors' that had cost her a world title she could have won. 'I was very hard on myself', says Cooke, 'at the time I could only see disappointment.'

She threw herself into winter training with the 2004 Athens Olympics front of mind. After the disappointment of missing out on the Sydney Games in 2000, Cooke was determined to seize the opportunity to make an impact on the British public that only comes around once every four years. Her achievements in 2003 had won her some followers, but Cooke recalls that she would often get asked by general sports journalists (i.e. not the cycling writers) why it was that her achievements received such little coverage in publications like *Cycling Weekly*?

'No one said it but the view seemed to be that women's racing was basically akin to "housewives go cycle racing at the weekend"', says Cooke. 'One female sports writer took the time to find out how many full-time riders there were on the world circuit at this time, when both the women's Giro and Tour were two-week events. She told me that the circuit was bigger than women's golf, and only exceeded in all sports by women's tennis. She was incredulous that the media didn't follow my story.'

The Olympic year started slowly for Cooke, with the pain in her left knee returning. It meant more scans and far less riding than she would have liked, with the days ticking by to the Athens Games. Seeing no improvement, Cooke opted to have surgery four months before the Olympics, vowing to come back 'stronger than ever'. Her return to action came at the British Championships, where she dominated from start to finish to win her fifth national road race title, crossing the line nearly three minutes ahead of her closest challenger. She even had time to plant a kiss on her troublesome left knee as she approached the finish line.

The next day Cooke flew to Italy for the women's Giro d'Italia – her second race in eight months and her only other major target in 2004 aside from the Olympics. The most prestigious stage race on the women's calendar, the Giro has been a part of the women's calendar since 1988, with the 2004 version held over 10 consecutive, and brutal, days. With Cooke having raced once all year and recording a DNF (did not finish) at her last big stage race – the 2002 Tour de France – few considered her a realistic challenger.

Going into the decisive penultimate stage, five riders were within 30 seconds of one another in the general classification, but Cooke was prepared. She had focused on this day since her return to training, driving up and down the stage's climb of the Ghisallo to memorise its hairpin turns and varying gradients. Her homework paid off. Cooke chose the perfect moment to attack and drove hard all the way to the finish line, taking the stage win and overall lead of the race. She would ride in the Maglia Rosa (the pink jersey worn by the race leader) until the race finished the following day, securing her first grand tour victory and a winners' cheque for £240 (plus a team bonus, naturally).

No Briton – male or female – had ever won any of the three big Tours (French, Spanish or Italian) before and yet here was Cooke, in her second year as a professional cyclist, proving that it could be done. She was also the youngest ever winner of the Giro, which that year had been run at the fastest-ever average speed. Despite all her history-making, however, Cooke's win garnered minimal coverage in Britain.

'A fact of life for a British female road race athlete was that only the Olympic road race counted', says Cooke. 'This was where the BBC would cover women's road cycling and my exploits could be relayed direct to the public without the specialist journalists imposing arbitrary censorship. Once every four years I would get a chance to show my talents.'

Cooke was well aware of the impact it would have upon her career if she could carry her Giro form into the Olympic road race in Athens. With just a few weeks in between the end of the former and the start of the latter, she felt confident that she was in with a good chance of winning what would be Britain's first Olympic road race gold medal.

But the race did not go to plan. Cooke finished fifth, believing that her 'desperate desire to win' had clouded her tactical judgement. 'I'd failed in what had been my ultimate aim in life since I was 12', she says, 'I felt devastated'. Cooke presented a brave face to the disappointed group of British journalists who had gathered at the finish line expecting to witness the first British gold medal of the Games, but later on she cracked, sobbing as she got changed alone.

'I had never contemplated what would happen after the Olympics. While others went on with life and the world kept turning, I wondered what I was supposed to do now.'

Fortunately, the world of elite sport provides almost immediate answers to such questions. There will always be a 'next big race' to focus on, and while the scars of Athens would not be easily erased, Cooke shifted her gaze towards working out how she could emerge from the next four-year Olympic cycle capable of winning in Beijing in 2008.

While 2005 brought another knee operation, this time on her right leg which required the same surgery she'd had on her left the previous year, Cooke still emerged with a handful of World Cup wins, a sixth British road race title and a silver medal at the World Championships – Britain's sole medal of the competition. She also played a part in the UCI's new commission that had been set up to help move women's road racing forward.

The hot topic of debate at that time was the Olympic programme where the addition of BMX had meant the removal of two track events, leaving the men with seven and the women with three. A petition was set up calling for the reinstatement of the events that had been scrapped to make way for the BMX (the 1km for men and 500m for women), but Cooke wanted more. She wanted parity: 'I wrote to the UCI, highlighting the inequality in track events and asked them to address this. It became clear that there was no support or desire to listen to the women's commission on this or many other issues and it was disbanded by the UCI before the end of the year [2005].'

Cooke's desire for equality on the Olympic programme was eventually satisfied in time for the 2012 Olympics, but as she says: 'The sexist bias could have been sorted out four years earlier.'

With the Beijing Olympics never far from her mind, Cooke reached the halfway stage of the Olympic cycle in the perfect position, finishing the 2006 season as the number one ranked rider in the world and having led her Univega team to top spot in the World Team rankings.

But at the Commonwealth Games in Melbourne in March of that year, Cooke – the defending champion – was without a team of any sort as she was the only Welsh rider selected to compete in the women's road race. The men's team, meanwhile, consisted of the full complement of six riders. 'I could have understood it if the men's team stood a better chance of bringing back a medal than the women's,' says Cooke of the Welsh selection committee's decision not to provide her with any teammates, 'but in fact, the opposite was the case.'

She reveals how throughout the build-up to the 2006 Commonwealth Games, the male riders had been taken on warm weather training camps, and trips to races, while the girls were left with nothing – 'over four years, not a single camp or supported race.' Cooke had won the biggest race possible while wearing the Welsh jersey and yet, she says, Welsh Cycling responded by 'depriving Wales's female riders of the means to succeed.'

Cooke's solo assault on the Commonwealth Games road race left her battling against teams of six riders. 'My chances of gold were zero', she says. It was a challenge requiring smart tactics from the lone Welshwoman whose plan of attack was to focus on the Australian team that was favourite for gold.

Her plan worked well enough to secure her a bronze medal, putting Cooke on the podium alongside all six members of the Australian team – an image that only served to highlight the disadvantage she had been at. Cooke herself accepted that this was a rare example of a bronze medal being as good as gold. 'It is everything I could have hoped for', she told the media after the race. 'Thinking about the support the other teams had and the different possibilities they had at their disposal, I am over the moon. There were six Canadians and six New Zealanders in that race, and not one of them made it on the rostrum.'

Neither did any of the Welsh men's team. In fact, not one rider from their six-strong squad managed to even finish the race.

By the time the Tour de France came round (now called the Grande Boucle Feminine) Cooke had a 49-point lead at the top of the World Cup standings. She was a different rider to the one that had started the same race in 2002. The race itself was also much changed, having suffered the consequences of the sport's many drugs scandals.

'Up until 2003 it was still a very prestigious race', says Cooke. 'That was the last edition when it was two weeks long. It didn't take place in 2004 because of it clashing with the Olympics, but I think it was already starting to struggle then. In 2005 it came back and it was a week long up until 2009. But at that time it wasn't getting TV coverage in France or on the internet, and it wasn't attracting the riders because it wasn't as prestigious as it used to be. Then it just slid away. It's an awful reflection of the sport that the race was just left to crumble.'

Despite its truncated length, in 2006 it remained an event Cooke desperately wanted to add to her palmarès. The race included six stages, starting with a time-trial in Font Romeu, high in the Pyrénées. Cooke won it, ensuring she would don the race leader's yellow jersey as she had dreamed of doing since she was a little girl. Once Cooke put it on, the yellow jersey was hers to the end as she led the race from start to finish.

But her finest moment arguably came the day before she crossed the finish line on the final stage, when she would get to tackle 'a climb of special magic to all British riders' over Mont Venoux. 'As we assembled on the start line … I saw this quiet figure of a 12-year-old wish me well, she would be watching me from her TV in her lounge, and she would be with me every pedal stoke today … Today was the day, above any other in my life, which I owed that little girl.'

Cooke attacked hard as soon as the peloton reached the steep slopes of Mont Ventoux, wanting to ride it alone, emulating the images of great riders past that she had grown up poring over in books and magazines. Once at the top she pressed on, thrilling in the rapid descent and increasing her lead further still. Cooke crossed the finish line six minutes ahead of her closest rival. With her overall victory confirmed the following day, Cooke had won her 'dream race', becoming the first British winner of the Tour de France.

Understandably, it upsets Cooke when she reads headlines proclaiming Bradley Wiggins as the first British winner of the Tour (even the British Cycling website was guilty of doing just that, until Cooke corrected them), but she notes that it's not something that is exclusive to her sport. When Andy Murray won Wimbledon in 2013, many of the initial news reports called him the first Brit to win Wimbledon in 77 years, neglecting to mention Virginia Wade's win in 1977. 'It's in the psyche', shrugs Cooke, noting the importance of celebrating female victories if future generations are going to be inspired to follow the lead of Cooke and so many others.

'There is a very obvious lack of women role models and that is because, mostly courtesy of the male sporting press, they are invisible. There are lots of female athletes out there achieving great things, but they aren't presented as role models to aspire to like their counterparts are on the men's side. That can be addressed and would have a very big impact on giving youngsters encouragement.'

The invisibility issue became even clearer when shortly after Cooke's victory in the 2006 Grande Boucle she climbed to number one in the UCI's world rankings – a position no British rider, male or female, had ever held before. How was this historic achievement celebrated? In the weekly *Cycling News* magazine it merited a mention on page 14, overshadowed by the reporting of Floyd Landis's fantastic exploits at the Tour de France.

Cooke swiftly turned her attention to adding the 2006 World Cup to her successes for the year. But before she could do that, her world – the cycling world – was rocked by two drugs scandals. News of Operation Puerto broke first with Spanish doctor, Eufemiano Fuentes, forced to hand over his collection of blood bags to the police, and a number of riders suspended. This was followed by the news that Floyd Landis – who had ridden a clearly unbelievable race to win the 2006 Tour – had tested positive for performance-enhancing drugs (PEDs).

For Cooke's professional team the timing could not have been worse. 'We're trying to sort out sponsorship for the next two years with people who are doubting whether it's even worth putting money into cycling', she told the *Guardian* at the time. 'So my team manager is having to fight quite hard and say that women's cycling isn't in the same state as men's cycling.'

Landis protested his innocence and appealed for funding to help his legal fight against the doping charges levelled against him, collecting over $1million in public donations. Cooke's manager, meanwhile, could not even raise a fraction of that to help fund what she says was 'the best women's team on the planet'. The overwhelming feeling of injustice would stay with Cooke throughout the rest of her career, while the cases of Fuentes and Landis inflicted wounds on women's cycling from which she says, 'parts of it would never recover'.

Amid the drama, Cooke wrapped up her second World Cup title and headed to the World Championships in Salzburg where she won bronze. She was disappointed, but took solace in the positive response from the media, who she says were 'generous in praise of how I rode the race … I was alone but had repeatedly taken the race to the rest, despite the odds. This was admired by those knowledgeable enough to understand the situation.'

One such example came in a report in the *Guardian*. Under the headline 'Cooke wants more company on road to Beijing', cycling writer William Fotheringham wrote: 'Cooke was isolated in the 14-woman lead group that she dragged clear on the penultimate lap … the scenario was the same as when she took bronze in Hamilton in 2003, fifth in the Olympic Games in 2004, and silver last year in Madrid. It is an impressive record of consistency, but it must also frustrate her.'

The performance director at British Cycling at the time, Dave Brailsford (who had replaced Peter Keen), admitted the need to 'develop riders who can support Nicole in the finale of a major event', while Cooke called for more British riders to follow her lead and race full time in Europe. 'There is no need to be afraid of it', she said, 'it's the only way to learn'. Cooke noted with delight, though, that in Salzburg a GB junior women's team competed for the first time since she had won the race in 2001. With the Beijing Olympics just two years away, Cooke sensed that at long last, she might have the support necessary to achieve her Olympic dream.

The following summer, Cooke's build up to Beijing appeared to be on track. She led the 2007 World Cup standings, retained her Grande Boucle title and won her eighth national road race title in nine years, establishing a period of dominance not matched by anyone since legendary British cyclist Beryl Burton (who won almost every race she competed in throughout the 1960s). But Cooke's victory that year masked an underlying problem: her knee pain had returned.

Determined not to let it stop her from winning an unprecedented third World Cup title with just two races to go, Cooke decided to manage the problem for as long as she could. A second place in the penultimate round ensured she had an 80-point lead with one race to go. In previous years this would have been enough for her to be declared the champion before the final race, but in 2007 the UCI decided there would be double points on offer at the final race of the World Cup, meaning the winner would collect 150 points instead of 75.

Cooke made it through the first lap before the pain started. From then on it grew with each of the following nine laps, and she crossed the line in 34th place, handing the World Cup to a woman who had become her nemesis in recent months: Marianne Vos. The Dutchwoman is four years younger than Cooke, but had already made her mark on the international scene by 2007, winning two world titles in 2006 (one in cyclo-cross and the other on the road). But the 2007 World Cup title was the first of five that Vos has won in her career so far – before then, she had never even finished the season in the top three.

The Dutchwoman's victory in 2007 was a tough one for Cooke to swallow. She had led the competition from the start to the closing metres of the final finish line. As if to rub salt into an already stinging wound, the UCI would remove their double points rule the following year.

Another knee operation followed, ruling Cooke out of 2007 World Championships and leaving Vos to usurp her as the World's top-ranked rider. Her health aside though, the Olympic year started with positive news. Halfords were to sponsor a British women's professional team which would be led by Cooke, and that ensured Britain's young female riders would get the chance to race with and learn from one of the world's best.

It was not until March, however, that Cooke was able to ride pain-free, and it was May by the time she had her first win, on the first stage of the 10-day Tour de L'Aude. Overall, Cooke finished fourth, but with her strength and fitness returning and other British riders around her proving they were capable of contributing at the top level, Cooke's Olympic preparation was back on track.

But at a GB team meeting in Manchester ahead of the Games, the performance manager, Shane Sutton, informed Cooke that her teammate Emma Pooley was to be the one riding for Olympic gold, with Cooke instructed to remain in the bunch as 'the false decoy for the others to watch'.

'I felt an anger building inside of me', says Cooke. 'I had come all this way without a team and constantly had to take on the might of the cycling world, single-handedly, and had delivered in virtually every race I rode for my country. Now, when there was finally some support on hand, it was being denied.'

The Olympic Road Race got underway beneath leaden skies, with Cooke keeping herself near the front to avoid any crashes as the rain began to fall. With Russian rider Natalia Boyarskaya taking an early lead, Pooley set about closing the gap with Italian rider Tatiana Guderzo for company – they had the perfect three for a winning break. The rest of the field gave chase though and toward the summit of the final climb the leaders in the field were back together in one large group.

Knowing that she was now free to go for gold, Cooke manoeuvred herself into a break of five riders. Ignoring the torrential downpour, she took the lead with just over 200m to go, putting every last ounce of energy she had into the uphill sprint finish that would secure her Olympic gold.

'I crossed the line. I looked right and I looked left, double-checking with my eyes what my senses were telling me. I had won! I was Olympic champion!'

Cooke collapsed off her bike, gasping to get the air back into her lungs. Once recovered, she applauded the British Cycling support staff and her teammates. It was Britain's first gold of the Games and the first road medal of any sort won by a British female road rider at the Olympics. 'It was perfect', said an elated, and soaking wet, Cooke afterwards.

Cooke left Beijing shortly after her triumph to prepare for the World Championships, which would take place in Italy at the end of September. She was the only British gold medallist to come out of the Games and get straight back into training, but having won three World Championships medals since 2003 and not one of them gold, Cooke was on a mission.

With the course just an hour's ride away from her adopted home in Lugano, Cooke rode on it two or three times a week, getting a feel for the hills and memorising every twist and turn in the final kilometres. It proved to be time well spent. As the race built to a thrilling crescendo, Cooke and Marianne Vos – the former and current world number ones – found themselves out alone in front, locked in a sprint for the line with 200m to go. It was the sort of 'heavyweight battle' Cooke had dreamed of. In the last 50m Cooke found the energy to edge ahead of Vos, flinging her arms high in the air as she crossed the finish line.

Winning the Olympics had freed Cooke up in a way that made her even harder to beat: 'It's great to have achieved everything and not have that desperation', she said afterwards. 'At times the difference between desperation and wanting to do your best is a very fine one, and most of the time I've been in the desperation category, losing control of my tactics.'

Cooke's success ensured her name would be written into the history books. She had become the first person ever to achieve the double of Olympic and World champion in the same year, and ended a 26-year wait for British success at the senior event since Mandy Jones's win in 1982.

Having secured her status as one of the greatest female cyclists of all time, Cooke decided it was time to take matters into her own hands regarding her professional future. 'The most obvious thing to do would have been to use my status as World and Olympic Champion to negotiate for the best year's pay of my life and join an established team', she says, 'but my dream was to create a team that would act as a development opportunity for young female British riders. I wanted others to have an easier route than I had.'

Cooke set up a meeting with British Cycling supremo Dave Brailsford to gauge his interest, but left disappointed (though not surprised). With the men's road team Team Sky taking shape, there would be no resource available for embarking on a similar project for the women. Cooke pressed on regardless, announcing the launch of her team, Vision 1 Racing, in October 2008.

Containing a mixture of young and experienced riders, including an 18-year-old Dani King (who would go on to become Olympic and double World Champion as part of Britain's all-conquering team pursuit squad), Cooke's team came together for the first time in February 2009 after a winter spent chasing sponsors – a challenge that was equal to any Cooke had ever faced on the road.

'The problem was countering the perception that no one was interested in women's cycling', says Cooke, citing the lack of coverage given to the sport outside of the World Championships and Olympics. She met with the BBC sports department to discuss how they might follow the road scene, but a polite refusal was all she could prise from them: 'They felt their coverage of track cycling gave quite enough time to cycling … I can only marvel at how the nation and the BBC have now taken the sport to their hearts … but unfortunately in 2008 and 2009 my voice could not be heard.'

Before long, Cooke found herself needing to dig into her own pocket to cover the vast array of costs that come with running a professional cycling team. Financial strains aside though, the year still brought some highs for Cooke. Racing in the famous Rainbow Jersey of the world champion, she added the Giro di Trentino to her palmarès before winning a 10th national road race title.

Not long after that success however, Cooke was laid low by illness and exhaustion. She was at breaking point physically and psychologically, bowing under the strain of managing a team on a shoestring: 'Now that I was ill the enormity of what I had taken on hit me. If I didn't do it, the show stopped.'

In August 2009 Cooke took stopped the show herself, cancelling Vision 1's racing programme for the rest of the season. Now, she admits that she should have also called a halt to her own season at that point, allowing her body to regain full health. But with her spot at the World Championships waiting, and the No. 1 race number hers to defend, Cooke could not bring herself to miss the race.

'I was stubborn and I was wrong', she says, looking back. 'I had no strength in my body … I should not have been there, and dropped out halfway through.'

Towards the end of 2009 though, Cooke was getting back on track. She had a contract with Team Nurnberger – one of the two best-established teams on the women's circuit, with 16 years of unbroken sponsorship. But in December 2009, Cooke received a call from the team management. They had lost their sponsor. 'I was asked to ride for free', recalls Cooke. Instead, she looked around for alternatives, but with teams already finalised by this stage of the season, her options were limited.

Cooke's only real option was to ride as part of the Great Britain under 23 squad – the drawback being that this group would not ride all the big races and even when they did, would not be able to offer full team support to a race leader. She reached the latter part of the year with just one race win to her name all season, and a third place finish at the National Championships (behind Emma Pooley and Lizzie Armitstead), leaving her motivation at rock bottom.

Only the lure of another World Championships could inject some spark into her training, although she remembers the event in Geelong in 2010 less than fondly: 'It reflected the emaciated state of the women's peloton at that time', says Cooke. 'The race tactics were poor and as a spectacle it was uneventful for the most part.' With Cooke given free rein to ride her own race (Emma Pooley was the one whose chances were being talked up by the press on this occasion), she took advantage of a lack of action and attacked on the final climb, establishing a 15-second lead alongside the German Judith Arndt who had gone with her.

With 150m to go, however, the pair were caught. Cooke finished in fourth place, 'devastated' to have been just metres away from winning gold. Overall though, a strong British team had achieved their best collective showing ever in a women's world road race, with Lizzie Armitstead, Emma Pooley and Sharon Laws all finishing in the top 20 – a far cry from the days when Cooke was battling for Britain alone. Although, Cooke adds: 'None of the three disrupted the chase behind her and Arndt in the closing kilometres' – something that could have helped her to secure a medal.

Her season ended with a fifth place finish at the Commonwealth Games in Delhi, after another four-year cycle during which Cooke says Welsh Cycling had again 'done nothing', despite her best efforts to provoke them into action. 'At one stage they agreed to appoint a women's coach to work with the other girls', says Cooke. 'They interviewed people, made an appointment and even asked me to prepare a press release. But then they decided to cancel the programme. They told me that Shane Sutton had suggested there was no need for it.'

When it came to race day in Delhi, Cooke did have some Welsh teammates after the Welsh cycling team management made some last-minute appointments. 'They selected some very nice girls who I had never met and who had never raced at that level before, and put them in Welsh jerseys', says Cooke incredulously. 'It was all about male administrators trying to salve their consciences. Another generation of Welsh riders let down.'

Had it not been for the lure of the London Olympics, now just 18 months away, Cooke says the 2010 Commonwealth Games would have marked her retirement. But her position was now very different from the one she had occupied at the same stage of the last Olympic cycle. This time, the GB women were ranked third in the world, with Emma Pooley, Lizzie Armitstead and Sharon Laws all having progressed their careers since Beijing. It was the scenario Cooke had longed for when she was at her peak, but at this stage in her career it meant she was far less likely to be the one riding for Olympic gold on home turf.

At the World Championship road race that year, the record shows that Cooke once again finished fourth. The plan, which had been decided on at a team meeting held in the week before the race, was that five of the seven-strong British team would work for Lizzie Armitstead, with Cooke claiming she was given the freedom to ride her own race. But the night before the race, Head Coach Shane Sutton held a team meeting. 'Despite not attending any of the earlier meetings he revised the tactics', says Cooke.

'He now announced that Armitstead insisted that I should lead her out [for the sprint over the final part of the race].'

The race did not go to plan, however, when Armitstead got held up behind a crash on the final lap. She did well to move back up the field, but Cooke – who was waiting for her towards the front of the peloton – was unable to spot her. The Olympic champion rode on, finishing just out of the medals in fourth. Armitstead meanwhile recovered to finish seventh.

While the rest of the team went back to the hotel, Cooke was called to anti-doping. When she arrived back at the hotel, she says that Shane Sutton brought the whole team into her bedroom for a team meeting, before she could even change out of her racing gear. 'Shane was in no mood to let facts cloud his judgement – his mind was made up', says Cooke. 'We had failed to win a medal. And I was the scapegoat on the road. The facts are that while no stone was left unturned for "Project Rainbow" [the name given to the successful attempt by Britain's men's cycling team to win the World Championship Road Race in the same year], British Cycling did very little to develop any strategy for the road girls.'

With the Olympics just months away, Cooke felt herself being pushed even further away from the British Cycling setup. In response she pushed herself harder in winter training, beginning the Olympic year mentally and physically fatigued. Her form was such that she was surprised when the phone call came informing her that she was indeed a part of the GB squad for London 2012. This time there was no quarrel about who was the team leader: Lizzie Armitstead.

'It was clear that no matter what I hoped to achieve, my form was not good enough', says Cooke, 'I was not the rider on whom the team could rely for the gold medal'. When race day arrived, however, Cooke felt the 'heart-thumping desire to give absolutely everything I had and race for the win'. But without the physical condition to take the race on, Cooke knew she would have to ride carefully and concentrate on helping the team to perform in front of the eyes of the nation.

With the race taking place in pouring rain, just as it had done for Cooke's victory four years earlier, Armitstead secured Britain's first medal of the games, taking silver behind Marianne Vos. For Cooke, the Olympics marked the perfect point at which to confirm that her ride was over. She had seen at close quarters how the British public 'valued their daughters equal to their sons', and left the sport hopeful that their opinion would eventually prevail and remove some of the obstacles that she had confronted during her own career.

Given the endless struggles with injuries, finances, the lack of support from her governing body and the prejudice of the media, would Cooke go down the same path if she was a young girl taking up cycling today? She pauses for thought before answering: 'I would first like to know what state cycling is in at the moment in Britain.'

'If I hadn't come through and got British Cycling to put on the first under-16 girls track championships, the first junior road race and junior track championships, and if I hadn't come through and rewritten the BC team agreement where the cyclist had no rights to a fair selection and a fair appeal – if all these things hadn't happened – I wonder what BC would be like today? Would it still be like it was in the 1990s? Would it still be that sexist? Would it just be about the men? Would there be a non-existent women's track scene because they just didn't want to breathe any life into it? So I can't answer that question because I don't know what it would be like.

'If I'm asking myself, do I love cycling, do I want to race, do I want to try and get to the top of the sport? Yes, to all of those things. But when I turned professional there was a Tour de France. The World Cup had rounds in New Zealand, Australia, the USA and Canada. Now the World Cup is in Europe. So I don't know if cycling would have the same appeal today. Yes, there were tough challenges and obstacles I had to face, but I got to race in an era of cycling when it had not long peaked and I had some amazing years racing. I don't know if that would be the same with women's cycling as it is today.'

6: Mind the (participation) gap ◎

Whether it's with a warm smile or a look of sheer horror, we all remember our childhood PE lessons: the awkwardness of parading in ill-fitting nylon shorts and plimsoll shoes, the red-cheeked shame (for some of us) of being the last one standing when it came to picking teams, and the overwhelming feeling of injustice (for most of us) when we realised that, however hard we tried, we'd simply never be the quickest runner in our school.

For some, these are the days that ignite a passion for sport that lasts for the rest of their lives. For others, these are the days that turn them off sport for good, with research consistently showing that this latter group is largely made up of females. It happens worryingly early on too, with young girls dissociating themselves from sport before they have had the chance to discover its vast and varied benefits. As they mature into women, sport remains something with little more appeal than a trip to the dentist.

This goes some way towards explaining the figures from Sport England's latest research into sport participation which show that while 40.8 per cent of men currently play sport at least once a week, just 31 per cent of women do the same. Why does this matter, you might ask? Should we really expect the entire UK population to share in an overwhelming passion for sport?

Obviously not, but we can – and should – do whatever we can to ensure everyone has the tools that are necessary for a healthy lifestyle. Sport is only one part of this, but it's one that can play a huge role in improving lives and impact upon physical and mental health. It can also help to develop life skills that are invaluable when it comes to coping with the stresses and strains of life in the 21st century.

Creating a bigger pool of young girls who grow up to become women with a passion for sport would also be an important step forward for women in sport. It would certainly have a dramatic impact on the vicious cycle of women's sport that we've been looking at in the previous chapters – who knows, it could even stop it from turning altogether. Because if you boost the number of women who love sport and want to watch or be involved with it, then it will become increasingly difficult for television and newspapers to ignore women's sport, for sponsors to withhold funding and for event organisers to offer pitiful prize money.

For Baroness Sue Campbell, who is Head of the Youth Sport Trust in the UK, the task ahead is clear: 'We have to get this right in schools.' At present, the number suggests we are far from doing so, with a 2012 report by Women in Sport finding that a massive 51 per cent of all girls are put off physical activity by their experiences of school sport and PE.

The numbers tally with a 2013 study conducted by University College London researchers, which found that while half of all UK seven year olds don't do enough exercise, there is still a stark difference between the amount of activity boys are doing compared to girls. Of the 6,500 children they monitored, 63 per cent of the boys achieved the recommended hour of daily physical activity, while just 38 per cent of the girls did the same.

'The findings are particularly worrying', said Professor Carol Dezateux, one of the lead authors of the study, 'because seven year olds are likely to become less active as they get older, not more. We need to really think about how we are reaching out to girls. The school playground is an important starting point. Often you will find it dominated by boys playing football.'

This is nothing new. The drop-off in girls' participation in PE and sport was first identified in 1957 (in a report produced by British educationalist, John Wolfenden). But while much of the research into the reasons for it has focused on girls in their early teenage years, some argue that we should be concentrating on a much younger age group. David Turner, who is Development Lead for Coaching Children at Sports Coach UK, tells me: 'Admittedly, the drop off can be seen to accelerate among girls as they reach approximately 14, but this is an acceleration which could easily be exacerbated by the social effects of earlier drop-out among peers.'

Turner believes it would be more beneficial to focus on the origins of the drop-off, a period that he says seems to coincide with the transition from primary school (Year 6) to secondary school (Year 7). His view is supported by the 2012 Women in Sport report, which highlighted the fact that in Year 4 of primary school (age 8/9), girls and boys are doing similar levels of physical activity. However, by Year 6 (age 10/11) girls are doing considerably less exercise than boys – a gap that widens as girls reach Year 9 of secondary school. By this point in their lives, at the tender age of 14, it seems a large number of girls have decided that sport is simply not for them.

In a 2011 survey of 1,500 children from across primary and secondary schools, The Institute of Youth Sport at Loughborough University found that 45 per cent of girls believed that sport was too competitive. An even higher percentage said that getting sweaty was 'not feminine', while over half of all the boys and girls agreed that 'there are more opportunities for boys to succeed in sport than girls'.

Tackling these issues requires schools to recognise the barriers that Baroness Sue Campbell says are making girls fearful of PE. Among them, she includes lacking the confidence to take part and being too body conscious to do so. 'Schools that deliver PE well recognise these challenges', says Baroness Campbell, 'and offer a wider variety of sports and physical activity that make girls feel included and encourages them to get involved.'

Not all girls are sold on the idea of team sports like football or hockey, just as not all boys are. But while boys are likely to find other options that do suit them (perhaps because they are more encouraged to do so), it seems girls need a little more help to find an activity that they enjoy. The quickest and easiest way to help is simply to ask girls what it is they want, says Managing Director of the Youth Sport Trust in the UK, Alison Oliver: 'Many girls are simply not interested in traditional PE and sport, and unless schools give their students a voice, and ask them what they would like to take part in, they risk putting them off physical activity for life.'

This is an approach that Judy Murray – tennis coach and mother of Britain's number one, Andy Murray – agrees is the way forward. For her, the key to getting children into sport from an early age is to make it a fun learning experience for them. And that, says Murray, involves looking at what girls want and doing our best to provide it: 'Dance, for example, being an incredibly popular physical activity for girls, is a great way of encouraging them to get active. It's non-competitive, can be delivered easily to large groups and is accompanied by music (another massive influencer on girls). Not everyone likes dance ... but the general principle of making activity enjoyable remains the same – the answer lies in a variety of fun, lively classes, led by fun, lively teachers.'

In 2015 I visited Blackheath High School for girls in south London, where the pupils are presented with a vast array of options for being active. There are the usual offerings like netball, hockey and athletics (though not football. The head of PE tells me that none of the all-female PE staff at the school are qualified to teach it, and they clearly don't think the interest is there from the girls that would persuade them to hire a specialist football coach). But the girls are also given off-site choices like horse riding, tennis, rowing and canoeing. On-site, the school employs specialist coaches to teach activities like fencing, boxercise, basketball, self-defence and the dance fitness phenomenon, Zumba. There's also a small gym with treadmills, cross trainers and weights. On a noticeboard in the sports hall I spy a collection of photographs showing pupils taking part in extracurricular events like organised 5k runs or ski trips. The message is clear: Being active is something to be proud of.

And yet, when I speak to the Head of Upper School, Paul Atkinson, he tells me that from around the time pupils reach Years 10 and 11 being 'sporty' is viewed as being not 'cool'. Pupils are obviously more focused on exams and results by that stage, and Atkinson tells me that in some cases parents contribute to the problem. He gives the example of a mother who once rang up the school after her daughter had missed an exam through illness. Her suggestion was that she could miss PE to take it – something Atkinson says he ensured didn't happen (he arranged for her to do it, just not at the expense of skipping PE). No matter how hard the school works to get girls into sport, it seems the attitudes of those around them (friends and family) will always have the ability to trump their efforts.

Atkinson also points out that a lot of girls are put off by the idea of getting hot and sweaty during school hours and then having to go back to lessons. He tells me that the school used to have showers on site but that they were removed because the girls weren't using them (and they were ancient). He believes that installing new ones in the style of a gym changing room with hairdryers, cubicles and plug sockets for hair straighteners would make a big difference in terms of encouraging the older girls to take part in sport and physical activity. Such things are often overlooked but in reality, they are factors stopping many girls from embracing sport in schools – even more frustratingly, they're probably the simplest ones to fix.

At primary school level, where teachers in charge of PE lessons are rarely specialists and teach it alongside other subjects, hairdryers aren't a priority – but getting help from sports specialists can be crucial. Alyssa Gunn is an old school friend of mine who now teaches at a primary school in Bedfordshire, where pupils range from Reception age (between four and five) to Year 4 (ages eight to nine). She tells me that they too brought in external specialist PE teachers to take one of the two PE lessons children were given each week, with the other one being taken by the class teacher. But as of the current school year that started in September 2015, Gunn tells me they are no longer needed. Instead, the school has trained up a member of staff to become a specialist PE teacher, meaning that is the only subject she'll teach. It's clear from this willingness to spend money on bringing in outside expertise and spend time training up a member of staff that Gunn's school recognises the importance of school sport – something that will help show the pupils that they too should consider it an important part of their lives.

According to the most recent figures from the UNESCO Institute for Statistics released in 2013, some 87 percent of primary school teachers in the UK are female. Indeed, at Gunn's school in Bedfordshire, they all are. Not all of them will have an interest in or passion for sport, and in the past many wouldn't have even bothered to change out of their teaching attire to take charge of a PE lesson. But some schools are starting to address these issues. For example, at Gunn's school, teachers come to school dressed in their 'PE kits' when they are teaching it.

When I ask Gunn whether she has noticed a difference in the way the boys and girls at her school engage with PE lessons, she shakes her head, telling me they have an equal number of girls and boys who take part in the after school sports clubs and enter inter-school tournaments. She does, however, add that this could be down to the fact that the children are still very young (the oldest are in Year 4, so are between eight and nine years of age), and ponders at what point down the line it is that the girls she sees – 'who have that lovely joy and enthusiasm for PE, sport and games' – might lose it (if the research mentioned earlier is correct, then it is usually just a year or two after Gunn's pupils move on from her school).

Gunn's overwhelming belief is that as long as PE is totally inclusive for all, then the notion that sport isn't really for girls shouldn't even enter young girls' minds. If school was the only influencer on the minds of children then her ideal might be feasible, but the majority of what they see and hear in everyday life is sadly far more likely to leave them believing differently.

The home is one obvious place that plays a critical role in shaping the minds of young girls. It's there that the words and actions of their parents will be absorbed, and when it comes to sport this can go one of two ways. In June 2015 the Football Association released the results of a survey in which they asked 1,000 dads which sports they would encourage their sons and daughters to play. When it came to their sons, football topped the list of sports that dads would want them to play. But they were less keen on the idea of their daughters kicking a ball around. In a list of sports dads wanted their daughters to play, football came seventh behind swimming, athletics, gymnastics, tennis, netball and martial arts.

Asked to explain their choices, a quarter of the dads surveyed said they believed other sports were 'better suited' to their daughters, while just under a quarter said that they thought their girls would prefer to play other sports. Just over 20 per cent said that they didn't encourage their daughters to play because 'football is a man's game' while some even said that it was 'unladylike' to play football, or that their daughter would be perceived as 'butch'. Finally 13 per cent of the 1,000 dads interviewed took the pre-historic view that 'women aren't built to play football'.

What hope does a girl have of breaking free from the stereotypes if her immediate family are the ones reinforcing them? This can also go the other way of course, and there are plenty of examples of sportswomen whose fathers have been instrumental in putting them on the path to sporting greatness – even in traditionally 'male' sports. Former England cricketer Beth Morgan is one such example. I was at high school with Morgan (before she became an international star) and remember her playing cricket on the school's boys' team as there was no girls' cricket team.

She tells me that as a child she was too shy to play cricket in a local boys' team (at school it was easier as the boys all knew how good she was and the teachers encouraged her), and was content to play in her back garden. But when she was 13 her dad noticed an advert in a local paper about a girls' taster session at Gunnersbury Women's Cricket Club and took her along. She's been there ever since and can look back on her pivotal role in England's World Cup wins in 2009 as well as the victorious Ashes campaigns of 2005 and 2008. Beth says that if her dad had not been so supportive and interested in sport she would probably never have followed up her passion for the game.

Of course, not every child pays close heed to what their parents say or do – some make damn certain to do exactly the opposite, in fact. But encouraging parents to present all sports as being equal, no matter what gender their child happens to be, is key to withering away the traditional notions of what is for girls (and boys) and what it not.

In recent years there has been no shortage of debates and discussions about these different ways in which we can encourage more girls to participate in sport and activity. Talking is never a bad thing, but sometimes it can get in the way of more useful, practical, things, like action. After attending a Women in Sport Conference in 2014 at Stirling University, where she works as the Head of Sport Management, Professor Leigh Robinson came to the conclusion that it was time for the talking to stop.

On the Thoughts in Sport website that belongs to her research group, Professor Robinson wrote an article headlined 'Women in Sport: We have to do something different'. In it she said that, although she agreed wholeheartedly with much of what was said at the Women in Sport conference, a lot of it had been very familiar, ultimately because she's heard it all before: 'Despite decades of programmes and initiatives aimed at improving both the participation of women in sport and their role in the leadership of sport, we are not winning.

'The statistics associated with participation and leadership have barely changed during the past two decades, despite initiatives, interventions and programmes designed to change the situation … We are still facing the same barriers, talking about the same issues and seemingly unable to do anything about it. "Running like a girl" is still an insult!'

In order to make a real change, she continues, radical thinking is required. Her first port of call is funding: specifically, focusing funding on increasing the participation of young girls: 'We should limit funding to initiatives that focus on building participation in young girls – not a popular thing to do – but we need to stop spreading the resource too thinly.'

Positive discrimination is used in other areas of life, so why not in schools? Shaun Dowling is the Head of Sport at United Learning (a group of schools across the country), a role that sees him help 50 state academies and independent schools to improve the quality of their PE offerings. Like Professor Robinson, he too believes that investment in school sport needs to be weighted in favour of getting more girls active, telling listeners at (yet another) seminar on women and sport that his company is over-investing in girls' sport in 2015. It would be too bureaucratic, says Dowling, to aim for equal expenditure (not to mention impossible to regulate). And above all, he says, over-investing on girls' sport and PE is simply the right thing to do given the 'historical inequalities'.

Professor Robinson echoes the need for more options in terms of the sports and activities offered on school grounds (as opposed to externally), saying that 'the need to leave school to take part in sport provides too many points where girls can just opt out'. For boys there is often a stronger bind to extracurricular activities – if they're in a football or cricket team, then it's normally something they're part of with a group of friends, meaning they're less likely to give it a miss if the weather is bad or their parents can't take them. Keeping girls at school instead, in what they feel is a familiar and safe environment, cuts down the chances of them ditching it in favour of time at home or with friends.

She suggests that, like Blackheath High School and Alyssa Gunn's school in Bedfordshire have done, external help could be brought in from sports clubs, local authorities and commercial providers, to provide opportunities. Ensuring that all this happens within the school environment helps to 'reinforce the importance of participation', says Professor Robinson, because children inherently understand that 'things done at school are important and part of education, leading to a good future'.

Professor Robinson's final suggestion is that sport should be mixed, as much as possible: 'If we want to tackle the "run like a girl" belief, we need to show girls and boys (and men and women) that running like a girl looks pretty much the same as running like a boy.'

Surveys often reveal though that for many girls – particularly those that have reached puberty - mixed PE classes are actually part of the problem. These girls are so self-conscious about their bodies and appearance that they don't like to be seen exercising, particularly by boys. It is also difficult to push for mixed classes when it comes to contact sports because of the physical differences between the genders.

So while mixed PE lessons at primary school aren't delivering Professor Robinson's message (because as she says, the "run like a girl" belief persists), research doesn't offer much hope that combining girls' and boys' PE lessons at secondary school is a solution.

One aspect that mixed lessons could help with, though, is the traditionally held idea of some sports being 'girls' sports' and others 'boys' sports.' At secondary school, boys and girls are often offered different sets of activities, based on the perceived appeal of various sports (as well as arguments around the differences in physical capabilities). But the idea of separating boys and girls on the basis that certain sports only appeal to one gender becomes a faintly ridiculous notion when you consider that in the UK, football is considered to be a 'boys' sport' and rounders largely a 'girls' sport', whereas in the USA, soccer is a 'girls' sport' and baseball is 'for boys'. Unless girls and boys are physiologically different on each side of the Atlantic, then this alone shows up the sporting stereotypes for what they really are: nonsense.

Shaun Dowling says that in the UK progress is definitely being made towards breaking these stereotypes. He points to the fact that decisions on separating activities by gender are now made locally, as opposed to forming part of a nationwide 'system' on how to offer sport in schools. His observation, having worked with around 50 different schools for United Learning, is that girls are increasingly taking part in activities that were historically considered the male preserve. He notes lots of girls' football going on (he clearly hasn't been to Blackheath High School), lots of girls' rugby (something that was never offered to me as a schoolgirl), lots of girls taking part in cricket and so on. While it's perhaps idealistic to believe these girls will leave school believing that 'boys' sports' and 'girls' sports' don't exist (as I mentioned earlier, those beliefs are projected onto them in lots of other ways), it is a definite step forwards.

From what I have seen, the variety of sports on offer in schools seems to vary hugely depending on the interests/experience of the teachers. At Blackheath the girls don't get to play football because there's no one there who wants, or feels able, to coach it. At my own primary school, I spent my lunch times playing football in the playground with the boys and (I think) was pretty good at it. But the sport I ended up pursuing was table tennis, not football, because while we had no girls' football team, we did have an after-school table tennis club. It was there that the teacher in charge encouraged me to start playing at a local club, and from there I went on to compete for my borough, county and country. But who knows what might have been if I'd had the same encouragement on the football pitch? It all seems so arbitrary. Should it really come down to 'luck of the draw' as to whether a young girl is able to find a sport she can enjoy?

The UK is by no means alone in its struggle to get more girls playing sport. In America too, girls have been found to take up sport (meaning joining clubs or teams outside of school) later than boys (at 7.4 years compared to 6.8 years for boys), and give it up sooner. Research by the US based Women's Sports Foundation in 2012 found that by the time they reach the age of 14, girls are dropping out of sports at twice the rate of boys.

This is despite the US introducing a revolutionary piece of legislation called Title IX in 1972. Often seen by those outside of America as a sort of 'cure-all' for issues relating to sports participation, Title IX was signed into law by President Nixon on 23 June 1972. It stated that 'no person in the United States shall, on the basis of sex, be excluded from participation in, be denied the benefits of, or be subjected to discrimination under any education program or activity receiving Federal financial assistance'.

The upshot of which was that, suddenly, doors that had been closed to women wanting to take part in sport at schools, colleges and universities across the US were blown wide open. Once Title IX was passed, all government-funded institutions had to provide female students with equal opportunities to participate in educational programmes, including physical education.

'Athletic scholarships for women did not exist before 1972', said Billie Jean King when I met her in Singapore in 2014. 'When I was in college at Cal State in Los Angeles I had to work two jobs to have a little money while also playing tennis. But Arthur Ashe and Stan Smith had full scholarships 30 miles away. So Title IX was huge. Probably one of the most important pieces of legislation of the 20th century in the United States.'

One only needs to glance at the numbers to understand King's point. Since Title IX was passed, the number of girls participating in secondary school athletics in the USA has increased from fewer than 300,000 to more than three million – from 7 per cent of the relevant female population to nearly 41 per cent. In comparison to this 10-fold increase in numbers, the proportion of male high-school athletes grew just 22 per cent over the same time frame.

Three-time Olympic track and field gold medallist, Jackie Joyner-Kersee was 10 years old when Title IX was passed. She recalls her days in elementary/primary school, when cheerleading was about the only sport girls were allowed to do. 'By junior high, they let us play', she says, 'but we had to come back after 6:30pm to practise because there was only one gymnasium and the boys used it first.' Not that Joyner-Kersee let that put her off. She went on to star on the track and basketball court for UCLA before winning six medals over four Olympic Games between 1984–96.

Title IX led to an explosion in the number and quality of female high-school and college athletes, but its work is far from complete. Between 2008 and 2013, the gap between male and female athletic participation at high-school level grew, with 1.3 million more spots available for male athletes on high-school and college teams than there are for female athletes.

'Title IX hasn't finished its job', says former Olympic swimmer Nancy Hogshead-Makar, who is now a professor at Florida Coastal School of Law. She explains that while most schools have the same number of teams for boys and girls, there are not the same number of spots available within those teams. 'So if you have boys' sports like [American] football and baseball [which don't have women's teams at college level], with lots of numbers, and you compare them with girls' sports like golf and tennis, that's where you get the big gaps.

If you're going to have football, you need to have three more girls' sports in order to give girls the same opportunities.'

The discrepancy can also be seen at college level in the total value of athletic scholarships that go to men and women. Overall, female college athletes receive $183 million less than male athletes ($965 million female vs. $1.15 billion male). Again, this can be skewed by the arms race that is college football and men's basketball – two sports that dominate the college sports landscape (while colleges do have women's basketball teams, they don't attract the same level of attention and thus funding as their male equivalents).

Would introducing a UK version of Title IX help to solve the issues around girls' participation? On this evidence, probably not, and many don't believe it is actually necessary. Alexandra Kyrke-Smith is co-founder of the Sporting Speak website, which focuses on issues of policy, development and participation. She says that current legislation in the UK is adequate, thanks to the Sex Discrimination Act of 1975, which makes good provision for the legal challenge of any inequality by sex in the provision of services, and is framed in such a way that programmes of sport and physical education are covered.

Kyrke-Smith says the main issue is that no one knows for certain whether boys and girls are equally provided for at school, or not. A government report on women and sport published in July 2014 cited 'overwhelming anecdotal evidence that funding in the UK was given primarily to boys' sports in schools', adding that 'anecdotal evidence was the only evidence available because neither the allocation nor the impact of spending was appropriately measured.'

The report suggested that the Youth Sport Trust could step in to monitor funding allocation, resource and opportunity in terms of gender equality and provide some hard facts before any decisions regarding legislation are made – something that Kyrke-Smith says would be the right approach: 'The difference between the UK and the US is not that the US has Title IX, it is that the relevant legislation has been backed up with hard data on the allocation of resources and provision of opportunity which in turn allows the legislation to be adequately enforced.'

The Department for Education did collect some facts and figures on the differences in the provision of sports for boys and girls, in their 2009–10 PE and Sport Survey. They found there was no difference at all in terms of the sports offered to boys and girls at primary school level – so the same sports were available to both genders. At secondary school level, boys and girls had access to an equal number of sports, but (as mentioned earlier), there were differences in the *types* of sports on offer to them. For example, cricket and rugby union were both more likely to be offered to boys than girls, with boys 11 per cent more likely to be able to play the former and 15 per cent more likely to be offered the latter. Levelling up the numbers, though, were sports like dance, rounders and netball, which were all offered to girls more than boys. Interestingly, there was only a marginal one per cent difference in the allocation of football to boys and girls at secondary school level.

For now though, a spokesperson for the Youth Sport Trust told me they have no plans to undertake any deeper investigations into the allocation of funding that goes into boys' and girls' sports in schools. Having that kind of information would undoubtedly add to the overall picture on girls' participation in sport, but in its absence there are other factors that we can focus on to help fill in the gaps when it comes to understanding why so many girls choose a life without sport.

Jo Pavey is an Olympic athlete and proud owner of the moniker 'the oldest woman to become a European Athletics Champion' after she won 10,000m gold at the age of 40 in 2014. But even she recalls her experiences of school PE lessons with a grimace: 'When I was younger we had quite a strict PE kit. We had to wear little short skirts and a lot of young girls were quite self-conscious. If your starting point in sport is that you feel uncomfortable, then it's always going to make you feel negative towards doing sport.

'Obviously the message should be that it doesn't matter what shape you are or what you look like, but at that age it's not about that. You're not mature enough to think that way, you're just thinking how uncomfortable you feel. At that vulnerable age, girls shouldn't have that as an issue when it comes to doing sport.'

Pavey says girls should be given a choice of what to wear when they take part in sport (these days some schools do allow a modicum of choice, i.e. over the type of shorts pupils wear, for example). Her view was supported by research that Virgin Active did for their Active Inspiration campaign in 2014. Their study found that 46 per cent of 16-year-old girls say they enjoyed being active but hated their school PE kit, while over a quarter of the girls surveyed said they avoided doing sport because the kit 'made them feel ugly'.

It's clear that girls' school days are a critical period in forming their relationship with sport and that there is plenty of scope for improving their experiences of school sport. It would be hugely beneficial if the Youth Sport Trust were to dedicate their resources to finding out the hard facts on spending in schools so that we are not just relying on anecdotal evidence. Knowing the numbers would allow for plans to be put in place to ensure resources are spread more equally among girls and boys.

Choice is also key, whether that's in terms of the activities on offer or the kit girls wear; give pupils a say and they are far more likely to respond in a positive way. More schools are realising this now but the age-old tendency to label sports as being either 'for girls' or 'for boys' remains a tough one to eradicate.

Looking back, one wonders what the impact has been of the coalition government's decision to cut spending on school buildings by 60 per cent in 2010. Is this the reason why schools like Blackheath have failed to replace old changing room facilities, deterring girls from getting involved in any activities that might cause them to break sweat? Investing in such resources would not only make girls more enthusiastic about P.E but would also send them an important message that they will hopefully remember even after their school days are over: sport is worth the effort.

Sadly, no amount of money can heal the body image issues that are so rife among young girls (and boys, too). A 2012 enquiry into body image by the All Party Parliamentary Group (APPG) found evidence that body dissatisfaction in the UK was 'on the rise', and that while it affected a huge range of people, children and young people were found to be particularly vulnerable to body anxiety.

Girls as young as five years old were found to be worried about the way they look and their size, while one in four 7-year-old girls had tried to lose weight at least once. Evidence submitted to the APPG suggested that 'from about the age of five, children begin to recognise that they are different from other people, and to understand that they may be judged because of this ... children of this young age are aware that certain body types are more acceptable in society than others.'

In the US, researchers report a similar scenario, finding that when 'kindergarten-age children are asked to indicate their ideal body size, nearly a third of them choose a size that's smaller than their own. But by age six, kids are aware of what "dieting" means and may have tried it. By age 10, 80 per cent of American girls say they've been on a diet.'

Girls' dissatisfaction with their bodies is undoubtedly a barrier to participation. Research from Women in Sport has shown that 76 per cent of girls agree with the statement that 'Girls are self-conscious about their bodies'. The same study reported that just over a quarter of girls agreed with the following: 'I feel my body is on show in PE and this makes me like PE less.' This rises to over a third of the least active girls. The irony here is that taking part in sport or physical activity plays a huge role in developing a positive body image and raise self-esteem, once you allow it to.

Breaking down the initial barrier is notoriously difficult, however, especially when so many girls are still growing up believing that sport is for boys. Some 48 per cent of girls surveyed said that getting sweaty was not feminine, while a third of boys questioned said that they too didn't think sporty girls were very feminine. While sporty boys are valued and admired by their peers, sporty girls are not (at least not in the same way), and, for many, the fear of falling foul of this 'social norm' is a big enough barrier to stop them from taking part in sport.

This could have been the case for Olympic athlete Jo Pavey, who tells me: 'At school I was really determined to do my running, and I loved going to my athletics club where I had a whole new group of friends. But at school I felt almost alienated – like I wasn't in with the in crowd. It made me feel like I wasn't cool because I did sport.'

Pavey pursued her passion regardless though, displaying the single-minded focus that has taken her to such heights during her athletics career. She believes one way to change things is to ensure that young girls see plenty of examples of how sport creates strong, successful women: 'It [being sporty] needs to be seen as a positive thing so young girls can feel self-esteem from doing sport. But I think that with all the role models coming through now, more girls should see it as something to be proud of.'

Pavey mentions the success of Team GB's female athletes at London 2012 – an event that is widely thought of as one that put Britain's sportswomen in the spotlight like never before. During the 2012 Olympics female athletes suddenly appeared all over mainstream television and on the covers of magazine titles like *Zest*, *Vogue* and *GQ*. Indeed it was a woman – Lizzie Armitstead – who won Britain's very first medal of the Games in the women's road race, while Jessica Ennis-Hill's gold medal winning performance in the Heptathlon sent the nation into raptures on 'Super Saturday'.

There can be some pretty vicious downsides to the attention for female athletes, however. Those who are considered to not conform to what is considered to be the 'athletic ideal' can find themselves the subject of social media abuse, or even be ridiculed on prime time television by comedians looking for a cheap laugh. Both of which have happened to former Olympic champion swimmer, Rebecca Adlington.

Not long after she won Olympic gold in 2008, the comedian Frankie Boyle invited widespread criticism for making a joke about Adlington's looks ('The thing that nobody really said about Rebecca Adlington is that she looks pretty weird. She looks like someone who's looking at themselves in the back of a spoon'). Adlington made a formal complaint and Boyle was reprimanded by the BBC Trust, who branded his comments 'humiliating' and 'offensive'.

In online spaces like Twitter and Facebook, such comments might not get the same huge audiences as those made on the BBC, but they are no less hurtful. In the lead up to London 2012 Adlington spoke out about the abuse she frequently received on Twitter, which was almost exclusively based around how she looks (this is discussed in more detail in the next chapter, on body image). Adlington is by no means the first (or last) female athlete to be judged on how she looks, over and above how she performs. It is incredibly sad that sportswomen cannot just enjoy the rise in profile they deserve without the unwelcome addition of increased scrutiny over how they look. And even sadder for the young girls who might read or hear comments like those made by Frankie Boyle, and believe that their appearance will always speak louder than their achievements.

In the aftermath of every Olympic Games, maintaining the raised profile of female athletes is a serious challenge (as Chapter 1 discussed). 'If you can't see it, you can't be it' is an oft-quoted phrase when it comes to women in sport, but it's an accurate one. If young girls grow up with reality television stars and celebrities bursting out of every programme they watch and adorning every magazine they read, then why would they aspire to be the next England football captain or gold-medal-winning Olympian?

Creating strong media profiles for sportswomen is a challenge that is now being met with more positive action than ever before. For example, women's magazine *Glamour* launched a campaign in January 2015 titled 'Say no to sexism in sport', with the aim of introducing their readers to these amazing sportswomen who often go under the radar. Putting this kind of coverage in front of an audience that might not necessarily consider themselves to be 'sporty' could play a key role in helping to change the views of those girls who still see sport as being something for the boys.

As noted at the beginning of this chapter, it isn't only young girls who are shying away from sport: women of all ages are less inclined to take part in sport and activity than their male counterparts. The difference in participation levels might narrow slightly as we get older (largely because the participation levels of men drop off after the age of 30), but the gap remains. 'Sport isn't working as well for women as it is for men', was the simple message conveyed by Sport England's Director of Insight, Lisa O'Keefe, at a seminar on Women and Sport in 2015.

Sport England's research into why this is happening identifies three main barriers that stand in the way of women doing more sport or physical activity. Firstly, there are the emotional issues that often develop early on (during school days, for example) and can take many years to change. Secondly, there is the anxiety over capability. Few men will ever admit to worrying they are not good enough to take part in a weekend kick about or round of golf, but for women it's often a real sticking point. If they don't feel confident that they can do something 'well enough', then often that is all it takes to stop them from taking part. And thirdly are the practical issues that often get in the way of women being sporty or active – the lack of free time to do so or challenges over cost and location.

This last point is one that many mothers struggle with – the concept of 'free time' becoming something of an alien one after having children. Mumsnet CEO Justine Roberts says that time for yourself goes out of the window when you have a family, and that sport 'falls squarely into that category'. She does add that dads do still somehow manage to enjoy their 'me time': 'Not surprising, given Mumsnet research shows that working women undertake double the number of chores as working men.'

Even for those women who can find the time to go out for a run or visit the gym, the creeping feeling of guilt at sacrificing family time for it often haunts them. One mum I spoke to, who has a two-year-old son and was regularly active before his arrival – playing hockey for a local team and regularly going out for runs – told me she gave up the hockey because matches are at weekends, which is precious family time, and she only occasionally makes it out the door for a 20-minute run after work, usually preferring to spend time with her son before he goes to bed.

There are of course exceptions. As I write this, Jessica Ennis-Hill has just won a gold medal in the heptathlon at the World Championships, 13 months after giving birth to her first child, Reggie. While Ennis-Hill has the excuse that sport is her job, rather than a pastime, her victory is evidence that it is possible to be a mum and still devote time and energy to something else that is important to you – and training for seven different events requires a huge amount of both those things.

Another mum I spoke to (this one not an elite athlete, but a woman who took up running only *after* having her two daughters), told me that she has never really understood the idea that some women feel guilty for taking time out to exercise: 'I'm sure the same people who say that don't feel guilty about, for instance, going out with friends. Nor should they – but time devoted to health and fitness is crucial. It's good for your health and it's good for your mental state.'

She also sees it as a way to set an important example for her children, wanting her daughters to grow up thinking that sport and exercise is fun and gender neutral: 'I want them to view it as a normal part of life.' Still, finding the time is not easy – she works full time, as does her partner, who also travels a lot for work – but she says being 'determined and a bit ruthless' allows her to find a way: 'For me, that includes running to or from work and at lunchtimes. Or sometimes extremely early in the morning, or after the kids have gone to bed. But you do have to prioritise it above other things. My social life in the week is fairly minimal!'

Obviously not all women share this mum's enthusiasm for running (or any other form of exercise), but Sport England's research did show that many do *want* to do something. Of those women who claimed to be currently inactive, six million expressed a desire to play sport. That desire, coupled with the fact that the health picture for British women was not a good one – according to a 2013 study, they (ok, we) were the fattest in Western Europe and ranked in the top 10 in Europe for inactivity among young women – inspired Sport England to launch their #ThisGirlCan campaign in January 2015. Focusing solely on getting more women in the 14–40 age bracket to be active, the campaign was designed to tackle one of the most persistent themes in women's attitudes towards sport and activity: fear of judgement.

After holding focus groups with women aged between 14 and 40 around the UK, Sport England reported that women's concerns covered a vast range of areas, from how they looked to whether they were fit enough to get fit, whether they knew the rules, whether they were too fat or too thin, and even what others might think about them taking time away from childcare responsibilities or similar to spend time on themselves.

The message the #ThisGirlCan movement was designed to send is best summed up by Tanya Joseph, who is the campaign's Executive Director: 'It was launched to say to women, if someone has a problem with me doing sport, let it be their problem: it really doesn't matter if you run like Phoebe from *Friends* or Paula Radcliffe, the point is you are running and that is worth celebrating.'

Sport England used images of real women – women who Joseph says 'are proud to show that they sweat, that they jiggle, that they have, wait for it, cellulite' – and brought them to life by linking them with strong, confident slogans, like: 'I swim because I love my body. Not because I hate it.', and one of my personal favourites: 'I jiggle, therefore I am.'

The campaign had an immediate impact, with 13 million views of the advert on Sport England's YouTube and Facebook channels in the first two and a half weeks after its launch. But Sport England's Director of Insight Lisa O'Keefe admits that judging the results of the campaign won't be quite as straightforward as counting viewing figures: 'I've been asked, how long do think it will be until you see the results of the campaign, and my simple answer is, I don't know – because we've never done anything of this size and scale before. But also because, for every woman that watches the campaign, the reaction will be different.'

Some women might have already started the year thinking about starting to exercise. For them, the campaign might have been the final push they needed to take that crucial first step. For others, who might have spent years believing that sport or exercise was not for them, it might take a little longer for the inspirational messages from #ThisGirlCan to take effect. Sport England's ultimate hope, though, is that the campaign succeeds in speaking to women in both of these camps, and everywhere in between.

It certainly made an impressive splash initially – even beyond Sport England's own social media streams. In the first few weeks of the campaign, Twitter was awash with the #ThisGirlCan hashtag. Even American rap star Missy Elliott tweeted about it (although admittedly it is her song, 'Get Ur Freak On', that can be heard in the #ThisGirlCan television clip). The hashtag has maintained a constant presence on Twitter since then too, with women using it to celebrate stories of sporting exploits (of their own and of others), and event organisers putting it in tweets letting women know where and when they can get active.

As with any campaign that aims to speak to a large group of people though, there were some who were unhappy with certain aspects of the #ThisGirlCan approach. One of the main points of concern was over the use of the word 'girl'. In an article on news and commentary website The Conversation, authors Simone Fullagar (Professor of Sport and Physical Cultural Studies at University of Bath) and Jessica Francombe-Webb (Lecturer in Sport and Education at University of Bath) argued that referring to women of all ages as 'girls' 'undermines' the campaign's 'empowering intent'.

They quoted American philosopher, Iris Marion Young, who said, '"Throwing like a girl" is a common insult that excludes women from feeling strong, capable and respected', and argued that using such language would prevent many women from engaging with the campaign's key message, writing: 'The marketing staff of Sport England appear not have considered how older women might respond to this less than inspiring form of address. Yes, there are older women depicted in the video, but how would they feel about being called a "girl"?'

Sport England's Lisa O'Keefe believes that the tone of voice used in the hashtag #ThisGirlCan is consistent with the campaign's imagery. She says it reinforces the fact that the women pictured are 'somebody like them, somebody they can really resonate with as opposed to high-performing athletes who, in many cases, exist in an unattainable world'.

The word 'girl' was also the one that came out on top when they asked women for their views, says O'Keefe: 'We tested it with our audience and that's the one that resonated most with the age group that we were targeting. What we are trying to create is a conversation amongst women where they kind of take it as their own ... that was the kind of terminology that women were using when they were discussing how they would talk to their friends. They said that was the one that felt most authentic if we were trying to get this feeling of, let's do this. It would be: Right, come on, girls, let's do this. That was the feeling behind it.'

Fullagar and Francombe-Webb's criticism doesn't end there, however. They claim that the campaign is 'still all about women's flesh', and doesn't consider that 'such symbolism might have the opposite effect to what was intended: normalising the slender body, accentuating the desirable and undesirable, what belongs and what doesn't.'

Dr Jo Welford is a research associate in psycho-social health and wellbeing at Loughborough University. When I speak to her about #ThisGirlCan, she too takes a critical stance: 'The message from the campaign is that being self-conscious is a big problem for women, and that they don't want to go to gyms because they're full of people who are going to judge you because of your body shape.'

The adverts encourage women to have the confidence to say: I don't care who's judging me, I'm going to the gym anyway. 'That's brilliant,' says Dr Welford, 'but it's not changing the context of the gym. It's just one person saying: "I don't care what other people think." What we should be more concerned about doing is trying to change the way people think.'

Dr Welford says she is uncomfortable with the idea that women need to change their attitude and then everything will be ok. 'It brings the responsibility back to women, when it shouldn't be the individual who has to take responsibility for getting over that – more about society.'

Sally Moss is a personal trainer who is playing her part in trying to effect that change in society. In 2010 she set up a training group called Ladies Who Lift, aiming to get more women involved with weight training. 'I felt that women were missing out on a lot of the fun as well as the benefits of strength training', Moss tells me, 'and that's because of the myths and misconceptions surrounding women lifting weights … The myth that just won't die is the fear that lifting weights will make you "bulky" and is unfeminine.'

So even though Moss has heard comments from women at her classes, such as 'Being stronger makes you better at everything physical – not just being strong', 'I was not prepared for the huge positive effect it had on my life outside of the gym', 'Lifting changes your mindset to "I can" rather than "I can't", making you mentally stronger and more confident', the growth has ultimately been disappointing. 'These women are still a small minority compared to the whole population', says Moss. 'Truly, I thought there would be *more* interest now than there actually is.'

Moss's experiences aside, there has been a shift in attitudes of women towards lifting weights in recent years. The #strongnotskinny movement has been gathering momentum, helped by a stream of female celebrities who have decided they would rather be able to bust out 10 press-ups than be a size zero. Gradually, more women are starting to understand the benefits of challenging their body's muscles and are realising that burning off calories on a treadmill is far from the only way to feel (and look) good. But for those women (myself included) who do decide that they enjoy being able to lift their own bodyweight and squat even more, there are still fears that it marks us out as – at best – different and unfeminine at worst.

Even elite athletes like UFC fighter Ronda Rousey and tennis star Serena Williams have had to deal with being told that they look 'masculine' because they have strong biceps or powerful shoulders. While Williams has mostly chosen to ignore the slurs, Rousey launched a fine riposte to them in 2015, when during an interview with the UFC's Embedded series, she let the world know that she takes great pride in her body and what it's capable of, saying: 'I think it's femininely bad**s as f**k because there's not a single muscle on my body that isn't for a purpose.'

The concept of femininity can be a divisive one, as the Minister for Sport and Equalities, Helen Grant discovered when she discussed it in relation to getting women active in February 2014. In an interview with the *Telegraph*, Grant was asked about the problem of many women viewing sport as an 'unfeminine' pastime. She responded: 'You don't have to feel unfeminine. There are some wonderful sports that you can do and perform to a very high level and I think those participating look absolutely radiant and very feminine, such as ballet, gymnastics, cheerleading and even roller-skating.'

Grant then echoed the suggestions of many who have spoken on the topic of engaging more girls in school sport when she said: 'We really need to take a step back and actually ask women what they want and give it to them. Whether it's a Zumba class or a game of rounders after they've dropped the kids off. That's the approach we need to take – what works for them.'

Grant believed she was simply pointing out the wide variety of ways in which women can be active – that there are options for those who might not enjoy the more 'traditional' sports or going to the gym. But some felt that her suggestions were simply another example of women being told that looks should always come first.

'It's actually discouraging for a minister to say this', wrote Laura Bates, founder of the social media-based Everyday Sexism Project. 'With our great athletes performing fantastically at the Olympics, we still see media outlets focusing on looks and femininity, which the comments seem to do too.' Bates's view was backed by a maelstrom of tweets accusing Grant of making 'sexist assumptions'.

While Grant tried to comprehend how her well-meaning comments had been turned into something so negative, a spokesperson for the Department for Culture, Media and Sport said: 'It is nonsense that the minister suggested women's participation in sport should be based on looks. The point is that there is a sport or physical activity out there for all women. For some it will be tennis or football, for others judo or dance. Women decide what they want to do based on their interests and own lives, and that choice is up to them.'

Nonsense it might have been, but the brief furore did at least ensure that Grant's message was heard by more people than it might have been, without the misinterpretation and misquotation that accompanied it. The debate also serves to illustrate just how complex the issues around participation in sport and activity are. The barriers preventing people from taking part and the motivations others have for doing so vary hugely between individuals, meaning that in terms of both a solution and a campaign designed to help change things, it is impossible to find a 'one size fits all' remedy.

Before 2012 there was great hope in the UK that the London Olympics would be just such a remedy – that it would 'inspire a generation'. And while Sport England's figures do show that the number of adults playing sport once a week is on the rise, they also show just over half of all adults play no sport whatsoever, with far fewer women doing so than men. While young girls will surely remember the golden moments featuring Jessica Ennis-Hill, boxer Nicola Adams and track cyclist Laura Trott, to name just a few of Team GB's successful women, their inspirational impact will have a limited effect if girls don't see the 'normal' women around them including sport and activity in their everyday lives.

Indeed the Olympic legacy has not had quite the impact that Chair of the Youth Sport Trust, Baroness Sue Campbell, had hoped for. In an interview with the *Independent* in 2013 she posed the question: 'In a generation's time, will we look back and think "that was the moment"?'

Speaking almost a year after London 2012, Baroness Campbell went on to say: 'I don't think we've grabbed [these issues] in the way we could have done. I think we can still do it, but it's about getting real focus on some of these big transformational issues.' One of which is improving the numbers of women doing sport. 'What we can't do is work under the assumption that they'll participate because we tell them that sport's good for you.

'You've got to get into their minds, which is, "I want to look good. I want to do better at work. I want to be attractive to the opposite sex." You've got to get into people's minds and think "how do we present activity as a way of helping you do that"? Not "Sport's good for you, come and have a dose of it" like a medicine. No. That's not going to do it.'

The motivations Baroness Campbell lists above only account for a tiny fraction of the reasons women might have for exercising. For the mother of two who I spoke to about 'guilt-free exercising' earlier in the chapter, her journey into running was a way of finding the precious 'me-time' that she felt she'd lost after having her daughters. 'At the beginning,' she says, 'I started running because I wanted to lose a bit of weight – nothing dramatic, just to feel a bit more like my pre-pregnant shape. But once I started to actually enjoy the running, the "me time" element became more important. When you go on maternity leave, people often ask you: "Don't you miss adult conversation?" My answer – with two kids at any rate – was always "No, I miss NO conversation!" I think you desperately miss (or I did, anyway) having no one to look after, no one to talk to, no one to follow you to the loo ... basically just no time whatsoever by yourself. I've always quite liked the odd bit of time by myself, and running kind of gave that back to me.'

So the methods, motivations and school sport nightmares vary wildly from woman to woman, but one thing remains constant: the need for real, radical change in how girls and women engage with sport and activity. It starts at school, where the Youth Sport Trust should step up and find out exactly what's going on in terms of allocation of funding and resources to boys and girls in relation to sport so that we know exactly where we are and what needs to be done. And beyond that, we need to keep the dialogue going between women of all ages and bodies like Sport England to ensure that every possible angle is covered when it comes to encouraging them to get active. For some, that might mean introducing them to activities like Zumba or roller skating. For others it might mean pointing them in the right direction of classes that suit their lifestyle (i.e. ones with a crèche on site for mums or options that fit around their work hours). And for many it could just mean providing reassurance that you don't have to be great to start, you just have to be there with a pair of trainers on and the willingness to have a go.

The Back to Netball campaign run by England Netball has been a resounding success and that's largely because the governing body asked what is was that people wanted from the sport. They knew that for many women, netball was a sport left behind in their school days (along with those terrible pleated miniskirts), but England Netball were convinced they could show it was worth revisiting. By delivering friendly and flexible sessions run by passionate coaches the campaign has seen fantastic results – bringing more than 60,000 women back to netball since 2010.

Without these changes, it's likely that the debates and discussions on why women are shying away from sport will still be raging 10 years from now, and another generation of girls will be well on their way to becoming women for whom sport just doesn't work.

Becky Hammon

THE LEADER OF MEN

'I very much look forward to the addition of Becky Hammon to our staff.' With this one sentence, Gregg Popovic – the head coach of NBA team, the San Antonio Spurs – sent the sports world into a spin. 'Having observed her working with our team this past season,' Popovich continued, 'I'm confident her basketball IQ, work ethic and interpersonal skills will be a great benefit to the Spurs.'

Popovich, or Pop, as he is widely known, was announcing that he had hired former WNBA star Becky Hammon to be a full-time assistant coach at San Antonio, a team that had won its fifth NBA Championship two months earlier. It was a move that secured Hammon a place in sporting history as the first woman ever to hold such a position in any of America's four major professional sports (Major League Baseball, National Football League and National Hockey League being the other three).

'Honestly, I didn't realize it was gonna be this big of a deal', said Popovich after Hammon's hiring made headlines around the world. 'People kind of went crazy, like we'd saved the world from fascism or something', he chuckled. 'It was much more important to reward her for who she is, what she's done and what I believe she can do, than worry about the reaction of people.'

Who she is and what she has done are relatively simple things to account for: Hammon is a six-time All-Star in the WNBA (the women's version of the NBA), an Olympic bronze medallist, and in 2011 was named as one of the 15 greatest WNBA players of all time. In short, she is one of the finest female basketball players the world has ever seen.

But what these top line facts don't reveal is how many times Hammon was knocked back, how often she had doors slammed in her face or how this all-American girl ended up playing on the opposing team when the USA women's basketball team faced Russia in the 2008 Olympic semi-finals.

Hammon has lived and breathed the game since she was a child, growing up in a rural part of South Dakota. She could hardly have been any other way, with a dad who had spent three decades as a basketball coach. Whenever Hammon had a few spare hours, she'd spend them with her basketball, practising her jump shots and lay ups, or playing hundreds of passes off an outside wall of the Hammon home. 'I didn't need anybody else', she says. 'I had a ball, and I had my hoop, and I didn't have to have somebody to go play catch with or throw me pitches. I grew up in the woods, I didn't have neighbours. So it was a sport that you could get really good at by yourself.'

If Hammon's older brother was around, she would join him and his friends, playing two-on-two games and testing her skills against the bigger boys who gave her nothing for free, and knocked her to the ground whenever she dared to venture 'into the paint' (the area underneath the basket on a court). It was during these childhood games that Hammon picked up the knack of exploiting angles to beat quicker defenders off the dribble and using her body to shield taller, stronger defenders when she went for lay-ups at the rim.

In those days, Hammon idolised NBA legends, Earvin 'Magic' Johnson and Michael Jordan. There was no WNBA back then – not until Hammon reached her late teens – so her dream was to play in the only professional basketball league that she knew of, and the one that had turned Johnson and Jordan into megastars – the NBA. That dream lasted until Becky reached the age of 10, when her father broke the news to her that the NBA was not for her (nor any other girl): 'No matter how good you become and no matter how hard you work at it', he told her, 'you'll never play in the NBA.'

Now, things are different, says Hammon – now, young girls have the WNBA. The league started in 1997 and since then has provided any young girl growing up with the same passion for basketball that fuelled Hammon, with countless female role models to look up to. 'There was no WNBA when I was growing up', says Hammon. 'My dad told me if I was really good, then maybe I could go to college on a scholarship, and that was kind of the end of it.'

Hammon later discovered that she could also play in the Olympics. Women's basketball made its first appearance at the Games in 1976 – a year before she was born – and the USA has dominated the competition ever since (one or two notable exceptions aside). Coupled with her basic love of the game, Becky's Olympic dream drove her on – it was what she thought about on the early mornings when she would get out of bed at the crack of dawn to 'shoot a couple of hundred shots before school'. And it was the reason she was back to do it all over again after a full day of lessons.

By the time she started high school, Hammon had already shown herself to be better than most other kids her age – boys and girls. Since the age of eight she had competed in a mixed YMCA league where the teams were made up almost entirely of boys. But when her skills marked her out as being way ahead of others her own age, her parents moved her up two age groups – something the league officials were not too happy about. Until they saw her play, that is.

'When I was better than all the boys who were even a grade, two grades ahead of me, they were like, "Oh yeah, she can stay … she can even bring up the ball".'

KICKING OFF

At Stevens High School in her hometown of Rapid City, Hammon continued to dominate on the court. She seized the starting point guard job in her second year, and by the time she graduated in 1995, she owned every significant record in the Stevens High record books, going on to be inducted into the South Dakota High School Basketball Hall of Fame. It was outside of school, though, where Hammon first realised that she had something her peers did not. And it wasn't just talent.

At basketball camps where the days started at nine in the morning and ran through to 10 o'clock at night, Hammon says the other girls were 'sick and tired of basketball' by the end of the day. While they spent their evenings chatting or watching films, she would head back to the gym, putting in the extra work that helped to set her apart. 'That's when I knew I was wired a little bit differently', she says. 'I was constantly learning, because I was constantly putting myself in situations where I could learn.'

Hammon's high school coach describes her as 'by far the best player I've ever coached' (and he spent 21 seasons coaching the girls basketball team at Stevens High). And yet when the college scouts went looking for new recruits during Hammon's senior year, the highest-profile institutions overlooked her. With her talents, Becky might have expected to be scouted by one of the major Division I programmes (the highest level of college sports in the USA), but Rapid City's remote location limited the number of college scouts who saw her play. And those who did make it left with the impression that Hammon was not of the right proportions – at 5'6" she acknowledges the fact that she 'hardly looks like a basketball player'.

But one woman looked beyond Hammon's stature and saw the passion and the potential within. Kari Gallegos-Doering was the assistant coach at Colorado State University and first spotted Hammon in the summer before her senior year of high school. While other scouts were watching more highly rated guards, Gallegos-Doering was impressed with Becky's habit of finding teammates in just the right spots, saying: 'Becky had mojo. She's just got this something special that you don't see [often].'

Gallegos-Doering saw Hammon play again at a national basketball camp a few months later, where she was among 24 high school prospects. The second viewing only confirmed her initial impressions: 'She made them look silly ... Everybody's sitting in that gym, and saw her do what she did and they missed out on her ... because of her colour, because of her size, because, yeah, she comes from South Dakota and she's not a big name.'

'I'm a typical underdog story', reflected Hammon in an interview with the *Washington Post* in 2015. 'My journey has been one of a lot of doors being closed, a lot of people saying I wasn't able to. Yet if you know me – my character, my personality traits – you know I love challenges. I love proving people wrong. Just trying to be the best that I could possibly be was a big enough motivating factor for me. It got me through a lot.'

Hammon's determination ensured that Colorado State's women's basketball team – the Rams – finally made it onto the college basketball map after years of mediocrity. During her four years as a student, the Rams made three NCAA tournament appearances (the annual National Collegiate Athletic Association tournament, which is only open to the top 64 teams in the country), including their first Sweet 16 showing in 1999 (meaning they reached the last 16 of the tournament).

A glance at the statistics shows that Hammon's influence was crucial to those results. She holds the school career record for (deep breath) points, points per game, field goals, field goal attempts, free throws made, free throw attempts, three pointers, three-point attempts, steals and assists. She also holds nine single season records including points, free throws and assists and finished her college career as the leading scorer, male or female, in Western Athletic Conference history.

In most cases, such a gilded college CV would ensure a smooth transition into the world of professional basketball. But during the 1999 WNBA draft, Hammon went unpicked, again regarded as too slow and short to have an impact at the top level. Not many undrafted players go on to make it on to the roster of a WNBA team but Hammon was fortunate. New York Liberty's first-year head coach, Richie Adubato, had spotted her during her senior year, when he just happened to watch one of Colorado State's games. For the rest of the year, Adubato tracked her progress. When she went undrafted he signed her up, primarily to fill a hole the Liberty had at the position of backup point guard.

'The thing that impressed me most was her aggressiveness and her toughness', says Adubato. 'She had to go against [US Olympic team star] Teresa Weatherspoon and Vickie Johnson. Both of them were physical, tough, fierce competitors. Her willingness to fight against those two every day amazed me. She looked about 16 years old when she came in, and to pit her against those two really told me a lot. She was fearless, a great competitor and she had the heart and the will.'

Adubato tells one tale from Hammon's rookie season in the WNBA which reveals that, from the earliest stage of her career, she had the mental fortitude needed to succeed. The Liberty made it to the WNBA Finals that year, but in the opening game, Adubato left Hammon on the bench for the entire second half, believing a fresh-faced rookie would not be capable of handling the occasion as well as his more experienced starting guards.

Adubato made his apologies to Becky after the game – which the Liberty lost – telling her that as it was their only home game in the series, they were facing the best team in the league and had to win, he thought it was 'maybe a little too much pressure for her to handle'.

'She looked me in the eyes and said, "Coach, don't ever worry about putting me in tough situations. You're going to find out that I thrive on pressure."'

In that first season under Adubato, Hammon earned her way into the rotation and thrived as the spark off the bench whenever she was called upon. In her second season, she started half of the Liberty's games at point guard, and by her sixth season, she had taken over as the team's full-time starter.

Hammon's coaching career might have been more than a decade away at this point, but Adubato saw the basis for what she would go on to become: 'Usually you can tell if someone has a desire, somewhere along the line, to go into coaching. They ask questions all the time – when you're in film sessions and going over your scouting reports, they're involved in understanding the details of the game and really wanting to know a lot about coaching.

'I saw that in Becky because she would question me a lot on certain things. She had a very nice way about her, but she was always asking questions, trying to learn more about the game ... She also was a player-coach on the floor – she really understood the game and really knew how to play the game, so I think that all carries over.'

After eight years in New York, during which time she won a place on the All-WNBA Second Team, Hammon was traded to the San Antonio Silver Stars in 2007. It was a move that she says was crucial in putting her on the path to the Spurs' head coach, Popovich: 'Without the WNBA, Pop doesn't get to observe me with my teammates ... I think him watching me play was, for him, like, "Hey, this girl, she thinks the game. She's small."

'He likes the underdogs. He likes the guys that have a little bit of a chip on their shoulder – the last kid picked at recess, you know? I think he just saw something in my game and in me, as a person and as a leader, that he identified with and said, "Hey, you know, that girl knows her stuff."'

Hammon's impact in San Antonio was immediate. She had the best season of her career in 2007, posting career high averages of 18.8 points per game and 5.0 assists per game (the highest in the league). The honours duly followed. Hammon finished second in the vote for the league's Most Valuable Player (MVP) that season, was selected as one of the five players to make the All WNBA Team, and received WNBA Peak Performer honours for leading the league in assists.

With the 2008 Olympics on the horizon, Hammon's future looked as bright as ever. She was arguably the best female player the USA had, considering that the player who had pipped her to be named MVP in 2007, Lauren Jackson of the Seattle Storm, hailed from Australia. And yet when the 23-person roster for the USA's Olympic team was announced, Hammon's name was missing.

'She was devastated', recalls Becky's mother Bev Hammon. Her daughter's agents put in numerous calls to the selectors to try and get some explanation, but according to Bev 'they never answered the phone'.

Once again, Hammon had been overlooked, only this time the reasons for it were far harder to ascertain. Friends and family suspected favouritism on the part of the national coaches – that they had selected guards from their own teams – but that type of suspicion is almost impossible to prove, especially when those under suspicion choose to maintain a deafening silence.

Months of turmoil followed as Hammon considered her options. She could sit at home and hope that USA basketball would have a change of heart or she could grab a different opportunity that presented itself – one that would give her a ticket to the Beijing Olympics in the colours of a different national team.

Since 2007, Hammon had spent the WNBA off-season playing for Russian club, CSKA Moscow. It gave her extra court time to hone her skills and meant she could earn some extra cash. Her contract with the club, which Hammon signed after finding out she was not on USA Basketball's list of potential Olympic squad members, included the possibility of playing for the Russian Olympic team – whose coach also happened to be CSKA's Sporting Director. According to an ESPN report, when Hammon later received an invite to try out for the US team, she replied that 'contractual obligations left her unable to attend'.

Before Hammon made her final decision about who to play for in Beijing, ESPN claims that she and her agent asked USA Basketball to clarify her position and were given the impression that 'she was not in serious contention to make the team'.

Despite having no ancestral ties to Russia, Hammon was able to take advantage of Russian league rules that stipulate a player can obtain a passport and become a naturalised citizen, providing they have never played for another country in an event sanctioned by the sport's international governing body, FIBA. For Hammon, who had only ever played for her country at the William Jones Cup in Taiwan in 1998, this meant she was eligible to represent Russia on the international stage.

In April 2008 Hammon ended months of mental wrangling. She would play under the Russian flag in Beijing. After making the announcement she tried to explain that in her view, it didn't make her any less of an American, telling ESPN: 'The jersey that I wear has never made me who I was. It has nothing to do with what's written on my heart … I'm 100 per cent still an American. I love our country. I love what we stand for. This is an opportunity to fulfil my dream of playing in the Olympics.'

Even now, Hammon describes it as 'one of the hardest decisions' she has ever made, but says, 'Once I made it I was very resolute. I was taking the opportunity that was given to me.' That resolve helped to keep her positive when the inevitable criticism came her way. Some labelled her a 'traitor'. The US women's basketball coach did not hold back either, saying: 'If you play in this country, live in this country, and you grow up in the heartland and you put on a Russian uniform, you are not a patriotic person in my mind.'

Hammon dug her heels in. She also made it clear that if it came to it, she would not think twice about taking a shot to knock her home country out of the Olympic tournament: 'I'm going to take that shot. I'm going to play to win. You have to be honest to the game and yourself. Sure, it will be awkward, but I wouldn't have made this decision if I wasn't ready to take that shot.'

One part of that scenario did come to pass, when Russia met USA in the Olympic semi-finals. But Hammon never got to take that shot. The USA triumphed 67-52, and went on to beat Australia in the final to win their sixth gold medal in Olympic women's basketball. Hammon meanwhile scored 22 points in a win over the host nation, China, to help Russia win the bronze medal.

Some seven years later, Hammon told the *Washington Post* how the Beijing Olympics – and the build-up to it – affected her: 'I remember being on the bronze medal stand and looking back, realizing I was a lot stronger and I could take a lot more than I ever thought I could take. It changed me, and it settled me in a way. When you know you're doing the right thing in your heart, you can take a lot of crap. The areas when you grow the most are the hard parts, not the easy parts. It's the hard parts that nobody sees, and the struggles that you go through behind closed doors that nobody has any idea about.'

By the time she went to the 2012 Olympics in London, again as part of the Russian national team, the outcry was far less. That was perhaps partly because by then, Hammon had firmly established herself as a WNBA legend. In 2011 she had earned a seventh WNBA All Star selection and become the only player in league history to participate in three different All-Star games with two different teams.

At the London Olympics, Hammon avoided a showdown with the US team. Both nations reached the semi-finals stage again, but this time Russia faced France in the final four, losing to leave themselves facing another playoff for bronze. This time there was to be no podium moment though, and Hammon flew back across the Atlantic empty handed, alongside a US team that had won yet another Olympic gold medal.

Hammon's flight home is one that will live long in her memory. Not because she spent it musing on what might have been, but because when Hammon arrived at her seat on the plane, she found a familiar face in the adjacent one: San Antonio Spurs Head Coach, Gregg Popovich. One of the NBA's most experienced and successful coaches, Popovich is also renowned for being a straight talker. 'He has no interest in playing cute or dabbling in small talk', writes Jason Gay in the *Wall Street Journal*. 'During interviews, he's as straightforward as a sledgehammer through drywall.'

Gay labels the 66-year-old as 'basketball's brilliant crabby uncle', but to Hammon, his straight-shooting attitude was more comforting than intimidating. And in Hammon, Popovich found someone with whom he could converse happily on a range of topics, with basketball merely a footnote on a diverse list featuring politics, wine and Russian culture (Popovich was born to a Serbian father and Croatian mother).

'She was very thoughtful and worldly, and could have a conversation that didn't just revolve around how to guard the pick-and-roll', said R. C. Buford, the Spurs' general manager. 'That made a very impactful impression on Pop.' The pair did, however, have one brief conversation about basketball, which Hammon recalls started with the following question from Popovich:

'So if you were an assistant for me and I asked you something, you'd tell me the truth?'

'I don't know why else you'd ask if you didn't want me to tell the truth.'

'Good, I don't want a bunch of yes men.'

This simple exchange formed the foundation of a mutual professional admiration between the pair that put Hammon on the path to an opportunity she never dreamed would come her way.

Hammon's 2013 season – her 15th as a WNBA player – got off to a delayed start after she broke her finger during a pre-season training camp, forcing her to miss the first 10 games of San Antonio's campaign. She finally took to the court on 6 July for a game against Los Angeles Sparks. But after playing for just 12 minutes, her match – and her season – was over. Midway through the second quarter she went down near the baseline and was carried off the court with a bad injury to her left knee.

Hammon had torn her anterior cruciate ligament (ACL). It meant surgery and a long period of rehabilitation before she could get back on the court. At the age of 36, many people doubted whether she would ever make it back to the WNBA. But to the seven-time All-Star who was so often told she was too small and too slow to make it, this was just another challenge for her to overcome.

'When you get physically knocked down, it also takes a toll on you mentally', she told the *Washington Post*. 'To try to come back and play in a league that is full of 21, 22 and 23-year-olds, as a 36-year-old coming off a major surgery, was certainly challenging. But

I thought: I'm going to get up every day, go to rehab, do my reps and do the best I possibly can. When you're able to have that discipline physically, you train your mind mentally. And being strong in your mind is probably, first and foremost, the thing that a great leader possesses.'

With the benefit of hindsight, Hammon now considers that injury a 'blessing in disguise'. It gave her the opportunity to take a step back, look at her life and ask: 'What can I be doing here to make the most of today?' The answer presented itself to her in the form of the NBA's 'crabby uncle' Popovich, who called up his old plane friend Hammon and said: 'You know, you can come in anytime you want.' It was an invitation she didn't need to hear more than once.

Hammon spent the season attending Spurs' team practices, listening in on video analysis sessions and observing how Popovich interacted with his team. 'She wants to coach after she's done', Popovich told ESPN in May 2014, 'and because she's not just a good player but a smart player, a great person in our community, and somebody that we respect so much, we gave her the opportunity to sit with us during the year. She came to our coaches' meetings, argued with us. She did everything.'

Asked whether he believed a female coach would ever make it in the NBA, Popovich played a trademark straight bat in response: 'I don't see why not. There shouldn't be any limitations. It's about talent and the ability to do things. It's not about what your sex is or your race or anything else.'

Hammon's informal 'internship' at the Spurs was an invaluable opportunity to learn from a man considered to be one of basketball's greatest leaders. 'It's kind of something you're born with or not born with', she says of Popovich's ability to guide and motivate the same team for 15 years (he took over as Spurs coach in 1996). 'Coach Pop is born with it, he does it naturally. To see him in his natural element and see how he interacts with the guys to me is really beneficial.'

When the 2014 WNBA season got underway in May, Hammon was back on the San Antonio Stars roster and played her part in helping them reach the playoffs, averaging 8.3 points per game, 4.2 assists per game and a perfect record from the free throw line. But by the time San Antonio faced Minnesota Lynx for the first game of a three-match series in the Conference semi-finals that August, Hammon had already decided this would be her final season as a WNBA player.

With her 16th season in the WNBA coming to an end, and despite having shown she still had much to contribute on the court, Hammon decided it was time to hang up her jersey. In an official statement released on 23 July 2014, her team announced that she would retire at the end of the season, finishing her career as the Stars' all-time leader in assists, points per game and three-point field goals made.

'To give it some perspective,' Hammon explained in an interview with the *Seattle Times*, 'our rookie [Astou Ndour] was four years old when I started in the league. You know it's getting to be that time and my body is telling me it's time. People see you out there playing at such a high level and there's definitely a price you pay body-wise ... the worst part is things hurt and our trainer will ask why and I won't even know why. I don't remember anything happening. I just wake up and it hurts.

'When I was in my mid-twenties, I said I didn't want to be that player who just sat the bench at the end and was just taking a roster spot. I want to go out as someone who still contributes.'

A little less than two weeks later came another announcement from San Antonio, this one from the city's NBA team. It was the groundbreaking news that Popovich was hiring Hammon as an assistant coach at the Spurs. His welcoming words made mention of her 'basketball IQ, work ethic and interpersonal skills', but failed to touch on the one factor that made his announcement headline news: Hammon's gender.

The local news report, however, was a different matter: 'The Spurs have made a major announcement', began an excited Joe Reinagel of Kens 5 Eyewitness News in San Antonio, 'they've hired a new assistant coach, but this one's a little bit different. It's history-making. Becky Hammon has been hired by Gregg Popovich. She becomes the first full-time female NBA assistant coach. She used to hang around with the Spurs while she was recovering from her injury, that's how Pop got to know her, plus the fact she's played eight years here in San Antonio for the Stars ...'

Hammon meanwhile was reluctant to accept the 'trailblazer' label that was being thrust upon her, telling the press: 'This is basketball. There are women who have trail blazed much bigger paths. Women are in every area – they're in surgery rooms, they're doctors, they're lawyers, they're COOs. Even me sitting here today, to be able to have the playing experience that I have as a professional basketball player, is thanks to the women who went before me to pave the way. I'm really just reaping all the benefits of their hard work.'

Hammon's position as an assistant coach gives her numerous responsibilities says Neal Meyer, who has more than 16 years' coaching experience in the NBA, including at the San Antonio Spurs. He tells me that the role can range from 'working players out' (training them physically on the court) to 'creating game plans for each opponent that you're assigned'.

'A coach might have 10 teams they're responsible for, so any time you play one of those teams you watch all the video footage of the opponent and do the prep work that you then give to the head coach before the game so he can use it to finalise the game plan.' Meyer says assistant coaches might also have 'on-bench responsibilities' during the game, offering the head coach advice and suggestions based on their scouting report. Or they might be sat behind the head coach, 'watching the other team and trying to get their "play calls" so you can give the coach a heads-up on what they might be doing'.

Another 'huge part' of the assistant coach's role, says Meyer, is developing a relationship with the players. 'You're the middle man between the head coach and them, telling them: "This is what the coach is saying", or "This is what you need to work on." It takes the pressure off the head coach having to do that all the time with the 15 players that he has.'

So, why Hammon? Many other WNBA players have gained equal amounts of experience in the game at the top level as the San Antonio star, but Hammon is the first to have moved across to work in the NBA. Meyer points out her – now renowned – 'high basketball IQ', but also says that during the season she spent with the team while recovering from her knee surgery, Hammon developed a strong working relationship with the Spurs players. 'I think Pop saw how she interacted with them, even though she wasn't hired as a coach at that time, and it made him realise the value of having her in that position.

'It's not always easy to take that risk to be the first team to hire a woman as an NBA assistant coach, though. Pop is one of the best coaches in NBA history so he has the weight to say "I'm gonna do it" and people respect that. If it was another coach who wasn't as successful, people might have questioned it more. Mainly, though I think they hired her because she knows what she's doing, she has a proven track record playing and they saw that she could gain the respect of the players when she was there prior to being hired.'

Hammon takes a similar view: 'I don't think the Spurs ever set out to hire a woman. It just happened. And it was never really a goal of mine to be a female assistant in the NBA. But, through the course of getting to know Coach Popovich and the staff and the players, they decided I was the right person for the job. I don't really think gender had any role in them hiring me. I think it was: "Does this person fit in? Does this person bring something to the table that could help our team win?"'

One of the key questions that Hammon's story raises (and she touches upon it in the above quote) is why a clearly talented basketball coach has stepped away from the women's game to work for a men's team? Hammon says that it was 'never really a goal of hers' to move into the NBA but when the opportunity came calling, she was never going to turn it down in favour of taking a job in the WNBA.

To understand why, it's helpful to compare the two leagues in terms of stature and profile. While the WNBA is a well-established professional league (at time of writing, its 19th season has just come to a close), it is still very much in the shadow of its male counterpart. In 2014, the NBA's top-rated broadcast (Finals Game 5) drew 18 million viewers. The WNBA's most-watched game (Game 2, West Finals) had 828,000 viewers. That's less than five per cent of the NBA's audience, and on the same network.

More viewers means more money for TV deals, which in turn creates more cash for player salaries. The WNBA forbids public disclosure of player contracts or salaries but what we do know is that the league has a minimum salary in place of $37,950, with a maximum (available only to players who have played for at least six seasons) of $107,000. Using these figures, a report on the BuzzFeed website estimated that, across the entire 12-team WNBA league, a total of around $10.3 million was being paid to players in salaries.

The report put this number into context by standing it up against the salaries of top NBA players including LA Lakers star, Kobe Bryant. In the 2013–14 season, Bryant made $30,453,805 – a total that's almost three times as much as the entire WNBA. His salary alone amounted to the average salaries of 423 WNBA players.

I'm not suggesting that Hammon was in any way motivated by money in her decision to join an NBA team. But looking at the hard facts it's easy to understand why she would consider it a better career move than taking a similar job at a WNBA team. It's about status. Hammon (and many basketball fans) consider Popovich to be one of the best basketball coaches the game has ever seen. Hammon told ESPNW that the opportunity to learn from him was one that she simply couldn't turn down. 'To be able to sit there and be a student and just listen … I knew this was somebody that could teach me a lot, not just about basketball, but about life … This is one of those opportunities that is kind of bigger than life, like, "Wow, pinch me". For me, to step into that kind of learning space was a no-brainer.'

It's a sad fact that while there might be female coaches out there with just as much knowledge and ability as Popovich, they don't have the same opportunities to reach his levels of fame and acclaim. If Hammon is to achieve a similar position in basketball, then for now, there is only one place that will take her there: The NBA. The hope is, though, that Hammon's presence and influence in the NBA will lead to this changing and mean that eventually, the same status available to Popovich and his colleagues will be achievable by a coach in the women's game, too.

The high-profile nature of her job at the Spurs means she is under more pressure than any male coach would be in her position – if she fails, it won't be because she's 'not a good coach' but because she's a woman. Equally, if Hammon succeeds (which at time of writing she certainly is, having led Spurs to victory in the annual NBA Summer

League – when teams typically try out different players ahead of the next season), her success will show that gender is no barrier when it comes to leading a team.

It will also show the current crop of WNBA players that there is a future in the game for them once they stop playing. The question is, by the time these young players reach that stage of their careers, will the disparity in profile and pay between the two leagues have narrowed? Will they see becoming a WNBA coach as a career that will bring them the same level of respect that Hammon has garnered from her time at the Spurs? Hammon has broken a barrier by becoming the first female assistant coach in the NBA, and that is something worth celebrating. But at the same time we can also be a little saddened by the fact that her job is considered to be so much better than it would be if the league she worked in started with a 'W'.

When Popovich offered Hammon the position at Spurs it was the first time that a door had opened for her at a first attempt, without several others being slammed in her face first. Whether it was the college coaches who believed she was too short and slow, the WNBA directors who ignored her in the draft, or the Olympic coaches who left her out in the cold, Hammon had always faced a fight to get to where she knew she belonged. Not this time, though.

On the day Popovich called to offer her the job, Hammon could hardly contain her emotions.

'She actually had tears in her eyes', recalls her mother, Bev. 'She says, "Mom, they picked *me*. Nobody has ever picked me. They picked me."'

Hammon says that for now, she does not know what the 'end game' is for her as a basketball coach: that for now, she's happy to be learning and 'becoming a better basketball mind'. But what she does know is that her story is one that sends out a strong message to young girls today. 'If I had five dollars for every guy that walked up and challenged me to one-on-one, maybe I would have been retired by now and I wouldn't need a job. But for me, there's a bigger message: the idea that you can do anything you want to do. I mean, the sky is really the limit. I'm doing basketball. You can be a CEO of a company. You might even be the president of the United States someday. I think women are just scratching the surface of what we can accomplish.'

7: Body matters

In 2013 the former Olympic champion swimmer Rebecca Adlington broke down in tears on national television, admitting to suffering from crippling insecurities over her looks. Viewers were stunned. This was a world-beater, a woman who had reached the absolute pinnacle of her sport and someone whose strength of body and mind had played an intrinsic role in getting her there.

'It makes me very, very insecure that I have to look a certain way', Adlington revealed in a teary conversation with her campmates on the reality TV show, *I'm a Celebrity ... Get me Out of Here!* 'For me, I was an athlete, I wasn't trying to be a model, but pretty much every single week on Twitter I get somebody commenting on the way I look.'

Perhaps it should not have come as such a surprise. In the lead-up to the London 2012 Olympics, and some 18 months before Adlington entered the jungle for the ITV show, she said she would be removing herself from Twitter for the duration of the Games. Adlington explained that she had already stopped looking at articles about herself online because reading the comments section often left her feeling upset or angry. 'Most things that I read about myself are not swimming related. They are to do with how I look', said Adlington. 'It's just nasty comments about things I cannot control. I can't help the way I look or who I am.'

Elite athletes are often presumed to be hardened individuals. We expect them to shrug off criticism in the same way as they ignore the aches and pains that come with pushing their bodies to the limit in training. But when almost 10 million women in the UK admit to 'feeling depressed' because of the way they look, should we really be surprised that female athletes are equally susceptible to suffering from body anxiety?

In some ways, they are perhaps even more vulnerable. Sportswomen are effectively 'on stage' every time they compete, and usually wearing clothing that is not exactly forgiving of any extra pounds. In an ideal world it would only be their sporting performance that is scrutinised but, in reality, that is rarely the case. 'Your body is the media's property and it's commented upon more than others' would be', says four-time Ironman World Champion Chrissie Wellington, when I ask her about the challenges female athletes face. 'That makes you increasingly aware of what you look like.'

The same survey that found 10 million women were depressed over their looks revealed that men were also affected by body image anxieties but to a lesser degree, with three quarters of men saying they were satisfied with their appearance. Men also seem to find it easier to break free from any negative feelings towards their bodies. Researchers at the University of Essex examined the effect of activity on self-esteem and body image in men and women, and found a significant difference between the genders. While men showed an improvement in body image perception after six weeks of regular fitness work, there were no significant differences in terms of body image or self esteem for the majority of the women.

The researchers speculated that this could be because the women in the study didn't feel there was enough of an 'improvement' to warrant a change in self-esteem or body image. For this, they pointed a finger of blame at the media for communicating what they called a 'cult of thinness and femininity'. Basically, women are putting themselves under pressure to attain levels of perfection that they see in airbrushed magazine photos and manipulated Instagram images, while men have traditionally set their sights on something far more achievable (although recent studies have shown that this is changing, with one in 10 men training in UK gyms found to suffer from something called muscle dysmorphia – meaning they are consumed by the idea they are not big enough).

The University of Essex researchers said that the focus for women in the study was on how their body looked, while the men were more likely to focus on what their body could do – how strong they were or how fast they could run. These body image anxieties don't only apply to people like you and me, but also to elite athletes – women who dedicate their lives to honing a physique that's capable of delivering them success. This fact alone proves the power of these images of perfection that we are bombarded with on a daily basis.

Olympic champion heptathlete Jessica Ennis-Hill has admitted that the pressure to conform to society's norms threatened to impact on her athletics career while it was still in its infancy. 'When I started doing sessions in the gym I just did not want to be good at it', she recalls in her 2012 autobiography, *Unbelievable*. 'I would not push myself because I felt big muscles were unattractive and none of my friends at school had them.'

These feelings led her to defy her long-time coach, Toni Miniciello. 'I don't want to lift this', she would tell him, despite his insistence that it was the only way she was going to improve. It was only as she got older that Ennis-Hill started to listen more to her coach and less to those outside of the sport: 'As time wore on I realised Chell [Miniciello] was right and that, if I wanted to be successful, then I needed to do the gym sessions properly ... but as a teenage girl I was more self-conscious.'

Even now, after all that Ennis-Hill has achieved (becoming an Olympic and World heptathlon champion), she admits to still feeling conflicted about her appearance, saying she will usually cover her arms when not competing: 'I look at myself in the mirror and think I am a bit butch, but you get to a point where you finally understand that looks do not matter so much.'

If any further evidence was needed of the mental challenge that female athletes face, this is surely it. Instead of Ennis-Hill looking in the mirror and feeling pride and satisfaction at the sight of a body that is clearly well nourished, strong and healthy, she sees a body that is out of step with what society says is 'feminine'.

For sportswomen like Ennis-Hill, there is an almost constant conflict of interests raging in their heads. On the one hand, they want to build a physique that will help to bring them the most success. But on the other, they fear this same physique will cause the rest of society to see them as less feminine, less attractive and less 'normal'. (Though there are of course exceptions, such as UFC star Ronda Rousey, who responded to critics of her powerful physique by making a video in which she said her body was "femininely badass").

When you consider the cases of track athletes Caster Semenya and Dutee Chand, it is little wonder that some female athletes are conflicted. Both women were found to have rare conditions giving them natural levels of testosterone that were normally only found in men. Semenya's condition was discovered after the International Athletics Federation (IAAF) subjected her to a gender test in 2009. They claimed their suspicions had been aroused by the huge breakthroughs the South African teenager had made on the track (she had run a world leading time for the 800m at the African junior championships, taking seven seconds off her best time).

But in a statement, the African National Congress suggested the IAAF was basing its decision on something other than Semenya's performances, suggesting there was a racial dimension at play: 'Caster is not the only woman athlete with a masculine build and the International Association of Athletics Federation should know better.' There was universal condemnation of the way in which the IAAF handled Semenya's case, with the details being leaked to the world's media hours before she lined up for the 800m final at the 2009 World Championships (a race she won by a huge margin). She was also banned from competing while the IAAF completed their investigation, ruling her out of competition for 11 months. Semenya was cleared to return in July 2010 after the IAAF accepted the conclusion of a panel of medical experts that she was eligible to compete with immediate effect but the medical details of the case were kept confidential.

In the wake of Semenya's case, the IAAF decided that it needed a plan for dealing with women with 'excessive androgenic hormones', or hyperandroginism (androgenic hormones are those that control the development of male characteristics and include testosterone). They imposed new rules dictating that if a female athlete was found to have testosterone levels above a certain amount (and was able to derive a competitive advantage from it), she would be offered an 'effective therapeutic strategy'.

In 2014, one of India's brightest young sprinting talents, Dutee Chand, was subjected to medical testing by the Sports Authority of India (SAI). The request for her to be tested for hyperandroginism had reportedly come from either an official or a competitor at the Asian Junior Athletics Championships where Chand had won two gold medals. The 18-year-old was found to have levels of testosterone that exceeded the IAAF's prescribed limit for women, and was barred from competing. The only way she would be allowed to return to competition was if she agreed to take drugs that supressed her body's production of testosterone, or had surgery to limit the amount of testosterone her body produced.

Chand refused both and instead chose to fight her ban, filing an appeal with the Court of Arbitration for Sport (CAS). In an interview with the *New York Times* in October 2014, she said she believed it was 'wrong to have to change your body for sport participation', adding defiantly: 'I'm not changing for anyone.' Chand described how the speculation had affected her, revealing that she had cried for three straight days after reading what people were saying about her on internet forums: 'They were saying, "Dutee: Boy or girl?" and I thought, how can they say those things? I have always been a girl.'

A year after she was banned, Chand was cleared to compete by a landmark ruling in which the CAS questioned the validity of the IAAF's guidelines around hyperandroginism. They also suspended the IAAF's rules on hyperandroginism for two years, saying that unless the IAAF could provide new evidence that high levels of naturally occurring testosterone provided a significant competitive advantage (something that has been a topic of heated debate among scientists), the rules would be scrapped.

The cases of Semenya and Chand are extreme (and relatively rare), but they are revealing of how sport scrutinises female athletes in ways it never would with men. 'There has been a long current in modern sport that there must be something wrong with strong women', said Canadian academic Bruce Kidd, in an interview with the BBC. 'It has become a kind of biological racism.'

Strength – both physical and mental – is a prerequisite for any elite athlete, but when weight categories come into play it is often an athlete's mental fortitude that is tested the most. I was at a photo shoot with Olympic weightlifter Evelyn Stevenson when she told me she had been fighting a constant mental battle after making the decision to move up a weight class a year or so earlier. She explained that as she had gotten older, dropping weight had become increasingly difficult: 'It was no longer about taking 30g of nuts a day out of my diet and not having milk in my tea and coffee. I had to be really strict to the point where I would track my fibrous greens intake. It felt mad doing so and yet I still did it. Then after I had made weight [for a competition], I would binge.'

Knowing that moving up a weight category would be the best thing for her health, Stevenson made the decision to do just that. It allowed her to stop measuring every morsel of food she put in her mouth, but it didn't stop her from feeling fearful about standing on the scales. She tells me that seeing the weight creep up still causes her anxiety, even though she has had 12 months to get used to the increase. Sometimes she avoids the scales so that she doesn't have to see the number, but eventually she goes back to them and sees that another couple of kilos have crept on.

All the logical parts of her brain know it makes sense and that going up a weight was the right thing to do for her lifting and her health. And yet she still struggles to accept it. 'All of a sudden I'm a heavier athlete', she says. 'I find myself thinking, "I wish I was lighter and yet I have no justification for why. Learning to just accept that I'm heavier, healthier, stronger and fitter – not fatter – is a total mental battle for me. I can list a million positives to moving up a weight, but this one unimportant negative has the power to cause what I can only describe as torment on some days.'

The irony in all of this is that most women – those in the sports world and those of us outside of it – will look at the likes of Ennis-Hill and Stevenson and be in awe of their physiques and what they are capable of. Even former Olympic track cycling champion Victoria Pendleton has admitted to looking on in admiration, saying: 'If you asked me whose body I would want, I would say Jess Ennis's at the Olympics. It was absolutely banging – abs, toned. That's my perfect body. I can appreciate how much hard work goes into that.'

Pendleton herself has revealed that throughout her own career she maintained a determination to 'retain her femininity'. In an interview with the *Guardian* in 2012 she recalled wearing miniskirts with her GB top and finishing the outfit off with a pair of sparkly sandals – 'The boys would be like: "Oh my gosh, this girl cannot be serious".' Pendleton explains that, for a lot of women in sport, taking on a 'very masculine, aggressive look' is a way of ensuring they are perceived as being strong and powerful, but that she never lost that sense of wanting to retain her femininity.

While Pendleton made a concerted effort to adorn herself with the 'added extras' that she felt kept her in touch with her feminine side, she developed an appreciation for what was beneath them, too. Describing the moment she took part in a nude photo shoot for *Observer Sport Monthly* (OSM) magazine in 2008, Pendleton wrote in her 2012 autobiography, *Between the Lines*: 'I didn't feel ashamed. This is who I am, I said silently, this is the product of everything I've done and everything I've denied myself for so long … I did not feel vulnerable. I felt strong.'

She described how as a teenager she would be so embarrassed by her 'flat and unwomanly' body on the beach that she would hide herself beneath a baggy t-shirt and shorts. But by the age of 27 she had learned to feel at ease with her body. 'At last,' she wrote, 'I was ready to show myself.'

When the *Observer* image was published, Pendleton was a World Champion and the picture of her in the nude, hunched low over the handlebars of a bike with her gaze fixed straight ahead, caused quite a stir. In the *Guardian* newspaper, cycling writer Richard Williams wrote that 'a world champion track cyclist, even a drop dead gorgeous one, should have no need to broaden her appeal by stripping off … playing the glamour card might not look quite so astute if, in this Olympic year, she suddenly runs into a streak of poor form.'

For Pendleton, though, the shoot was not about 'playing the glamour card'. The image was intended to portray power and strength. 'It didn't look very sexy to me,' she says, 'but I liked the stark and honest way in which I was depicted.'

In her autobiography, Pendleton says that when she asserted her femininity at her place of work (the velodrome), she was belittled and told she was too 'girly' to make it in the world of professional cycling. But when she tried to assert her strength and show her pride in what she had achieved (as was her intention with the *Observer* photoshoot), it seemed she was also onto a loser.

If she wasn't being depicted as attention seeking, Pendleton was being 'toned down' for public consumption. In her column for women's magazine

Zest she wrote: 'It still surprises me that we have such a narrow view of what makes women attractive. I've been photographed lots of times over the years, but one picture sticks in my mind. I wore a dress that exposed my whole back, and when I saw the photo on a screen at the shoot I thought, "Wow! My back looks muscly", and I felt really proud. But when the picture was printed, my back was smooth and practically muscle free.

'They'd softened it all, and I was so disappointed because I'd put a lot of work into that! I guess, in their opinion, being muscly isn't that attractive in a woman. But surely if you take a picture of an athlete, you'd expect to see some muscle, wouldn't you?'

Pendleton's experience shows just how ingrained the notion of the 'ideal' female body has become. It also illustrates just how difficult it is going to be to change. Some consider Pendleton's cover shoot for OSM as a significant step in the right direction, though. Chrissie Wellington tells me that the more the media 'capture women in their natural state and celebrate that', along with celebrating what they've achieved and their power, success and athleticism, 'then I think we'll start to see a change'.

Wellington herself has taken part in photo shoots for US magazine *ESPN* and *Women's Health* magazine in the UK that were both designed to highlight how her physique has been finely tuned to satisfy the rigours of competing in Ironman events. She describes the images as a celebration of the athletic form as opposed to anything sexual. 'I think women need to see those images and for those to be the norm rather than the über skinny", says Wellington. 'Female sportspeople make fantastic role models, not just because of their appearance but their tenacity, and achievements and determination. They can be used in a range of different contexts and I think if we do that, it could change perceptions of what females and female sportspeople are capable of.'

The super close-up photograph of Wellington's muscle-hardened legs that appeared in *ESPN*'s *The Magazine* was part of the publication's annual 'Body Issue'. Launched in 2009 with an edition that included naked (but cleverly posed) photographs of Serena Williams, NBA star Dwight Howard, mixed martial artist Gina Carano, and track and field athlete Lolo Jones among others, the Body Issue was designed to help boost advertising revenue by creating a buzz around a 'special issue' of the fortnightly magazine.

'These days, people are sceptical enough about print, or at least wary enough about print, that they're looking for executions that differentiate print', claimed the magazine's editor in chief at the time, Gary Belsky, when the Body

Issue was launched. 'Print can't deliver music [or] video, but what print can deliver is beautiful, in-depth visuals and journalism that explores subjects in a particular kind of way.'

ESPN's exploration of the athletic physique involves photographing male and female athletes in the nude, but with the subjects posing in such a way that nothing is ever on show that should not be. UFC champion Ronda Rousey has posed for both *ESPN*'s 'Body Issue' and *Sports Illustrated*'s famed 'Swimsuit Issue' and says the two magazines are far removed from one another in terms of tone: 'The *ESPN* Body Issue is about celebrating the peak of human potential and the kind of form the human body, when specialised, can really look like. The Swimsuit Issue has a lot more [of a] sexual side to it. I don't think the Body Issue is overtly sexual, whereas *Sports Illustrated* is ... when I posed for *ESPN* Body, I really tried to be a lot more cut and a lot closer to my prime fighting shape because I was being photographed as a fighter and trying to look more like a fighter.'

For Olympic champion snowboarder, Jamie Anderson, taking part in the Body Issue was as much about learning to be happy with herself as it was about revealing to the world what the body of an elite snowboarder looks like: 'I've never done any naked shoots or even bikini shoots so it was new for me to do that', Anderson said. 'At first I was a little bit terrified, but it was really good practice for me to accept everything about myself and love my body, and not judge the little things that we do as women or anyone and just embrace where I'm at ... I got to step back and embrace myself and how I am and not try to fit this Hollywood image of being really super skinny.'

If there is one criticism to be made of *ESPN*'s Body Issue, it is that for all the diversity in terms of gender and sports featured, the female athletes featured have not deviated much in terms of body type. In the 2014 edition, 275lb baseball player, Prince Fielder was pictured in all his 'big guy' glory. In the interview that accompanied his photograph, Fielder said: 'A lot of people probably think I'm not athletic or don't even try to work out or whatever, but I do. Just because you're big doesn't mean you can't be an athlete. And just because you work out doesn't mean you're going to have a 12-pack. I work out to make sure I can do my job to the best of my ability. Other than that, I'm not going up there trying to be a fitness model.'

Fielder's words epitomise what the Body Issue is supposed to be all about: Proving that fitness and sporting prowess come in all sorts of different packages. But the issue has not yet featured a female athlete of similar proportions. Some have been slightly more muscular than others, some have been amputees, one has even been pregnant, but none have yet challenged society's assumptions about what a (non-pregnant) female athlete looks like.

The implication is that while a male athlete who doesn't quite fit the mould will be accepted and his athletic proficiency unquestioned, the outcome would be different for a female athlete. For women in sport then, it seems that appearance and sporting prowess are simply more closely entwined than they are for their male counterparts.

While the Body Issue has largely steered clear of sexualising the female athletes it features (although some images admittedly tread a fine line), there have been countless examples over the years of sportswomen who have chosen to go down that path. Most recently, tennis player Caroline Wozniacki donned a white bikini and swimsuit for *Sports Illustrated*'s Swimsuit Issue. The Danish former world number one told *USA Today* that it had always been a dream of hers to be in the Swimsuit Issue. While many assumed the magazine had approached her about posing, Wozniacki revealed that she actually went to them, visiting the *Sports Illustrated* offices and 'throwing herself out there'. 'I said, "If you need a model or want one, I'm here." It must have made a pretty good impression.'

As one of the world's best-known female tennis players, Wozniacki's decision to swap tennis whites for tiny whites is unlikely to have been driven by a need to boost her profile – tennis is, after all, one of the few sports that affords its female competitors an impressive level of fame. But all too often, sportswomen have been led to believe that the best way to drive interest in their sport and increase their chances of bringing in sponsorship revenue is to use their looks. 'I don't think there's any question that there's a double standard', says Kevin Adler, Chief Engagement Officer at sports marketing agency Engage Marketing. 'For male athletes, it's primarily about their performance. And for female athletes it's definitely as much about their looks as it is about their performance.'

This was evident from the actions of five female German footballers who stripped off for their nation's version of *Playboy* in the lead up to the 2011 Women's World Cup in Germany. On the cover all five women can be seen wearing see-through crop tops, tiny knickers and football socks (obviously). Although none of the players featured were in the German squad for the tournament, Selina Wagner (20), Annika Doppler (19), Kristina Gessat (20), Ivana Rudelic (19) and Julia Simic (22) claimed the photo shoot was their opportunity to 'disprove the cliché that all female footballers are butch'.

Inside the magazine, midfielder Simic said: 'I think we are well on our way to getting rid of that image. There are more and more cute, pretty women playing women's football, who also like shopping and taking care of their looks'. The players were approached directly by *Playboy* (meaning the magazine didn't run it past the German Football Association first), but according to a spokesperson for *Playboy*, when the German football authorities did find out about it they didn't put up any resistance.

In fact, according to online football magazine *When Saturday Comes*, the president of the World Cup organising committee, Steffi Jones, 'gave her blessing in April last year [2010], and the national team manager Doris Fitschen granted her permission in the press in January'. Considering Jones had explained the World Cup slogan 'The beautiful side of 2011' as meaning that the tournament is about 'attractive football and attractive women', it is perhaps less surprising that she was in favour of *Playboy*'s exposé of German football.

The month after *Playboy* hit the shelves, and with action already underway in the Women's World Cup, three members of the French squad followed the German's (naked) lead and posed without their kit for a Sunday edition of the German tabloid *Bild*. Gaetine Thiney, Elodie Thomis and Corine Franco said they took part in the feature to help draw more attention to the women's game: 'We wanted to provoke and to generate some discussion', said Thiney.

'Sex sells' has long been the motto of advertisers looking to make a quick splash and sports marketers looking to maximise ticket sales. But what exactly is it selling? Whatever it is, it certainly isn't sport, according to Mary Jo Kane who is the Director of the Tucker Center for Research on Girls and Women in Sport at the University of Minnesota.

'I don't disagree that when *Sports Illustrated* publishes its Swimsuit Issue males are quite interested in buying that particular issue of the magazine', says Kane. 'It does not automatically follow, however, that their interest in women's sports has increased. On the contrary, I would argue that what males are interested in consuming is not a women's athletic event but sportswomen's bodies as objects of sexual desire.'

To prove her point, Kane conducted a study, in which men and women from the ages of 18 to 55 were shown photographs of female athletes. The images ranged from depicting 'on-court athletic competence, to wholesome "girls next door", to soft pornography.' They were then asked which images had increased their interest in reading about, watching on TV and attending a women's sporting event.

Kane discovered that in most cases, the 'sex sells' approach actually offended the core fan base of women's sports – women and older men. And when younger males – a prime target audience – did look at the sexually provocative images, they stated that although the pictures were 'hot', they did not 'fundamentally increase their interest in women's sports, particularly when it came to attending a sporting event'. The key takeaway from this said Kane, was that 'sex sells sex, not women's sports'.

Research also shows that even when female athletes are simply going about their day jobs and not posing for nude photo shoots, their appearance is still a major talking point – a fact the athletes themselves are all too aware of. In 2014, BT Sport conducted a survey of 110 female athletes from 20 different sports on the topic of body image, and 80 per cent reported feeling under pressure to conform to a certain look and body type.

Unsurprisingly, the media took much of the blame for this, accused of being hyper-critical of all women – not just athletes – who don't live up to their expectations of perfectionism. As I write, I've just had a quick look at one national newspaper's sports section online. I scrolled down, down, and down again until I found the first piece on women's sport – it's an interview with British tennis player Heather Watson ahead of the US Open. 'Watson as you've never seen her before!' is the sell on the main sports page. When I click into the article the headline reads: 'Heather Watson has a stunning new look as Britain's number one female heads to the US Open.' This is just one example of how the most widely read English-language news website in the world presents sportswomen: It's looks first, sport second.

Some athletes also felt they were responsible for putting that pressure on themselves. Downhill mountain bike racer Rachel Atherton described it as 'the feeling that I do not deserve to call myself a professional athlete if I am not the owner of a stick thin body with visibly bulging muscles attached, zero body fat or gorgeous skin that isn't weathered from the elements!'

Atherton might take full ownership of those feelings, but she wouldn't have them if it wasn't for the media's continued propagation of how female athletes are 'supposed' to look. And it's this idealised image that many sportswomen feel they are constantly judged against, with 67 per cent of the athletes quizzed in BT Sport's survey saying they believed that the public and media valued the way a sportswoman looks above her achievements in sport. One athlete said: 'Women are still first judged on their physical appearance before their talent, personality and achievements.'

Former Wimbledon women's singles champion Marion Bartoli can certainly vouch for this. As she stood on Centre Court in July 2013, cradling the trophy she had dreamed of winning since she was a little girl, the Frenchwoman was blissfully unaware of the storm that was brewing.

It had started a few hours before her triumph when BBC broadcaster John Inverdale told Radio 5 Live listeners what he made of Bartoli's qualities as a player: 'I just wonder if her dad – because he has obviously been the most influential person in her life – did say to her when she was 12, 13 or 14: "Listen, you are never going to be, you know, a looker. You are never going to be somebody like a Sharapova, you're never going to be 5ft 11, you're never going to be somebody with long legs, so you have to compensate for that. You are going to have to be the most dogged, determined fighter that anyone has ever seen on the tennis court if you are going to make it". And she kind of is.'

Inverdale's comments sparked universal outrage and led to calls for him to be sacked. Instead, he returned to the airwaves for the men's final the following day and proceeded to explain what he referred to as his 'clumsy' phrasing: 'The point I was trying to make, in a rather ham-fisted kind of way, was that in a world where the public perception of tennis players is that they're all 6ft tall Amazonian athletes, Marion – who is the Wimbledon champion – bucks that trend.'

He added that she was 'a fantastic example to all young people that it's attitude and will and determination together, obviously, with talent that, in the end, does get you to the top. So I have apologised to Marion by letter if any offence was caused and I do hope that we can leave the matter there now.'

The BBC also apologised, accepting that his 'remark was insensitive'. But that was where it ended. Inverdale kept his job (he was removed from Radio 5 Live's Wimbledon coverage in 2014, but continued to front the nightly highlights show on BBC Two), and Bartoli very (perhaps too) graciously let him off the hook: 'I'd known John a long time, and I knew what he was trying to say', said Bartoli. 'At the end of the day I am a tennis player, I know I'm not 6ft tall, I'm not the same long, lean shape as Maria Sharapova, but the beauty of tennis is that anyone can win, tall or short.

'Everyone starts with their own assets, not everyone is born the same way, but the point is that in sport – in life in general – the message is, if you have determination you can still make it happen. In my mind it was never really a story.'

While comments like Inverdale's will always sting, Bartoli brushed them off with the confidence of an athlete who knows that her appearance has no bearing on her sporting prowess – after all, she had just won the biggest title of her entire career. But in some cases, thoughtless comments like Inverdale's can have a far more dangerous effect.

A Norwegian study from 2004 looked into eating disorders among elite athletes (from all sports) compared to the general population. It found that the prevalence of eating disorders was higher among athletes than non-athletes, and higher in female athletes than male. The study estimated that 25 per cent of female elite athletes in endurance sports, aesthetic sports (like dance, diving, gymnastics and figure skating), and weight-class sports had clinical eating disorders. These numbers are compared to nine per cent of the general population.

Certain disciplines have been labelled as more high risk than others, with endurance athletes inevitably more focused on staying light and lean in view of the performance benefits. Other sports earn the label because of the necessity for the athlete's body to be on display when competing, the focus on aesthetics (as in those sports mentioned above), or the need to fit into a certain weight category as in weightlifting and boxing.

The psychological make-up of athletes can also be a contributing factor, according to Dr Alan Currie, who is a consultant psychiatrist and a trustee of eating disorder charity Beat. He says: 'People have commented on the psychological similarities between a good anorexic (i.e. one capable of severely restricting their food intake for a long period of time, thus becoming dangerously underweight) and a driven perfectionist person who can tolerate high levels of pain and is very compliant and easy to coach. Some of those characteristics might make a very good long-distance runner, and they overlap a little bit with some of the psychological traits that might help you towards an anorexic life.'

Dr Currie also discusses the competitive nature of athletes, which he says can create a culture of 'competitive thinness' among teammates or training groups: 'Sometimes they get attracted towards trying to be thinner and thinner. You want to be faster or stronger than everyone on the team, but you want to be leaner as well. For some vulnerable people that is an additional risk factor.'

For some female athletes, disordered eating can be just the start of a dangerous spiral that leads to them suffering from a syndrome known as the female athlete triad. Made up of three interrelated conditions – low energy availability (from an eating disorder), amenorrhea (the absence of a menstrual period for more than three months) and decreased bone mineral density (caused by low oestrogen levels and poor nutrition) – the female athlete triad is something that is thought to mostly affect young female athletes taking part in sports that emphasise leanness. It's a disorder that often goes unrecognised, but the consequences can be devastating. According to a research carried out at the University of Cincinnati in 2000, lost bone mineral density may never be regained and can lead to a lifetime of bone health issues.

Returning to an appropriate diet and moderating the frequency of exercise can result in the natural return of an athlete's menstrual cycle, but in some cases experts advise hormone replacement therapy to prevent the loss of bone density. The problem is that the disorder often goes unrecognised, with many female athletes unwilling to divulge information about their menstrual cycles to coaches (especially when those coaches are male). So it requires a collaborative effort from coaches, parents, athletes and doctors to be alert to the symptoms (which can include hair loss, fatigue, cold hands and increased healing time from injuries, as well as the more obvious weight loss) in order to prevent what is a potentially life-threatening illness.

For British triathlete Hollie Avil it was an ill-judged comment from a coach – not her own – that set her on a destructive path to disordered eating. In 2006, a then 16-year-old Avil, who was still flitting between specialising in swimming or triathlon, was discussing the size of female triathletes with teammates, telling them jokingly that she had 'big swimmer arms' and 'needed the body fat to be buoyant'. At that point, food was fuel for Avil. She barely knew what a calorie was.

One of the coaches listening in on the conversation spoke up to offer what he misguidedly believed was sound advice. It was to have a disastrous effect on Avil: 'Swimming is not going to make you quicker Hollie, if you want to get quicker you should watch your weight.'

It was at that moment that Avil says she became 'a bit more switched on to it and started looking at other athletes and what they were eating, their shapes and sizes – what they were doing.' In an interview with the BBC in 2012 she explained that at the time she was living at home with her parents but found ways to hide her issues from them: 'My mum would make me lunches, and I would throw away half of it and hardly eat. Then I took control of making my own lunch and all I would really eat was salad. From 2006 to around January 2007 I must have dropped 8 or 10kg.

It was Avil's coach Ben Bright who eventually took action. He spoke to her family and supported her as she began her recovery with the help of a nutritionist and psychologist. He also showed her the hard facts about how her deteriorating health was impacting upon her performance. Her running times had been quicker when she was heavier, as were her swimming times, something she said she had known at the time: 'When I got light I could barely swim, I had no buoyancy … I was cold getting in the water.'

Avil's recovery was good enough that in 2007 she won World and European junior titles, and added the World under 23 title in 2009. The future looked bright. But changes in Avil's coaching and squad structure in 2010 left her feeling unsettled and unhappy, and eventually that led to a return to her old ways. 'What I ate became the one thing I could control in my life. I kept everything secret. I lost a lot of weight, but kept lying to people that it was just because I was running more.'

This time the illness lasted longer and took more time to overcome. By the time she felt mentally healed, Avil's body decided it had been through enough trauma. In February 2012 with the London Olympics on the horizon, Avil was diagnosed with stress fractures in both shins, something that she believes was a consequence of reduced bone density caused by her diet. Her initial determination to overcome the injury lasted a month, she says: 'And then I cracked.'

This time she didn't resort to controlling her emotions through food, but was diagnosed with depression. It was the final straw for Avil, who at the age of just 22 announced her retirement from elite sport in May 2012, saying: 'I don't ever want to go back to those dark, lonely times … I don't want to risk my health again, not just my mental health but my physical health.'

Avil said she hoped one day to set up a charity to help young female athletes with eating disorders: 'I feel it is rife in our sport and lots of girls suffer in silence.' Those that do speak out act as warning signs that this is still a problem that needs addressing. It was during the lead-up to the 2014 Commonwealth Games in Glasgow that Scottish high jumper Jayne Nisbet opened up about the eating disorder that almost robbed her of her sporting dream. Suffering from bulimia, Nisbet's weight plummeted to seven stone at the height of her illness, forcing her to miss out on the 2010 Commonwealth Games in Delhi.

In an interview with Scottish newspaper the *Daily Record*, Nisbet explained: 'People say they don't understand why you'd be so worried about how you look, but I think when you are wearing a crop top and pants on television, if you are even a little bit overweight, you are going to get criticised … I became really aware of the other high jumpers. I thought, "All those other girls look lighter than me, that's how I need to jump higher."'

Sporting administrators are now realising that the issue of eating disorders among female athletes is one that urgently needs addressing. In 2014, UK

Sport and other bodies, including the English Institute of Sport and British Athletics, set up a dedicated group to explore the risks of eating disorders and consider how sports organisations can be supported.

The topic of menstruation is one that has been mentioned in relation to eating disorders, but until fairly recently it was one that the sports world otherwise tried hard to ignore. With women now able to control their cycles through the use of the Pill, it might have been assumed that for most female athletes, their periods weren't an issue. But in January 2015, tennis player Heather Watson attributed her poor performance at the Australian Open to what she called 'girl issues', complaining of feeling light headed and low on energy.

It might have confused the male journalists present at Watson's post-match press conference, but the entire female population knew what she was on about. The ensuing discussion led former British tennis player Annabel Croft to question whether periods were 'the last taboo in sport?' In an interview with CNN she said: 'We talk about sex quite openly, we talk about breast enlargements, we talk about so many things that people don't even bat an eyelid about these days, yet this particular subject never gets discussed.'

It seems that Watson's semi-openness has at least started the discussion, with many athletes coming out to talk about their own experiences. Paula Radcliffe revealed that she broke the marathon world record in 2002 when she had her period, while former England footballer Sue Smith told the BBC she'd played with some players who would wear cycling shorts beneath their white England shorts to avoid any embarrassments when on their periods.

And now some research has even been done into the true extent of the menstrual effect in sport. The Female Athlete Health Group – a collaborative project between St Mary's University and University College London – carried out two surveys in 2015, including one on London Marathon competitors. They found that of the 1,862 women surveyed, including 90 who were considered elite level, 41.7 per cent said their menstrual cycle affected their performance, but only 22.3 per cent had sought help for period problems. 'Many females are clearly suffering in silence, so don't realise they have a problem or if they do, they deal with it alone', said Dr Charles Pedlar from St Mary's University.

For some female athletes though, opening up about such issues can cause more problems than it's worth. Professional cyclist Inga Thompson told CNN that she believed there was a fine line between openness and undermining women's sporting abilities: 'I feel very protective of our sport. You don't want to pull the "girl card", because we've fought so hard for equal representation.

It's true that the day before or the day after I started my period, I was a little weaker. Was I ever so weak that I felt I lost a race because of it? No.'

The key to this debate though is that female athletes should at least feel free to discuss periods, if and when they want to and feel that it is relevant. They should also be able to do it in such a way that it doesn't leave a room full of male sports journalists scratching their heads in bafflement.

Despite some of the evidence in this chapter so far, it should be remembered that for many sportswomen, training and competing has had a positive effect on their body image. Before Chrissie Wellington became a world champion Ironman triathlete, she strived for perfection in all other areas of her life – in her studies, in her work and in her body shape. What she calls a 'craving for control' manifested itself as bulimia by the time she was at university. Later on, when studying for a Master's degree, it developed into anorexia. Wellington would work late into the night and wake up at dawn to go running, losing more and more weight and depleting her body of nutrients to the extent that her hair started to fall out.

'The victims of such illnesses are often very ambitious, outwardly successful young women who pursue these ideas of control and achievement', she says, echoing the words of psychologist Dr Alan Currie, quoted earlier. 'We're driven, compulsive, obsessive, competitive, persistent and seek perfection. That can be channelled incredibly negatively.'

While it was the reaction of Wellington's family in 2001 that initially helped shock her into seeking help, she credits her sporting career with helping her in different ways. Competing, says Wellington allowed her to channel those 'feelings for control into something else that has enabled me to be very successful. I think the eating disorder was just another reflection of my desire to achieve perfection.'

It also allowed Wellington to view her own body in a way she had not done before she took up Ironman: 'Sport has given me a different perception and respect for my body. I cannot judge its success by whether I can fit into a pair of skinny jeans. I look at other women and, yes, they're beautiful with stereotypically wonderful figures but I can think, "Yeah, but you haven't won what I've won." I might not be perfect but I can love my body now.'

Even for athletes who have never suffered from the same issues that affected Wellington, sport can still have an almost transformative effect on how they see themselves. Olympic rower Anna Watkins won gold with teammate Katherine Grainger in the women's double sculls at London 2012, and told afterwards of how training alongside a group of women all focused on one outcome – Olympic gold – helped her develop a new appreciation for her physique: 'There are 30 of us [in the Great Britain Olympic rowing team] training every day and we actually appreciate building up muscle, being strong. The atmosphere is great: when we're weightlifting, there's a great cheer when someone does a personal best.

'For us, the female ideal is athletic. We want to make our bodies look as strong and capable as possible, partly because then they are and we can win, and partly because it gives the opposition something to think about. I've got quite muscly shoulders and I wouldn't normally wear a vest-top, but now I feel proud to show them.'

In stark contrast to some of the experiences discussed, Watkins believes that 'sport is uniquely able to strip away common body insecurities, as you stop aspiring to look like something in a catalogue and instead want to look capable and healthy.'

This is exactly the way it should be for all female athletes. But in reality there are still many who find themselves trapped in the no-man's land between where Watkins says they should be and a far darker place, where they strive to match up to an idealised picture of perfection. Ennis-Hill's long-time coach, Toni Minichiello, has a message he sends out to his female athletes as regularly as he needs to in order to ensure they stay on the right side of that mental divide: 'You're building a body to perform and do particular things that not a lot of human beings can do.' In time, hopefully it's a message he won't need to impart quite so often.

For that to be the case a real change in the way sports women are talked about, written about and pictured is required. And the athletes themselves need to believe they are more deserving of coverage when fully clothed, red-faced and sporting a hairstyle that can only be achieved via dried-on sweat than when stripped down to their smalls in a photo studio. Achieve both of these things and we will be one giant step closer to helping women – not just sportswomen – develop the kind of relationship with their bodies that will make us all a lot happier, healthier and so at peace that we might even forgive John Inverdale his 'clumsy' words. Possibly.

Clare Connor

THE POWER PLAYER

When England's Women won the Cricket World Cup in 1993, they could never have predicted where their victory would lead. The day after England captain Karen Smithies (taking time off from her nine-to-five job as a manager at Coral Racing) led her team of police officers, several teachers, two clerks and a van driver to victory against New Zealand at Lord's, their success was splashed all over the front and back pages of the daily newspapers. In a summer that had brought a 4-1 defeat for England's men in the Ashes, the press welcomed the opportunity England's women had given them to praise the high standards of cricket on show.

'Suddenly the sport had some profile', says Smithies' successor as England captain, Clare Connor, who is now the Head of Women's Cricket at the England and Wales Cricket Board (ECB). 'The team appeared on breakfast news and the front pages of the papers. It was a big deal and I barely knew that women's cricket existed.'

Connor's passion for cricket started early. As a toddler she would go to watch her dad play for his club team, absorbing everything she saw. Her mum tried to broaden her sporting horizons, taking her to swimming and tennis lessons, but Clare was not to be persuaded, sitting on the doorstep crying because she couldn't go to cricket with her dad.

When England won the Women's World Cup in 1993, Connor was in her mid-teens. By then she was playing cricket for the first XI at Brighton College – a boys' team. For a girl at public school to be playing alongside boys in the first team of one of the major sports was extraordinary, but for Connor it simply felt like a natural progression: 'All my formative experiences were of playing in boys' teams,' she tells me, 'whether it was my club team – Preston Nomads [in the South Downs] – or my school team.'

At Brighton College Prep School, Connor played in boys' teams from the age of nine up to the College's first XI, when she was 18. 'All of my most important learning years in cricket were in those teams', she says. 'All my coaching experiences, all my team practice and match day experiences were with boys. I didn't even really know there was such a thing as girls or women's cricket until I was in my mid-teens.'

'I had dreams and ambitions back then. Cricket was my life. But as a girl playing in boys' teams all the time I just thought, if I can play for Brighton College first XI, then why can't I play for the England men's team?'

The World Cup win by England's women in 1993 showed Connor that there was another route to playing at the top level – one specifically for female cricketers. And while she would change nothing about the way her own cricket career started, Connor is pleased that the situation for young female players today is very different: 'Not every girl wants to play sport with boys – it's a real character or personality thing. Now, girls can progress into girls-only teams when they're young. If that opportunity wasn't available I don't think the sport would be as accessible as it is now to girls.'

The gender of the players around her was never an issue for a young Connor, though. 'For me it was just the most natural thing. I was doing what I loved and I'll be forever grateful that I was supported to do that because it gave me such confidence. I was never made to feel like an outsider.

'Obviously there were some practical issues. The first year I was in the Brighton College first team they gave me no option but to share the dressing room with them. Our coach, John Spencer, the former Sussex fast bowler, said: "Well, Clare, if you want to be part of it ... You can't pick and choose." So I said ok, and just made sure I turned up to games pretty much fully changed.'

Coach Spencer's approach was to treat Connor as simply another member of the team. He would tell her that like everyone else, if she was good enough, then she would be in the team. 'It was completely meritocratic', she says. 'He made it very simple. He said: "If you can hold your own, if you're strong enough and technically good enough, then you'll play."'

Connor was more than good enough. During her second year in the team she opened the batting, and became a well-known face on the school circuit. Not only because she was 'unusual', but because she was a talented player. Opposing teams rarely even mentioned the fact she was female once they were used to her presence. But when it came to the parents of her opponents, things were a little different, says Connor.

'If I got their son out, the boy wouldn't have a tantrum, he'd take it and in the spirit of cricket accept he had been got out – whether it was by a boy or a girl. But the parents got shitty and often made comments. I suppose they felt their son shouldn't have been bowled out by a girl. I remember my mum telling me about some uncomfortable conversations she heard around the boundary, but it didn't affect me. I got the odd comment here and there, but ultimately I felt that I belonged.'

There was one exception, though. A few months after finishing her A-levels in 1994, Connor went to Zimbabwe with the College first XI. She was the only female on a touring trip of 25 boys and four male members of staff. While the boys all shared dorms together, Connor was set up with lodging alongside female members of staff at the schools they played against. 'I remember realising then, in that male environment, that actually Clare, this is quite odd what you do.'

Nevertheless, Connor was so at ease in the men's game that when she first started playing alongside women it took a while for her to adjust. 'Just being in an all-female environment was very different', she recalls. 'It didn't feel the same at all. I liked the banter of being in a boys' team and lots of my closest best friends were boys, so to go to Sussex women's trials and start to make my way in a different environment was probably more challenging in a way than doing the boys thing.

'The way the women's game is played is a bit different, too. Not in terms of the techniques, but the actual tactics and the pace of the game. It has different nuances and there are slightly different skills needed, so it took a bit of adjusting to.'

Running the Sussex trials was a woman called Ruth Prideaux, who at the time was the England Women's Coach (she had also been the coach of the England team that won the World Cup in 1993). She spotted Connor's potential almost immediately, watching her bat in the nets and telling her: 'If you carry on playing like that, one day you'll play for England.' Prideaux had no idea how rapidly her prediction would come true.

Despite still being a junior, Connor broke into the Sussex women's team almost immediately. It was a selection that led equally quickly to her being picked for the England under 18s squad. It all happened so fast that Connor barely had time to get used to the fact she was no longer playing against men, but with and against other women. By the age of 20 she was captaining the full women's Sussex side and had made her full England debut, in a One Day International against Denmark.

'It was a quicker thing for me back then than it would be these days, with the numbers that are playing now', she says. 'There's far more competition for places today. My grounding in boys' cricket obviously stood me in good stead because I made those steps into the women's game really quickly, but when I think about it, I probably didn't do as well as I expected at first, given the amount of training and opportunities I'd had compared with the other girls my age.'

Connor's England debut in 1995 came after a period during which women's cricket had dropped completely off the sporting radar. 'The sad part of England's World Cup win in 1993 was that it was followed by a real lull. I don't think there was any international women's cricket played between 1993 and 1995, so winning that tournament wasn't a springboard. We didn't capitalise on it or make the advances we could have made as a sport given that there was lots of interest in that World Cup victory.'

The England setup was going through a period of great change at the time that Connor's international career was getting started. It was around then (in the late 1990s) that the volunteer-led Women's Cricket Association, which had run the game since 1926, merged with the ECB, leaving the latter to take over the running of the women's game. 'Perhaps,' muses Connor, 'there was more time spent considering what the national governing body remit was going to look like for the women's game than there was on making the most of the performance of the World Cup winning England team.'

Connor's England debut came in the summer of 1995 and it went well; the new girl took two wickets in a victory against Denmark. Shortly afterwards, Clare was called up for an eight-week tour to India during which she would make her Test bow. It was a trip she describes as 'turbulent', featuring torn thumb ligaments, a trip to hospital with dysentery ('a fairly brutal experience'), and getting 'very choked up' by her first Test wicket.

Connor had just turned 19 and was in her first term at Manchester University when she parted with the £500 that every female England player had to contribute towards the trip in those days. 'We had to pay for our own England blazers, too', recalls Connor. 'The girls now have all their sponsored kit with a different piece of clothing practically for every hour of the day. I think we went to India that year with a couple of pairs of shorts, each sponsored by different companies and a mishmash of sponsored T-shirts.'

Not that the clothing options bothered her. Connor was just thrilled to get the chance to play in India, where cricket draws huge, impassioned crowds. The tour was a somewhat chaotic experience, as Connor remembers it: 'Even if you're the most professional organisation under the sun it can be that way. But for us, with this change in administration taking place and the lack of finances, it was a real adventure.

'If you had 11 fit people to put on the pitch it was a bit of a miracle. Everyone was struck down by all sorts of lurgy at one point or another. But some of those memories are as precious as winning back-to-back Ashes [as Connor later experienced with England in 2013–14], because that's where you get your sense of perspective.

'For me to play international cricket for 10 years – to go from 1995 through to standing in Trafalgar Square in front of thousands of people having regained the Ashes after 42 years – was an amazing journey. It all has to begin somewhere. And while yes, it was fairly chaotic and you could say unprofessional and not well organised at times, India was where it all started and I remember it as an amazing adventure.'

By the time Connor played in her first senior international tournament – the 1997 World Cup – which was also held in India, some of the changes from the ECB's merger with the Women's Cricket Association were starting to take effect. In August of that year, England played their first match wearing trousers instead of skirts, which at long last had been recognised as somewhat impractical on the field of play (yep in 1997, not 1917).

That pivotal moment came during the summer home series against South Africa. It was one that Connor says had a more professional feel than previous series. 'We played at first-class grounds like Bristol and Lord's. Suddenly there was a difference in how international women's cricket was organised, with the ECB having the resources to organise it at first-class venues. Previously, the Women's Cricket Association didn't have that.

'Some things changed almost straight away. There was a sense that we were part of the national governing body for the sport and there were some immediate improvements in terms of training camps and that move to a proper kit. But other things took a bit longer, like the infrastructure and the development of the women's cricket programme.'

Throughout the late 1990s and early 2000s, England slowly started playing more internationals and were given access to expertise in the form of nutritionists and fitness coaches. But Connor pinpoints the introduction of Lottery funding at the turn of the millennium as having perhaps the biggest influence: 'It was one of the things that helped to create more of an accountable, high-performance environment. The funding wasn't enough for us to go part-time or anything, but at least it was some financial support to train and travel and cover loss of earnings. We all still had full-time jobs.'

England went to the 1997 World Cup in India as the defending champions from 1993. Connor believes it was a position that made their task of winning the tournament again even harder: 'I think the organisers gave us a tough schedule because we were the holders. They had us making some bonkers journeys on buses, and taking internal flights at 4am. We weren't really the favourites to win it anyway – both Australia and New Zealand were stronger than us by the late 1990s.'

Indeed it was those two countries that made it through to the final, with England going out to New Zealand at the semi-final stage. It was a tournament that left a lasting impression on Connor, though with packed stadiums – 'we had 20,000–25,000 people watching us play' – and the chance to travel all over India. 'In some ways I look back and think I was a bit too young to have taken it all in, but it was amazing to be part of a World Cup and see Australia win the final in front of 70,000 people in Calcutta. It was remarkable to see the sport that I had started playing on school pitches in that sort of environment, on a proper global stage.'

At the time, Connor would never have imagined that by the time England were back on that World Cup stage in 2000, she would be there as the team's captain. Her ascension to the role came in February 2000, mid-way through a disastrous tour of Australia and New Zealand. England had been thrashed 4-0 by Australia in the one-day series, with the final blow coming at Newcastle's No. 1 sports ground when England, chasing 300 for victory, were bundled out for 79. It was their lowest score in one-day international history.

The next day, Karen Smithies (who had led England to World Cup glory in 1993) quit her job as captain and handed the role over to Connor, who had been vice-captain since the start of the 1999 home season. 'It was an interesting time', reflects Connor. 'I was young – just 23 – and I probably wasn't quite ready for it, but there was no way I was going to say, come back to me in a couple of years when I'm a bit more mature.

'It was an absolute honour, so I grabbed the opportunity with both hands. Karen had been a successful player and captain for a decade or so, but on that tour things went dreadfully for us as a team. The leadership – her leadership – was undermined.' During the four-match series against Australia, Smithies had come under fire on a number of different fronts, including her strategy as opening batsman. When England needed 4.84 runs per over to win, she took 40 deliveries to score two runs, and finished the series with the slowest scoring of any recognised batsman on either side. She was also criticised for her field placings and bowling changes, which many argued took whatever pressure existed away from the Australian batsmen.

For Connor, it was obvious that bad tactics were just the tip of the iceberg – there were deeper issues at play. 'There was a bit of a bad culture among the group,' she says, 'a bit of a blame culture between the batsmen and the bowlers. We weren't a very united group of people. We had a brutal time on that tour and it was clear that … with some of the older players either having retired in the late 1990s or about to retire, a change was needed.'

Connor was offered the position of captain in between the Australia and New Zealand legs of the tour, with ex-captain Smithies staying on the team to serve under her successor for the five one-day internationals. 'It was a baptism of fire', admits Connor, with a wry smile. Her tenure as England captain began in the worst possible way, with a 5-0 series whitewash in New Zealand. 'Those early days were my toughest time as captain, without doubt. We'd been absolutely trounced out of sight by Australia – didn't even look like getting within 100 runs of them in most of those games. They were bleak days.

'When you're playing any sport and playing for your country as an amateur, things are pretty bad when the joy goes out of the dressing room. And it had. I got my head down and did my best, but when I sit down and really think about it now, they were tough days. I was desperate to try and help turn it all around and make playing cricket for England a joy again, but those first couple of years were not easy.'

At the age of 23, Connor was younger than most of her teammates, whom she was charged with leading. 'It's hard to know what people think of you, but I can guess they thought I was probably a bit young to do it. I think I had their trust, though. They knew that I lived and breathed cricket and playing for England so I would give it my best shot, and I think that's all you can really ask for in a new captain. In any leadership role, people need time to evolve.'

Asked what type of captain she was, Connor pauses for thought. 'I was an open book, really', she surmises. 'In fact, I was probably a bit too open. I wore my heart on my sleeve and I didn't hide things, so I think everyone knew where they stood and exactly how I was feeling. That openness was probably quite welcome at the time because things had got a bit tetchy and a bit bitchy. There were chats going on in hotel rooms behind closed doors and a bit of two-faced behaviour going on. I tried to communicate a lot and unpick that a bit. But crikey, let's be honest, who at the age of 23 knows how to really sort those kinds of things out? I just did my best.'

With the 2000 World Cup just 10 months away when she became England captain, Connor did not have much time to turn things around. Nor did she have many opportunities to do so, with a home series against South Africa in June England's only preparation at full international level after their hammering in New Zealand.

While she adjusted to life as captain, Connor was still working full time as a teacher at Brighton College, although it quickly became clear that doing both jobs to the best of her ability was not going to be easy. 'I was managing a full teaching load while training as an individual, working in the nets and in the gym and also being captain and trying to do that role properly. Doing it all became untenable by about 2003.'

Connor was fortunate to have a boss – the headmaster at Brighton, where she had spent her formative years as a pupil – who was also something of a mentor. When she opened up to him about her predicament, he told her to take an unpaid sabbatical from 2003 until after the Ashes in 2005, something that Connor remains endlessly grateful for. 'He basically told me that I had a limited time to be an international cricketer and captain my country, so I should go and do it properly. It meant that for those two years I had a taste of what the current generation have got (18 of England's women now have central contracts), and experienced what it was like to be a male cricketer.

'I had a season playing overseas in New Zealand and did a bit of work in the media [Connor worked on Radio 5 Live and became a key member of the Channel 4 team, working on *The Cricket Show*]. So I managed to earn as much money doing two days a week of various media bits and pieces as I had teaching. I really landed on my feet.'

Despite her busy schedule and the team's limited competitive action ahead of the 2000 World Cup in New Zealand, Connor was confident that England were better prepared for the tournament than in previous years, telling the BBC: 'Preparation for the last World Cup was nothing like as intense as this one. We have now merged with the ECB and that has made an enormous difference in terms of organisation and coaching. The regularity of training sessions was nothing like it is now. There wasn't the opportunity or funding back then, and hopefully we are as best prepared as we can be.'

It was a disappointment then when England failed to reach the semi-finals. In one of the biggest upsets ever seen in women's cricket, they lost to South Africa – who had re-joined the international fold only three years earlier – by five wickets in the group stage. When they followed that defeat with another to India two days later, England's early homecoming was decided. 'It was a massive under-performance', says Connor.

But with seven members of the 18-strong England squad that disappointed in New Zealand still in their teenage years, the hope was that by the time of the next World Cup in four years' time, they would be a far stronger, and more experienced unit.

'Our results did gradually start to pick up after that tournament', says Connor, pointing to victories against India and South Africa in the early noughties. Indeed, England recorded their first Test series win on home soil since 1979 when they beat South Africa at Taunton in August 2003, and followed that up with a 2-1 victory in the one-day series.

'By 2003 we were winning 80 per cent of our games', recalls Connor with the typical statistical recall of a captain. But it was a one-day series victory against the World Champions, New Zealand, in 2004 that really proved how far England had progressed. 'That was our first win against them in a decade [in a series], so it was a huge confidence booster. And looking ahead to the Ashes in 2005, it felt like we had moved a step closer to finally being able to beat Australia. Looking back at it now, I can really chart our progress. I know what things worked and what didn't during that period leading up to the 2005 Ashes.'

England went to South Africa the following March for the 2005 World Cup determined to prove how far they had come since the previous tournament: 'People who haven't seen England for a while will be in for a shock', promised the ECB's media manager, Andrea Wiggins. With the improvements made to fitness levels and funding, and the introduction of more specialised coaching, the team had climbed to second in the world rankings.

After winning all four of their warm-up games, Connor's side were full of belief heading into their opening game against the tournament favourites, Australia. With that game washed out by heavy rain, England were forced to wait until the semi-finals to gauge their improvements against Australia. 'I knew we were playing well and that we had developed', says Connor. 'Our game plans were better than they had ever been, so we felt we were on the right curve.'

Even so, England fell to a five-wicket defeat in that semi-final, leaving Australia to go on and beat India to lift the trophy. Connor, though, remained bullish about their chances in the forthcoming home Ashes series: 'I don't think we've got much to fear', she said after the match. 'Over a series back in England with a chance to play them five times, I'm confident we'll do well. It's easy to be doom and gloom and say, "where do we go from here?", but a World Cup is a tough tournament.'

By the time of England's momentous Ashes summer in 2005, Connor had played for England for a decade, and never beaten Australia. 'It's almost impossible to describe what a hold they had over us', she says. 'At the start of my career, you knew that you didn't stand an earthly and that all the self-talk and positive attitude in the world couldn't ever get you over that feeling of: "we've got no chance". Then it progressed in 2004–5 to thinking that we had a chance. We knew it was going to take something bloody special and that we were probably still not as good as them on paper, or quite where they were in terms of their skills and abilities. But I knew we were edging ever closer going into that Ashes. It felt like we were on the cusp.'

The 2005 Ashes started with the First Test at Hove, in which Connor made the slightly surprising call to select 15-year-old Holly Colvin for the squad. 'Holly was about to go on a geography field trip', recalls Connor. 'But because the Aussies had a good left-arm orthodox spinner, we brought Holly in to training. We were in the nets at the top of the ground and she got everyone out. She got Lot [current England captain, Charlotte Edwards] out, she got Tails [Claire Taylor] out, she got everyone out – comfortably. So everyone was sort of looking at each other, thinking, well, this is just a bit outrageous.'

After canvassing the thoughts of then England coach Richard Bates and Edwards (who was Connor's vice-captain), Colvin was picked for the first XI that would take on Australia in the First Test. 'It was opportunistic and it worked – she was on a hat-trick in the first innings', smiles Connor. England's batting let them down though, and they looked to be in trouble when they lost three early wickets. But a match-saving innings from Arran Brindle, who compiled her first Test century to make 101 not out, salvaged a precious draw for England.

Three days later came the first instalment of a five-match one-day series, which saw Australia triumph by 12 runs in a thrilling contest at Cheltenham. Connor's side felt they could – and should – have won it, having been 198-4 at one stage, and took confidence from that going into the second match. That one went the way of the World Cup winners too though, leaving England 2-0 down in the one-day series with three to play.

'Then we won a game', says Connor. 'We beat them at Stratford which was amazing. I will never forget the emotions of that day. It was the first time we'd ever been on a cricket pitch and beaten Australia. We just didn't know what to do with ourselves.'

It was the perfect way for England to go into the second and final Ashes Test at Worcester – one that Connor's side had to win if they were to regain the Ashes for the first time in 42 years. And when they were set a score of only 75 to win, it seemed as though history might even be made in a straightforward manner. There were still a few anxious moments though, as they struggled to 3-2 and 39-4 before Arran Brindle and Lydia Greenway hauled them across the finish line.

'I'll never forget the sight of Arran clipping a single off her legs mid-afternoon on the final day to take us over the line', says Connor. 'Every player leapt in unison, before scrambling on to the pitch to share the winning feeling. It was an historic Ashes win in the context of the most magical summer for English cricket. The curse had finally been lifted.

'After 10 years of hurt and 10 years of never really getting close, what we achieved that summer was massive. It was the first series win against Australia since '63 and the first time Australia had lost a Test match for 21 years. It really catapulted women's cricket into a new place, too.'

That same summer, England's men also triumphed in an Ashes series for the first time since 1987. To celebrate, the two teams shared a victory parade on an open-top bus through the streets of London, finishing in Trafalgar Square where huge crowds gathered to celebrate the historic victories.

'The summer of 2005 was epic', says Connor. 'The memories of the men's team were so fantastic and you have to remember that in terms of the ECB, this was only eight years on from the merger, and suddenly we were part of an Ashes celebratory parade around the streets of London and going to Downing Street. The ECB really did drive change during that period so we could have that sort of profile.'

The 2005 Ashes proved to be the final high point of Connor's England career, as she retired from international cricket the following March. It was not a huge surprise as she had been hampered by a persistent ankle injury that kept her out of England's post-Ashes winter tour to India. Fortunately, Clare had a ready-made successor in place in Charlotte Edwards – a player who had been an integral part of the side for a decade.

Still, Connor says that stepping down as England captain was not an easy decision. 'I have spent the last six months undergoing an agonising decision-making process', she wrote in her retirement statement, 'and actually penning these words is the hardest moment of it all. I have fulfilled the dream I had as a young girl: I have played for my country, led my country and we have won the Ashes. I firmly believe that women's cricket in this country, at every level, is in the healthiest state it has ever been in and I am so proud to have played a part in that success and rise in profile.'

With Connor now approaching 40, she looks back on all the experiences she had as a young leader and knows they have stood her in good stead for the position she now holds as the ECB's Head of Women's Cricket. 'They gave me some really valuable experiences and lessons. I suppose that's the beauty of sport – it's not life or death but it can teach you a hell of a lot.'

With Connor in reflective mood, I ask whether she thinks her style of captaincy changed from the time she was first handed the role amid that disastrous tour Down

Under in 2000? 'I think I probably changed a little as a person', she says. 'I matured. And in the last couple of years of my tenure I probably did evolve into a slightly more sophisticated captain, by which I mean my plans were better and my tactical planning in terms of the actual game and decision making improved a huge amount.

'I also learnt to handle people better. I was very raw at first and didn't understand people's differences very well. When you're 23 and are an enthusiastic, confident person, you just expect everyone to be like you. It's not until you get older that you start to learn how to lead people, how to treat them differently and push their buttons to help them get the best out of themselves. Understanding and appreciating that everyone is different is something that probably only came to me in the last couple of years and in a way, that's a shame. I think you need to be older to understand all that stuff and as a 23-year-old who's just graduated, what do you know about the world and what do you know about people?'

After retiring, Connor returned to her teaching job at Brighton College. She had a passion for teaching English and held ambitions to one day become a deputy head or head teacher. Towards the end of 2007, however, an opportunity arose that she simply could not ignore – to become the ECB's Head of Women's Cricket.

'I had never even thought about going into the administration side of the game before', says Connor. 'I always thought my future would be in teaching. It was a career that had given me so much support, too, allowing me that space to have a couple of years away from the day job to focus on cricket. I had a real loyalty to teaching as well as a real love of it. But then this job came up, and almost two years after I had retired, the timing felt perfect.'

For a second time, Connor was forced to choose between her two passions: teaching and cricket. 'While I could see this was an amazing job, I had no idea what it entailed or where I'd start. All I knew was teaching and dabbling with a bit of media stuff, so I prevaricated for quite a long time because it felt like a big departure from what I had always planned to do.'

Despite the leap, Connor says she has no regrets about the choice she made: 'I'm 100 per cent delighted I did take that step into administration. I love it. I'm immensely proud and privileged to work in sport at a time when the women's side of it is enjoying some huge advances in terms of increased attention from media and government, and hopefully that will continue to develop.'

One of the earliest 'big wins' of her tenure at the ECB relates to the issue of player contracts. 'When I joined the ECB there were no contracts at all,' she says, 'but then we contracted half the England women's squad to Chance to Shine [a scheme started in 2005 which makes cricket completely accessible to boys and girls through the national curriculum] as coaching ambassadors. I think there are around eight or nine players now who are not only fully contracted to the ECB through their playing contracts but also still have contracts with Chance to Shine.

'There has been a really long-term relationship between England women's cricket and that scheme, which I think is something to be really proud of, because for young girls to see Charlotte Edwards or Lydia Greenway coming into their schools on a daily basis is remarkable.'

Since taking on the role at just 31 years of age (bringing down the average age of the ECB's leadership team by a significant amount), Connor has established herself as one of the most powerful women in the game. In 2011 she was appointed as Chairwoman of the International Cricket Council's (ICC) Women's Committee, and two years later she was being talked up for one of the most senior jobs in the ECB, when Managing Director Hugh Morris announced his resignation.

'I did think about it', she says. 'But I decided it wasn't the right time. I have lots I still want to achieve within the women's game and women's sport in general. It's a really exciting time and I have a real affinity with the whole movement and the progress we're making. Maybe one day, though. It would be the ultimate role.'

It is interesting that a sport which would not be the first one you think of as progressive or forward-thinking has shown such a readiness to embrace the women's game. The ECB itself was only established in 1997, yet by 1998 it had assumed responsibility for women's cricket – something that the governing bodies of other sports prevaricated over for years. And with Connor now occupying such a high-profile and influential role in the organisation, the ECB is again defying its image as the stuffy home of striped ties and tea-time snoozes.

'Lots of sports have reputations, stereotypes and prejudices,' says Connor, 'but I don't think many people realise how young the ECB is and how quickly it took the women's game under its leadership.' It is imperative, she tells me, that sports like cricket and others are genuinely accessible and appealing to every single member of our society.

'They have got to be representative. I'm not a fan of tokenism or quota systems, but I think it's vital that sport moves forwards in terms of sports administration and leadership. In a very challenging, modern world, sport has got to survive and continue to inspire. And I don't think it's as easy to be inspired by sport now as it was when I was a kid, because there are so many other distractions for young people.

'The more that sport can relate to everyone and make itself open and accessible, the better its chances of appealing to potential future players. Sport is one of the most powerful, galvanising things that we've got, so it's vital that it continues to move into what will probably be even more dynamic and challenging times with good leadership and crucially, representative leadership.'

Connor is quick to praise the ECB for 'where it has taken the women's game so far', but her own role in the journey has been just as crucial. As a player and captain she guided England through challenging, turbulent times to become a powerful force in the women's game, and now as a leader she is driving women's cricket forward with the same momentum.

'The most powerful lesson I have learnt', she says, 'is that winning is not the only beacon for success. Success is about perseverance, it is about honesty, it is about learning from disappointments, it is about being brave and it is about picking yourself and those around you up when you don't think you can.' Her career as a teacher might be on hold, but there are many who would benefit from taking lessons on the world of sport from Ms Connor.

8: Guiding lights

'You are going to have to be twice as good as the men to be considered even half as good.' This was the warning given to 23-year-old Karren Brady by David Sullivan after the media magnate hired her as the Managing Director of Birmingham City Football Club in 1993. Her response at the time – 'Luckily, that's not difficult' – reflected the self-belief that was crucial in helping Brady to navigate a world where women were banned from boardrooms and tagged with one of two labels: ball-breaker or bimbo.

More than 20 years on, women are still a minority when it comes to leading and running all sport – not just football. In the boardrooms and on the training grounds, female presence remains a rarity. And for those who are there, the challenge of doing their job well is always compounded by that of being a woman in what is largely a man's world.

Even the sports that many consider to be relatively 'equivocal' in their treatment of men and women fall down when they open up their boardrooms for inspection. Take the International Tennis Federation (ITF), for example. The governing body of world tennis is made up of 210 national tennis associations, sanctions the four Grand Slams throughout the year and operates the sport's three major team events – the Davis Cup (for men), the Fed Cup (for women) and the Hopman Cup (mixed).

And yet despite this broad reach across the entire game, the ITF has a grand total of zero women among its 14 board members. Not one. For a sport that is regarded as one of the most forward-thinking in terms of equality, it is baffling that the game's highest level remains run 100 per cent by men.

This fact was revealed in a report published in the lead-up to the 2014 Commonwealth Games by Women on Boards (a social enterprise group aiming to 'lower the barriers to entry to the boardroom and build the pipeline of board-ready women'). And it wasn't just the ITF that was found lacking.

The report found that on the majority of sporting boards at international and national levels women remained under-represented, with fewer than 20 per cent of board seats being held by women at many of the world's top sports governing bodies.

Women on Boards looked at International Sports Federations (where 15 per cent of board members were women) and National Olympic Committees (16.5 per cent).

So much for the target put in place by the International Olympic Committee before the 2000 Games, stipulating that by 2005 a minimum of 20 per cent of all board members of National Olympic Committees must be female.

The report also shows the breakdown of all 34 International Sports Federations that were included in the study. While the ITF's zero count strikes a particularly sour note, swimming's international governing body (Federation Internationale de Natation, or FINA) does not come out of it much better. Just one woman sits on FINA's board, alongside 34 men who have the responsibility of overseeing not only swimming but also diving, synchronised swimming, water polo and open-water swimming – none of which can typically be described as 'male-dominated' sports.

The report's author, and Executive Director of Women on Boards, Claire Braund, pointed out that fewer female voices at the top level in sport means female athletes will continue to be treated like second-class citizens in terms of salaries, sponsorship and media coverage. 'Sport has the power to change the lives of young women,' she added, 'opening up opportunities for leadership and development and transforming gender norms. It is equally important to have female role models in the corporate boxes and the boardrooms as it is to have those who represent their country.'

We are well accustomed to applying the term 'role model' to those on the field of play, but as Braund says, the women who attain positions of leadership in sport should be viewed as equally inspirational for younger generations. For the chief executive of Women in Sport, Ruth Holdaway, improving these percentages is 'not just about having women sitting on the board, it is about opening the eyes of young girls to the possibility that working in sport, being a leader in sport, is something that you can achieve.'

Holdaway says that while it's obviously important to focus on getting more women and girls playing sport, it is just as crucial that we don't ignore the non-playing side of things. Because if more women and girls are going to benefit from sport, then that has to be about the number of women working in sport as well as playing it – whether that's in coaching roles or on the administrative side.

Increasing the numbers is not quite as straightforward as it sounds though, says Holdaway, who notes two main sticking points. Firstly, she explains that there are structural reasons why boards can't just suddenly advertise for new board members. And secondly, she says: 'Actually, we don't currently have loads of women knocking on the door saying, "I want to sit on the board of a national governing body."'

This shortfall is finally being addressed, however. In 2006 the British Olympic Foundation together with UK Sport and the Sport & Recreation Alliance launched the Women and Leadership Development Programme. This was aimed at giving 11 women involved in British sport the skills and experience required to take on senior decision-making roles. The first instalment ran until 2009 and was followed by a second one that ran from 2010 to 2013.

When I spoke to chief executive of the British Olympic Foundation, Jan Paterson, about the programme that she played a key role in setting up, she said it was a way of opening up pathways to women who might have otherwise seen little opportunity for progression: 'It was about looking at middle-management women and saying to them, if you'd like an opportunity to grow and develop, please come on board with this programme.'

The idea, adds Paterson, was to make them aware of what the opportunities were in the marketplace while upskilling them, giving them a mentor and providing them with international opportunities to build their own network. 'I think that's the key', says Paterson firmly. 'Once women get to a specific level in an organisation, it's up to the company and other women to be able to keep them going.'

That's just half the story, though. Raising the number of women in sport leadership roles requires getting more young girls excited by the possibilities that the sports world can offer them. It requires getting to them early, before they even enter the world of work, and showing them that women who were once schoolgirls like them can go on to find great and varied careers in sport. It requires role models.

But according to research by Girlguiding UK (initially carried out in 2011, but more recent surveys have revealed the same figure), 55 per cent of girls aged between 11 and 21 say they feel there are not enough positive female role models. It was this figure that shocked lawyer Miriam Gonzalez Durantez (a partner at law firm Dechert, and the wife of former Deputy Prime Minister, Nick Clegg). 'In reality', wrote Durante in the *Telegraph* in 2013, 'there are not only enough female role models, but a surplus of them. There are legions of female role models in our workplaces, in our own families, in the street.'

She was writing to explain why, in 2013, she decided to set up the Inspiring Women campaign. Aimed at a range of professions (including sport), the campaign set out to get 15,000 women from a wide range of occupations to go into state schools and talk to 250,000 young women about the range of jobs available and how they can get into them. Durantez hoped that this would be good start in removing 'the stereotypes and absurd labels that still today surround women'.

Professional golfer Kelly Hanwell took part in an Inspiring Women event in London, where 300 girls from 18 state schools were gathered. When she told them what she did for a career, Hanwell says that hundreds of very surprised little faces looked back at her: 'Golf was clearly not on their radar.'

Sports broadcaster Clare Balding was also there that day, telling tales from her many experiences as one of Britain's best-known broadcasters – including working across the London 2012 Olympic and Paralympic Games. 'There are so many options across the board, whether it be in event management, coaching, marketing, sports science, journalism or governance', says Balding. 'And I know that when you are in your teens deciding which path to take, it can make all the difference to have access to worlds you may not have considered.'

It will take some years before we know the true impact of these type of events, but Gonzalez has certainly delivered her message loud and clear to the nation's teenage girls: 'I believe that every single woman can choose what they do with their lives – as men do – and not have to give explanations to society about what they have chosen', she told the BBC in 2014. 'I am being asked all the time, do you want to have it all, and, I don't want to have it all – I want to have what men have.'

Gonzalez's final words would no doubt send then FIFA president Sepp Blatter into meltdown. 'Football is very macho', he said on the eve of the Women's Under 20 World Cup in 2014. It's so difficult to accept [women] in the game. Not playing the game, but in the governance. It's easy in basketball, it's easy in volleyball, it's easy in athletics. It is no problem. But in football, I don't know. There's something very reluctant [*sic*].'

Football writer Sonja Cori Missio was present in the room where Blatter gave this speech in August 2014. Her report of it in the *Guardian* made clear that she was shocked by his words, but not because they were sexist, politically incorrect or out of touch: 'It was shocking because it seemed heartfelt, genuine, and – above anything – honest.'

Missio presented Blatter as being sincere (though not apologetic) about the 'difficulty' of fitting women in at the top end of the international football hierarchy. Blatter, she wrote, was 'only one part of FIFA's poly-head hydra'. Despite his presidential role, she claimed he was not the only one responsible for change at executive level.

It would be easier to go along with Missio's way of thinking if Blatter hadn't spent most of his 18 years in charge of FIFA blurting out things like, 'Let's get women to play in tighter shorts'. This was probably his most famous faux pas (made in 2004), but there was also this, on the allegations that then England captain, John Terry had been unfaithful to his wife with the ex-girlfriend of a teammate: 'If this had happened in let's say Latin countries, then I think he would have been applauded.'

Blatter's blathering makes it difficult to accept the idea he put forward in May 2015 that he was a 'godfather to women's football'. But even his staunchest critics have to accept that during his tenure, there has been some change – slow change, but change. Perhaps the most publicized of these changes came in May 2013 when FIFA elected a woman to its powerful executive committee for the first time in the governing body's 109-year history.

President of the Burundi FA, Lydia Nsekera, collected the most votes from a trio of candidates that also included Australian Moya Dodd and Sonia Bien-Aime, of Turks and Caicos Islands, meaning she's currently serving a four-year term on the committee. Dodd and Bien-Aime, meanwhile, both served as co-opted members for a one-year term.

Their presence suggests progress. And Blatter has (of course) put himself in prime position to take all the credit for it. Had it not been for his intervention, he said, they might not be there at all: 'If you look at the organization of FIFA, the President is elected by the congress, and all the other members of the executive [are elected] by the confederations. And the confederations never would have proposed a lady.

'Finally, [I] said: "Now we go to the congress and ask the congress to [elect] at least one lady." It was in 2011 and they said "Yes!" So we now have one fully elected and two appointed ... It took more than 100 years for FIFA to elect a woman in the executive committee, it's not easy to change these attitudes.'

Whether Blatter was the driving force behind this that he claims to be, or whether he was simply bowing to external pressure, the result remains the same – a significant step forward for women in football. And there is more to thank Blatter for, says Juliet Macur of the *New York Times* – a journalist who has devoted much time to writing about FIFA and its long-time President.

Writing on the eve of the 2015 Women's World Cup in Canada, Macur penned a piece titled 'A Little Praise for Sepp Blatter. Very Little'. In it she credited him with overseeing 'an explosion of growth in the women's game', using the Women's World Cup itself as an example. In its early years, the tournament consisted of 12 teams (in 1991 and 1995), but expanded to 16 teams from 1999 onwards, and then up again to 24 in 2015.

Eight of those 24 teams that competed in the 2015 tournament were from nations making their Women's World Cup debuts, something that Macur believes Blatter can also take plaudits for: 'It would be hard to argue to those squads that some portion of the much-maligned FIFA development money – funds that people routinely accuse Blatter of passing out as bribes — had not been used to develop women's teams where they never existed before.'

It's true that women's football would probably have thrived in many places without Blatter. But in others, it has needed a helping hand and as Macur adds: 'For years, Blatter has been the one providing it.'

It's difficult though, this notion of applauding a man whose sexist remarks have been a recurring theme throughout his career for advancing women's football. Even the players can't bring themselves to do it. In Macur's piece, United States midfielder Megan Rapinoe points out that Blatter has really only done the things he *should* have been doing (and that he probably could have done far quicker) 'You can't look at it and say that he's done nothing for women's sports', says Rapinoe. 'But I don't think you should be congratulated or patted on the back for doing the right thing. He has said he is the godfather of the sport, but I think he just sort of allowed it to grow, and it was going to do its own thing anyway.'

Blatter's point about the inherent difficulty of making changes at executive level is echoed by Claire Braund, the Executive Director of Women on Boards. She points out that in most organisations, board members are elected by members or via nomination from a club, regional or country sports body. It's an election process that Braund says rewards 'those who have participated in elite sport or served time with the sports' governing bodies, rather than those with the skillsets for the job.'

To help shift the balance, she calls for 'better governance,' particularly in board election and selection processes. Better governance and gender imbalance on governing boards are twin issues, according to Braund, who believes that ensuring the former – for example, by limiting terms in office and ensuring at least two independent board members - is the only way to improve the latter. The compliance of governing bodies to these mandates should, adds Braund be tied to funding outcomes, where appropriate.

Government-imposed laws like quotas require corporations to have a certain number or percentage of women on their boards. Many countries already have them – Germany became the latest to introduce them in 2015, following Norway, France and Spain on to a growing list of countries that have introduced quotas in a bid to force corporations to boost the number of women directors.

Braund stops short of calling for quotas to be introduced in the UK, but others believe that they are the only way that real diversity will be achieved in the boardrooms of sporting organisations. FIFA executive committee member Moya Dodd is one such believer. 'In an ideal world there would be no need for quotas because you'd have well-functioning, merit-based systems providing equal opportunities', she said. 'But I think quotas are useful if you think that those systems are not working, or not working quickly enough to ensure outcomes.'

A former footballer turned lawyer, Dodd also became the first female board member of the Asian Football Confederation and Football Federation Australia in 2007 – positions that she believes she only attained because a conscious effort was made to diversify: 'I am sure I am only a member of the Asian Football executive and the FIFA executive committee because those positions were created for female members. I think it would be a long time before women started turning up at executive committee level if it were not for those seats.'

In September 2015, as FIFA's Reform Task Force gathered to try and pick its way through the mess that preceded the elections earlier in the year (when seven FIFA officials were arrested on charges of accepting more than $150million in bribes), Dodd added her suggestions to the mix, asking FIFA to consider setting a target of 30 per cent for female members of its decision-making hierarchy.

She revealed that when the women's football community gathered at FIFA's Symposium in Canada before the Women's World Cup in 2015, the message that emerged was clear: 'We want an inclusive FIFA, with a 30 per cent participation target in committees and senior roles, and non-discriminatory resourcing of the women's game in fair financial proportion to our participation and our potential. These asks have been passed up to the Reform Committee, and we are hopeful of favourable consideration in the reform process.' In December 2015, FIFA's executive committee approved a number of changes, including replacing the executive committee with a FIFA council. This new body would have responsibility for setting the organisation's overall direction and at least six women will sit on it. It's a start.

FIFA's gender imbalance is not solely the fault of the governing body though, says Dodd. In 2014 she told the *Guardian* that she believes the lack of women in governance is partly down to the fact that there simply aren't as many ex-players with the longevity in the game that so many men have: 'Women weren't able to play the game in so many parts of the world for decades. So it's an evolving thing, where you get women emerging and graduating from the playing side of the game and into the boardrooms. And that's still a work in progress.

'The reality is, there's thousands of male ex-pros, some of whom turn up in boardrooms and many who do not. But with women, they are presently in much smaller numbers … Football was a game for men for so long, that opening it up to women requires conscious effort in all of those areas: grassroots, leagues, coaching, off-field and commercial development.'

For some women, introducing quotas has far too many downsides for it to be a positive step. Helena Morrissey is one of them. The chief executive of Newton Investment Management – the company behind taking the Women's Boat Race to the same stretch of the River Thames as the men's – believes that quotas can cause women to be seen as less deserving of their place in a company's hierarchy, regardless of whether they have earned the right to be there: 'I think they can end up with a lot of tokenism and questioning someone's ability to serve on the job', says Morrissey. 'It's very off-putting for others but can also diminish a woman – to be there because she's a female.'

Morrissey's stance is one that the British Olympic Association's Jan Paterson can understand. In 2010 she became Britain's first female Chef de Mission (the person considered to be the 'head' of the national Olympic Committee during a Games, and responsible for all athletes, officials and other staff) at the Singapore Youth Olympics, telling me that she was simply the right person, in the right place at the right time.

So, why did it take so long for a woman to have that role? 'A lot of it is down to history', explains Paterson. 'British sport was once based on grey flannels and navy jackets, and it's not any more. I think it was probably timing plus my experience that contributed to the fact that it was the right time to have me as the Chef for Team GB. All the stars aligned. I don't think it was because I was a woman at all, I think it was because I had the right skillset.'

Like many people, Paterson is torn on the idea of quotas. On one hand she says, they are a step forward: 'It puts it in people's minds. It's a sign that we recognise where we are in evolution.' On the other hand, she also recognises the negative of quotas, saying: 'Depending on who's administering them, sometimes the impact that quotas lead people to appoint a woman just because they have to, rather than putting together a competency framework and choosing the right person.'

In America, Title IX could be considered as a sort of quota system in the way that it focuses people's minds on the issue of gender equality. Sophie Goldschmidt, who is now Chief Commercial Officer for the Rugby Football Union (RFU), spent the early part of her career working in the USA, initially for Adidas and then for the Women's Tennis Association, before joining the NBA as Senior Vice President for Europe, Middle East and Africa Operations.

She tells me that professional women – not just those involved in sport – are treated differently in America compared to the UK, saying: 'I think it's more progressive over there … there are many more women in senior positions across the board and more opportunities. I think a lot of that is to do with legislation. It's definitely more male dominated here [in the UK] than in the US.'

Title IX led to a huge boom in the numbers of females playing sport, when the legislation was signed more than 40 years ago (something discussed in more detail in Chapter 6). In theory, it should follow that in time this boom will lead to a second (albeit smaller) one at leadership level in American sports.

Yet despite Goldschmidt's own experiences, it seems the theory has not yet become reality. The Racial and Gender Report Card is produced by The Institute for Diversity and Ethics in Sport (TIDES) every year, and awards a grade (like A+ or B-) to many of the leading professional and amateur sports and sporting organizations in the United States on the equality and diversity of their hiring practices.

Of the three major sports in the USA – NFL (American football), NBA (basketball) and MLB (baseball) – it was the NBA that emerged on top in 2014, receiving an A+ for their racial hiring practices and a B+ for gender. In real terms, the B+ translates as 40.9 per cent of employees in the NBA league office being women, while 42 women served as vice presidents during the 2013–14 season.

These figures sound positive, but Richard Lapchick, the director of TIDES and primary author of the report, sees room for improvement in the numbers of women operating at team level: 'Women are still not well represented at the senior team levels', he says, pointing to the figure of 21.4 per cent that reflects the number of women who held team senior administration positions during the 2013–14 season.

The NBA still outshines the NFL and MLB though, with these leagues receiving a C- and C+ respectively for their gender hiring practices (both received A grades in terms of racial hiring). The report surmises that this leaves both leagues lagging behind the NBA in both a business and athletic sense. Having a diverse organisation, it claims, 'can provide a different perspective and possibly a competitive advantage for a win in the board room as well as on the field'.

The hope is that, in another 40 years from now, we will see the full effect of Title IX. Add all those young girls who grabbed their chance to get involved in sport at school or college into the US sporting landscape and those C grades could become As. 'It all comes back to leadership', says Mechelle Voepel, a writer for ESPN's dedicated website for women's sports, ESPNW. She believes that if Title IX is to have the impact on women's sport that it's capable of, it is down to those who have benefited from the educational opportunities it has provided to 'give back to those who follow them by providing even greater opportunities'. And they can only achieve this by holding positions of power and influence.

The idea that a better-balanced boardroom can be advantageous on and off the field of play is one that both UK Sport and Sport England, who between them are responsible for supporting sport at elite and grassroots level, firmly believe in. Both have set targets for the governing bodies that they fund to ensure that by 2017 women comprise at least 25 per cent of those boards. These aren't quotas though, insists UK Sport Chief Executive Liz Nicholl. She believes that using the word 'quota' implies that any female with a pulse and a passing interest in sport would fit the bill (she might have phrased it a little differently, but that was the drift), when really it's about finding the right women to create balanced boards.

'Because better balanced boards have a broader perspective', said Nicholl, 'and frankly, they will make better decisions'. She claims that UK Sport sees a direct link between a sport's success (in terms of medals, etc.) and how successful its governing body is in terms of its make up (meaning how well balanced it is). So while Great Britain has done pretty well in recent years in terms of what we've achieved through our elite success, Nicholl says that UK Sport sees room for vast improvement: 'As we look across the sports, we know and the sports know, we can be even better. It presents a fantastic opportunity for us if we can address it.'

If UK Sport's targets aren't technically quotas though, what can they do about those governing bodies that fail to meet them? Nicholl says that the figures will be re-examined after the 2016 Olympics in Rio, and that they 'might consider sanctions at some point'. It is after Rio that UK Sport will make their decisions about how sports will be funded in the next Olympic cycle, so it is then, says Nicholl, that they will decide 'whether or not to make [female representation] a funding requirement.'

Women in Sport's chief executive Ruth Holdaway says that UK Sport's 25 per cent target is 'helpful', but not quite enough to force real change. 'We want to push further', she says, 'and the evidence from business is very clear, the point at which you get better decision making is at 30 per cent. So you need to have at least 30 per cent of your board made up of women if those women are going to be able to have real impact and to affect decision making.'

Numerous studies have been done into the results of a balanced boardroom, and as Holdaway says, the evidence is clear: Boards with better gender diversity get better results. In 2014 Morgan Stanley Capital International (MSCI) carried out a survey into Women on Boards in 2014, and found that those boards with gender diversity above and beyond regulatory mandates or market norms had fewer instances of governance-related scandals like bribery, corruption, fraud and shareholder battles.

Sandrine Devillard is a director of Mckinsey & Co. in Paris. She explains that they started researching gender diversity in corporations for two reasons: Firstly, women represent half of the talent pool, so they believed it was critical to have the best brains, of both men and women, at a time of talent shortage. Secondly, says Devillard, there was a big question being asked: Does it really matter for corporations to have more women at the top? Does it matter for performance?

Since 2007, McKinsey & Co.'s Women Matters research has consistently shown that, yes, it does matter. The reasons range from 'getting the best brains to work on the problem' to having a workforce that better matches customer demographics. It's common sense really: Diversify your boardroom and you get a broader range of thoughts, opinions and ideas, which can only be beneficial to business.

Beyond this basic summation, McKinsey & Co. have also found that companies benefit from certain behavioural aspects that are distinct to women. In 2009 they surveyed 800 business leaders worldwide, and found that certain leadership behaviours typically adopted by women are critical to perform well in the post-crisis world.

Claire Braund of Women on Boards has pored over the research done over the last decade and more, and says that it offers a vast array of reasons why gender diversity if good for business: 'The research tells us about the dynamics of the discussion in the boardroom and the quality of decision making when women are present. It tells us the range of issues canvassed increases and includes usefully different perspectives from female board members. Boards with women also are more likely to be best practice in terms of board evaluations, codes of conduct, conflict of interest guidelines and looking more closely at executive remuneration arrangements.'

In short, placing more women on the boards is good for business. It's also good for future generations of females, says Ruth Holdaway of Women in Sport, who advocates having boards of at least 30 per cent women: 'In order to generate a sustainable pipeline … it's not just about putting one or two women on a board. It's about growing that, it's about showcasing those women and making sure that there are other women coming through to take those places in the future as well.'

Karren Brady is a prime example of how one woman in the right position can sometimes be all it takes to generate the pipeline that Holdaway talks about. Now Vice Chairman of West Ham FC (a position she holds among many, many other positions at various companies and organisations), Brady became the first woman to run a top-flight football club when she was made the Managing Director of Birmingham City FC in 1993 – at just 23 years of age. In her 2012 autobiography, *Strong Woman*, she explained why she views clearing a path for future generations of women as one of her key responsibilities: 'If you are the first woman in anything, then that's something to take heart from because you have opened a door. The trick is to hold that door open as wide as possible, for as long as possible, to allow other women to march through it.

'I can say, with my hand on my heart, that I have tried to do that. When I joined Birmingham City Football Club I was the only woman. When I left, three-quarters of my senior management team were women. Similarly, when I joined West Ham United there were no women on the senior management board, however, now 50 per cent of the board are female. If I don't do it, then who will?'

Brady might have been the first lady in football, but others have now joined her, including Sunderland's Chief Executive Margaret Byrne, Charlton Athletic's Chief Executive Katrien Meire and Mansfield Town's Carolyn Radford, who became English football's youngest CEO when she was appointed in 2011 at the age of 29. Chelsea also appointed a woman to their executive board for the first time ever in 2013, in the form of Marina Granovskaia, who was immediately labelled by the press as 'Roman Abramovich's right-hand woman'. And further afield, change is starting to appear too, with former US women's national team star Mia Hamm named as a new member of Italian club AS Roma's board of directors in October 2014.

A small, select group of women they may be, but they are a sign that even the male-dominated world of football is starting to change its views. There are a growing number of powerful individuals within the game who accept that there is more to be gained from having a female influence in the boardroom than by shutting it out completely, or even banishing it to the ladies' room. This was the area reserved for directors' wives, and the place where women would be sent to in the days before they were allowed into football boardrooms. 'With me coming along and making a fuss', writes Brady, 'ladies' rooms were closed and women were finally allowed to go into boardrooms. I had made my first major breakthrough, and had had my first chance to change things for women in the game.'

One area of football that does escape Brady's powerful influence is that of coaching. It is not surprising that there has never been a female coach at the top level of the men's game, but the following statistic is more of a head-scratcher: Out of all 18 FA Women's Super League clubs, just one – Chelsea – has a female manager in Emma Hayes.

There are women involved in various other senior positions: Julie Chipchase is the Director of Football at Doncaster Rovers Belles, while Kelly Chambers combines her role as General Manager of Reading Ladies with working as the assistant first team coach. Yeovil Town Ladies also have a female assistant manager, Michelle Yeowell. But invariably, the top coaching positions at the elite level remain largely filled by men.

'Up until now there haven't really been too many opportunities in coaching on a full-time level', Emma Hayes said at a conference run by Kick it Out (football's equality and inclusion organisation) in October 2014. She took the reins at Chelsea Ladies in 2012, but spent large chunks of her early career in management working in the USA. 'The game in America is on an equal footing', she explains. 'There's equal funding, equal access. If women are good enough, they will get an opportunity. It's a great place to develop as a women's coach.'

Hayes points out that the women's game has not been professional – or even semi-professional – for very long in England, and that as the current crop of players progress, we will see more moving into coaching as well as other areas of the game. 'We are in a profession where it has been in the dark ages. It is changing, but it is changing slower than other professions. But as boards diversify, then coaching appointments will diversify.'

'Ultimately', says Hayes, 'it is up to clubs and The FA to continue their investment so that we have a place to go.' Never a woman who's afraid of demanding what she feels is deserved (just ask her players at Chelsea), Hayes also asks for 'a bit more courage' from team owners. They have to understand that 'in order for women to get better at coaching, you have to put them in positions.'

When it comes to hiring a female head coach for a men's side, this courage needs to be accompanied by a solid dose of bravery and unshakeable belief in one's own decision making. It might not be something that has happened in English football yet, but it has happened somewhere not too far away – in Stirling, to be exact.

Former Arsenal Ladies manager Shelley Kerr became the first woman ever to manage a British senior men's team, when she took charge of Scottish Lowland League side at the University of Stirling in August 2014. 'I've always had aspirations of working in the men's game', Kerr told BBC Scotland, 'and right now this seems like a really good fit for me'. Her appointment might not have invited the same level of scrutiny that would accompany a similar move in the Premier League or even the Football League, but that didn't stop people from questioning the reasons for Kerr's employment, with some wondering whether it was a ploy to get more media exposure for the club.

Not so, says Raleigh Gowrie, Stirling University's Sports Performance Manager. He pointed out that Kerr was one of 15 candidates for the job and was simply the standout applicant: 'Shelley had the very highest level of coaching qualifications: a UEFA Pro Licence. She also had experience of coaching at the highest level, including coaching in the Europa League, albeit in the women's game. The interview panel were impressed by her CV and the vision she demonstrated for the club.'

For her part, Kerr had no qualms about moving into the men's game: 'I'm confident enough … It shouldn't be about gender, it should be about your ability as a coach.' Unlike some though, Kerr does believe that coaching men can present a different test to coaching women, telling BBC Scotland: 'I think women can sometimes be a little bit more difficult than men.'

Kerr's belief is one that Sports Coach UK – a body set up more than 30 years ago to provide support to the coaching industry – have challenged. When it comes to coaching women's sport, Sports Coach UK claim that many of the so-called 'facts' are based on stereotypes and that the common assumption that women are more difficult to coach is one example of this. In a fact sheet put together by Sports Coach UK to help advise coaches working with female athletes, they write that women are actually "often more open to being coached and to new ways of doing things, especially if it will help them perform better."

Michael Bradley is the Basketball Strength and Conditioning Coach at Florida State University and has worked with female athletes at college level in the US since the early 1990s. In his book, *Coaching the Female Athlete*, he writes that coaching women is no different from coaching men. "In each case the coach must deal with people as individuals. Each person responds to different motivational styles in their own way. It's up to the coach to discover how to best motivate and get points across regardless of whether the athlete is a man or a woman."

He adds that in his experience, female athletes can be 'extremely tough minded,' but explains that this is an overwhelmingly positive thing from a coaching perspective: 'My experience has been that female athletes will train just as hard or harder than most men … If the activity is presented in the correct way, there will be a great "buy in" and they'll be some of the biggest proponents of a programme.'

The differing views of Kerr and Bradley undoubtedly come down to their own experiences. It's possible that their genders could also be relevant here. Do female athletes sometimes respond better to male coaches and vice versa? It's a complex topic with many strands to it, including the attitudes and beliefs of the athletes themselves (have they grown up surrounded by stereotypical views on gender roles, for example?) But it's also potentially very simple: Athletes are individuals, and male or female; they will respond to coaches in the way that individual would, not as 'a man' or 'a woman' would.

It's not just in Scotland that a woman has broken through the previously impenetrable barrier between men's and women's football. Former French international Corinne Diacre took over as manager of French Ligue 2 side Clermont Foot in June 2014, following another woman, Helena Costa into the role. Costa hit the headlines just over a month before Diacre's arrival when Clermont Foot president Claude Michy hired her as the new manager, making Costa the first woman in Europe to be appointed as manager of a top-level club.

The media excitement over Costa's appointment outlasted her reign as manager, though. After just one day in the role she quit, saying it had become clear to her that she was expected to be 'the face of the club', but without any of the power or control to go with it. 'There were a series of events that no trainer would tolerate and a total lack of respect as well as amateurism', she said in a statement released after her resignation. Costa also claimed that

Michy's adviser Olivier Chavanon had signed players without her knowledge – 'for a team I was supposed to lead and be responsible for.'

Many dismissed the whole episode as a cry for publicity by Michy, who had previously bemoaned the fact that the club was operating 'in a city where the number one sport is rugby'. But his decision to appoint Diacre almost immediately after Costa's departure suggests otherwise. Indeed, before Costa's time ended so sourly she described Michy as 'a visionary but also a brave man'.

When Michy initially hired Costa, he explained that doing so would give the club an 'opportunity to create a sporting challenge and to use something that hasn't been done before to try to give a different image to our club … It's a great challenge, and on top of that, I met a person who really wanted to try this experiment, someone with a real will and character and certainly lots of competence.'

Costa's appointment might not have worked out, but while Corinne Diacre remains the Clermont manager (as she does at time of writing), Michy's 'experiment' continues. The pressure on him to make a change should the club have a bad season (they finished 12th in her first season, two places above their position from the previous year) will be immense, as it would be if a male manager was in place. But it will be interesting to observe if, as and when her time in charge does come to an end, Diacre's gender is one of the headline reasons given for her departure. If not, and it's any of the million and one other excuses that are trotted out whenever a football manager gets the boot, then we can finally say we are getting somewhere – that women in football are treated just the same as men.

This is a scenario to which rugby coach and former England international Giselle Mather has given some thought. At present, she is employed by Aviva Premiership side London Irish as manager of their academy programme, but she has also worked as the head coach of a senior men's amateur side, Teddington RFC. Her success with both squads – six players from the last two seasons have graduated from the academy programme into the Senior Academy at London Irish, while Teddington RFC had two of the most successful seasons in their history between 2009 and 2011, winning 62 consecutive games – has led many to suggest that Mather could one day become the first female Premiership coach.

She is too modest to say it will be her, but Mather tells me she does believe a female coach will eventually get a job in the Premiership. 'It will happen when the skillset is right and the right individual is there', says Mather. 'It's evolutionary. It takes time. It's all about opportunity and having people with the courage to say, "I'm going to give this person the job because they are the right person, not because they are a man or a woman."

'But being female, if you are given that opportunity, you have to get it right. That is the pressure. And at times I do feel that I have to do this well, because I'm the first to do it and you want other people and yourself to get more opportunities.'

Mather pays tribute to former London Irish boss Toby Booth for having 'broad enough shoulders' to absorb all the comments he got when her hired her. 'He judged me by what he saw, how I worked, how I saw the game and didn't see that I was female doing it. He didn't care what people thought and for the first few females to get on, you need innovators prepared to do the same. Then it is down to people like me to show what we can do.'

The thing is, there aren't currently any other women out there quite like Mather. She is the only female to hold a Level 4 coaching qualification from the Rugby Football Union (RFU), be a World Cup winner (Mather was part of the England team that won the tournament in 1994), and will go down in RFU history for taking her six-week old daughter along to her Level 3 coaching course.

'I rang the RFU and said I would be bringing my little one along, just a courtesy call to let them know', recalls Mather with a grin. 'You can imagine the reaction. But I just told them that if she starts screaming and I have to take her out and I fail, then so be it. Still, I don't think it has been done before or since.'

Throughout the years it took to get her coaching qualifications, Mather was always the only woman in the room. It's something she learned not to take much notice of though, telling me: 'As long as I've prepared for it, meaning that in my head I've gone "Yep, usual scenario", then I'm fine. I don't see myself as the only female in the room. I see myself as a rugby coach in a room with other rugby coaches.'

There were times though, Mather admits when she was forced to confront the obvious. Her Level 2 coaching course was largely practical based, and she chuckles as she recalls one session out on the field when she found herself stuck in a maul with a group of large, rugby-shaped men: 'There was an ex-Scottish international in there. To protect me, he just picked me up, put me out to the side and dropped me. It was hilarious.'

During her time as a coach, Mather says she has encountered players who have initially struggled with the idea of having a female coach, particularly with the senior men's teams. 'For some of them I think it was like, wow, I've never been coached by a woman before. For 10 or 15 minutes, it's novel, but then I'm challenging them and pushing them, and they forget that and get on with what they're doing.'

One or two have proved to be more obstinate characters, however: 'Out on the field I can see it straight away', says Mather. 'They may challenge me directly over something I've said so I'll answer that, then continue to work them, and then I'll be asked again. But by the end of the session it's gone. I've never had it where it continues constantly in terms of my athletes.

'I think people who work around me or maybe against competitively find it weird initially because they don't know me and culturally it's not the norm. And there are moments where I think, ok, that's happening because of my gender so I've just got to work hard, keep proving myself and it'll go away. Over years though, opinions do change and people now accept me for who, and what I am. They don't necessarily see me as a female, I'm just the coach.'

Mather's experiences with the older men that she has coached will be familiar to any woman who has operated in sport at any level – whether that's as an athlete, coach, medical staff or even as a sports writer (I know of female football journalists, for example, who have been asked by a man alongside them in the press box if they need help understanding certain aspects of the game). This 'mansplaining' (meaning to explain without regard to the fact that the explainee knows more than the explainer, and often done by a man to a woman) can mean that female coaches often find themselves questioned more frequently by their athletes than their male counterparts would be.

For this reason it's critical that any female coach taking on a men's team has the absolute backing of those above her. Dr Justine Siegal now works as the Director of Sports Partnerships at Northeastern University in Boston, MA, but her background is in baseball. In 2009 she became the first woman to coach men's baseball professionally as the first base coach for the Brockton Rox team in the Boston area. In an interview with CNN in 2015, Siegal said that during her time in charge she realised how key it was for a woman in her position to have the full backing of senior management: 'When that leadership is not behind [you], all of a sudden there's space [for dissension], and maybe one player tries to go through it and brings more players along, so that's why it's so important to be backed.'

Male coaches aren't immune from being questioned by their athletes, but there's a difference, says Siegal: 'Men step on the field and it's assumed they know. I found [as a woman] you have to step on the field and prove yourself.'

This is true even away from typically male-dominated team sports. When Amelie Mauresmo was announced as the new coach of Britain's number one tennis player Andy Murray, in June 2014, it marked the first time that one of the top-ranked male players had hired a female coach. The usual spate of questions followed: Will she be allowed in the locker room? Will she be able to hit with him on the court (er, yes, she's a two-time Grand Slam champion). Will Murray still let the f-bombs fly in the direction of his box during a match that's not going his way?

Murray didn't care one bit. He hired the coach he felt was best placed to advance his game. Having grown up with a female coach (his mum, Judy), it didn't feel like anything out of the ordinary. But when Murray's 2014 season failed to deliver the successes it had done in the past, he realised that for others, his employment of a female coach was a far bigger deal.

After watching Murray get pummelled by Roger Federer at the World Tour Finals in London in November 2014, Sky Sports pundits Greg Rusedski and Annabel Croft discussed the changes they felt Murray needed to make to his game. Croft suggested he looked 'confused' on the court, and lacking in direction. Rusedski added that Murray needed to go back to the way he was playing under his former coach, Ivan Lendl. 'He needs to find the right person who can instil that in him', said Rusedski. 'Go call Lendl.' For them, the fact that Murray was still working his way back to top form after undergoing back surgery the previous year was secondary to the fact that his coach wasn't someone they considered to be capable of leading him there.

'Her competence was always under fire', wrote Murray of his coach in a column for French newspaper, *L'Équipe*, six months after he was soundly beaten by Federer in London. 'I felt embarrassed. That's why I made a point of repeatedly saying she was doing an excellent job. The real low point hit at the Masters when I lost 6-0, 6-1 against Roger. Rather than blaming me, they pointed the finger at Amelie. I still remember what some players and coaches said about her – I wasn't impressed and I shan't forget in a hurry.'

Murray's return to form in 2015 acted as vindication for his choice (although he has always said that even if the relationship hadn't worked out it wouldn't have had anything to do with Mauresmo's gender). And he has done much to advance the case for female coaches, writing in *L'Équipe* how it's 'a crying shame there aren't more female coaches. I hope this changes even if this isn't the reason I chose Amelie. Whilst a female coach might not gel so well with others, it wouldn't hurt for everyone to be a little more open-minded.'

Clearly, that applies not only to the other men in the locker room, but those discussing the sport in the media, too.

Giselle Mather tells me she is well aware that, like Mauresmo, her gender could become the headline story if she was to become the Premiership's first female coach: 'I do feel that if I was to fail, people will say "she wasn't able to cope"', says Mather. 'They would blame my gender rather than my lack of skillset, so instead of assessing the reasons why I might have failed, they would immediately say, well, how could a woman be expected to survive in that environment? If a male fails though, it would be put down to his lack of skillset.'

She says the thought of such scrutiny doesn't deter her, though. After all, she has already bulldozed her way through a number of barriers to get to where she is now. 'When my players go out on the field, the big thing is how they cope with pressure. If I can't cope with pressure, then why am I coaching them? Rugby is a game of chaos, with an 80-minute outcome, and you have to deliver in that 80 minutes with someone physically trying to stop you – that's pressure. I see my job as challenges and opportunities to do things I haven't done before. It's exciting.'

While rugby and football are the most obviously male-dominated sports, female coaches remain a rare species all over the wider sporting world, particularly when it comes to high-performance sport. Sports Coach UK reported that at the London 2012 Olympics just 10 per cent of Team GB's coaches were female, and they all coached female teams or individual female athletes.

The story is a similar one in the US. Of the five sports in which America fielded a women's team under a single head coach at London 2012 – basketball, field hockey, soccer, volleyball and water polo – only the soccer coach was a woman. This was despite the fact the USA Olympic team contained more female athletes than male for the first time in its history.

But the US coaching scene was once very different. When Title IX was passed in 1972, 90 per cent of women's teams were coached by women – it was the norm. By 2012, however, that figure had fallen to 43 per cent, with the number of women coaching men's teams as low as two to three per cent. Somehow, at the same time as Title IX was creating a huge increase in women's participation in sport, it was also causing the number of female coaches to dwindle.

The picture becomes even more baffling when you consider that by 1978 – the year the federal government designated as the deadline for compliance with Title IX – the number of women's sports teams at all levels had more than doubled – from an average of about 2.5 teams to 5.6 teams per school.

How can this be? For many the answer is simple: by bringing women's sports up to speed in terms of facilities and funding, Title IX made it a much more attractive prospect for male coaches who might previously have turned their noses up at getting involved in women's sport. Suddenly, women's sports had attained a new level of respect and offered significantly higher salaries, transforming them from 'passion projects for the most dedicated women's sports advocates to serious career paths', according to *Washington Post* reporter Megan Greenwell. She highlights the examples of legendary college basketball coach Pat Summit, who earned $250 a month when she began her career at the University of Tennessee in 1974. By the time she retired in 2012, Summit was earning a salary of more than $2 million.

Once Title IX had taken full effect, things snowballed rapidly. Assistant coaches of men's teams saw an opportunity for faster promotion by applying to head coach jobs on the women's side. And for graduating male athletes looking to stay in the college game, the availability of jobs had suddenly doubled. Finally, both of these groups found it far easier to impress the directors of college sports, who had always been predominantly male, than female coaches who might have been applying for the same positions.

'In too many cases, athletic directors take the easy way out', says Judy Sweet, who became the first-ever female athletic director of a combined men's and women's program at the University of California in 1975. 'Instead of actively recruiting outside of their networks, they hire the people they already know, and their networks are likely to be male-dominated.'

The shortage of female coaches is inextricably linked to the shortage of females at the very top of the sporting food chain. Put them together, and these factors show young girls that unless they are going to be a professional athlete, sport is not for them once their days as a student are over. It also robs young girls of the strong, female role models who could potentially encourage them to continue participating in sport – as a player or a coach – long after they have left their schooldays behind.

Christine Bowmaker is one such strong female. The former sprinter is one of the few female coaches operating at the top level of British athletics, and one of even fewer females working as a sprints coach. On the day I visit her at the Lee Valley Athletics Centre, where a significant proportion of Britain's top athletes have their training bases, she is the only female coach in the building – the same as it is on most days that Bowmaker is working there.

At present, she is responsible for guiding top young British talent Jodie Williams through the tricky transition from being the fastest girl in the world at junior level to a world-beater as a senior athlete. Bowmaker acknowledges it's a 'great responsibility', but it's one she is used to, having worked with former World and Olympic champion Christine Ohuruogu (which Bowmaker did alongside Ohuruogu's long-time coach, Lloyd Cowan), as well as former world youth champion Asha Philip.

What she has found harder to accept, however, is the feeling that somehow she is not worthy of the same respect as her male counterparts. 'You feel like you have to achieve much more in order to get recognition', she says. 'I've achieved quite a lot in female sprinting, but I'm not recognised. I don't feel there is as much respect for me as there would be if I was a male coach. But I've realised that I can't wait for them to put me up there because I'm not in it for that. I'm in it to make sure that I'm a better coach.'

She's also in it to make sure that Britain's young female sprinters have the kind of guidance that she did not have in her own days as an athlete: 'I coach men and women, but my passion is for female sprinting. I think women are harder to coach than men because there are a lot of obstacles you have to overcome like menstruation, change in body, boyfriends and your image. When I was at school women with muscles were seen as masculine. I want to make them realise that you can be feminine, be successful and be a high-profile athlete – these are the things that motivated me to go into coaching. I made a decision that I would come into the sport to raise the profile of female sprinting and empower women.'

Bowmaker provides a sharp insight into some of the reasons why coaching can be a challenging occupation for women. As the primary carer for her two young children, she tells me she often has to bring them along to the track with her while she is coaching. They have also had to accompany her on some of the warm-weather training trips she has needed to go on with her athletes. The job is hard, says Bowmaker. She works late into the evening and at weekends for modest pay, but she is in it because she believes she offers something different to what is on offer from other (male) coaches.

'I'm quite hard on the girls, and I don't differentiate between male and female athletes. If you're training, then you're training. Male coaches think they are being hard, but they don't really know women's capacity for work. I think a lot of male coaches go easy. But they look at me and think that I'm the one that's soft because I talk to my athletes and we laugh together. There's many ways to skin a cat, though. I don't have to shout at you to get what I want.'

Bowmaker says she was elated when Andy Murray hired Amelie Mauresmo as his coach. But the doubting voices and relentless questions about whether Murray had made the right choice left her seething. 'They were suggesting women couldn't coach at that level', she says incredulously. 'Why not? People think that because you're a woman you're weak. But you've had to overcome adversity to get to where you are so you've had to be tough and motivated. You've had to be focused and driven. If you've gone through all that, then why can't you be a good coach?'

It's a good question, and one that the sport's governing body, British Athletics, has been asked many times in recent years. The questions became more pointed after the 2013 World Athletics Championships in Moscow, where just two of the 43 British coaches involved were female (Bowmaker was one, and former athlete Liz McColgan the other). A report in the *Guardian* called for 'urgent action' to bridge the gender divide among coaches in British athletics, claiming 'a change in the system is badly needed'.

The Moscow World Championships came the year after British Athletics set up the Female Coach Legacy Programme in 2012 to try and address the discrepancy. Eight coaches already working within the sport were selected for the first cycle of the programme, which British Athletics said would provide them with the extra knowledge, skills and confidence required to work at the highest level. With the programme now in its third cycle, the governing body is clearly making an effort to clear a path to the top for female coaches.

Even so, Bowmaker still doubts that female coaches will ever become the norm in her lifetime, particularly in her event: 'Sprinting is the hardest thing to break', she says, reeling off the names of former sprinters Linford Christie and Mike McFarlane who are as well-known and highly regarded as coaches now as they were as athletes. 'And then you have me. But if I can break through in this, then anyone can break through in any other event. And I want women to think they can do it. It's important for the girls to see they can do it and that it is attainable.'

Outside of athletics, UK Sport has also made moves to try and add to the numbers of female coaches at the elite level of British sport, with the body's Chief Executive Liz Nicholl seeing it as an area that represents 'a real opportunity' to retain talented athletes in the system once they retire. UK Sport launched their Athlete to Coach programme in February 2014 with a view to encouraging female athletes to transition into coaching once they retire. 'In coaching only about 15 per cent of coaches in high-performance sport here in the UK are women', says Nicholl.

She points out the imbalance in the fact that 41 per cent of Team GB at the London 2012 Olympics was female, and yet only 10 per cent of the coaches were women. 'That signals untapped potential, and an opportunity to get a more diverse coaching workforce supporting our women athletes to help them to achieve greater success on an ongoing basis'. The aim, says Nicholl is to attract a 'balanced intake – ideally 50 per cent of female athletes and 50 per cent of male athletes transitioning into coaching through the Athlete to Coach programme.

'If you look at our elite coach programme, it is male dominated. Those that are close enough to be fantastic elite coaches, those who are coming forward for these development opportunities are nearly all men … So we have got to start with the Athlete to Coach scheme to get more women coaches coming through the high-performance system.'

It has to start with numbers, then. Women like Karren Brady, Giselle Mather and Christine Bowmaker are already showing that it is possible, and are doing what they can to encourage others to follow in their footsteps. The barriers that have stood in the way of women for decades are still in place, but there appears to be a growing willingness and desire to see them breached. Not just because it is 'the right thing to do', but because it is the smart thing to do.

'I want to believe that, in the future, opportunities in whatever field, in whatever circumstances, will be equal', says Karren Brady. She believes that the best decisions (in any realm – whether that's business or sport) are made by boards that represent a wide and diverse mix of people, including those who are not afraid to offer a fresh perspective – something that is often desperately needed in the sporting sphere, where the word 'change' is treated with serious suspicion.

While Brady's vision of the future might still be some way off, the work that she and others are doing to ensure that there is now an ongoing debate and discussion surrounding the issue of female leadership lends hope to the idea that Miriam Gonzalez Durantez will one day get her wish, that 'every single woman can choose what they do with their lives – as men do.'

Afterword

Not long after this book hits the shelves the women's Boat Race between Oxford and Cambridge universities will be held on the tideway alongside the men's Boat Race for the second time in the event's long history. Last year's race marked the first time that the women raced on the same day as the men and for many, it was also the first time that they realised a women's Boat Race even existed, despite the fact it had done so for the past 88 years (I'll admit, even I only discovered its existence when I entered the world of sports journalism in 2006).

Not only were the 250,000 people who packed out the banks of the Thames on the day of the race able to watch the 18 super women in both boats go head-to-head in a battle to make history, but millions more were too, with the BBC broadcasting the women's race for the first time.

It was a hugely significant moment for women's sport, but one that many could not believe had taken quite so long to happen. The uncomfortable truth is that it only happened in 2015 because of the determination of one woman – Helena Morrissey – to make it so. As the CEO of Newton Asset Management – a subsidiary of the men's Boat Race sponsors, BNY Mellon – Morrissey was frustrated by the discrepancies in funding, facilities and recognition between the men's and women's races. Knowing that she had the power, and money to make a difference, Morrissey did just that, ensuring that the women's Boat Race is finally getting the recognition it deserves.

This is just one example of how tangible and lasting change can be made. But it is overly optimistic to expect that where Morrissey has led, others will simply follow. As has become clear throughout the previous eight chapters, women's sport is surrounded by a complex web of issues that cannot be untangled by one woman, one solution or one momentous occasion.

Instead, it needs what Chrissie Wellington calls 'a joined-up approach', and one that 'doesn't just work in the women's sport silo'. While there is a place for lobbying and advocacy and raising awareness, Wellington says there is also the need for deeper institutional changes including changes in governance, because these are what set the foundations. 'The make-up of the boards of national governing bodies and the number of female sports journalists – those kinds of things need to change', says Wellington.

What is ultimately needed, though, is action. In researching for this book I came across countless studies, conferences and debates on women in sport. Of course these are valuable and many have provided strong practical recommendations that need taking forward. Now is the right time to do just that. In Wellington's words, we need 'less navel gazing and discussion, and more concerted action. I think we know what we need to do'.

Helena Morrissey knew it, Wellington knows it, and in recent times, more organisations have emerged that know it, too. Women in Football, Women in Sport and the Women's Sport Trust are three that come immediately to mind as proactive groups that are making excellent use of social media and supporters in positions of influence and power to continue the push for equality in women's sport.

It is a battle that the likes of Roberta Gibb and Billie Jean King have been fighting for decades. We owe it to them – and to the many others like them – to continue their work in a similarly dedicated and determined fashion. My own five point action plan is below – some of these things might already be happening to some extent but it's time to up the ante:

1. Improve media awareness and the profile of sportswomen. This can be achieved by encouraging the governing bodies of sports to work closely with marketing experts and advisors to ensure that outlets have everything they need to cover sports and athletes to the best of their ability. That means regularity of scheduling, good imagery and proper communication of when and where events are taking place, to those in the media and the general public.

2. Ensure that incidences of sexism are treated with the same level of seriousness as other forms of discrimination. Only this way will women working in sports like football feel they too are being taken seriously, whether that's as players, officials or staff. At present, Women in Football are one of the lone voices speaking up on this issue – more voices are needed to force a real change in attitudes.

3. Put more pressure on sporting bodies to improve gender balance on boards. UK Sport can make as many suggestions as they like but without the threat of sanction, little is likely to change. Equality in the boardroom has the potential to play a huge role in levelling the playing field elsewhere.

4. Dedicate time and resources to making changes to secondary school sport. At the moment it's clearly not working for girls who are being turned off sport in their droves after they leave primary school. Public health chiefs can tax sugar

all they like but if we can't get more girls to see the value of staying active, the obesity crisis will continue to grow.

5. Following the success of the This Girl Can campaign, let's have other campaigns that focus on families, providing parents with ideas and inspiration for how they can raise active children and enjoy being active with them. By approaching sport from a family perspective, gender becomes less of an issue and the notion that some sports are 'just for boys' or 'just for girls' will hopefully die out as future generations grow up doing whatever sport they choose.

The power of sport to influence lives in so many positive ways is immense. Our target must be for future generations of young girls to have the chance to experience that positivity just as much as their male peers.

Further Reading

Billie Jean King, *Pressure is a Privilege*, Lifetime Media (2008)

Bobbi Gibb, *Wind in the Fire*, The Institute of Natural Systems Press (2nd edition, 2011)

Bobby Riggs, *Tennis is my Racket*, Simon & Schuster (1949)

Carrie Dunn, *Female Football Fans: Community, Identity and Sexism*, Palgrave Pivot (2014)

Donald Walker, *Exercises for English Ladies*, Thomas Hurst (1836)

Jo Welford and Carrie Dunn, *Football and the FA Women's Super League*, Palgrave Pivot (2014)

Jessica Ennis, *Unbelievable*, Hodder & Stoughton (2012)

Karren Brady, *Strong Woman*, Harper Collins (2012)

Kathrine Switzer, *Marathon Woman*, De Capo Press Inc (2009)

Kelly Smith, *My Story*, Bantam Press (2012)

Nicole Cooke, *The Breakaway*, Simon & Schuster (2014)

Victoria Pendleton, *Between the Lines*, HarperSport (2012)

Acknowledgements

Writing *Kicking Off* has taught me a lot. Not only about the complex issues around women's sport but also about the number of people who have dedicated themselves to helping untangle them. Many of them are in this book, whether that's on the page or behind the scenes. I am grateful to them all for the expertise they kindly passed on and that was crucial to creating a book that provides a realistic outlook on women's sport today.

Thanks in particular to Alison Donnelly, the founder of women's rugby website, Scrumqueens.com, golf writer Matt Cooper and boxing writer John Dennen for their excellent insight, endless knowledge and admirable patience in answering my many, many questions.

Four-time Ironman World Champion Chrissie Wellington applies the same unrelenting energy and fierce determination that she did to her sporting career to helping more women enjoy sport and activity. I am hugely grateful to her for taking the time not only to write the thought-provoking Foreword at the beginning of this book, but also for passing on her fascinating views that are mentioned throughout many of the chapters.

If it was not for the efforts of literary agent supreme, David Luxton, this book would not exist so I'm forever grateful to him for that, and for the priceless advice he's given me over the past couple of years. Much the same can be said of Charlotte Croft and Sarah Connelly at Bloomsbury who have helped create a book that's detailed and informative while remaining an entertaining read (that's the dream, anyhow).

My day job at *Sport* magazine means that writing *Kicking Off* has required countless late nights and weekends at my desk (i.e. the kitchen table), but I have also been fortunate to have the support of my editor, Tony Hodson. He and the rest of the team have not complained (well, not much) about me leaving them in the lurch on numerous occasions and without their backing I would either be unemployed or still catching up on months without sleep.

While ours has never been a conventional household in terms of gender norms (I record the boxing, he records MasterChef and we both curl up on the sofa to watch Match of the Day), it has become even less so over the past year. My husband Simon has kept me fed and watered (with tea, mostly) and ensured our house remains clean and tidy while I have done embarrassingly little other than write. He has also read every word of *Kicking Off* (more than once), been my chief sounding board and hauled me back to my feet when I've felt overwhelmed by the task at hand. I simply could not have done this without his unwavering support.

Finally, thank you to all the women in sport who feature in this book and all those who do not, but who have played just as important a role in showing time and time again why women's sport deserves so much more than it has traditionally received. Thanks to you future generations will have fewer battles to fight, more plaudits to win and the freedom to pursue their dreams – whatever they might be.

Index

INDEX